About Island Press

Island Press is the only nonprofit organization in the United States whose principal purpose is the publication of books on environmental issues and natural resource management. We provide solutions-oriented information to professionals, public officials, business and community leaders, and concerned citizens who are shaping responses to environmental problems.

In 2001, Island Press celebrates its seventeenth anniversary as the leading provider of timely and practical books that take a multidisciplinary approach to critical environmental concerns. Our growing list of titles reflects our commitment to bringing the best of an expanding body of literature to the environmental community throughout North America and the world.

Support for Island Press is provided by The Bullitt Foundation, The Mary Flagler Cary Charitable Trust, The Nathan Cummings Foundation, Geraldine R. Dodge Foundation, Doris Duke Charitable Foundation, The Charles Engelhard Foundation, The Ford Foundation, The George Gund Foundation, The Vira I. Heinz Endowment, The William and Flora Hewlett Foundation, W. Alton Jones Foundation, The John D. and Catherine T. MacArthur Foundation, The Andrew W. Mellon Foundation, The Charles Stewart Mott Foundation, The Curtis and Edith Munson Foundation, National Fish and Wildlife Foundation, The New-Land Foundation, Oak Foundation, The Overbrook Foundation, The David and Lucile Packard Foundation, The Pew Charitable Trusts, Rockefeller Brothers Fund, The Winslow Foundation, and other generous donors.

About the Natural Resources Law Center

The Natural Resources Law Center is a research and educational program at the University of Colorado School of Law. The mission of the Center is to promote sustainability in the rapidly changing American West by informing and influencing natural resource laws, policies, and decisions. Through a comprehensive program of research, education, and advice, the Center seeks to inform and influence legal and policy decisions on western natural resources. Center constituents include all levels of government, community and environmental groups, attorneys, Native American tribes, academics, students, and the general public. Through a network of leading legal and policy decision makers, natural resources administrators, researchers, stakeholders, and concerned citizens, the Center focuses substantial intellectual and practical expertise on natural resources issues of importance in the American West. Center activities aim to promote real and immediate policy innovation in natural resources decision making and also to address the long-term and incremental nature of more fundamental reform. The form, content, and distribution of Center activities and products mirror the diversity of public and private decision makers associated with natural resources.

JUSTICE
and
NATURAL
RESOURCES

JUSTICE

and

NATURAL RESOURCES

Concepts, Strategies, and Applications

Edited by

Kathryn M. Mutz, Gary C. Bryner,
and Douglas S. Kenney

ISLAND PRESS

Washington • Covelo • London

Library of Congress Cataloging-in-Publication Data
    Justice and natural resources : concepts, strategies, and applications /
edited by Kathryn M. Mutz, Gary C. Bryner, and Douglas S. Kenney.
        p.   cm.
    Includes bibliographical references and index.
    ISBN 1-55963-897-4 (hardcover) — ISBN 1-55963-898-2 (pbk.)
    1. Environmental justice. 2. Conservation of natural resources.
I. Mutz, Kathryn M. II. Bryner, Gary C., 1951–   3. Kenney, Douglas S.
    GE220 .J87   2001
    333.7 21   2001005666

British Cataloguing-in-Publication Data available.

Printed on recycled, acid-free paper ♲

Manufactured in the United States of America
10 9 8 7 6 5 4 3 2 1

To all those who care about the land,
its resources, and its people
and who work to protect them

Contents

Acronyms

ADR	alternative dispute resolution
ARPA	Archaeological Resources Protection Act
AWQC	ambient water quality criteria
BAD	Backcountry Citizens Against Dumps
BIA	Bureau of Indian Affairs
BLM	Bureau of Land Management
CAFO	confined animal feeding operation
CALFED	California-Federal
CAMPFIRE	Communal Areas Management Programme for Indigenous Resources
CBEP	community-based environmental program
CDCA	California Desert Conservation Area
CEQ	Council on Environmental Quality
CERCLA	Comprehensive Environmental Response, Compensation, and Liability Act
C.F.R.	Code of Federal Regulations
CITES	Convention on International Trade in Endangered Species of Wild Fauna and Flora
COPEEN	Colorado People's Environmental and Economic Network
CRAC	Concerned Rosebud Area Citizens
CWA	Clean Water Act
DMC	Dawn Mining Company
DOC	Dioxin/Organochlorine Center
DOH	Department of Health
DOI	U.S. Department of the Interior
DOT	U.S. Department of Transportation
EAB	U.S. EPA Environmental Appeals Board
EA	environmental assessment
EDR	environmental dispute resolution
EIS	environmental impact statement
EJ	environmental justice
EPA	U.S. Environmental Protection Agency

ESA	Endangered Species Act
FEMA	Federal Emergency Management Agency
FFDCA	Federal Food, Drug, and Cosmetic Act
FLPMA	Federal Land Policy and Management Act
FONSI	finding of no significant impact
IBIA	Interior Board of Indian Appeals
IBLA	Interior Board of Land Appeals
LULU	locally undesirable land use
NEPA	National Environmental Policy Act
NHPA	National Historic Preservation Act
NMED	New Mexico Environment Department
NPDES	National Pollutant Discharge Elimination System
NIMBY	not in my backyard
QLG	Quincy Library Group
RCRA	Resource Conservation and Recovery Act
TAS	treatment as a state
TEPA	tribal environmental policy act
TMDL	total maximum daily load
TSCA	Toxic Substance Control Act
UNESCO	United Nations Educational, Scientific and Cultural Organization
U.S.C.	United States Code
USDA	U.S. Department of Agriculture
USFS	U.S. Forest Service
WWPRAC	Western Water Policy Review Advisory Committee

Cases

Statutes

Foreword

I have been an environmentalist most of my life. I never thought it odd that I would be committed to the civil rights movement and the environmental movement at the same time. The values of each movement always reflected two aspects of who I was and in my mind there was never a question whether these movements were linked in some important way. Each part was an essential element in my understanding of the world. Yet, despite this inchoate understanding, I had not explored the foundational linkage that I had assumed was there.

The environmental justice movement that has emerged over the past thirty years made the connection explicit. The movement forged this linkage through action at the grassroots level as well as through a challenge at the level of institutional advocacy. "Where," the National Urban League asked in 1978, "are the people of color in the leadership of the national environmental organizations?" In the neighborhoods of Chicago, Houston, Baton Rouge, and Los Angeles it was street level epidemiologists who first noticed the infirmities afflicting their communities. They tied these afflictions back to public and private decision making that caused poor and colored communities to bear a disproportionately larger share of our nation's environmental burdens. This connection caused these activists to ask new questions that threw down a challenge to the promise of democratic decision making. It is this challenge to democracy with its promise of equal dignity to all members of the polity that is the continuing contribution of the movement.

This book moves the inquiry into new direction. It takes the insights of the environmental justice movement out of the urban or rural southern setting where the focus has been on toxics issues and locates them in the natural resources realm and at the level of policy. This book takes the insights of the movement and applies them to natural resource issues, particularly as they have been shaped in the West. That new focus tests the policy implications that have implicitly shaped discourse in environmental justice.

This book thus takes up one of the distinct challenges to the envi-

ronmental justice movement. Helen Stacy, a philosopher and environmental lawyer, suggested in a 1999 article entitled "Environmental
Justice and Transformative Law" that because the environmental justice movement has been driven largely by activism it has not had the
need to theorize itself. Yet, because of the need to construct policy, the
luxury of that time has passed and the complexity of the task is
revealed in the essays in this book.

The first step in the creation of policy that contained implicit (if
also somewhat inchoate theories of the movement objectives) came
with the adoption of Executive Order 12898. I consider my work on
Executive Order 12898 and its accompanying Presidential
Memorandum a continuing source of pride. The Executive Order was
in many ways the direct result of a movement that had begun at the
neighborhood level, but that now demanded national attention. The
policy embedded in the executive wove together many of the strands
of the environmental justice movement that were produced by local
activism. Through the force of over twenty years of community
activism the movement had changed the course of both civil rights
and environmental advocacy.

The adoption of the executive order was also the beginning of a
new phase in the movement. Community advocates would now
receive support from the federal government and their actions would
be subjected to increased academic and critical scrutiny. Yet, despite
the addition of new characters with increased institutional clout, its
fundamental quality as a community based movement remained
intact.

The impact of the challenges that the movement launched is still
being felt. It is too much to assert that any fundamental transformation in the conception of environmental protection has occurred, yet
even the marginal differences are important. By redefining the notion
of transparency in terms of the fundamental fairness of substantive
outcomes, the environmental justice movement has contributed to the
vitality of democratic decision making. Because the politics of the
environmental justice movement are rooted in a fundamentally ethical critique of decision making, the notion of transparency spawned
by that movement necessarily has a substantive component. Instead
of merely requesting more process, movement activists have demanded that agencies responsible for environmental decision making
consider a different range of consequences than they had previously
contemplated. The environmental justice movement said: look at
cumulative impacts, look at the nature of the subject community, look
at sensitive subpopulations, look at mortality and morbidity in a com-

munity, and ask, How is this decision affecting those factors? When looking at the cumulative impacts, do not just consider those things that have conventionally been considered within the environmental domain. Take account of all of the factors in public and private decision making that have contributed to the current conditions of the community. The movement activists have asked, What is the balance between this proposed use and the other possible uses of this property? In a direct confrontation with the claims of the property rights movement, environmental justice advocates have added the normative questions, Shouldn't members of the community, even those who are not property owners, have a say in the way the community is developed? Isn't one of the foundations of property rights found in accommodations between neighbors?

Although some have treated these claims as if they are extraordinary, in fact their roots can be traced back through the basic private as well as public law governing both neighbors and land uses. That environmental justice advocates posed these questions from a novel position should not obscure their nature as fundamental. The questions and the political activity that suggested them are challenges to conventional conceptions of what environmental protection means, and they should thus be understood as part of the evolution of environmental activism. This is true even if environmental justice advocates did not initially consider themselves environmentalists.

The introduction suggests that the contributors to this volume are asking three basic questions: 1) What claims are (and should be) the concerns of environmental justice? 2) What communities should have their interests championed under the banner of environmental justice? 3) How do we remedy existing injustices and prevent future ones?

Each question implies a range of contested normative claims. To begin with the first one, for example: What claims are (and should be) the concerns of environmental justice? We could begin to sketch out an answer by cataloging the current objections that have characterized the environmental justice movement. There is something to that method. It is empirical and it is grounded in contemporary practice. Yet to assemble such a catalog would do nothing to illuminate the normative question that lurks in the parenthetical. To answer the normative question requires that we have some way of answering whether the inclusion of the word "environmental" modifies "justice" in a way that matters. Does it convert our conception of justice in this context into a subspecies of our conception of justice in any other setting? Or does it give us a fuller understanding of the nature of justice in a legal setting? The cataloging would help to this extent: it tells us how we have been remiss in assessing the justice claim implicit in environmental protection generally. It also provides an answer to those critics of the environmental movement who claim that environmental activists put nature ahead of people. The environmental justice movement instead reasserts the priority of understanding the intricate bonds between concern about the natural environment and concern about the human environment. It provides a vital linkage between three traditional sources of American commitment to environmental protection: pollution reduction, protection and conservation of natural resources, and protection of wild spaces and wild things.

What environmentalism has helped us do is to understand our relationship to the natural world, to assemble guidelines to help us understand how that relationship ought to be constructed and its imagined impact on social life. The progressive era brought us the lessons of scientific conservation. Those lessons have been modified by the science of ecology, and our politics and our law have slowly been modified to reflect the changes in our knowledge. Advances in engineering and environmental management, like the emergent field of industrial ecology, presage further transformations in the law. Yet environmentalism, whether manifest as pollution control, resource conservation, species protection, or preservation of wilderness has never been completely at the service of science. It has been directed by and informed by science, but its impulses come from deeper within the American character. As Patricia Limerick reminds us in the concluding chapter, the American character is not one thing, but a complex of competing and contradictory desires and inclinations, so that exploring what expressions of environmentalism tell us about justice is a tricky business.

Yet, if the modifier "environmental" tells us anything about justice beyond locating the grounds upon which claims of justice will be contested, it tells us this: that the transformation of the American commitment to environmental protection has been profound, but it has been partial. By asserting that there are justice claims embedded in environmental protection or resource decisions, the environmental justice movement highlights how the mainstream environmental movement discounted the claims of the disadvantaged to a clean natural environment and the wealth of natural resources. That there would be differences in focus is understandable. The political climate within which each movement evolved drove their priorities.

As the final moments of the abolitionist movement were being fought out in the civil rights struggles begun in the American South, America was awakening to the impact of our industrial culture on the quality of life and the natural world. Though both these impulses were translated into mass social movements, the leadership of each came from radically different segments of the American people.

Though both groups drew from the same stream of American values, they were standing at very different points on the bank. The normative judgments they made generated different ideas of priority and approaches to transforming the social landscape of the United States. Yet when they finally encountered one another, it seemed to each as though the other had merely encoded provincial prejudices and tried to elevate them to normative centrality. These differences were compounded because each shared a fascination with litigation and the courts.

Environmentalists and civil rights activists turned to the courts because they felt our representative institutions were slow to respond to the demands of the American people. The structure of representative decision making permitted small groups resistant to popularly supported changes to resist and obstruct the desires expressed by the American people in mass demonstrations and in individual changes in daily life. Most Americans wanted a cleaner environment as is evident today; most want protection of the natural resources that have, in important ways characterized our self-image. That self-image also included a commitment to racial justice, even if the full expression of such a commitment remained blurred.

In the context of the civil rights movement, the litigation centered on giving meaning to the civil war amendments that promised an equal place in American life for black people. For the environmental movement, the courts were a place for public meaning to be inscribed on what were once considered to be private remedies. The movements converged in the demand for inclusion of their values in the calculus of legislation affecting their interests. This was especially evident in the remedies advocates sought. Environmentalists wanted decision makers to include the consequences for the environment in their processes and civil rights advocates wanted decision makers to consider the implications for communities of color. Each wanted the right to enforce these values.

In some ways it was only a matter of time before consideration of the distribution of environmental burdens would come to be seen as central to the question of environmental protection. It had already been a part of the private law of nuisance, and the takings clause of the Constitution drew lines around the legislative jurisdiction of the

Congress and the states. Similarly, the expansion of the congressional authority to regulate private activities under their power to regulate commerce, a central feature in regulating air or watersheds, also provided a basis for extending federal protection to black people and other minority groups in those areas of the country that were resisting the social transformation that was afoot. In short, once the distributional effects embedded in resource or environmental protection decisions take center stage, we can only understand them by understanding how they are necessarily linked to the question of which communities should have their interests championed under the banner of environmental justice.

The conflation of these two questions occurs in the following way. To avoid the claim that the demands of the environmental justice movement are just a different form of the NIMBY (not in my backyard) syndrome, we have to assess the ways in which its claims are different. Noting a superficial similarity is insufficient because all opposition to a particular project or a siting decision is going to look the same: *we don't want this here.* The difference lies in their genesis. There is a significant difference between "I don't like this" and "This is yet another burden this community must bear." The first may state a strongly held preference, the second is rooted in a claim about equal treatment. We can only distinguish the two by inquiring into the nature of the group making the complaint.

As Luke Cole and Sheila Foster persuasively demonstrate in *From the Ground Up,* one of the central features of the environmental justice movement is its character as a grassroots driven phenomenon. They show that it arose out of community-based concern over the cumulative health effects of environmental decision making. While its local manifestation as activism was usually in response to a specific decision or facility, the community's action has to be understood within the context of the larger claims that the movement is making: that there are communities that share specific characteristics and are made to bear a disproportionately larger share of the environmental burdens. Thus the specific complaint is tied to a larger critique about environmental decision making as well as the substantive content of environmental protection.

In addition to these components, the environmental justice movement asks us to consider the nature of the groups who have been subject to the larger burdens. What do they have in common? What is their relationship to power? How does their predicament reflect on general issues of democratic accountability? Who are the natural allies in making this critique of environmental or resource decision making. In answering these question you are required both to assess the kinds of claims that are justified as being part of the environmental justice critique and to assess which groups are situated to make environmental justice complaints that we are required to take seriously as an expression of the environmental justice critique.

I am not saying that the no complaints about environmental protection or resource use should be taken seriously unless they are rooted in environmental justice concerns. I am saying that when a complaint is posed as an environmental justice critique, there are specific ways to evaluate that claim, and that environmental justice claims implicate more than the specific decision, although they may require action as to a specific decision. Environmental justice thus is a basic policy critique as well as an indictment of specific decision making. Its foundation in a commitment to democratic equality as well as to equal treatment points the way to generalizing the insights of the movement to improve environmental protection and resource use generally.

Thus we get to the last question posed by this volume: How do we remedy existing injustices and prevent future ones? The answer to this inquiry is suggested by our consideration of the first two. Once there is an awareness of the distributional effects of current land use, pollution control, trade, and resource use policies, it is easier to ask which of those effects are the avoidable consequences of decisions made with incomplete knowledge. I am not merely restating the problem of regulating under conditions of uncertainty; that issue will always bedevil environmental decision making at the margins. Instead, I am suggesting that policy that was made without consideration of the distributional impacts can no longer be considered well-made policy. We cannot know all of the effects of a particular decision, but reviewing past impacts can give us a clue about what we ought to be on the lookout for. For those communities that continue to suffer higher mortality and morbidity rates than the norm for reasons that are traceable to environmental decision making, we ought to be focusing, at a minimum, on reducing those manifestations of past policy. What this volume does is to show how resource decisions are fundamental to our full understanding of the environmental justice consequences of past policy. The decision to divert water from the San Joaquin River delta increased the selenium concentrations in the waters, for example, leading to bioaccumulation in the fish and increasing the risk to people who ate the fish from that river. Of course, health issues are not the sole issue. What the environmental justice movement has shown us is that questions of equity pervade environmental decision making, including resource decisions.

What we have learned from the environmental justice movement, and what this volume exemplifies is that meeting the demands of environmental justice does not require a single response but encourages local experimentation. It also allows for the implementation of least cost solutions where the gains in efficiency might be used to benefit the burdened community. This approach also encourages the cooperation of various levels of government, because a federal permit may have resulted in a cascade of local consequences, each of which must be attended to separately and through the web of social effects within which it is embedded.

This volume continues the inquiry into all three questions, but pushes them into new policy areas. It proves that the light shed by the environmental justice movement still has corners of our environmental and resource policies to illuminate. There is no better place to begin this effort than in the essays that make up this book. The writers here understand the nuances and implication of resource policy and with that provide a unique contribution to the development of the theory of environmental justice. The debate will be changed by the efforts found here.

GERALD TORRES
H. O. Head Centennial Professor of Real Property Law,
University of Texas at Austin

Acknowledgments

The Natural Resources Law Center initiated its justice and natural resources project in 1999 with funding from the Ford Foundation. Center staff met first with faculty of the University of Colorado School of Law and Center of the American West who were interested in either natural resources or social justice issues. Based on the initial recommendations of the faculty members, and dozens of phone calls, e-mail exchanges, and personal contacts, we eventually brought together the twenty-one individuals represented in this volume. Only a few of the authors—Luke Cole, Sheila Foster, and Barry Hill—had been active in what we term the "traditional" environmental justice movement. The rest—drawn from academia, government, and field-level practice—had focused their scholarship or work on either natural resources or Native American issues. We asked the authors to reflect on equity issues within their own realms of expertise.

With draft manuscripts in hand, the authors met at a workshop in Denver in April 2000 to discuss their initial work among themselves and with a variety of natural resources professionals and social justice activists. The workshop, cosponsored by the Colorado People's Environmental and Economic Network (COPEEN), Region 8 of the Environmental Protection Agency (EPA), and the University of Colorado Office of Diversity and Equity, provided the authors with real-world perspectives to ground their arguments. In the subsequent months, contributed essays were transformed into chapters with funding from the William and Flora Hewlett Foundation.

We acknowledge first the contributions that the authors, our many advisors, and the workshop participants made in directing this project and preparing manuscripts. We also thank Center research assistants Robert James, Chris King, Heather Corson, and Miriam Stohs, who helped prepare the manuscripts; Mel Munoz of COPEEN, Deldi Reyes and Elisabeth Evans of Region 8 EPA, and Center intern Dana Sevakis, who helped coordinate the workshop; and staff and research assistants of each contributing author. Special thanks go to Todd Baldwin of Island Press for his patience, insights, and skillful diplo-

macy in leading us through the process of publication. We also grate-
fully acknowledge the generous support provided by the Ford
Foundation and the William and Flora Hewlett Foundation for the
Center's justice and natural resources project. Without the vision of
these foundations, the dialogue would flounder.

Introduction

Environmental justice brings together two of the most powerful social movements of the late twentieth and early twenty-first centuries: environmentalism and civil rights. These are particularly potent movements due to the compelling moral arguments they convey and the ways in which they complement each other. This is not to say, however, that attaining the goals of either movement necessarily satisfies the other's cause. Advocates of social justice recognize the importance of eliminating environmental hazards that affect health, reduce economic opportunity, and diminish quality of life for people of color and the poor. But policies that strengthen the political power and decision-making influence of disadvantaged communities may not improve environmental conditions, and actions taken to improve overall environmental quality may exacerbate existing inequities. Much progress has been made in reducing pollution, but progress in reducing race- and income-based disparities in environmental conditions has been limited. Minority and low-income communities continue to bear a disproportionate share of environmental burdens.

However, environmental inequity is not solely the result of the pollution burdens that first galvanized the environmental justice movement. Our natural environment also bestows many benefits on those able to use and enjoy it. Access to land and water—either for preservation or for consumptive use—can be a vital economic input and a critical determinant of a community's quality of life. Failure to provide equitable access to the nation's natural resources and degradation of those resources through development and use can also constitute injustice.

This book is inspired by the simple observation that the inequitable distribution of the burdens and benefits of environmental protection reaches well beyond the facility siting and pollution focus of the traditional environmental justice movement. Charges of inequity involving natural resources extraction, management, and preservation are heard increasingly throughout the nation, often emanating from the public lands and American Indian reservations of the rural West. These natural resource equity issues—as distinct from environmental issues—are typically outside the scope of traditional environmental justice inquiries, even though they often exemplify traditional environmental justice themes: namely, the inequitable distribution of harms and benefits along lines of race and class.

Expanding the concept of environmental justice to include a broad range of natural resource issues and fusing the agendas of the environmental and civil rights movements are compelling, but problematic, goals. Environmental justice is rooted in claims of rights that invoke corresponding obligations and duties that can outweigh majoritarian interests; minority rights are to be vindicated even if the majority does not wish to pay the costs or have its options limited. Further, the power of these claims of rights may be diluted by their too frequent invocation. An inflation of rights might weaken the moral power that the rights represent. Consequently, conceptualizing environmental justice in ways that expand its reach while preserving its political potency and moral claims is a daunting task.

Devising solutions to environmental injustices is also fraught with challenges, especially when equities are unclear and resources are limited. National and local priorities for energy development, open space, and species protection may conflict, or the community itself may be internally divided on the optimal balance of resource development and resource protection. Expansion of access to land or water for groups that have been denied full access in the past may threaten long-held existing rights or preclude preservation of undeveloped resources for future generations. Pursuing the goal of environmental justice requires innovative remedies that balance the goals of community empowerment with improved environmental quality and that promote their mutual reinforcement. Strengthening tribal sovereignty and the capacity of tribes to govern their lands, for example, may be an essential step in remedying past injustices, but tribal governments may choose to focus on other issues besides preserving natural resources.

There is also the inevitable need to set priorities, to allocate scarce financial and law enforcement resources. Budgetary limitations may mean that fewer land protection or restoration projects can be undertaken if forest workers are paid a fair, living wage. Enforcement efforts taken to ensure a low-income community's access to quality water may strain government resources available to respond to other problems of injustice—for example, exposure to toxic wastes—or to meet the water quality needs of the larger community. A broadened agenda of environmental justice can and should generate support for more resources and expanded effort, but choices of allocating resources and efforts are inescapable and trade-offs inevitable.

This book seeks to contribute to the integration of environmental and equity issues across a diverse range of natural resources concerns. The chapters that follow strive to engage the reader in the debate over whether natural resource equity issues should be integral elements of the environmental justice agenda, and if so, how they can be addressed. The authors of these chapters do not always agree on how to define environmental justice in the context of natural resources; nor do they concur on remedies. The common goal is to describe concepts, identify a range of strategies, and examine efforts to devise solutions. Contributing authors propose ideas that others can test, assess, and refine by focusing on three integrating questions:

- What claims are—and should be—the concerns of environmental justice?
- What communities should have their interests championed under the banner of environmental justice?
- How do we remedy existing injustices and prevent future ones?

These questions probe the roughest edges of our topic, providing frameworks for the understanding of environmental justice in Part One; focusing on specific contextual and conceptual issues of defining justice in Part Two; and providing strategies for identifying and remedying injustices in Part Three. Readers will quickly realize that this delineation between *Frameworks, Concepts,* and *Strategies and Applications* in the three parts of this book is imprecise, a fortunate (and intended) fiction produced by challenging our authors to jointly consider and embrace alternative perspectives and, perhaps more importantly, to always retain focus on the interplay of people, resources, and government.

Outline of the Book

The chapters of Part One, Frameworks, provide a structure for classifying and understanding both the existing environmental justice movement and how an expansion of it might incorporate the special problems associated with natural resources development and protection. Chapter 1 begins with a brief introduction to the environmental justice movement and the range of natural resources equity issues that might be addressed by a more broadly defined movement. In their chapter, David Getches and David Pellow provide perspective on the first two of the book's three questions, asking "how large a tent to erect in the name of environmental justice." According to the authors, the answer is relevant for "determining the reach of government policy, the agendas of nonprofit organizations, and the kinds of solutions that can and will be pursued under the banner of environmental justice." While advocating that the field evolve to recognize natural resources issues more fully, they urge that the environmental justice movement "maintain its focus on communities that exhibit traditional characteristics of disadvantage—where high poverty levels, large populations of people of color, or both are concentrated."

In Chapter 2, Gary Bryner identifies five theoretical frameworks that can be used to understand alternative ways of defining injustices related to natural resources and the environment. His review suggests how environmental justice can be approached from different perspectives and explores how environmental and social justice goals might be more effectively pursued together. Bryner's literature review and broad theoretical framework is rooted in concepts widely found in legal, political, and environmental philosophy and ethics.

Chapter 3 provides a more focused framework—constructed by James Wescoat and coauthors Sarah Halvorson, Lisa Headington, and Jill Replogle—for addressing justice and natural resources in the context of water and poverty in Colorado. The authors developed their framework by asking how public officials, nongovernmental organizations, and scholars have conceptualized water problems faced by low-income people in Colorado. The authors' inductive approach to the problem helps to clarify the distinction between the terms *water resources equity* and *environmental injustice* and other alternative conceptual approaches to water and poverty and suggests how each might lead toward different public forums and potential remedies to low-income water problems.

In the final chapter of Part One (Chapter 4), Tseming Yang explores the parallels between domestic environmental justice and international environmental justice in the context of natural resources management activities, offering a framework that broadens the inquiry across national boundaries and cultures. A close examination uncovers similar historical roots of race and wealth dynamics. Yang's comparative examination highlights the importance of both race and poverty in defining the environmental justice field and provides important suggestions for resolving environmental justice problems domestically and internationally.

Part Two, Concepts, turns from the broad perspectives that will help readers understand the wide range of natural resources–based equity issues to more focused discussions on institutional causes of injustice. In Chapter 5, Jeff Romm pursues the causes of environmental injustice and the means to reduce it with specific attention to forest governance in California. He argues that the causes of environmental injustice, and thus its potential solutions, are embedded in the social order of environmental governance itself. Romm's "just environment" would frame natural and social relations so as to equalize benefits and influence among all affected people, rather than to privilege those who own and control property.

In Chapter 6, Sheila Foster tackles the critical issue of public participation in natural resources and environmental policy and management decision making. Government officials, academics, and community leaders across the country are currently rethinking the appropriate scale—both administratively and geographically—of decision-making processes for addressing environmental and natural resource problems. Increasingly, these inquiries promote a more community-oriented mode of governance known as devolved collaboration. Foster's critique investigates the ability of this decision-making approach to identify and equitably distribute costs and benefits of resources management, comparing these outcomes to the traditional top-down, command-and-control strategies.

In Chapter 7, Sarah Krakoff introduces readers to the unique status of Native American environmental justice claims. Krakoff describes the ways in which tribal sovereignty complicates the typical "disparate impact" approach to environmental justice, arguing that environmental justice for tribes must include the norm of supporting tribes' unique political status. She proposes a definition for environmental justice claims involving tribal sovereignty, then explores that definition using examples involving tribal decision making. Is there an environmental justice concern when a tribe imposes higher standards under the Clean Water Act than non-Indian neighbors, prompting those neighbors to attack the tribe's sovereignty? Is it an environmental justice issue when a tribe decides to site a solid waste dump within its boundaries and non-Indian neighbors object?

Chapters in Part Three, Strategies and Applications, continue the discussion of this book's three central questions, with a greater use of case studies to illuminate the potential strategies for eliminating injustice. In Chapter 8, Luke Cole explores a civil rights theory for preventing environmental injustice, examining the potential for using Title VI of the Civil Rights Act of 1964 and its implementing regulations to address damage to natural and cultural resources. Cole examines definitions of the term *impact* under federal case law and federal agency guidance documents to discern whether they are pliable enough to include cultural and natural resources damages. He then applies his analysis to a Native American nation's challenge to a proposed freeway through sacred petroglyphs. Cole argues for broadening the legal basis for environmental justice claims but concedes that the prospects remain uncertain.

In Chapter 9, Henry Carey focuses on the issues of environmental justice raised by forest management in the remote mountains of northern New Mexico, where U.S. Forest Service policies and the goals of preservationists have had little regard for the traditional forestry practices of the local land-grant community. Carey describes problems both of distributive injustice related to timber supplies and of procedural injustice in the management of roads. He asserts that environmental justice requires that the quality of the forest—the habitat of the community—be maintained in a manner that meets the cultural priorities of the community. Carey further asserts that "community forestry" offers a promising approach for sustaining both communities and their forests.

Dean Suagee deepens our understanding of the unique situation of tribes in Chapter 10, exploring a specific class of Native American environmental justice claims through application of the National Environmental Policy Act (NEPA) in American Indian country. Suagee points out that environmental impact assessment systems like NEPA can be important tools for integrating the values of low-income populations and communities of color but, as in the case of the Rosebud Indian Reservation hog farm, they also can be misused. Unless the assessment is conducted competently, and unless decision makers act on information about adverse impacts, the exercise is meaningless.

Jan Buhrmann follows in Chapter 11 with another look at NEPA, applying a four-point framework—developed by Region 8 of the U.S. Environmental Protection Agency (EPA)—for evaluating environmental justice implications of federal projects and for incorporating community concerns into NEPA impact analysis. Her study reveals how Native Americans and low-income communities could be unfairly burdened by a proposed federal water project in North Dakota. Buhrmann's study also underscores how natural resources management can impact a range of stakeholders quite differently, distributing benefits to some and burdens to others. The EPA's methodology can be adapted by other federal and state agencies, academia, and community organizations, and it illustrates the role of federal agencies in ensuring that environmental justice considerations are an integral part of natural resources and land use decisions.

In Chapter 12, Barry Hill and Nicholas Targ discuss how authority under existing environmental law can be used by federal regulators to address a broad spectrum of environmental justice concerns. The authors illustrate their thesis with three case studies, which involve standards for fish toxicity, a visitor center on public lands, and a reservoir project, respectively. The cases illustrate the potential for addressing environmental justice concerns under the Clean Water Act and NEPA. Hill and Targ conclude that if statutes are applied using broad, generic averages, people of color and low-income communities may be disproportionately impacted and environmental injustices may result. Only if regulators view the communities' environmental resources from the communities' points of view can health and the resources upon which human health depends be maintained.

In the final contribution of Part Three (Chapter 13), Kathryn Mutz examines environmental justice in the context of hardrock mineral development on federal lands. She begins with stories from three communities that have felt the negative impact of mineral development and have criticized mining companies and federal and state agencies for slow, inappropriate, or inadequate response. Mutz then analyzes the laws and regulations that federal land managers must work within to protect lands and communities, finding a great deal of potential and flexibility, but very little requirement, to deal with the special problems of environmental justice in the hardrock mining context. She concludes that achieving the goal of environmental justice depends on both the ability of traditionally disenfranchised communities to forcefully communicate their concerns and the willingness of the agencies to use their discretion to ensure that community needs are addressed.

In her concluding chapter, Patricia Limerick comments on several important themes of the book and what she considers its decidedly "optimistic" tone. From a historian's perspective, she explores the shifting meanings of the terms *race* and *nature* and the general disconnectedness between environmentalism and respect for human rights that has pervaded much of the history of the environmental movement. Limerick notes that mainstream environmentalism often seeks to separate nature from humanity, and that writers such as Joseph Wood Krutch and Aldo Leopold appear "tone-deaf" on the matter of racial justice. She concludes, however, that the early joining of human rights and commitment to nature by Thoreau can be repossessed by the environmental movement at any time.

Part One
FRAMEWORKS

Chapter 1

BEYOND "TRADITIONAL" ENVIRONMENTAL JUSTICE

David H. Getches and David N. Pellow

Over the last three decades, scholars, activists, and policy makers have begun to pay attention to the impacts of environmental pollution on disadvantaged communities. Research in the 1980s and 1990s highlighted the fact that hazardous waste facilities were disproportionately located in poor and minority neighborhoods. But it was the stunning finding in a 1987 United Church of Christ study that race is the single most significant predictor of the location of these facilities that caught the attention of civil rights leaders, environmentalists, and policy makers. Legal scholars saw the potential for claims under the U.S. Constitution or statutes prohibiting racial discrimination and became interested. The ambit of environmental policy and activism that focuses on patterns where the poor and "people of color bear the brunt of the nation's pollution problem" became known as "environmental justice."[1]

Characterizing the absence of environmental justice as environmental racism sharpened the appeal of the cause. A pioneer in the field, Bunyan Bryant, described environmental racism in terms that would move most Americans:

> It is an extension of racism. It refers to those institutional rules, regulations, and policies or government or corporate decisions that deliberately target certain communities for least desirable land uses, resulting in the disproportionate exposure of toxic and hazardous waste on communities based upon certain prescribed biological characteristics. Environmental racism is the unequal protection against toxic and hazardous waste exposure and

the systematic exclusion of people of color from environmental decisions affecting their communities.[2]

The intersection of racial discrimination and environmental insult,
both of which are eschewed in modern political rhetoric and public
opinion, is where the environmental justice movement began.

The connection between race and the impacts of environmental
harm is not news. Patricia Limerick's concluding chapter in this book
explores this phenomenon, and others have begun to do so as well,
through the emerging "new environmental history." One finding
from this research is that different ethnic groups often face different
forms of environmental inequality. For example, African Americans
and Latinos face greater threats from pollution *additions* in urban
areas, and many Native Americans who live on reservations confront
the problems of resource *extraction,* including mining and timber harvesting. Asian Americans and Pacific Islanders in the United States
often face environmental threats disproportionate to their numbers
from occupational hazards and from contaminated fish.

That the realm of environmental justice should include diverse
claims is, at first, an appealing notion. It seems no less an environmental justice issue whether the claim is to benefits or to burdens of
environmental policies. Poor populations and people of color are
harmed when there are no parks or open spaces near their neighborhoods or if high entrance fees limit their access to outdoor recreation.
Equal enforcement of laws can have perniciously unequal effects:
toxic pesticides are applied by predominately non-English-speaking
migrant farm workers, with warnings and instructions on proper use
printed only in English; Clean Water Act standards, as described by
Barry Hill and Nicholas Targ in Chapter 12, are set to protect people
ingesting an "average" quantity of fish but disregard American
Indian cultures or poor non-Indian people who eat large quantities of
fish for traditional or economic (that is, subsistence) reasons.[3] Market-
based pollution controls can be attractive but may produce unfair
results. For instance, emissions trading can reduce overall pollution
levels but leave "hot spots" near sources, typically in poor areas,
where pollutants remain heavily concentrated.[4]

Some communities are actually placed at a disadvantage by the
strong application of environmental laws, such as when a low-income
housing project is scrapped because it would violate a height limitation or obstruct someone's view. Consider, for example, a tribe that
struggles internally to make the difficult decision to cut timber in
wildlife habitat in order to provide income for its impoverished mem-

bers and then confronts objections from environmentalists.[5] In other instances, individuals or communities are excluded from environmental decision-making processes that impact their communities and their capacity to make a living from natural resource usage. For instance, in northern California, the U.S. Supreme Court allowed a highway and logging operation planned by the government to destroy a portion of a national forest after a study clearly concluded that the area was central to a tribe's traditional religion and would have a devastating effect on religious practices.[6]

This book explores efforts to expand the realm of environmental justice to include concerns in which natural resources are developed, managed, and used in ways that exacerbate social injustice or disadvantages of communities of low-income people and people of color. The examples explored in several chapters are western and rural, thus expanding the concerns of a field that began with problems arising in urban, industrialized areas. The seminal challenge, as the field evolves, is to allow it to grow without losing its focus. The recurring questions in the book are: First, what kinds of actions and what types of harms constitute environmental injustice? Second, which communities can claim the attention of the environmental justice movement? And third, how do we remedy existing injustices and prevent future ones?

This chapter addresses the first two by asking how large a tent to erect in the name of environmental justice. The answer is relevant to determining the reach of government policy, the agendas of nonprofit organizations, and the kinds of solutions that can and will be pursued under the banner of environmental justice. While recognizing that there is a compelling argument for expanding the notion of environmental justice, we caution that, as a movement, environmental justice must find its limits. Given the reality that resources are limited and the capacities of individuals and groups for problem solving are finite, we urge that the environmental justice movement maintain its focus on communities that exhibit traditional characteristics of disadvantage—where high poverty levels, large populations of people of color, or both are concentrated.

Because this book examines the changing boundaries of a relatively new movement, its premise is that the field should be broader than the "traditional" environmental justice issues, such as the concentration of polluting facilities in neighborhoods of poor people and people of color and the failure to enforce environmental laws against polluters in these areas as rigorously as in other areas. As awareness of the scope of environmental inequities has grown, the ambit of environmental justice issues has stretched well beyond attacking the classically urban problem of undesirable facility siting and unequal pollution impacts.

Origins: A Problem in Search of a Movement

Since the time of the first "civilizations," the refuse, effluence, and detritus in cities have been concentrated in the quarters where low-income populations and ethnic groups lived.[7] Today, the unsavory idea of dumping the waste of an affluent society on the poorest and most vulnerable neighborhoods is discomfiting to most people and is gaining greater political attention as a social problem.

"Discovery" of a Problem

Social scientists, activists, some government agencies, and the public health community long ago recognized the issue of disparate treatment of racially identifiable regions in waste disposal in the United States. Official, and then public, notice came more slowly. As early as 1971, the Council on Environmental Quality recognized the links between racial discrimination and the adverse effects of environmental quality on the urban poor. Sociologist Robert Bullard began his path-breaking work in 1979 with a study of one black community's battle against a landfill. The siting issue was finally elevated to national attention in the late 1980s, after the U.S. General Accounting Office revealed that three out of four hazardous waste facilities in one U.S. Environmental Protection Agency (EPA) region were located in African American communities, and the United Church of Christ issued its famous report concluding that race is the single most significant factor in waste facility siting (see Box 1.1). Later studies either almost universally corroborated these conclusions or added further evidence.[8]

As powerful and convincing as the evidence was, it did not immediately lead to an organized movement. This was probably because the problems raised issues at the intersection of two well-established movements with well-defined agendas: civil rights and environmentalism. As a result, the environmental justice movement struggled to find an identity of its own. Like other social movements, it was inspired by problems, and as those problems were demonstrated and gained public understanding, they should have been ripe for political action and organizing efforts. The civil rights movement, for example, could rally against Jim Crow laws and develop "programs" in such areas as voting rights and public accommodations. Likewise, the environmental movement was galvanized by its pursuit of a legislative agenda aimed at remedying palpable water and air pollution problems and cleaning up hazardous wastes. Organizations were formed to champion the needed litigation and legislative reforms. By contrast, even after studies alerted the public to the nature of environmental justice problems, it was difficult for people outside disadvantaged neighborhoods to see the problems, and legal remedies were hard to find. Environmental justice lacked a discrete, well-defined agenda around which dedicated organizations could coalesce. Some civil rights and environmental organizations were able to incorporate environmental justice issues within the larger causes on their agendas, but initially at least, they were relatively poor cousins of the core concerns that motivated these groups.

Looking to the Law: Wrongs without a Remedy?

Environmental justice cases found their way into the courts about twenty years ago. Claims under the civil rights laws, even when they were based on the demonstrable, racially discriminatory distribution of environmental impacts, were largely unsuccessful in the courts. From the earliest cases, it has been difficult to prove the facts needed to win such a case. One problem is the cost and difficulty of proving that the impacts are distributed along racial lines in a particular neighborhood. Even if the statistical proof can be made, there is a legal problem. Current U.S. Supreme Court law requires a showing of *intentional* discrimination to prove an equal protection claim.[9]

Accordingly, lower courts have denied environmental justice claims for failure to prove intentional discrimination. *Bean v Southwestern Waste Management Corp* (1979) involved a challenge to the decision by the Texas Department of Health to grant a permit to Southwestern Waste Management to operate a solid waste facility in a community of color.[10] While the court found that the statistical data the plaintiffs marshaled revealed "unfortunate and insensitive" corporate behavior, this evidence fell short of proving discriminatory intent. Ten years later, in *East Bibb Twiggs Neighborhood Assoc. v Macon-Bibb County Planning & Zoning Comm'n* (1989), plaintiffs used an equal protection theory to challenge a permit for landfill siting in a predominantly African American community.[11] This theory failed because, as in *Bean,* the plaintiff failed to show either discriminatory intent or a historical pattern of discriminatory conduct.

Title VI of the Civil Rights Act of 1964 prohibits "discrimination under any program or activity receiving Federal financial assistance." As implemented by agency regulations, Title VI seems to impose

BOX 1.1. Major Studies of Environmental Justice

1971

In its annual report, the U.S. Council on Environmental Quality noted that populations of low-income people and people of color were disproportionately exposed to significant environmental hazards. This is perhaps the earliest governmental report acknowledging the existence of environmental inequality in the United States.

1983

Research begun in 1979 by Robert Bullard was published in an article titled "Solid Waste Sites and the Black Houston Community." In this work, which culminated in the book *Dumping in Dixie: Race, Class, and Environmental Quality* in 1990 (discussed below), Bullard found that waste dumps were not randomly scattered throughout the city. Rather, they were more likely to be located in African American neighborhoods, particularly near schools. This was the first study to examine the causes of environmental racism. Bullard found that housing discrimination, lack of zoning, and decisions by public officials over a fifty-year period produced these environmentally unequal outcomes.

1983

A congressionally authorized U.S. General Accounting Office study revealed that three out of four off-site, commercial hazardous waste landfills in the southeastern United States were located within predominately African American communities, even though African Americans made up just one-fifth of the region's population.

1987

A study, "Toxic Waste and Race," by the United Church of Christ Commission for Racial Justice—the first national study to correlate waste facilities and demographic characteristics—found that race was the most significant factor in determining where waste facilities were located. Among other findings, the study revealed that three out of five African Americans and Hispanic Americans lived in communities with one or more uncontrolled toxic waste sites, and 50 percent of Asian–Pacific Islander Americans and Native Americans lived in such communities. A follow-up study in 1994 concluded that these trends had worsened.

1990

A Greenpeace report on incinerator siting practices concluded that communities with *existing* incinerators had minority populations 89 percent higher than the national average, and communities with *proposed* incinerators had minority populations 60 percent higher than the national average.

1990

Sociologist Robert Bullard published *Dumping in Dixie: Race, Class and Environmental Quality.* This was the first major study of environmental racism that linked hazardous facility siting with historical patterns of residential segregation in the South. This study was also one of the first to explore the social and psychological impacts of environmental racism on local populations and the growing environmental justice movement—a new response from communities against these environmental threats.

1992

A study by the *National Law Journal,* "Unequal Protection," uncovered significant disparities in the way the U.S. Environmental Protection Agency enforced its laws: "There is a racial divide in the way the U.S. government cleans up toxic waste sites and punishes polluters. White communities see faster action, better results and stiffer penalties than communities where Blacks, Hispanics and other minorities live. This unequal protection often occurs whether the community is wealthy or poor" (p. 12).

stronger protections than the U.S. Constitution's equal protection clause. Indeed, although the Supreme Court had said Title VI does not, by itself, vitiate the need for a showing of intentional discrimination, it held in *Guardians Ass'n v Civil Serv Com'n of City of New York* that Title VI regulations could prohibit unintentional discrimination.[12] Thus, black and Hispanic policemen who were disproportionately affected by a layoff policy could sue to enforce an agency regulation under Title VI that prohibited discriminatory effects. The EPA's virtually identical regulation under Title VI prohibits any recipient of federal funds from "administering its program [to] have the effect of subjecting individuals to discrimination because of their race."[13] After *Guardians Ass'n* was decided, environmental justice advocates seized on this regulation prohibiting discriminatory effects and attempted to apply it to the uneven impacts resulting from a concentration of waste facilities being located largely in black neighborhoods.

A federal court of appeals accepted this argument in *Chester Residents Concerned for Quality Living v Seif*. The court held that plaintiffs could sue under the regulations and would only have to prove disparate impact.[14] But then the proposal to locate the new waste facility was withdrawn, and the matter became moot. After this it was not necessary to address the question of whether such a suit was proper, so the U.S. Supreme Court vacated and remanded the decision. But this left the door open to such suits under Title VI. Then in 2001 the Supreme Court spoke directly enough to the issue to dash the hopes of environmental justice advocates for asserting Title VI unless they can prove that discrimination was intentional. In *Alexander v Sandoval*,[15] a case challenging English-only driver's license examinations, the Court ruled that although the Department of Justice had issued regulations prohibiting disparate racial impacts of state programs receiving federal assistance, private individuals have no right to sue to enforce the regulations. For further discussion of Title VI, see Luke Cole's discussion in Chapter 8.

Although it was clear that creative thought was needed to find effective remedies for apparently discriminatory impacts of environmental insults and uneven enforcement of environmental laws, legal scholars only recently have given serious attention to the field of environmental justice. Most scholarship has focused on the Equal Protection Clause of the Fourteenth Amendment and Title VI of the Civil Rights Act of 1964 as tools for protecting citizens against "disparate impact."[16] In the 1990s, major symposia were held that advanced scholarly attention to environmental justice, resulting in more publications on the topic. For example, the *University of Colorado Law Review*'s symposium "Race, Class, and Environmental Regulation," held in 1992, explored the melding of environmental and civil rights legal approaches. For many activists who had been involved in both the civil rights movement *and* the struggle for environmental justice, this fusion made sense.[17] Attorneys like Luke Cole, who were practicing environmental poverty law, were at the cutting edge of this approach.[18]

Some legal scholars have proposed a wider range of claims, suggesting that the Fair Housing Act would be more promising than Title VI as a tool for making legal claims to environmental justice.[19] Meanwhile, some litigants have pursued legal theories outside the civil rights laws. For instance, in *El Pueblo para el Aire y Agua Limpio v County of Kings,* a Latino community successfully used the public participation provisions of California's Environmental Quality Act to overturn a decision to permit a toxic waste incinerator.[20] The plaintiffs charged that the environmental impact statement and the public hearings required by the law were written and conducted only in English, producing a barrier to participation for the 40 percent of the population who spoke only Spanish (see Box 1.2).

Discussions among lawyers and scholars continue about the possible legal remedies for environmental injustice. Uncertainty persists for people of color who are disproportionately affected by environmental problems, and there may be even greater legal hurdles for poor white communities.

Whatever inadequacies exist in the law, there has been a growing consensus that there is something wrong when communities of color and poor people are the involuntary hosts for the rest of the nation's garbage. Whether or not they can muster proof of racially discriminatory intent on the part of industry or the government agencies that approved the siting of facilities in these neighborhoods, residents argue persuasively that they have been deprived of environmental justice. Where the insult is clearly concentrated on a racial group, the lack of a smoking gun of intentional racism may cause a judge to toss the matter out of court, yet these legal obstacles are unlikely to overcome our intuition that there is a problem to be solved. Whatever "the law" may allow, it is offensive when an insult is concentrated on poor people and people of color. With legal horizons limited, there is no less a cause, but advocacy and activism must concentrate on political fora and public information because the environmental justice movement cannot reliably look to the law to provide definition for its cause.

BOX 1.2. Watershed Events in the Movement for
Environmental Justice

1982
A major protest was staged in Warren County, North Carolina, over
a PCB landfill in a majority African American town. Several hundred protesters (many of them high-profile civil rights activists)
were arrested. The protestors called for a study of environmental
racism in the South, which the U.S. General Accounting Office conducted one year later.

1983
The Urban Environment Conference in New Orleans framed the
toxics struggle in terms of power, class, and racial inequality.

1986
Concerned Citizens of South Central L.A. and Mothers of East L.A.
successfully stopped the LANCER incinerator project and several
other locally unwanted land uses. This victory sent a surge of pride
through many Chicano communities and propelled the environmental justice movement.

1990
The Michigan Conference on Race and the Incidence of Environmental Hazards was held. This conference was attended by several
"activist-scholars" who, while working closely with community
activists, came together to present and debate the evidence for and
against environmental racism.

1990
Several environmental justice organizations sent scathing letters to
the "Group of Ten" beltway environmental organizations, criticizing them for a monocultural perspective on environmentalism; for
their lack of racial and ethnic diversity in their membership, staffs,
and boards of directors; and for ignoring the plight of people of
color struggling against environmental racism.

1991
The First National People of Color Environmental Leadership Summit in Washington, D.C., brought together hundreds of environ-

mental justice activists from around the nation and other countries to forge the "Principles for Environmental Justice." One of the goals of this conference was to advocate for local and regional environmental justice activism in the form of regional and ethnic networks. It led to the creation of the Asian Pacific Environmental Network, the Indigenous Environmental Network, the Northeast Environmental Justice Network, the Southern Organizing Committee for Economic and Environmental Justice, and the Midwest/ Great Lakes Environmental Justice Network.

1991

El Pueblo para Aire y Agua Limpio won a landmark case against Chemical Waste Management over a Kettleman City, California, incinerator that was proposed without public documents translated into Spanish.

1992

The United Nations Conference on Environment and Development in Rio de Janeiro brought together hundreds of human rights and environmental justice activists from communities of color, Third World communities, and indigenous nations around the planet.

1994

President Clinton signed Executive Order 12898, charging all federal agencies with integrating environmental justice concerns into their operations.

1997

Chester Residents for Quality Living (Chester, Pennsylvania) was given the green light by the courts to pursue its case against polluters for Title VI violations.

1998

The chemical corporation Shintech was defeated in its efforts to bring an $800 million polyvinyl chloride plant to Convent, Louisiana, a majority African American community.

A Place within the Civil Rights and Environmental Movements?

Civil rights groups eventually took up the cudgels of environmental justice. However, the work of environmental law and policy specialists was, and remains, somewhat foreign to the repertoire and experience of the civil rights movement. The nation's mainstream environmental groups had environmental law and policy expertise, but they were even slower to accept the link between racial injustice and the concentration of the burdens of environmental pollution. Indeed, a distinct environmental justice movement emerged partly because the major U.S. environmental organizations had turned a blind eye to the problem. Typically, they had been founded and financially supported by white, relatively affluent individuals and institutions that were largely unfamiliar with the particular environmental grievances of poor people and people of color. Moreover, environmental organizations were further deterred when legal scholarship and judicial activity exposed more problems than solutions.

Not surprisingly, the greatest activism in combating environmental injustice has been from locally based groups, closely connected with the affected communities, who could perceive the environment as the places "where we live, work, and play." Recently, however, some national environmental groups have begun to appreciate that solutions to most environmental problems—not just environmental justice issues—can be addressed wisely and effectively by the people closest to the problems. These groups are reforming their programs, and the idea of devolution and community-based conservation is beginning to bridge the gap between the mainstream groups and local communities. For some, the impacts on communities placed at a disadvantage by race and poverty is an area of particular emphasis for their community-based programs; for others, communities of poor people and people of color may be incidental beneficiaries of a more localized orientation of programs.

Today, civil rights leaders and environmentalists alike embrace the concern with environmental justice. Though sometimes uneasy, this coincidence of interests has encouraged a fuller examination of all social inequities, from poverty to employment to housing, for intersections with the benefits and burdens of environmental protection. Similarly, it has led environmental advocates to seek out inequities linked to race and poverty in the contexts of wide-ranging environmental issues, from undesirable land uses to exposure to health threats, and from resource development to limits on access to public lands. Although environmental advocates have barely scratched the surface in exposing the potential reach of environmental justice for traditionally disadvantaged communities, they have also struck a responsive chord with rhetoric that appeals to other individuals and interest groups who perceive that they, too, have been treated unfairly under environmental laws and policies.

Executive Order 12898: A Defining Moment?

The federal government has played a valuable role in defining environmental justice. In 1994, a presidential proclamation of national policy, Executive Order 12898, declared that every federal agency should make "achieving environmental justice part of its mission by identifying and addressing . . . disproportionately high and adverse human health or environmental effects of its programs, policies, and activities on minority populations and low-income populations."[21] This was a milestone in the institutionalization of environmental justice. It also served to animate activity within the government and made both civil rights and environmental advocates more comfortable with their entries into the environmental justice field. At least the government had handed them a statement of policy and practices that could be used to put pressure back on the government agencies.

The executive order was not limited to siting waste facilities, but it did specifically target minority and low-income populations for protection. It also prescribed practices for agencies that have responsibilities ranging beyond facilities siting issues. The EPA's application of the policy, however, has continued to focus mostly on permitting issues, that is, on "traditional" environmental justice matters. This narrower approach, in combination with a continued policy of permitting polluting facilities, has dismayed many activists.

On the sixth anniversary of the executive order, several organizations and citizens issued a report concluding that the problems to be addressed by the order had actually worsened. The report indicated that communities of people of color and low-income populations remain under siege, battling what one activist termed "toxic terrorism" at the hands of polluting federal facilities and chemical industries. It argued that the negative human health consequences of these activities are increasingly visible.[22]

A national task force was appointed to examine and recommend measures to be employed not only by the EPA but also by a wide range of state and local agencies receiving federal funding (that therefore are covered by Title VI of the Civil Rights Act). The task force arguably could have pressed for a broader definition of the types of actions and services of governments at all levels that would trigger claims of discriminatory treatment. It recommended only modest expansion, suggesting going beyond permitting of facilities into policies and practices for enforcing laws against facilities located in communities of poor people and people of color. It also recommended that the EPA look at the environmental justice implications of brownfields redevelopment and grapple with the problem of unregulated sources of pollution in communities of color. The task force did not, however, reach significantly beyond traditional environmental justice concerns in addressing the implementation of Title VI.[23]

Environmental justice as a concept for guiding government action can be extended if particular agencies have the will to frame policies that are not as limited as they have been in the past, and if interest groups advocate the expansion. Some agencies have read the mandate to include a wide range of activities. In a 1998 status report by the U.S. Department of the Interior on "significant environmental justice accomplishments," the agency listed the following activities, among others:

- Consideration of the effects of oil and gas exploration on the subsistence activities of Alaska Native tribes, including the effects of seismic activities on bowhead whale migration
- Training of professors at historically-black colleges on state of the art technologies in cartography, GIS, and other mapping techniques
- Representing Sandia Pueblo Indians in preventing adverse impacts on the Petroglyphs National Monument from a proposed highway
- Focusing on urban parks and related race issues
- Monitoring water quality for sources adjacent to a Nevada Indian reservation, and examining upstream non-Indian uses affecting water salinity.[24]

Although Interior's report illustrates some of the possibilities for expansion, government activity in the field continues to concentrate on facilities siting in communities of poor people and people of color, struggling to reach its potential even there.

Attainable Policy and an Operational Definition

The field of environmental justice has evolved, and now several opportunities for its ambit to expand have become clear. As the field expands, it becomes more important to have an *operational* definition of environmental justice to focus policies and programs and agendas for action. Groups and individuals, as well as government agencies, need to identify specific issues and to define them so that they can get their arms around the issues. The types of solutions that are feasible and within the expertise or jurisdiction of the people and institutions involved also inform the scope of a movement or cause. For environmental justice to be addressed effectively in practical and political contexts, its agenda must be distinguished from broader goals of social and economic policy. So we raise the question whether, at some point, the environmental justice movement risks losing focus and effectiveness by enlarging its tent.

The definition to the field that we propose in this chapter is intended to encourage substantial expansion of the *types of issues* that are within the realm of environmental justice concerns. But we would limit the *types of communities* who have a claim to environmental justice. Every community can claim that it deserves to be involved in decisions that affect its environment, and therefore inclusion and participation are goals for the entire environmental movement. But it is the additional factor of group disadvantage that merits the heightened attention of the environmental justice movement. Thus, the claims of poor people and of people of color, including tribal communities, are uniquely issues of environmental justice.

A Tent Large Enough for All That Is "Unjust"?

Framing an agenda in any sector requires a coherent and definable notion of what is and is not within that sector. One way to do this is to define environmental justice in terms of the kinds of problems that it will attack. Looking for the appropriate limits to environmental justice as a concept begins with imaginative searches for every conceivable "injustice" that can be related to environmental protection. Is environmental justice simply a door into virtually everything that is unjust in our society? Justice is an expansive concept, and in Chapter 2, Gary Bryner provides a variety of frameworks for considering whether an act or a situation is just or unjust. Justice also has different connotations and manifestations depending on whether the context is economic, social, cultural, civil rights, or environmental. At the same time, broad areas overlap.

In an effort to define environmental justice, Bunyan Bryant leaves out almost nothing:

> Environmental justice (EJ) . . . refers to those cultural norms and values, rules, regulations, behaviors, policies, and decisions to support sustainable communities where people can interact with confidence that the environment is safe, nurturing, and productive. Environmental

justice is served when people can realize their highest potential. . . . EJ is supported by decent paying safe jobs; quality schools and recreation; decent housing and adequate health care; democratic decision-making and personal empowerment; and communities free of violence, drugs, and poverty. These are communities where both cultural and biological diversity are respected and highly revered and where distributed justice prevails.[25]

Bryant is describing the vision environmental justice holds for society—its goals—not an agenda. A fuller understanding of the goals of the environmental justice movement entails understanding the multiple causes of injustice, and Bryant thus helps us see *why* there are environmental justice problems and identifies a set of social conditions that, if addressed, would alleviate or prevent those problems.

In the social science literature, historical analyses of specific cases offer the most revealing research on causes or driving forces behind environmental inequality. These studies indicate that environmental justice problems are linked to endemic issues like those in Bryant's formulation. They trace the causes to at least three problem areas: the workplace, housing, and transportation.[26]

Besides being subjected to disproportionately high environmental impacts in their communities, people of color, poor people, and immigrants tend to confront similar hazards at work. The literature relating environmental harms to the workplace depicts the struggles of farm workers—of whom 90 percent are people of color or immigrants—and their exposure to pesticides. This maldistribution of risk was brought to the public's attention by the United Farm Workers and their most visible spokesperson, Cesar Chavez, in the 1970s.[27] More recently, studies demonstrated that African Americans face greater health threats in the workplace than the average white worker of the same socioeconomic status.[28] In Silicon Valley's high-tech sector, 70 percent of the production workforce are Asian and Latino immigrants, the majority of whom are women. While making microchips, printed wire and circuit boards, and other computer components, these workers may be exposed to seven hundred different chemicals.[29]

Because most environmental justice conflicts have occurred over facility siting, housing and real estate markets surely play a role. The causes of environmental injustice include: the historically rooted tendency for corporations and governments to "follow the path of least resistance" in facility siting; "market dynamics"; institutional racism in housing; and discriminatory zoning and planning practices.[30] When neighborhoods become contaminated with pollution, people of color and poor people are less likely to be able to move "up and out" into cleaner communities. Whites, on the other hand, are more likely to be able to "buy their way into" more desirable areas. Housing markets reflect long-standing patterns of excluding people of color from certain neighborhoods, keeping them concentrated in other, less desirable communities. These patterns have been achieved by using restrictive covenants, redlining, real estate sales and lending practices, and outright violence.[31] Housing quality itself is also a contributor to environmental health problems. Fully 90 percent of all lead poisoning sufferers are African American and Latino children, and lead poisoning often occurs within the household through exposure to lead-based paint or dust. The EPA also estimates that indoor air pollution is, on average, several times greater than outdoor air pollution. And as James Wescoat and his coauthors discuss in Chapter 3, some marginal populations still lack basic access to drinking water in their homes notwithstanding improvements for the population at large over the last century.

Recent research also has begun to make linkages among race, environmental quality, and transportation systems. Robert Bullard and his colleagues at the Environmental Justice Resource Center at Clark Atlanta University have traced the history of America's two-tiered, racially biased transportation infrastructure, from early conflicts over "separate but equal" accommodations, through the "urban renewal" that followed development of the interstate highway system, which disrupted, displaced, bisected, and bypassed many inner-city neighborhoods, to today's "auto addiction" and sprawl that exacerbate the problems of pollution and ecological damage. Charles Lee, former director of the United Church of Christ Commission on Racial Justice, has described sprawl as "a scenario where we are literally driving each other apart."[32]

Bryant realized that the environmental justice problem was intertwined with multiple social and economic problems. He posited that environmental justice issues pervade all of public policy, and he related it to national industrial policy, public education, and "land use, housing, banking, energy, effective national health care, and indigenous peoples' needs."[33] The linkages can reach even farther. In a recent essay, Detroit-based activist Grace Lee Boggs went so far as to connect an elementary school shooting to what she termed "place-based consciousness" and thus to the broader goals of the environmental justice movement.[34] If policy is made right in all these areas, then the environment should be better off, and presumably so would people of color and poor people.

Seeing the causes of injustice as intertwined, and environmental injustice as but a symptom among other multiple manifestations of injustice, helps us to understand the interconnection of issues and to form a vision for a better society. It is, however, less useful in charting an agenda. To address the causes of environmental injustice that extend well beyond *environmental* policy confuses appropriately broad goals with the definition and mission of a movement. Given the way political and economic institutions operate, people and organizations involved in social change can be most effective if they target identifiable issues and operate in specific areas.

If the solutions to environmental justice problems must be systemic, they will necessarily exceed the capacity of most people and institutions to make a difference. Neighborhood groups are not likely to make a dent in national industrial or banking policy, but they can effectively demand community involvement in environmental decisions and policy making. National environmental groups are not well equipped to deal effectively with housing policy, but they can correct the exclusion of people of color and low-income communities from the dominant environmental movement. Moreover, the jurisdiction of the EPA is generally limited to the environmental dimensions of particular problems. Making the operational definition of environmental justice specific to what reasonably can be accomplished within the realm of environmental policy allows for setting agendas that make sense in the context of the opportunities and issues that will arise.

An operational definition of environmental justice distinguishes the work that must be done to achieve justice in the formulation and application of environmental policy. When agencies, nonprofit organizations, funders, and activists decide how to focus their perennially limited resources and time, they may benefit from understanding the deeper causes of social injustice. But ultimately, they must set realistic goals for their part of the overall struggle against injustice—and an agenda for achieving them. Agendas are practical, attainable programs that involve tough decisions about what kind of work will—and will not—be done by particular groups and agencies.

A Tent Large Enough for All That Is "Environmental"?

In this book, the authors of many chapters expand the concept of environmental justice beyond the traditional siting question. But is environmental justice concerned with everything "unfair" that is related to the environment? In fact, some activists and scholars have argued that environmental justice includes all claimed disparities in the distribution of benefits and burdens of environmental regulation and natural resources policy, as well as unfairness to anyone in access to and participation in decision making.

UNFAIR RESULTS

Almost everything about environmental and natural resources policy is arguably unfair to someone. Some people get more or less use of resources or more or less harm from pollution. Can anyone who is far from a park or close to a pollution source raise a claim of environmental injustice? What about a landowner who claims "unfairness" when a parcel of land loses much of its value because zoning or environmental laws prevent it from being fully developed? A recent study linked high levels of cancer among affluent women in the United States to their increased exposure to perc (a chemical used by dry cleaners) and lawn pesticides (used by landscapers). All of these claims could raise "fairness" issues, and all implicate the goals of environmental protection. Is that coincidence enough to constitute an environmental justice issue?

In Chapter 2, Gary Bryner discusses how to analyze whether an act or situation is just or unjust. He explains that an "ecological framework" uses the touchstone of ecology to integrate the values inherent in sustainability with the other theories of justice. The search for a meaningful cause in the merger of environmental policy and justice, he posits, can be informed by the ideal of sustainability. Sustainability links ecological, economic, and social issues. This, in turn, helps explain why the issues that we intuitively care about, and that may matter to environmental justice, are those that involve social or economic inequity as well as ecological concern.

The ecological framework thus incorporates consideration of the interconnections among social and economic concerns in a way that informs an understanding of what issues coherently fit within a concept of environmental justice. As such, the cause of environmental justice—especially focusing on economic and social dimensions of environmental issues—is essential to achieving sustainability.

FAIR PROCESS

A major concern of environmental policy as well as a vital component of sustainability is ensuring that the people most affected by decisions are not excluded from participating in those decisions. Environmentalism has therefore begun to stress solutions that require a deeper

commitment to economic and political inclusion, equity, and participation.

One perspective is that environmental justice is essentially the
subdivision of environmental policy that seeks to involve all
affected stakeholders in environmental decisions. Neighboring communities were left out of decisions in virtually every classic environmental justice siting case in the literature and in the courts. This
issue is also common to the wider class of environmental justice
cases discussed throughout this book. See, for example, Chapters 7,
9, 10, and 11.

When major decisions about resources (their extraction, use, or
disposal) are made, the prospect of doing injustice to affected communities increases enormously by leaving community members out
of the process. Sheila Foster persuasively argues in Chapter 6 that a
fundamental cause of many environmental justice problems is the
exclusion from significant participation in decision making of people
with a stake in the outcome. The goals of environmental justice certainly must include ensuring that communities have meaningful
involvement in decision-making processes, and that decision makers
give respectful consideration to their interests. One potential tool for
achieving this goal is the so-called "devolve and collaborate" model
of decision making, a central tenet in modern efforts to reform environmental law and natural resources management. This decision-
making approach is effective in remedying environmental justice
problems deriving from inadequate community participation remains
an open question.

Is exclusion from participation in decision-making processes sufficient to constitute a problem as an environmental justice issue?
Should the tent be enlarged to include pervasive complaints about the
process of environmental decision making that go well beyond situations normally considered within the scope of the term *environmental
justice?*

If environmental justice were considered to encompass the cause
of ensuring a fair *process* in environmental decision making for all
claimants, it would then become the cause of victim and polluter
alike. It would include anyone who, regardless of motive, seeks to
invoke environmental laws. This would include opponents of affordable housing in upscale neighborhoods as well as chemical companies
seeking to prevent expansion by their competitors. Everyone deserves
to be heard, but does this mean that they march under the banner of
environmental justice?

If the mission of environmental justice were to ensure effective participation of some, but not all, people with a stake in the outcome of environmental decisions, how would the line be drawn? Does environmental justice care only about the cause of those who argue for improvements in environmental quality? What then of the views of people who would at least consider the benefits of jobs added by development in a troubled African American neighborhood? The American Indian tribe that wants to develop its economy over the objection of neighbors? The Hispano community that wants to engage in community forestry in a national forest? (See Chapters 7, 10, and 9 for discussions of these issues regarding American Indian tribes and Hispanic land-grant communities.)

And is participation enough? Outcomes can be intolerable, even to those who were heard in the process leading up to a decision. If, at the end of the day, a hazardous waste facility is located in a poor African American neighborhood, or if Hispano communities in northern New Mexico end up losing their communal water rights in *acequias* to a federal water project, will it be enough that public objections were voiced before the key decision was made? Ensuring adequate participation may be a fundamental goal of environmental justice, but it is not the only one.

We urge that environmental justice is at once more and less than the portion of the environmental movement that demands more inclusion and participation in decision making. It is more because the problems and solutions suggested by many of the chapters in this book do not all begin and end with participation questions. It is less, we believe, because not every claim to participation or injustice in environmental decision making is one that the field of environmental justice can or should embrace. So we do not think that the boundaries of environmental justice can be drawn effectively in terms of either the outcome or the quality of participation in environmental decisions. Ultimately, lines must be drawn in terms of who—that is, which *community*—is raising the claim.

Environmental Justice for What Communities?

Whatever the boundaries of environmental justice may be, some claims seem more worthy of attention than others. Whose claims fit into a movement that was founded to ameliorate the effects of waste facility sitings in communities of people of color and in poor neighborhoods? Consider the possibilities: Does a largely African American, upper-middle-class neighborhood have the same claim to environmental justice that a poor, historically disenfranchised African American community would have? Can everyone, regardless of race or poverty, who has ever cried "NIMBY!" join the movement? Is it an environmental justice issue when a rancher complains that entitlements to graze cattle on the public land were reduced because of a new federal environmental protection policy? Is a business owner who legally sent toxic chemicals to a landfill years ago and now is retroactively liable under the Superfund law for costs of cleaning up the dump a victim of environmental injustice? When farmers' use of irrigation water is restricted by federal programs to protect endangered salmon, are they victims of environmental injustice?

First, we suggest that environmental justice claims should be seen in terms of *community* issues. The idea of ecological justice as framed by Bryner and the EPA's framework for evaluating environmental justice impacts, described by Buhrmann in Chapter 11, include the notion of community. If the wrongs to be addressed are essentially community wrongs, then communities, not individuals, can stake a claim to environmental justice.

But what then is a "community" whose concerns fit within the ambit of environmental justice? What distinguishes the neighborhood or group that raises an environmental *justice* issue from any other neighborhood or group? The definition of the term *community* connotes some commonality in interests, backgrounds, occupations, or legal treatment among people as well as the existence of ties to a particular place. Otherwise, any individual or family who has experienced problems or unfairness or inordinate costs because of the way environmental law or policy works could claim to be a victim of environmental injustice. And presumably, it would take more than finding a common cause in opposition to a particular decision to make a *community* of an otherwise eclectic group of individuals.

What is it, then, that compels us to devote additional time, resources, and caring to an issue in the name of environmental justice? We propose that the roots of this young movement should guide its development and expansion. Because of the circumstances of the traditional siting cases, most people understand environmental justice to be about the especially egregious injustice suffered when environmental laws disregard or disserve the interests of the "disenfranchised and dispossessed."[35] This criterion should be applied, as well, to evaluating whether a resource development matter far from the traditional case deserves the attention of the environmental justice movement.

Although environmental justice as a concept is expansive enough to deal with the full range of problems that arise in the realm of environmental and natural resources policy, it will have viability as a significant area of concern only if the injustices it addresses are focused on the claims of *disadvantaged communities*.[36] That is, to have a claim to environmental justice, a community should come to the table with a palpable and endemic disadvantage.

Why do we urge here that there must be some aggravating circumstance, such as race or poverty, that triggers a heightened concern for justice? First, environmental policy is plagued with hard choices and debates about priorities. Policy makers and scholars press competing environmental objectives and methods, arguing about the degree of health protection that should be pursued and whether and how much technology should be required. They struggle with assessing risk and how to fit market incentives and economic efficiency into pollution control and resource allocation programs. The problem of undefined priorities starts with a suite of uncoordinated statutes and agencies, and it is exacerbated by the intense involvement of multiple and conflicting interests, from industry to environmentalists to states to posturing politicians. The result is a huge expenditure of resources, time, and effort quibbling over competing methods and nuanced goals. If it is to succeed, the pursuit of environmental justice should not add another level of ambiguity but should instead be a clear priority within environmental policy, and this requires a clear understanding of what is and is not an environmental justice claim. Similarly, we urge the criterion of an aggravating disadvantage for a matter to come under the rubric of environmental justice, because a lack of participation would not distinguish environmental justice problems from other environmental problems. Ensuring fuller participation in environmental decisions is part of the solution to most environmental problems.

If environmental justice is conflated into the claim of *all* people—not just low-income populations and communities of people of color—to be free of *any* kind of inequity that occurs in the name of environmental and natural resources policy, then it aggravates the problem of undefined priorities that pervades environmental policy.[37]

Second, environmental justice, as a particular area of concern, risks dilution and even co-optation if it goes beyond the cause of victims with distinctive claims. The goals of environmental protection are to minimize adverse environmental impacts, and the aspiration of modern environmentalism is to maximize public participation. While these ends are within the broader vision of environmental justice, they are too general to define an environmental justice movement apart from the environmental movement. The ideal of environmental justice has a more particular mission, one that formed originally around the sense of injustice piqued by blatantly discriminatory sitings of waste facilities in communities of color and in poor neighborhoods. To say that the field ought to expand beyond sitings issues is not to say that it should forget the nature of the injustices that inspired the movement.

It is important for the environmental justice movement to know what it is and what it is not, just as the civil rights and environmental movements have had to define and limit their missions and the causes they would embrace. The civil rights movement has seen the ideal of "colorblind justice" co-opted by the "victims" of affirmative action, and it has no trouble excluding their cause. In environmental law, polluters and developers have won the right to bring lawsuits under statutes that require environmental impact statements, disclosure of information, public participation, and elaborate procedures. These procedural rights can be invoked to delay or weaken enforcement of environmental laws. The environmental movement, of course, has not even considered expanding its agenda to assert the procedural rights of polluters, although the rights being asserted are rights to participate under environmental laws.

Likewise, environmental justice cannot take on all environmental wrongs in all communities, or it risks being co-opted by its own rhetoric of inclusion and equity. It should focus, we believe, on championing the cause of communities for whom inequity in the allocation of benefits and burdens of environmental policy intensifies the social or economic disadvantages they already suffer. Thus, we conclude that environmental justice should comprehend the claims of poor communities because they suffer from economic disadvantage, communities of color because they have chronically been victims of discrimination, and tribal communities because they typically have been denied full protection of their rights to culture and self-government under the law.

We accept that this criterion is not unproblematic and that many communities may not fit neatly into the categories of areas that are in poverty or composed of people of color. Determinations will be case by case, and there will be close cases and hard choices. We also understand that the judgment calls regarding who is vulnerable or disadvantaged can be controversial and will raise the question of who should decide. But if environmental justice is as important as we believe it to be, this is a worthy and essential debate.

Conclusion

In this chapter, we have discussed the development and the possible expansion of the relatively new field of environmental justice. The other chapters in this book raise a broad range of issues that arguably belong within the concerns of environmental justice. The breadth of these concerns continually reminds us of the primary questions of what kinds of claims are the concerns of environmental justice, which communities should have their interests championed under the banner of environmental justice, and how we remedy existing injustices and prevent future ones.

As several chapters illustrate, inequitable distribution of the burdens and benefits of environmental protection for these groups can reach well beyond the traditional siting and pollution focus of environmental justice. The "new" issues treated here are predominately rural and western in that many of them emanate from American Indian reservations, public lands, and natural resources development activities. They often involve natural resources extraction or management rather than pollution and waste. Yet virtually all of the cases studied in these chapters exemplify the coincidence of inequitable distribution of environmental harms and problems of race and chronic poverty. This exacerbation of existing social inequities is the phenomenon that originally excited local activism and public concern over the traditional kind of environmental justice. We are mindful also of pleas to include the problems of anyone who is treated unfairly or left out in environmental decision making. But we believe that this could actually perpetuate injustice if it diluted the focus of the movement.

The particular circumstances of communities of color, poor communities, and of American Indian reservations distinguish their claims. Their disadvantaged status makes it more onerous and tragic when they suffer unfair burdens or are deprived of the benefits of natural resources management and environmental protection policies. And history has shown that it is more difficult for them to gain justice within political and legal systems than it is for other communities. That is why environmental justice has emerged as an area of particular concern. If these communities merely share in society's progress toward greater equity in administration of environmental laws, we doubt that they will get a fair share of the benefits.

Notes

1. Benjamin Chavis, "Environmental Racism," in *Confronting Environmental Racism: Voices from the Grassroots,* ed. Robert Bullard (Boston: South End Press, 1993), 1–8.
2. Bunyan Bryant, ed., *Environmental Justice: Issues, Policies, and Solutions* (Washington, D.C.: Island Press, 1995), 5.

3. Catherine A. O'Neill, "Variable Justice: Environmental Standards, Contaminated Fish, and 'Acceptable' Risk to Native Peoples," *Stanford Environmental Law Journal* 19 (2000): 3.

4. Lily N. Chinn, "Can the Market Be Fair and Efficient? An Environmental Justice Critique of Emissions Trading," *Ecology Law Quarterly* 26 (1999): 80.

5. Kristin Schrader-Frechette, "Environmental Justice and Native Americans: The Mescalero Apache and Monitored Retrievable Storage," *Natural Resources Law Journal* 36 (1996): 703; Kevin Gover and Jana Walker, "Escaping Environmental Paternalism: One Tribe's Approach to Developing a Commercial Waste Disposal Project in Indian Country," *University of Colorado Law Review* 63 (1992): 933.

6. *Lyng v Northwest Indian Cemetery Protective Association*, 485 U.S. 439 (1988).

7. Martin Melosi, *Garbage in the Cities: Refuse, Reform, and the Environment, 1880–1980* (College Station: Texas A&M University Press, 1981); Samara F. Swanston, "Environmental Justice and Environmental Quality Benefits: The Oldest, Most Pernicious Struggle and Hope for Burdened Communities," *Vermont Law Review* 23 (1999): 545.

8. Although social scientists made significant contributions to the field, quarrels have raged over the appropriateness and size of samples and methodologies used in some of their studies. Paul Mohai, "The Demographics of Dumping Revisited: Examining the Impact of Alternate Methodologies in Environmental Justice Research," *Virginia Environmental Law Journal* 14 (1995): 615; Don Coursey, "Environmental Racism in the City of Chicago" (paper presented at the Irving B. Harris School of Public Policy, University of Chicago, Chicago, Ill., October 1994). Extended discussions persist over whether zip codes or census tracts properly demark a neighborhood and what percentage of residents of color constitutes a "minority neighborhood." Glynis Daniels, "Ecological Fallacy or Environmental Fact?: An Investigation of Aggregation Bias in the Study of Environmental Justice" (paper presented at the annual meeting of the American Sociological Association, Washington, D.C., August 2000). Similarly, the courts have struggled with the evidentiary value of various studies cited to prove the disproportionate impacts of waste facilities on communities of poor people and people of color.

9. *Guardians Ass'n v Civil Serv. Com'n*, 463 U.S. 582 (1983); *Alexander v Choate*, 469 U.S. 287 (1985); *Alexander v Sandoval*, 121 S.Ct. 1511 (2001).

10. 482 F. Supp. 673 (S.D. Tex. 1979).

11. 896 F.2d 1264 (11th Cir. 1989).

12. *Guardians Ass'n v Civil Serv. Com'n*.

13. 40 C.F.R., sec. 7.35(b).

14. 132 F.3d 925, 936–37 (3rd Cir. 1997), vacated as moot, 524 U.S. 974 (1998).

15. 121 S.Ct. 1511 (2001).

16. Civil Rights Act of 1964, 42 U.S.C., sec. 2000d. For a critique, see Peter Reich's article "Greening the Ghetto: A Theory of Environmental Race Discrimination," *Kansas Law Review* 41 (1992): 281–87; see also Kelly Colquette and Elizabeth Robertson, "Environmental Racism: The Causes,

Consequences, and Commendations," *Tulane Environmental Law Journal* 5 (1991): 153–207; Sheila Foster, "Race(ial) Matters: The Quest for Environmental Justice," *Ecology Law Quarterly* 20 (1993): 721; Gerald Torres, "Class, Race, and Environmental Racism," *University of Colorado Law Review* 63 (1992): 839; Luke Cole, "Empowerment as the Key to Environmental Protection: The Need for Environmental Poverty Law," *Ecology Law Quarterly* 19 (1992): 619; Luke Cole, "Remedies for Environmental Racism: A View from the Field," *Michigan Law Review* 90 (1992): 1991; and Rachel Godsil, "Remedying Environmental Racism," *Michigan Law Review* 90 (1991): 394.

17. Symposium "Race, Class, and Environmental Regulation," *University of Colorado Law Review* 63 (1992): 839; see also Symposium "Environmental Justice: Mobilizing for the 21st Century," *Vermont Law Review* 23 (1999); and Symposium "Environmental Justice," *Fordham Environmental Law Journal* 20 (1999).

18. Arthur Hayes, "New Specialty Helps Poor Fight Pollution," *Wall Street Journal*, October 3, 1991.

19. Ralph Santiago Abascal, "California Rural Legal Assistance and Environmental Justice," *Chicano-Latino Law Review* 14 (1994): 44, 46.

20. 22 Envtl. L. Rep. 20,357 (Cal. App. Dep't Super. Ct. 1991).

21. Executive Order No. 12898, "Federal Actions to Address Environmental Justice in Minority Populations and Low-Income Populations," 59 *Federal Register* 7629 (1994), 3 C.F.R., sec. 859, reprinted in 42 U.S.C., sec. 4321. Available at www.epa.gov/docs/oejpubs.

22. Cat Lazaroff, *Environmental News Service*, February 11, 2000.

23. Environmental Protection Agency, "Report of the Title VI Implementation Advisory Committee," March 1, 1999.

24. Letter from Anne H. Shields, U.S. Department of the Interior, to Mr. Thurgood Marshall Jr. and Ms. Kathleen A. McGinty (April 14, 1998).

25. Bryant, *Environmental Justice*, 6.

26. See, e.g., Andrew Hurley, *Environmental Inequalities: Class, Race and Industrial Pollution in Gary, Indiana, 1945–1980* (Chapel Hill: University of North Carolina Press, 1995); and Laura Pulido, S. Sidawi, and R. O. Vos, "An Archaeology of Environmental Racism in Los Angeles," *Urban Geography* 17 (1996): 419–39.

27. One report estimates that one thousand farm workers die each year due to pesticide poisoning, while more than three hundred thousand become ill annually. See Ivette Perfecto and Baldemar Velasquez, "Farm Workers: Among the Least Protected," *EPA Journal* 18 (March/April 1992): 13–14.

28. African Americans are 37 percent more likely than their white counterparts to succumb to an injury or illness on the job. In California, African American men and Latino men are respectively 40 percent and 80 percent more likely than their white counterparts to suffer an injury or illness on the job. See James Robinson, *Toil and Toxics* (Berkeley: University of California Press, 1991). African Americans make up 20 percent of the steel industry workforce but occupy 90 percent of the positions in the coke

ovens—sites where exposure to the carcinogen benzene is known to produce high rates of leukemia. See Robert Bullard and Beverly Wright, "The
Effects of Occupational Injury, Illness and Disease on the Health Status of
Black Americans," in *Toxic Struggles: The Theory and Practice of Environmental Justice,* ed. Richard Hofrichter (Philadelphia: New Society, 1993),
153–62.

29. Studies estimate that illnesses in this industry are three times that of any
basic industry. Joseph LaDou, ed., *The Microelectronics Industry: State of the
Art Review—Occupational Medicine* (Philadelphia: Hanley and Belfus,
1986).

30. Vicki Been, "What's Fairness Got to Do with It? Environmental Justice
and the Siting of Locally Undesirable Land Uses," *Cornell Law Review* 78
(1993): 1001; Robert Bullard, *Dumping in Dixie: Race, Class and Environmental Quality* (Boulder, Colo.: Westview Press, 2000); Robert Bullard and
Beverly Wright, "The Effects of Occupational Injury, Illness and Disease
on the Health Status of Black Americans," in *Toxic Struggles: The Theory
and Practice of Environmental Justice,* ed. Richard Hofrichter (Philadelphia:
New Society, 1993): 153–62; Robert Bullard, Eugene Grigsby, and Charles
Lee, *Residential Apartheid: The American Legacy* (Los Angeles: CAAS Pub-
lishers, 1994); Richard Lazarus, "Pursuing Environmental Justice: The
Distributional Effects of Environmental Protection," *Northwestern University Law Review* 87 (1993): 787.

31. Bullard, Grigsby, and Lee, *Residential Apartheid*; Joe Feagin, "A House Is
Not a Home: White Racism and U.S. Housing Practices," in Bullard,
Grigsby, and Lee, *Residential Apartheid,* 17–48; Joe Feagin and Melvin
Sikes, *Living with Racism: The Middle Class Black Experience* (Boston: Bea-
con Press, 1994).

32. Personal communication with Charles Lee, July 1995; Robert Bullard,
Glenn Johnson, and Angel Torres, *Sprawl City: Race, Politics, and Planning
in Atlanta* (Washington, D.C.: Island Press, 2000).

33. Bryant, ed., *Environmental Justice,* 219.

34. Grace Lee Boggs, "A Question of Place," *WORT,* Madison, Wis. (March
27, 2000).

35. William A. Shutkin, "The Concept of Environmental Justice and a Recon-
ception of Democracy," *Virginia Environmental Law Journal* 14 (1995): 580.

36. Executive Order No. 12898, sec. 1-103, is specific about the types of communities that it intends to protect. It specifies "minority populations and
low-income populations."

37. Christopher H. Foreman Jr., *The Promise and Peril of Environmental Justice*
(Washington, D.C.: Brookings Institute, 1998), 116.

Chapter 2

ASSESSING CLAIMS OF ENVIRONMENTAL JUSTICE

Conceptual Frameworks

Gary C. Bryner

A lively debate exists about the nature of environmental justice, the extent and seriousness of the risks, and the causes and underlying factors. But just as important and difficult is the question of what kinds of responses we should pursue. What are our options, and how should we choose from among them? Natural resources laws and policies traditionally focus on encouraging development of resources, protecting natural systems, and ensuring the sustainability of resource development. These laws and policies are usually assessed by how well they achieve these resource development and environmental protection goals and how they interact with the economic goals of efficiency and growth. Environmental justice advocates argue that just as important as these environmental and economic goals, however, should be the consequences of natural resources policy decisions for the societal goals of protecting individual rights, promoting justice and fairness, ensuring fair participation, and fostering social equity. This chapter examines five theoretical frameworks that can be used to understand alternative ways of defining injustices related to natural resources and the environment, to suggest how environmental justice can be approached from different perspectives, and to explore how environmental and social justice goals might be more effectively pursued together.

The Problem of Environmental and Natural Resources Injustice

Environmental injustices go beyond the problems of inequitable exposure to environmental hazards that have traditionally been the focus of the environmental justice movement. However, it is not clear how the goal of environmental justice should be broadened to incorporate issues of natural resources. Expanding the reach of environmental justice to include access to natural resources is a compelling goal, but it must compete with other demands including greater emphasis on the environmental justice agenda. Setting priorities for the allocation of scarce financial and enforcement resources of government agencies and the efforts of advocacy groups is inevitable. Questions such as what claims are (and should be) the concerns of environmental justice and what injustices we should seek to remedy are inescapable.

Defining Environmental Justice

As David Getches and David Pellow argue in Chapter 1, environmental justice has been defined several different ways. Under their expanded definition, the problem might take either of these forms: (1) low-income and minority communities are disproportionately exposed to environmental risks; and (2) low-income and minority communities are less likely than other communities to benefit from natural resources access and development policies. Both cases are examples of injustices, primarily seen here as problems with the ways in which benefits and burdens are distributed in society.

Hazardous waste treatment and storage sites, representative of the first kind of problem, are often located in low-income and minority communities because of low land prices and little political opposition. As a result, community members are exposed to greater levels of hazardous emissions, odors, water contamination, and other environmental risks than those who live in other communities. Or, poor people may move into areas where these facilities already exist, because housing prices there are cheaper. People of color may have fewer housing choices because of discrimination and may have few options other than moving into areas with higher environmental risks. Because of their lack of political influence, low-income and minority communities may also have less enforcement, prevention, mitigation, and other efforts to reduce environmental hazards. Other communities, where residents have more political clout, are more likely to have more influence to ensure that government officials respond to environmental threats in their communities.

Despite these barriers confronting minority communities, these communities have been increasingly successful in raising awareness of cases of disproportionate exposure to environmental hazards. African American children in Chicago, for example, chained themselves to dump trucks filled with hazardous wastes; a multiracial group in Los Angeles blocked the construction of an incinerator in their community. Tribes have protested threats to subsistence fishing and hunting by pollution from mining operations that have poisoned fish, game, and reservation lands. Cases brought in the 1990s continued to focus on toxic waste but also expanded to reach other issues. In Boston, community members protested plans to expand Logan Airport, because of the impact of increased aircraft noise on working-class and poor communities. In Atlanta, environmental and community groups oppose highway projects that would increase air pollution in minority neighborhoods.[1]

The development of water and other natural resources in the arid West have been primarily aimed at politically well-connected communities, an example of the second kind of injustice. Subsidies and other policies benefit large, wealthy landowners more than they do small, low-income farmers and ranchers. The treaty rights of tribes have been regularly violated by states and private interests who have ignored fishing, water, land, and other Native American rights in order to increase their access to valuable natural resources. In other regions of the country, advocates have raised similar concerns about the impact of projects on minority and poor communities. The plan to restore the Everglades by redirecting freshwater into the area, for example, was criticized by some members of Congress for failing to give adequate attention to the impact of the loss of agricultural water on low-income and minority farmers. Members urged the Army Corps of Engineers, the agency responsible for the Everglades project, to establish a monitoring panel to represent the interests of low-income and minority communities and to involve them in the implementation of the restoration project.[2]

Frameworks for Assessing Environmental Justice Issues

A major challenge in environmental justice is deciding how to define the problem and then choosing a core strategy for developing a legal and political response. While other chapters in this volume more thoroughly identify and explore the causes and characteristics of environmental injustice, this chapter considers different ways of framing the problem of environmental justice. Five options for framing the issue of environmental justice seem to capture most of the approaches taken by advocates and scholars. These frameworks are not mutually exclusive, and they overlap considerably as they are used by proponents of the different frameworks. Table 2.1 summarizes the frameworks and outlines the issues raised in this chapter.

The Civil Rights Framework

Environmental justice is typically viewed as a civil rights problem, with remedies rooted in civil rights law and policy. Minority communities are targets for siting hazardous sites because of their lack of political power. Similarly, politicians who make resource development decisions and policies that distribute benefits to politically powerful interests or violate treaty or statutory rights and agreements may do so because of the perception that there is little political cost, and considerable political gain, in ignoring these rights and commitments. The interactions of race, income, and political power are complex. The location of facilities may be driven by market factors, such as the price of land, access to transportation infrastructure, availability of labor, and location of raw materials; the facilities may be located in areas where residents have less political power than in other communities; and they may even be intentionally located in minority or low-income communities. Site locations evolve over time: a site may originally be located in an urban, working-class community. As time passes, residents in this community who can afford to move to more pleasant surroundings do so, leaving poorer residents and depressed land prices. In turn, low-income residents move in because of cheap housing prices.[3] Market factors, discrimination, and the political powerlessness of marginalized communities that have little clout in policy-making decisions all contribute in complicated ways to environmental injustice.[4]

The civil rights framework is sometimes intertwined with broader notions of social justice. Robert D. Bullard, a distinguished environmental justice scholar, argues that several factors contribute to environmental injustice. These factors include concerns about the procedures by which rules, regulations, and criteria are applied; the location of meetings to inform the public; the publication of materials only in English; and the composition of decision-making bodies that does not reflect the racial and ethnic makeup of the communities affected by those decisions. There are geographical concerns about the distribution of jobs and income from industrial activities and the burdens caused by the disposal of industrial wastes; communities that house the waste sites receive fewer benefits than the areas where production occurs. Social inequity concerns focus on lingering racism in the United States and the extent to which communities of color are seen as sacrifice zones for pollution and hazardous waste. Bullard argues that race and class are "intricately linked in our society," but that race "continues to be a potent predictor of where people live, which communities get dumped on, and which are spared."[5]

Title VI and Fairness in Government Funding

The Environmental Protection Agency's (EPA's) Office of Civil Rights is responsible for receiving and investigating environmental justice complaints. The challenges confronting the agency in dealing with environmental justice complaints are daunting. A key challenge here is to determine what constitutes discrimination. Is every decision that results in disproportionate impacts a problem? Is exposure to pollution sufficient, or does there need to be evidence of actual adverse impact? In either case, what level of disparity is required to constitute a discriminatory impact? EPA officials do not have a great deal of law to guide them. They find in federal law clear authority for a disparate impact standard (rather than intent to discriminate), and they rely on analogies from employment, public services, and education law, even though there are important differences among the issues addressed by statutes in these areas.

In contrast to statutory law, complaints of discrimination pursued under constitutional provisions such as the Fourteenth Amendment's equal protection clause require a showing of discriminatory *intent* on the part of government actors. Providing such proof is a much more difficult task for complainants, since officials are unlikely to provide evidence of discriminatory purposes, making statutory complaints more common and more likely to be successful. But constitutional requirements are nevertheless important elements of legal strategies for environmental justice since they reach all government actions, not just those covered by statutes.

Much of the debate in interpreting Title VI of the Civil Rights Act of 1964 and other civil rights law and policy focuses on remedies for discrimination. Two competing principles might guide decision making: nondiscrimination and racial preference. The nondiscrimination standard prohibits any consideration of race in the making of environmental, land use, natural resource, and other policy decisions.

TABLE 2.1. Frameworks for Assessing Environmental Justice Issues

Framework	What the framework requires	Underlying assumptions	Some questions/ problems
Civil Rights	•Identify disparate impacts due to discrimination. •Devise remedies that make victims whole.	•Civil rights law provides legal tools and concepts.	•How is discrimination to be defined? •When does it occur? •What remedies are possible? •Should low-income communities be included? •Will problems just be transferred to another community?
Distributive Justice and Ethics	•Distribute benefits and burdens fairly or equally. •Ensure that differences benefit the least well-off. •Provide compensation for past injustices such as treaty violations. •Consider environmental ethics.	•Public policies should produce fair outcomes. •Policies should meet expectations of constitutional equal protection.	•What is fair? What is equal? Exposure to risks and access to benefits cannot be distributed equally, so how should they be shared? •What obligations do we have to those who are especially dependent on natural resources and rooted in the land?
Public Participation	•Devise fair procedures that give voice to all members of a community, especially the politically powerless. •Ensure that all groups have the social capital to participate effectively.	•Fair procedures for whatever outcomes are agreed to. •Participation allows affected parties to help determine what happens in their communities and how benefits and risks are balanced.	•Is a fair process enough? •Can all parties participate fairly and effectively? •Who should be involved in the process?

Framework	What the framework requires	Underlying assumptions	Some questions/ problems
Social Justice	•Comprehensively assess the interaction of economic, political, social, and cultural power. •Address the root causes of injustices. •Ensure the preservation of cultural diversity, especially groups with ties to the land.	•The economic, political, and social ideas, institutions, norms, incentives, and underlying assumptions that result in disproportionate risks and harms are addressed.	•With such a broad agenda, what are the priorities for legal and policy responses? •How can they be addressed in environmental and natural resources law? •What are the historical land use patterns and decisions that have contributed to injustices, and how can they be reversed?
Ecological Sustainability	•Require pollution prevention and conservation of resources. •Reduce pollution and risks for all people. •Ensure that economic, equity, and ecological values are intertwined. •Make ecological sustainability the primary value. •Use the precautionary principle in the face of uncertainty.	•The effects of environmental problems are to be eliminated rather than redistributed. •Environmental problems are dealt with directly, as ecological challenges, rather than more indirectly, as social, economic, or political problems.	•Pollution may eventually be eliminated, but what about its impacts in the interim? •Are there fairness, discrimination, and disproportionate impact issues that still need to be addressed beyond what sustainability implies? •What use of resources, especially nonrenewables like fossil fuels, is consistent with sustainability?

That standard raises the question of what constitutes a violation of the principle—how much difference constitutes a disparate impact? In environmental justice cases, the question may be, how does the environmental risk to health compare across minority and nonminority communities, or how do the natural resources benefits given to minority groups compare with those provided to nonminority ones? These and related issues are addressed by Luke Cole in Chapter 8 as well as in much of Part 2.

However, the nondiscrimination principle may be too conservative and acquiescent to the status quo. In embracing it, we commit to discriminate no more. But what about the impacts already in place? Preferential treatment or a race-conscious remedy, many argue, is required to compensate for past discrimination. This may take the form of offering compensation to communities for the existing facilities in their community or the lack of access to natural resources, and perhaps preferential treatment to ensure that the risks of environmental harms and the benefits of natural resources are spread more evenly. Those decisions turn on notions of distributive justice (discussed in the following section).

The civil rights framework will likely continue to guide efforts to pursue the goals of environmental justice. But problems with this framework must be addressed. For example, should environmental justice focus only on people of color, or should impacts on low-income people also be addressed? The civil rights solution may not work as well for income as it does for race. Race is well established in constitutional law as a suspect classification, requiring heightened or strict scrutiny by courts and a showing of a compelling government interest when it serves as the basis for policy making. In contrast, federal courts do not recognize class as a suspect classification or any kind of a problematic distinction. Poor people simply have fewer options than wealthy ones. They also bear more risks because they have less money to protect themselves against some risks. Neither constitutional nor statutory provisions provide any basis for claims that class or income status constitutes an actionable claim. Note that some have argued that affirmative action should be viewed as a remedy for income-based disadvantage, rather than racial status, but that view has yet to gain formal legal or constitutional acceptance. If income or poverty is the ultimate root of environmental and natural resources injustices, then we need solutions that go beyond the remedies available from civil rights law.

More broadly, should civil rights be at the center of the debate over the role of government in pursuing environmental protection policies, at least for people of color? We rely on a discourse of civil rights to discuss the values and concerns that are most important to our political, collective lives. But a politics of rights makes trade-offs difficult because it emphasizes entitlements that claimants make regardless of costs or competing concerns. A discourse of rights eschews the balancing that is inevitable when we have public demands that are contradictory or exceed the resources that are available. The controversies surrounding rights place into question their role in guiding public policy making. If rights are to play a transforming role in ensuring environmental justice, they will have to be thought of in different ways, not just as restraints on government, but as ways of empowering individuals, reinforcing our responsibility for one another and for the kind of society that we are part of, and asserting the moral and social responsibilities we have in common. Rights need not insulate individuals from one another but, rather, can be part of defining membership in a political society and reinforcing shared commitments. Rights can help foster common concerns and encourage us to commit to ensuring that each person enjoys access to natural resources and environmental quality, which are essential for realizing a meaningful life and enjoying real equality of opportunity.

The Distributive Justice and Environmental Ethics Framework

Another way of framing the problem of environmental justice comes from theories of justice devised by philosophers who grapple with such issues as how to distribute benefits and burdens, how expectations of equality are to be satisfied, and what ethical principles can guide natural resources policy making. Much of environmental justice's development is rooted in the expectations created by the idea of distributive justice. Distributive justice seeks answers to questions such as these: If an equitable distribution in the location of polluting facilities or access to natural resources is the goal, what definition of equity do we use? Does equity mean the polluter pays—that those who benefit from pollution should bear the burden of disposing of the accompanying wastes? If so, then should those who consume more have more polluting facilities near them or pay others to bear that risk? The "polluter pays" principle appeals strongly to a sense of fairness that links benefits and burdens. But following this principle presents numerous challenges, such as determining who bears the burdens, what those burdens are and how they should be valued, and what additional costs should be imposed on producers and purchasers.

One form of distributive justice is geographic equity, which requires fairness in the physical distribution of hazardous facilities. However, such a standard is impractical. It is not likely that everyone would be exposed equally, and some inevitably will be more exposed than others. Proposals to bury wastes or ship them to other countries simply impose the problem on future generations or on communities in other nations. One option is to give preference to those who have not benefited or who have been burdened in the past. Here, we encounter the same challenges faced by advocates of preferential treatment: Do we compensate actual victims of specific injustices, or do we compensate victims of general, societal discrimination? Do we compensate individuals or communities? How do we prove instances of past discrimination? How do we identify victims of societal discrimination? Are all people of color entitled to the same preference? Are low-income groups similarly deserving? How do we determine which persons are in fact entitled to the benefit? Violations of principles or expectations of distributive justice also compel calculations of compensation for past victims of injustices. Should those who have benefited from access to those resources, or benefited from reduced exposure to risk, pay those who have been left out of benefits or have borne risks? Perhaps so, but the calculation of who pays and who is compensated would be complex. Most of the following chapters provide examples of environmental justice as disproportionate and unfair impacts.

JUSTICE AND UTILITARIANISM

One of the most prominent forms of distributive justice is utilitarianism. Utilitarianism calls for a distribution of benefits, opportunities, and burdens that generates the greatest welfare for the greatest number. It is defended from at least two perspectives. First, utilitarianism is consistent with economic efficiency; a failure to maximize benefits would be unjust because of the unrealized potential for generating wealth and the consequential well-being. The goal of public policy here is to maximize the economic value of goods and services or economic utility. Second, utilitarianism is egalitarian: every person's utility or interests are given equal weight. Utilitarianism here is consistent with democratic theories of individual equality and majority rule.

Utilitarianism often shows up in environmental policy in the form of cost-benefit analysis. Cost-benefit analysis is a widely used analytical tool that appeals to commonsense notions and has deep roots in natural resources policy making.[6] The shortcomings of cost-benefit analysis and utilitarian calculations have been most prominent in natural resources and environmental law and policy. These shortcomings usually take one of two forms. First, many values cannot be easily quantified in dollars; those values that can be more precisely and unambiguously quantified and monetized will be given priority over those that are less certain. More precise economic costs, for example, may be given more weight than imprecise estimates of the value of ecosystem health, ecological services, public health, or aesthetics. Cost-benefit analysis's bias against values that are not easily quantified can be overcome by resisting quantification and laying out in qualitative terms the values to be compared. This systematic identification of the costs and benefits of alternatives can be a very useful decision-making tool and can help illuminate the consequences of policy choices, but its inability to generate an unambiguous bottom line—whether the benefits are greater than the costs—makes it less useful, at least to some users.

A second shortcoming of cost-benefit analysis is particularly important for environmental justice because it may produce unfair outcomes. A cost-benefit analysis is based on an *aggregate* of relevant costs and benefits, but these consequences may not be distributed equally. A facility that generates benefits to an entire community, for example, may also pose greater risks to some residents—such as those who live near enough to inhale toxic emissions—than others. More problematic is the case where benefits largely accrue to one group while burdens are primarily imposed on others. Even if the aggregate benefits clearly and strongly overwhelm the costs, it is hard to defend as fair such a mismatch between those who bear the burdens and those who enjoy the benefits of a particular activity. Utilitarianism does not prevent the designation of a minority of people to bear costs or risks in order for a majority of people to enjoy benefits.

Utilitarianism underlies much of environmental and natural resources law, and its consequences for how natural resources and environmental benefits and burdens are distributed have done much to spark interest in environmental justice. Other theories of justice challenge utilitarianism and suggest other ways benefits and burdens should be distributed. A rights-based theory of justice, for example, requires that no one be subjected to certain burdens or adverse impacts or restraints regardless of the overall benefits. Individuals may possess rights, such as the right to breathe clean air or have a safe environment, that trump utilitarianism. While there are no such constitutional rights, environmental laws create statutory rights and expectations that individuals will be protected from unreasonable risks or that their health will be protected with an adequate margin of safety. Even if social welfare is enhanced by concentrating risks in some areas and on some persons, the actions are unjust if they violate these individual rights.

INDIVIDUAL RIGHTS, EQUALITY, AND JUSTICE

Other forms of distributive justice suggest different definitions of egalitarianism. Perhaps the simplest notion is that benefits and burdens are to be distributed equally across all affected parties; everyone receives the same level of benefit, such as access to natural resources, and is exposed to the same level of environmental risk or pays the same cost. Alternatively, equality can mean that those who are similarly situated are treated the same, and those who are different are treated differently. That is, there may be some factors that justify different treatment, although there should be consistency within each category. For example, those who benefit from a risky activity should bear the associated costs. Or, equality can be understood to require a minimum level of equality or access to benefits or imposition of burdens or risks. A commitment to equality may conflict with simple utilitarian calculations and suggest different distributions to different persons, according to their merit, conditions, or needs. A socialist formulation links benefits and needs: everyone is to receive the level of benefits consistent with their needs. In contrast, a merit-based approach requires that benefits be distributed according to effort or contribution and burdens. Correspondingly, those who make only a partial contribution should receive partial benefits.[7] James Wescoat and his coauthors make this distinction, in Chapter 3, in which decisions may be equitable but not equal in terms of the benefits they provide.

The nature of risk is a complicating but important factor here. Risks that are voluntarily assumed and represent an informed choice pose less of a problem than risks involuntarily imposed on others. For example, the choice of individuals to live on the oceanfront and voluntarily accept the increased risk of damage or death from hurricanes and other storms does not pose a challenge to this notion of distributive justice. On the other hand, a decision to live next to a toxic emitting factory or incinerator is problematic because it may be in only a very narrow sense "voluntary"; low-income persons may have few options besides choosing to live in economically depressed areas where prices are low and environmental risks are high.

The dominant American understanding of individual rights is that rights are so important that, in the words of John Rawls, they cannot be outweighed by majority will: "Rights secured by justice are not subject to political bargaining or the calculus of social interests."[8]

Rawls argues that rights provide a framework that ensures individuals have the freedom to pursue their own vision of the good life as long as they respect the similar freedom of others. Government is to remain neutral toward specific ends in respecting the capacity of individuals to choose for themselves their own beliefs and values. Liberals, following Kant, argue that society should protect rights and liberties rather than promote "good" values. No one way of life should be affirmed or mandated, but society should be neutral in terms of what values individuals choose to live. Individual rights are trumps that persons possess against the majority.[9]

Rawls's theory of justice is an alternative to the dominant role of utilitarianism in moral philosophy. But Rawls provides no clear guidelines for determining when environmental injustices have occurred or how to remedy them. His theory of justice calls for interventions to remedy environmental or other injustices that place at a disadvantage those who are already less well-off than others. Priority must be given to the status of the least well-off, as long as this can be done without violating basic personal and civil liberties. People are placed at a disadvantage by social structures for which they are not responsible. The more fortunate should only benefit from social, political, and economic arrangements if the less fortunate benefit more. But liberal or individualist theories of justice may not provide a sufficient basis for the kind of shared morality that is best suited to deal with collective problems like environmental pollution and the preservation of natural resources.

There are other forms of justice besides the distributional version that should be mentioned here because they are sometimes used to identify examples of environmental injustices and to suggest remedies. Corrective or compensatory justice seeks to compensate victims of injustices in order to restore the victims to the conditions they were in before the injustice occurred or to make them whole, to remedy the damage inflicted, or to provide fair compensation for the injury suffered. Obviously, some harms can be remedied and conditions restored—hazardous sites can be cleaned up, for example—but in many cases, in which life or health has been lost, cash payments are a limited surrogate for making the victim whole. The repeated violation of treaties with Native Americans or the history of colonial exploitation, for example, may trigger demands for compensatory justice that have implications for natural resources policy (see Chapter 7, on tribal sovereignty, and Chapter 4 on North-South equity). Compensatory justice and distributional justice differ fundamentally from procedural justice in their focus on outcomes and consequences.

ENVIRONMENTAL ETHICS

Expectations created by different notions of justice do not exhaust the philosophical ideas that can serve as a basis to identify cases of unfairness in natural resources policies and in fashioning remedies. These ideas overlap significantly with the more critical variations of social justice theories discussed below. They deserve brief mention here because many of their proponents argue that an understanding of the interconnectedness of the environment that is rooted in ecology has implications for environmental justice. Some environmental ethics writers suggest how environmental policy should be shaped by notions of equality among all species and commitments to a biospheric, rather than an anthropocentric, perspective that are reflected in ideas of deep ecology.[10] Since the focus here is on the rights of and duties to nonhumans, the relevance for environmental justice here is only indirect as these ethical theories seek to broaden our thinking about the consequences of environmental and natural resources decisions.

More relevant are critical theories rooted in economics, ecofeminism, socialism, and other critiques of modern, industrial, male-dominated, high-consumption societies that offer alternative visions of environmental ethics rooted in equality, nurturing, and postmodern challenges to ideas of progress and materialism.[11] Environmental ethics is also rooted in spiritual ecology, such as that found in the writings of indigenous peoples. One of the great ironies of modern life is that as we come to realize the consequences of our Western model of consumption, industrialization, and hostility to nature, all of which are at the heart of the environmental crisis, we have begun to recognize that we have much to learn from those who have yet to embrace all the trappings of modernity. Much of the wisdom of native peoples is rooted in biological knowledge and how ecosystems function over time. Their commitment to considering the impact of decisions on generations in the future parallels the commitment to sustainability discussed at the end of this chapter.

The Public Participation Framework

The participation of those who are not represented well in political forums or who have traditionally been underrepresented is an essential part of environmental justice. But there is no consensus over what kind of participation is required, since there are different expectations or theories of procedural fairness and justice. One standard is that a "choice, made without prior consideration of the interest of all sections of the community would be open to criticism as merely partisan and unjust."[12] Justice may require the right to participate in a deci-sion-making process, the right to have one's interests included in the analysis, or the right to be represented by others. Participation may range from commenting on proposals formulated by others to being involved in the process of generating the proposals themselves and selecting from among options.

For many, environmental justice is driven by aspirations for com-munity empowerment, accountability of political power to those who are affected by it, and real democratic participation. For some advo-cates of public participation, the ultimate goal is to ensure that low-income and minority communities have the opportunity to partici-pate effectively in decision making and to ensure that their views are taken into account. The emphasis is on ensuring that those who have been underrepresented in past decision making because of racial dis-crimination are empowered to participate fully and effectively. For others, public participation represents a broader expectation of a strong, inclusive, egalitarian form of democracy that gives voice to every member of a community.

Full public participation creates procedural, rather than substan-tive, expectations for natural resources policy making; if fair proce-dures are established and all interests are represented, then the results, whatever they may be, are acceptable. This view is consistent with pluralist politics: policy making is to include all relevant inter-ests, they have the incentive to represent their interests the best they can, and out of the competitive clash of interests emerges the public interest. But critics have long warned that interest group politics has an upper-class bias, and that low-income people and people of color are not well represented. Pluralist expectations can be more closely approximated, however, by empowering people through access to technical information and other resources that are required for them to be equal partners—or at least to be competitive. Sheila Foster explores procedural expectations that contribute to the idea of justice in Chapter 6.

Christopher Foreman argues that the real concerns of environ-mental justice advocates "lie in the eternal yearnings for a more dem-ocratic and egalitarian society comprised of livable communities."[13] Their discourse of *justice, fairness, community,* and related terms clashes with the technocratic language that dominates environmental policy and the clash of environmental and industry groups that dom-inate its politics. According to Foreman: "For many activists, environ-mental justice is mostly about accountability and political power rather than the more technical issue of environmental risks facing communities. A major reason why one simply cannot accept advocacy claims of risk at face value is that they are often anchored, ultimately, not in the dangers posed by a site or substance ostensibly at issue, but rather in a desire for transformed power relationships to be achieved on behalf of politically energized and engaged communities."[14] In Foreman's view, remedies may not be accomplished simply by holding more meetings and hearing more voices but, instead, may require fundamental changes in the way in which economic power and political power are distributed.

One of the major debates in environmental justice, however, is whether procedural expectations are sufficient, or whether justice calls for certain substantive standards—as with the distribution of benefits and burdens discussed earlier in this chapter—to be satisfied as well. Some argue that a lack of consensus in the United States concerning kinds of policies and the role of government in economic and social activities may make judging policies nearly impossible. Without objective measures or widely agreed upon standards by which public policies can be evaluated, we turn to procedural values of pluralism, openness, and representation. Advocates of pluralist policy making in the United States have argued that since there is often little agreement over substantive goals, the best we can hope for is to design fair processes for making natural resources and other policies. If procedural norms are satisfied, then we judge policies to be largely successful.

Defenders of the public participation solution argue that if participation is truly inclusive and grants access to decision makers, it can empower people to make their own decisions and does not rely on paternalistic policy making by government. People can decide for themselves how to balance environmental risks and economic benefits rather than having those decisions made by others. This solution is also attractive because it does not require policy makers to come up with a set of substantive principles that are written into national laws and are to guide all decisions but, rather, allows participants to shape solutions that meet their specific circumstances.

Critics of the public participation solution identify several concerns. Critics of pluralism have emphasized that since all groups are not equal in resources and ability to shape outcomes, the result of pluralist politics is unequal and unfair.[15] Solutions that communities devise may be acceptable to them, but there may be spillover effects that threaten others who are not part of the decision-making process. Solutions may leave out future generations, and we may decide as a society that broader institutions of governance are required to intervene to protect those interests. (This then requires another difficult assessment about how the interests of current and future generations should be balanced: do the needs of current generations outweigh those of the future?) We may decide that there are fundamental rights at play here, such as the right to a healthy environment, that people should not be allowed to negotiate away or be forced to compromise because of poverty. And negotiations may result in acceptable cost-benefit calculations for some people, who are willing to be exposed to greater risks in exchange for more benefits, while others in the community are opposed to such calculations. Advocates of pollution prevention (see below) may argue that we should not allow people to negotiate some levels of acceptable pollution, but we should all agree to accept no pollution or waste so that producers will be compelled to prevent pollution. For these reasons, ensuring a more fair, balanced, and representative decision-making process may not be enough of a solution to environmental and natural resources injustices.

The Social Justice Framework

Environmental injustices are also a function of broader social inequity, the interaction of poverty and race, and the relative political powerlessness of low-income and minority persons and their lack of influence in policy making. Environmental injustices and disparities in the benefits that flow from natural resources development are a manifestation of more fundamental problems of poverty and political and economic disadvantage, democratic inequality and lack of participation, and other manifestations of social injustices and unfairness.

For many activists, environmental justice is mostly about the fundamental distribution of political power, not the environmental risks facing communities. While this is a view shared by some advocates of more inclusive public participation, who argue that people of color are underrepresented in public decision making, the critique reaches much deeper than race to address fundamental issues of class. Social injustices include disproportionate environmental risks and lack of access to natural resources benefits, but they go well beyond these to include jobs, housing, education, public services, health, and other areas where people of color and low-income persons are disadvantaged. These problems are interrelated because they are a function of racism, exploitation of the politically powerless, cultural and social practices that favor majority interests, laws that are written to benefit those who are already advantaged and can afford to invest in the political process and campaigns, and a host of other factors. Solutions to the complex problems of social justice require structural changes in political, economic, and social institutions; increased public participation in meetings is not enough. These solutions are also obviously beyond the scope of environmental and natural resources law and policy. The question here is whether there may be a modest role for natural resources law and policy in addressing these broader economic, political, and social concerns. If we can reduce environmental injustices, that is a step toward reducing injustice as a whole, and it might inspire other efforts.

Social Justice and Race

Two theories that address empowerment are critical legal and critical race theories. Critical legal scholars have argued that legal institutions, doctrines, and decisions "work to buttress and support a pervasive system of oppressive, inegalitarian relations."[16] Law is not neutral but, rather, is rooted in subjective and political choices that favor the interests of dominant political, economic, and social elites. Many critical theorists argue that law obstructs the goals of democracy, and their analysis encourages the realization of participatory democracy. They have emphasized how laws rest on an underlying layer of meaning that is not objective but, instead, depends on and reflects dominant cultural and social beliefs.

Critical race theory is based on the experience, traditions, culture, and perspective of people of color. It offers a race-conscious perspective by which legal doctrines and decisions are critiqued. Rather than color blindness, critical race theory calls for race consciousness—analysis that is rooted in the history of American race relations, that recognizes major economic differences between white and black communities, and that seeks to develop a distinctive set of legal theories and principles rooted in those differences. Part of this approach requires greater participation by minority scholars in the development of civil rights law, because they come from a perspective of racial oppression that gives their assessments the "authority of racial distinctiveness."[17] Some critical race theorists call for the rejection of the integrationist goal of some proponents of racial equality, in favor of a more culturally diverse, contextualized set of standards that recognize the uniqueness of minority experience.[18] The different experiences of racial groups in dealing with such problems as disproportionate exposure to environmental hazards—not the experience of majoritarian society—should, according to this view, become the base for formulating and implementing natural resources law and policy.

SOCIAL JUSTICE AND INDIVIDUAL EMPOWERMENT

Reducing environmental injustices can be part of a much broader effort to address social injustices, but it is not clear that environment-related efforts will have much of an impact on these more systemic shortcomings. Broader efforts that address poverty and related issues may more directly get at root causes. A social justice framework also suggests a more proactive approach in empowering people to choose how to live their lives and realize their ambitions. Reducing or eliminating hazards and burdens that prevent them from exercising choices is important in itself, but it can also provoke actions that promote choice and freedom more broadly among people who have traditionally had more limited options.

The difference between a social justice or class-based approach and a more narrow civil rights or race-based approach to environmental justice is clear in the writings of Nobel economist Amartya Sen. Sen argues that economic development should be understood as freedom, and that government plays a major role in helping people be in a position to exercise freedom and to be accountable for what they do. Expanding freedom is the primary end and the principal means of development. Development should have as its primary objective the expansion of the freedoms that people enjoy by empowering people and by removing the major limits on freedom, such as poverty, tyranny, poor economic opportunities, social deprivation, lack of adequate public facilities, and repression.[19] Freedom is the key to social development, since economic opportunities, political liberties, social power, health, education, and the encouragement and cultivation of initiatives all shape what people are able to accomplish. The ability of people to participate in political and social decisions affecting them shapes the opportunities that are available to them. According to Sen, "Freedoms are not only the primary ends of development, they are also among its principal means."[20] Freedom includes the processes that allow free actions and decisions and the opportunities that people enjoy. A freedom-based approach to development requires a public discussion of how different kinds of freedoms are valued and what priorities among different freedoms should be pursued.

The broader agenda of social justice goes well beyond environmental and natural resources issues to address the alienation citizens feel toward a government that is out of touch with real, immediate concerns, and toward a politics that produces little of value.[21] Advocates of political reform propose an ambitious agenda: encouraging a politics of deliberation, inclusion, and individual and shared responsibility; replacing entitlement with reciprocity and ideology and replacing partisanship with compromise; fostering a sense of community, neighborliness, hope, optimism, and a willingness to listen; and nurturing authentic democratic dialogue, civility, and a commitment to empower people to participate in real, meaningful political debate.[22] Part of the solution requires broader participation and inclusion of those whose voices are not usually heard, including those of future generations. This requires strengthening traditional institutions that serve as a buffer between the state and market forces—churches, voluntary associations, local schools, and other groups—in ways that reclaim our public, civic voices. It calls for finding common ground and overlapping interests and for tempering individualism with obligation. The agenda goes far beyond natural resources to cultivating the habits and attitudes—the culture—necessary for democracy and for a greater respect for human dignity.[23]

Environmental and natural resources policy, as currently constituted, can only address these issues at the margin. But the growing interest in ecological sustainability can broaden environmental and natural resources policy so that it is more relevant to addressing more of the root causes of social injustice. In Chapter 5, Jeff Romm explores this interaction of social justice and environmental policy in more detail.

The Ecological Sustainability Framework

Environmental injustices are sometimes a result of the way in which environmental policies are formulated and implemented. The injustices are not necessarily an intentional outcome of these policies but, rather, are a result of political compromises, limited resources, incomplete understanding, and other shortcomings that nevertheless contribute to unfair outcomes and impacts. For example, many environmental laws have been criticized for shifting pollution from one environmental medium to another rather than reducing or preventing pollution. Politically connected individuals are often quite successful in gaining access to the political system to ensure that at least most pollution and environmental risks occur far from where they live. Their success in getting pollution moved somewhere else may produce injustices because poor and minority communities are simply late in joining the political debate over how to deal with environmental risks. It is usually cheaper, at least in the short run, to shift pollutants from one environmental medium (such as air) to another form (such as solid waste) that then poses a new set of problems and risks, often to other groups of people and other ecosystems.

The traditional approach to environmental regulation has contributed to environmental injustice by its emphasis on treating pollution, since those efforts are, at least in the short run, usually less expensive than preventing pollution in the first place. Advocates of pollution prevention argue that there are economic advantages of reducing waste and improving efficiency. Those investments are initially costly, and if all parties are not compelled to make such investments, those who do not and who instead externalize some of their costs will gain competitive advantages. So collective action is required. But more important here is the solution to the problem of injustice: if threats are eliminated, then there is no disproportionate risk. (See Chapter 12 for Hill and Targ's discussion of pollution prevention.)

Part of what is most valuable here is an endorsement of the idea of true costs—prices should include the *real* or *true* costs of production, including the environmental and health consequences and impacts, rather than allowing sellers and purchasers to externalize those costs to others. In a system committed to markets as a way of allocating scarce resources, determining value, and making choices from competing needs and wants, it is critical that prices provide accurate information about the true costs of what is being sold. As real costs are better understood, those affected by them can have more of the information needed to make trade-offs and to balance competing concerns, such as environmental protection and economic development.[24]

The idea of sustainability goes beyond reforming environmental and natural resources laws to make them more effective to addressing the values underlying production and consumption. *Sustainability* is admittedly a broad and vague term, expansive enough to aggregate a wide range of interests under its umbrella, but specific enough to give some direction. Sustainability focuses on comprehensive solutions that reflect the interconnections of ecology. It respects the maxim "everything is connected to everything else," which is at the heart of ecology.[25] It requires that we deal with a broad range of problems that people are concerned about—sprawl, traffic, air pollution, pressure to develop open spaces, lack of access to recreation, overcrowding, and other ills that threaten our quality of life. Sustainability is largely a concept of community. There is considerable enthusiasm for the idea of sustainable communities. Sustainability is bound up with notions of strong democracy, participation, and community, and these social characteristics are fostered through a scale of personal interaction. So too is it a commitment to a land ethic. Aldo Leopold defined a land ethic, sounding much like a proponent of sustainable communities:

> An ethic, ecologically, is a limitation on freedom of action in the struggle for existence. . . . All ethics so far evolved rest upon a single premise: that the individual is a member of a community of interdependent parts. . . . The land ethic simply enlarges the boundaries of the community to include soils, water, plants, and animals, or collectively: the land.[26]

Sustainability seems promising as an idea for governing a community. The problem is how to extend the idea beyond our community. We may find that our own community is sustainable if we export our wastes or import unsustainable levels of resources. We may find that our own community thrives, while others live lives mired in poverty. How does sustainability guide us in these circumstances?

Proponents of a thick version of ecological sustainability call for a new vision of how humankind relates to nature. Ranji Kothari, for example, suggests that sustainability requires an ethical shift, not a change in the way we employ technology or financial resources, but a shift in viewing nature not in terms of resources to be turned into economic commodities but as valuable in itself and for the way it supports life. Sustainability is intertwined with social justice: "The ecological crisis is in large part a matter of treating nature's diversity as dispensable, a process that has gone hand in hand with the view that a large portion of the human species is dispensable as well. To reverse the ecological decline we require an ethical shift that treats all life as indispensable."[27]

The distribution of wealth and material resources is a concern of sustainability, both in terms of intergenerational equity, including the wealth and wealth-generating opportunities preserved for future generations, and in terms of the distribution within the current generation. Wealth matters because the lack of it causes people to engage in ecologically damaging practices to survive. But sustainability requires also a sense of limits and appropriate scale and of the distribution of resources. The same forces that exploit natural resources also exploit people, and sustainability calls for solidarity and social concern among all human beings. Sustainability also requires that the pressures of human populations and consumption growth be moderated. It is not enough to stabilize population growth. The ecological impact of population is a function of the kinds of technologies that are prevalent and of levels of consumption. One of the fundamental tasks of sustainability is to decrease poverty and increase consumption or access to goods and services, while at the same time decreasing the level of pollution produced and of nonrenewable resources used.

Conclusion

The five frameworks are not independent ways of approaching the problem of injustices; they overlap in many ways. Advocates of environmental justice will find that elements of each can contribute to their goal. Some remedies may come from within one framework, while others will be built through the interaction of different approaches. No one framework is sufficient, but in recognizing where those with other views are coming from, we can develop opportunities for creative solutions that bring together alternative approaches. The traditional civil rights approach, for example, is compelling and has a strong history on which it can extend its efforts. Advocates of this approach can find allies who come at the problem from other directions. Expectations of distributive justice pull powerfully on many people as a way to remedy past injustices and prevent future ones. Enhanced public participation by all members of a community is widely viewed as an essential part of any response to injustice and is also valuable in promoting democratic politics. Social justice addresses the essential needs of all members of a community to live lives of freedom, dignity, and promise. Advocates of solutions to such problems as access to adequate water supplies and exposure to toxic mine tailings can seek legal remedies rooted in civil rights or pursue more fundamental social and economic reforms that promise to give people more power over their lives.

The agenda laid out by the idea of ecological sustainability is particularly important for addressing natural resources injustices. Sustainability is intertwined with political and governmental renewal that encourages participation of citizens and engages them in identifying problems, designing solutions, and implementing them. A strong sense of political efficacy encourages people to become involved in devising solutions to environmental problems. A robust commitment to community motivates people to reduce adverse impacts they impose on others and contribute to a shared quality of life. The kinds of changes that are required by sustainability require motivation and commitment that are more likely to come from people who feel a sense of responsibility and accountability for how their actions affect others' quality of life. The changes also require engagement and empowerment, so that participants devise solutions they are then willing to comply with. A spirited, vibrant civil society, composed of effective government and committed nongovernmental organizations, works together to ensure that the common interests of all are realized.

Notes

1. Mark Murray, "Seeking Justice in Roads and Runways," *National Journal* (March 4, 2000): 712–13.
2. Brett Ferguson, "Implications of Restoration Project on Minority, Poor Citizens Should Be Weighed, Panel Told," *Environmental Reporter* 31 (March 10, 2000): 443–44.
3. Evan J. Ringquist, "Environmental Justice: Normative Concerns and Empirical Evidence," in Norman J. Vig and Michael E. Kraft, eds., *Environmental Policy*, 4th ed. (Washington, D.C.: CQ Press, 2000), 232, 244–47.
4. See Sheila Foster, "Justice from the Ground Up: Distributive Inequities, Grassroots Resistance, and the Transformative Politics of the Environmental Justice Movement," *California Law Review* 86 (1998): 775.
5. See Robert D. Bullard, "Anatomy of Environmental Racism and the Environmental Justice Movement," in Robert Bullard, ed., *Confronting Environmental Racism: Voices from the Grassroots* (Boston: South End Press, 1993), 15–40, quote at 11.
6. Edward M. Gramlich, *A Guide to Benefit-Cost Analysis,* (Prospect Heights, Ill.: Waveland Press, 1990), 2.
7. See Ellen Frankel Paul, "Set-Asides, Reparations, and Compensatory Justice," reprinted in Kenneth A. Manaster, *Environmental Protection and Justice* (Cincinnati: Anderson Publishing, 1995), 27.
8. John Rawls, *A Theory of Justice,* rev. ed. (Cambridge: Harvard University Press, 1999), 25.
9. For a thoughtful critique of Rawls, see Thomas Nagel, "Justice, Justice, Shalt Thou Pursue," *New Republic* 220 (October 25, 1999): 36–41.
10. For a broad overview of these issues, see Holmes Rolston III, *Environmental Ethics: Duties to and Values in the Natural World* (Philadelphia: Temple University Press, 1988); and Christopher D. Stone, *Earth and Other Ethics: The Case for Moral Pluralism* (New York: Harper and Row, 1987).
11. See Carolyn Merchant, *Ecology* (Atlantic Highlands, N.J.: Humanities Press, 1994).
12. H. L. A. Hart, *The Concept of Law* (Oxford: Clarendon Press, 1961), 162.
13. Christopher Foreman, *The Promise and Peril of Environmental Justice* (Washington, D.C.: Brookings Institute, 1998), 5.
14. Foreman, *The Promise and Peril of Environmental Justice,* 58–59.
15. Charles Lindblom, *Politics and Markets* (New York: Basic, 1977).
16. Gary Minda, *Postmodern Legal Movements* (New York: New York University Press, 1995), 106.
17. Minda, *Postmodern Legal Movements,* 172.
18. Minda, *Postmodern Legal Movements,* 177.

19. Amartya Sen, *Freedom and Development* (New York: Knopf, 1999), 3.
20. Sen, *Freedom and Development*, 10.
21. See Daniel Yankelovich, "Three Destructive Trends," *Ketterling Review* (fall 1995): 6–15.
22. Jean Bethke Elshtain, "The Politics of Displacement," *Ketterling Review* (fall 1995): 31–38.
23. David Zarefsky, "The Postmodern Public," *Ketterling Review* (fall 1995): 39–49.
24. Thomas Prugh, Robert Costanza, and Herman Daly, *The Local Politics of Global Sustainability* (Washington, D.C.: Island Press, 2000), 28–29.
25. See Barry Commoner, *Making Peace with the Planet* (New York: Pantheon, 1990).
26. Aldo Leopold, *A Sand County Almanac* (New York: Ballantine, 1966), 238–39.
27. Ranji Kothari, quoted in Dale Jamieson, "Sustainability and Beyond," *NRLC Public Land Policy Discussion Paper Series (PL02)* (Boulder, Colo.: Natural Resources Law Center, 1996), 16.

Chapter 3

WATER, POVERTY, EQUITY, AND JUSTICE IN COLORADO

A Pragmatic Approach

James L. Wescoat Jr., Sarah Halvorson, Lisa Headington, and Jill Replogle

This chapter deals with water problems faced by low-income people in Colorado and asks how public officials, nongovernmental organizations, and scholars have conceptualized those problems. Low-income water problems include inadequate domestic water supplies, unsafe floodplain occupance, vulnerability to industrial contamination, unsustainable community irrigation systems, and shutoffs by water utilities. Although often associated with developing countries, these problems affect significant numbers of transients, tenants, poor families, and minorities in the western United States.[1] These problems are generally neglected, and when they are addressed rarely involve claims for environmental justice. Our broader project, "Water, Poverty and Sustainable Livelihoods in Colorado," uses census, water rights, and water quality data to survey broad geographic patterns of water problems and poverty in Colorado. We interview local public officials and voluntary organizations to identify pockets of water-related poverty—from mountain hamlets to semiarid plains and from inner-city Denver to American Indian reservations.

This chapter focuses on several key theoretical questions in the project: (1) What types of low-income water problems constitute environmental injustices, as compared with other ways of framing those problems? (2) What are the conceptual strengths and weaknesses of alternative ways of framing low-income water problems? (3) What forums and remedies does each conceptual approach offer? Some conceptual approaches, for example, define low-income water problems simply in terms of physical standards, while others focus on political participation, equity, sustainability, or poverty.

The first section of the chapter briefly reviews previous research on water and poverty, including the pioneering study *Water and Poverty in the Southwest*, by F. Lee Brown and Helen Ingram, which was roughly contemporary with but independent of environmental justice movements and research. Indeed, our literature review documents persisting conceptual gaps between research on natural resources equity and environmental justice. We concur with Bunyan Bryant's definition of environmental equity as "equal protection of environmental laws," but we will also show how equity in western water policies allows dramatically unequal water allocations. While sympathetic with Bryant's definition of environmental justice "as broader in scope than environmental equity . . . refer[ring] to those norms and values, rules, regulations, behaviors, policies, and decisions to support sustainable communities,"[2] we develop a narrower, but perhaps more forceful, definition of environmental justice as fundamentally concerned with *equal* exposure to risks and access to resource benefits.

The second section of the chapter briefly surveys different conceptual ways of defining low-income water problems. This conceptual map helps us situate environmental justice in relation to complementary and competing approaches and thereby address the questions of this volume (that is, what is included in the idea of environmental justice, what constitutes an injustice, and what remedies are available?).

Our approach to these questions is "pragmatic" in two senses of the term.[3] First, rather than posit a theoretical definition of environmental justice and assess the extent to which it has been realized in water law and policy, we work inductively from the actual use of environmental justice and related concepts. We seek to document their denotations, connotations, and limitations in the water sector. Jumping ahead a bit, this method indicates that the rubric of environmental justice, as currently understood, denotes a relatively limited range of urban water quality problems and connotes some fundamentally unacceptable *inequalities*. Other conceptual approaches denote a broader range of water problems and connote basic physical standards or equity, rather than equality. These differences help clarify (but not justify) the current distinction between the terms *water resources equity* and *environmental injustice*. Instead of trying to conflate these approaches or argue for extending the scope of environmental justice to subsume a broader range of water problems, we first want to ask how these alternative conceptual approaches lead toward different public forums and potential remedies to low-income water problems. We hypothesize that a broader range of conceptual approaches may generate a broader range of potential remedies and strategies for low-income groups.

Our approach is thus "pragmatic" in a second, methodological sense. It begins with a messy situation, identifies alternative approaches to that situation (including environmental justice approaches), and traces out their potential implications and remedies for low-income water problems. The third section of the chapter demonstrates this pragmatic method of analysis.

Gaps between Water, Poverty, Equity, and Justice

Our study of water and poverty in Colorado began with two propositions: first, water resources researchers have given little attention to poverty; and second, researchers on poverty have given little attention to water. Aside from work on Native American water rights, most water resources struggles have involved "haves" and "have-lots," with much rhetoric but little resources or attention going to the "have-nots" (that is, parties with insufficient funds to hire staff, attorneys, and lobbyists).[4] Similarly, social scientists working on poverty have paid little attention to types, locations, or impacts of water problems faced by low-income social groups in the United States, with the important exception of differential exposure to fish consumption risks.[5] Colorado statutes and case law include only a few tangential references to water and poverty (two statutes and four cases).[6] Environmental justice research and activism would seem to have relevance for low-income water problems.[7] But, as will be shown below, water resources research in the western United States tends to frame these problems in terms of equity rather than environmental justice.

The benchmark example was the groundbreaking book *Water and Poverty in the Southwest,* by economist F. Lee Brown and political scientist Helen Ingram.[8] In the book, Brown and Ingram ask how water "flows away from the poor." They use the 1980 U.S. Decennial Census and other data to describe conditions of rural poverty in the four-state region of Arizona, Colorado, New Mexico, and Utah. They then present detailed case studies of water problems faced by the Tohono O'odham tribe in southwestern Arizona and by Hispanic acequia irrigation communities in the upper Rio Grande valley of northern New Mexico.

In theoretical terms, Brown and Ingram contrast "commodity" and "community" values in water. Commodity values include the following:

• Increasing economic value
• Transfer to higher-value uses
• Interstate commerce in water
• Full or marginal cost pricing
• Expanding water markets
• Individual decision making.

Community values include the following:

• Emotional and symbolic value
• Emphasis on fairness
• Participation and local control
• Opportunity (economic)
• Caring for the resource
• Collective decision making.

Brown and Ingram observe that the Southwest is on a historical trajectory from community to commodity values, and they argue that this shift in values disproportionately affects communities of color in the Southwest. They further assert that communities must develop new strategies that cope with this broader trend, as well as defend traditional values, if they are to reduce rural poverty.

Although the prevalence, dynamics, and implications of these ideal types of value among communities of color and low-income groups are important empirical issues that deserve additional research, the key point for our purposes is that Brown and Ingram do not use the terms *environmental racism* or *environmental justice*, although those social and intellectual movements emerged at about the same time and presented arguments applicable to the water problems and discrimination faced by tribes and acequia communities.[9] Similarly, the early literature on environmental justice did not address low-income rural (or urban) water supplies, except insofar as they were polluted.[10] Both lines of research were innovative, had little previous research to draw upon, and had few points of contact with each other. Even if they had initiated contact, it would have been difficult to achieve a coherent focus because they addressed, at that time, different environmental problems and regions. One movement focused on resources, the other on wastes; one on the South, the other on the West.

More importantly for this chapter, they also invoked different rights and claims: property rights in the water resources field and civil rights in the environmental justice field; claims for equity in the water resources field and claims for equality in the environmental justice field. Later in this chapter, we shall examine these substantive differences—especially the distinction between equality (focusing on the equal distribution of benefits and burdens) and equity (fairness of distributions that may actually be unequal)—which persist today.

Notwithstanding this historical gap between water resources equity and environmental justice, Brown and Ingram's study has relevance for environmental justice research by showing how ethnicity and class shape vulnerability to irrigation problems as well as community-based opportunities for irrigation development. In addition to influencing subsequent Latino and Native American water resources research, it continues to be cited in most major water policy studies.[11] However, it has not stimulated a sustained program of research on water and poverty of the sort that developed in the environmental justice field. Subsequent research has been conducted on Native American water rights and acequia organizations that has affinities with environmental justice research.[12] But research on water and poverty (that is, income and class) has declined. Important exceptions include research on water problems in the U.S.-Mexico borderlands, especially the Tijuana River basin, lower Colorado River delta, Ambos Nogales, and *colonias* of the lower Rio Grande.[13] Interestingly, these studies do not often emphasize concepts of environmental justice.

The conceptual gap between *resource equity* and *environmental justice* is also apparent in western water policy studies. The report Water in the West: Challenge for the Next Century is a good example. One of the report's main principles for water management is to "promote social equity," as articulated below:

> **Promote Social Equity.** Determining and fulfilling tribal rights to water and providing universal access to safe domestic water supplies should be a priority. We must also recognize that local economies have developed throughout the West as a result of government policies designed to encourage certain land and water uses. As those policies evolve, regardless of the reason, people and communities affected by such changes may need

time and assistance to make a transition. Water transfers should be done with full consideration of the communities of origin, third party transfers, and unintentional consequences and should be open to participation by affected parties.[14]

This passage highlights four equity issues: (1) fulfilling tribal rights; (2) ensuring universal access to domestic water supply; (3) considering third-party effects of water transfers; and (4) calling for full participation by affected parties. However, the report and much of the related water policy literature address these four issues in very different ways. Tribal water rights are discussed further in the report, which cites the example of the Animas–La Plata project. In the entire report, this project alone is described as an issue of "justice" and as a case of "injustice."[15] Curiously, universal access to domestic water supply is not mentioned again in the report, perhaps because it again refers to unsafe domestic water and sanitation conditions on reservations. By comparison, the report discusses the social impacts of water transfers—citing the 1992 National Research Council report *Water Transfers in the West: Efficiency, Equity and the Environment*—as issues of "equity" rather than "justice." The report frequently mentions public participation, and it presents "participatory decision-making" as a major recommendation: "National, regional, and local resource decision-making must be open to involvement and meaningful participation by affected governments and both interested and affected stakeholders."[16] Although public participation is not framed as an issue of equity or justice, it clearly resonates with the principle of promoting social equity and will be discussed later in this chapter.

The report briefly offers several additional examples of equity issues. It cites *Water and Poverty in the Southwest* as a key study of equity—and inequity—in water resources allocation and management. It also mentions that Gilbert White's classic 1968 National Academy of Sciences study, *Water and Choice in the Colorado River Basin*, was "one of the first major studies to question whether water resources development promotes regional growth and equity."[17] *Water in the West* notes that "the amount of protection each state provides for equity and the public interest varies, and it is important to remember that the highest economic use is not necessarily the same as the highest public good."[18] An electronic search of *Water in the West* documents (more than twenty reports to the commission) yielded no reference to "environmental justice."

Notwithstanding this limited treatment of equity, less attention to justice, and complete omission of environmental justice, the report drew heavy criticism from some western states' representatives to Congress. The critics supported a "Rebuttal," which stated the following:

> This principle ["Sustainable Use of Water"], when combined with others such as "Maintain National Goals and Standards," "Promote Social Equity," and "Restoration of Aquatic Ecosystems," is fundamentally inconsistent with the principle of "Respect Existing Rights" which is only briefly mentioned in the Report. It is also a central defect in the Report.[19]

Although critics might also have framed "respecting existing rights" as a matter of equity or justice, they stressed instead that it has "served the West well by meeting beneficial use requirements and providing certainty to water users."[20]

This lack of formal debate about issues of equity and justice also extended to issues beyond the water sector. A report on social trends commissioned by the Western Water Policy Review Advisory Commission asserted the following:

> People appear to consistently value these things [environmental concerns] over economic well being and over concern for social matters, such as crime, homelessness, social injustices of one kind or another, integrity of public organizations and elected officials, and so forth.[21]

This statement suggesting that mainstream environmentalism has greater salience than race and poverty should not be accepted uncritically. Much of the early environmental justice literature documented joint concerns for environment, race, and poverty. However, the terms *environmental equity, environmental justice,* and *environmental racism* are not even mentioned in water policy studies such as the *Water in the West* report.

To assess whether this omission of environmental equity and justice, and seemingly different connotations of equity and justice, is indicative of broader patterns of water resources inquiry, we searched seven electronic libraries for research on "water" *and* "environmental equity," *or* "environmental justice," *or* "poverty." Many of the "hits" listed in Table 3.1 are activist publications (including films, Internet guides, and news items) and government agencies (for example, Environmental Impact Statement compliance with environmental justice regulations). *Water Resources Abstracts,* the leading water research

TABLE 3.1. Database Search Results

Electronic Library	Environmental Equity	Environmental Justice	Poverty
WorldCat (books)	17	26	2
Article1st (articles)	1	5	1
UnCover (articles)	2	8	1
GEOBASE (articles)	37	15	701
Diss (dissertations)	28	7	1
Water Resources Abstracts	3	2	86
Univ.Law.Rev (articles)	4	8	1

Keywords: "water" *and* "environmental equity" *or* "environmental justice" *or* "poverty"

Search date: March 21, 2000

database, has the fewest citations to equity and justice, which suggests that these issues remain outside mainstream water science and management.[22] The most references occurred in law review articles. Interestingly, law review articles refer more often to *environmental justice* than to *environmental equity*. Journals from other academic fields, by contrast, refer more frequently to environmental equity than to environmental justice. It seems reasonable to infer that environmental justice may be more closely associated with legal forums and remedies, while environmental equity is associated with policy forums and remedies.

The search identified surprisingly little research on water and poverty in the United States.[23] Although GEOBASE listed 701 articles on "water *and* poverty," a sample of the first seventy references indicated that all of them dealt with developing countries and none with the United States. *Water Resources Abstracts,* which does emphasize the United States, yielded eighty-six references, 95 percent of which involved developing countries.

Shifting from publications to field research, we have undertaken structured interviews with county officials and water district commissioners in Colorado to understand how they conceive the relationships among water, poverty, equity, and justice. The interviews covered a broad range of issues, including the following:

Water problems
1. Domestic water supply problems
2. Agricultural water supply problems

3. Water quality problems
4. Hazards (including hydroclimatic variability)

Social groups
1. Low-income rural Anglo-American households (household income lower than $16,600 for a family of four)
2. Low-income rural minority households (African American, Asian American, Hispanic, Native American)
3. Low-income urban and suburban Anglo-American households
4. Low-income urban and suburban minority households
5. Transients and homeless persons
6. Migrant workers

Geographic areas
1. Mountain watersheds
2. Urbanizing valleys
3. Rural plains

Although the survey research is still in progress, we may draw upon preliminary interviews, along with the water resources literature discussed above and theoretical arguments about environmental justice, to survey the range of conceptual approaches currently used to define severe low-income water problems.

Conceptualizing Water, Poverty, Equity, and Justice

This section distills the range of conceptual approaches currently used to address low-income water problems in the western United States. It follows the pragmatic tradition of inquiry in geography and law by starting with a problematic initial situation—in this case, western water policies that have given little attention to environmental justice.[24] It is useful to clarify the difference between this pragmatic approach and more deductive approaches to environmental justice. For example, whereas pragmatic approaches begin with a problematic "initial situation," more deductive approaches, such as John Rawls's *Theory of Justice*, commonly begin with an "initial position" for defining justice. In Rawls's initial position, justice is defined as, "the principles that free and rational persons concerned to further their own interests would accept in an initial position of equality as defining the fundamental terms of their association."[25] In the "initial position," actors do not know their respective resource entitlements and are therefore more likely to agree on rules that are "just." The pragmatic approach, by contrast, begins with an "initial situation" that is uncertain, pluralistic, and thus problematic, which gives rise to inquiry.[26] It focuses on actual patterns of thinking to identify the range of remedies that a society might be able to currently generate. In Rawls's terms, the pragmatic approach aims at partial justice. To date, this approach has identified seven ways to conceptualize relations among water, poverty, equity, and justice. These conceptual approaches (described in the following sections) are as follows:

1. What problem?
2. Physical degradation
3. Lack of political participation
4. Inequity as unfairness
5. Inequality and environmental injustice
6. Unsustainability
7. Poverty

What Problem?

Some officials question our concern about low-income water problems. For example, water rights administrators often argue that water policy is and ought to be blind to race and class, and that water rights must be strictly administered by seniority. This approach emphasizes a type of present-day procedural justice. They know that water rights appropriations are unequal, and that water rights seniority reflects unequal processes of appropriation and subsequent inequalities in the ability to pay for senior water rights, but they adopt a strict procedural approach.

A second set of arguments common among county officials is that low-income water problems often involve private choices that properly lie outside public purview. The officials cite examples of mountain residents who choose to live "off the grid," to have primitive plumbing, or to haul their drinking water from a distance in order to live more independently than they would in an incorporated municipality. "People have a right to live how they choose," the argument goes, so long as they do not create a public nuisance or jeopardize the health and welfare of children.[27]

Similar arguments have been directed against environmental justice claims. Initially, it was deemed rational to site noxious facilities in low-income and minority areas. Historical studies showing that low-income people subsequently *chose* to live in degraded areas offered further justification for rebutting claims of environmental injustice, even if not the degradation.

Physical Degradation

The most common approach we have encountered in our project to date frames low-income water problems in physical terms: a dry well, an eroded ditch, a disconnected tap, a broken sewer line, and so on. These problems are conceived as the failure of a physical system to function properly. Some of these physical problems might reasonably be regarded as environmental injustices. They include grossly inadequate domestic water supply and sanitation, shallow wells contaminated by industrial effluent, and varying standards and practices of basic public works maintenance.

However, aside from cases of severe exposure of communities in the Denver metropolitan area to public and private health hazards, these conditions of physical and environmental degradation are rarely described as environmental injustices.[28] Instead, they are viewed as problems of "public works" if they involve streets, sewers, and ditches, or as problems of "public health and welfare" if they involve wells, septic fields, and indoor plumbing. In contrast to questioning whether there is a problem, this approach acknowledges severe physical problems and seeks physical remedies for them (discussed in a later section). However, the physical approach does not probe underlying causes of degradation, which can be explained in several ways.

Lack of Political Participation

A prevalent explanation for low-income water problems focuses on political participation. According to this view, the "have-nots" do not effectively participate in political and economic processes that secure water benefits (for example, water rights or water infrastructure). They do not have strong representation on legislative committees or strong influence upon capital budgeting processes that allocate public resources. Many water issues in the West are framed in terms of competing interests—urban versus agricultural, recreational versus environmental, and so on. These competing interests are supposed to be reconciled through open democratic processes that depend upon free participation in public forums.

The *Water in the West* report certainly stresses openness to participation and access to water information. This line of explanation accords well with Gary Bryner's public participation framework for environmental justice discussed in Chapter 2.[29] In addition, water resources and environmental justice groups have both fought hard for access to information (for example, "right to know" legislation), standing in the courts, and participation in public hearings. However,

Water in the West and other water policy initiatives have given less attention to differences among the relative political access of different social groups. As Bryner argues in Chapter 2, participation is also constrained by social and financial resources that raise basic issues of equity and justice, which finally begin to intersect with concerns for environmental justice.

Inequity as Unfairness

An earlier section of this chapter discussed *Water in the West*'s goal of promoting social equity. Equity concerns all income groups, especially low-income communities with limited means of political participation. It should be noted that the report's four examples for promoting social equity all entail a standard of fairness. Although the goal of open participation would seem to go further toward calling for *equal* access to information and the public forum, the previous approach cited unequal political power and participation as a source of low-income water problems.

Conceptions of equity as fairness (and, conversely, inequity as unfairness) prevail in western water policy. Under the prior appropriation doctrine, people do not have rights to an equal or even minimum share of water but rather to their fair share, which is most commonly defined as what they have appropriated, paid for, or otherwise deserved as a water customer. In conditions of scarcity, it is currently deemed fair and equitable that junior water rights holders be completely curtailed until senior water rights holders obtain their entire share (riparian and other water rights regimes, by contrast, may require proportional or equal sharing of scarcity). If a "call" is placed on the river in times of scarcity, it is deemed unfair (a "futile call") to shut down juniors unless it makes a material difference for meeting senior water rights.[30] If a water rights transfer injures third parties, it is a matter of fairness that those parties be equitably compensated.[31] If some win and others lose, a court may seek to weigh or balance the equities.

Principles of equity apply to other realms of water and environmental law as well. The doctrine of "equitable apportionment" guides interstate adjudication.[32] Robert Bullard describes fair share legislation addressing environmental risks and harms among states but also argues that "states need also to begin to address intrastate siting equity concerns."[33] In some contexts, equity has come to imply minimum standards of water supply and quality. In international forums, such standards are increasingly framed as "human rights" to water, but in the western United States, there are no human rights to water.[34]

Instead, society has a moral duty to provide minimum standards of access and care, especially for children but also for adults and even animals.[35] Although it is sobering that low-income water problems are rarely defined in terms of inequality, the next section demonstrates that environmental justice often entails claims for equality above and beyond what society currently deems equitable.

Inequality and Environmental Injustice

Concern about inequality lies at the heart of environmental justice movements. Unequal exposure to toxic hazards, unequal treatment under the law, and unequal mitigation of water pollution problems are key examples. Antitoxics campaigns, in particular, have shifted the debate from equity to equality, exemplified by the change in slogans from "not in my backyard" (implying that some equitable site exists) to "not in anybody's backyard."[36] While the latter slogan also implies a demand for pollution prevention, it does so on the argument that there is no equitable siting solution.

Similarly, water quality inequalities differ from water supply inequalities (for example, between senior and junior rights, which society in the western United States currently deems fair for the most part). Colorado water officials recognize the importance of treating unequal junior and senior water rights alike in procedural terms, but this does not extend to equal sharing of surplus or scarce water supplies. The federal Clean Water Act and Safe Drinking Water Act establish uniform national water quality standards.[37] But because Colorado water law is largely separate from state water quality regulation, there is a gap between principles of equity in water law and something approaching equality in water quality regulation. As noted above, environmental justice movements are also more likely to assert claims for equality, either because they believe there is no equitable solution for differential toxic exposure or to redress inequalities based on race. Thus, we would also expect a gap between state water laws and environmental justice movements. In fact, the gap between environmental justice policy and state law is wider still; despite increasing concern that unequal exposures to water pollution are related to inequalities of race and class, the terms *environmental justice* and *environmental racism* do not appear at all in Colorado case law or statutes.[38]

Thus, whereas claims for social equity have a limited but established role in state and federal water resource policies, claims for environmental justice are advancing in different sectors, primarily at the federal level. Environmental justice claims are initially conceptualized in local social movements, supported by national networks, and are subsequently recognized and incorporated in federal laws and policies. There are important intersections between resource equity and environmental justice, as Laura Pulido has shown in a case study of the Ganados del Valle struggles in New Mexico.[39]

The similarities and differences between the patterns of environmental justice and natural resources equity movements discussed thus far indicate that environmental justice movements have focused on the following:

• Unequal racial exposure to toxic hazards
• Unequal class exposure to toxic hazards
• Unequal racial access to water resource supplies
• The joint effects of racial and class inequalities.

Resource equity movements have focused on the following:

• Inadequate class access to water resource supplies
• Inequitable class exposure to natural hazards
• Inequitable racial exposure to natural hazards
• The joint effects of inequitable exposure to toxics, resource constraints, and natural hazards.

In highlighting these patterns, we do not want to entirely conflate environmental justice with inequality. Bullard, Bryant, and others have framed environmental justice as claims for equity as well as equality.[40] However, claims for equality distinguish, and add substantial force to, environmental justice movements as compared with resource equity movements.[41] A later section of this chapter explores strategic implications of these distinctions for choices about forums and remedies, but first it is important to discuss two less well-developed conceptual approaches to low-income water programs.

Unsustainability

To a limited extent, federal, state, and local water programs have also begun to grapple with concepts of sustainability, which may have special relevance for low-income water problems.[42] Although the most vigorous research on sustainability to date has focused on developing countries and global environmental change, interest in communities and watersheds of the western United States is growing. "Ensuring sustainable water use" is the first principle and overarching challenge addressed by the Western Water Policy Review Advisory Commission.[43] Among the major challenges, they highlight overallocation of surface water, groundwater overdraft, and finding ways to increase supplies, increase water use efficiency, manage shortages, modify federal water project operations, and privatize federal water facilities.

Lawrence MacDonnell has employed concepts of sustainability to analyze social and environmental transitions under way in rural communities of the western United States.[44] His concept of sustainability entails (1) reducing the gap between water diversions and consumption, (2) allowing rivers to function ecologically as rivers, (3) changing water use patterns to meet emerging urban demands while supporting more efficient agricultural uses (for example, through water salvage, dry year agreements, and leasing), and (4) forming watershed partnerships that lead toward collaborative solutions to environmental problems.

The literature on sustainable, community-based watershed management has expanded dramatically during the 1990s, but it has not yet engaged issues of environmental justice, perhaps because sustainability movements strive for long-term conservation of resources that have not yet been terribly degraded while environmental justice movements seek to rectify long-standing or imminent environmental crises. Although there is no reason why sustainability criteria might not be developed and applied as standards for environmental regulation, they have to date had limited salience in the United States for addressing issues of poverty per se.

Poverty

There are low-income water programs in the United States administered by the Bureau of Indian Affairs, Indian Health Service, Environmental Protection Agency, and Department of Agriculture.[45] The State of Colorado also maintains water and sewer needs lists, which are prioritized by health criteria.[46] These programs tend to rely on physical infrastructure criteria when providing loans, grants, and technical assistance. Local assistance programs employ "eligibility" requirements based upon income and other socioeconomic criteria, but they do not probe the social causes or water-related consequences of poverty. Social services programs have a more detailed understanding of poverty, but they have little awareness of water problems faced by low-income and minority groups. We have not encountered any policy initiatives that define low-income water problems in terms of the socioeconomic processes that lead to poverty.

Research on environment and poverty in the United States makes surprisingly little reference to theoretical debates about "development," "entitlements," "capitals," and "capabilities" internationally.[47] Working in the Andean highlands, for example, Anthony Bebbington defines the term *capital* as encompassing natural resources (such as water), produced goods (such as water infrastructure), and various types of social capital (such as water organizations, political participation, and water-related values) that constitute the "assets" of impoverished groups.[48] He articulates strategies of capital formation that include efforts to "claim," "defend," "transform," and "receive" assets; that "challenge rules" that govern assets in the state, market, and civil society; and that build "capabilities" for reducing poverty and enhancing livelihood. Research on tribal, migrant worker, and other low-income water problems in the western United States, however, rarely addresses the economic causes and water resources effects of poverty and might benefit from international perspectives on poverty reduction.[49]

One Approach or Many?

The seven ways of conceptualizing low-income water problems discussed in the previous sections intersect with environmental justice movements in various, but generally limited, ways. They describe how the participants and literature we have encountered currently frame low-income water issues. As with most typologies, these conceptual approaches are not independent of one another. Scholars, activists, and officials draw upon them strategically when presenting their claims. But while environmental justice advocates may use many of the seven concepts, local water officials make strikingly little reference to claims for environmental justice as such.[50] Although we share our colleagues' view in this volume that environmental justice concepts and claims could be extended to natural resources management, in this case to address low-income water problems in Colorado, we are less clear about the potential advantages and disadvantages of such extensions. In the next section, we employ the pragmatic method to assess how the seven conceptual approaches lead toward different forums and different remedies to low-income water problems.

From Conceptual Approaches to Forums and Remedies

Each of the seven ways of defining low-income water problems presented here gives rise to a distinct chain of inquiry.[51] Each chain of inquiry includes a set of actors, public forums, and potential remedies. These actors, forums, and remedies influence the strategies that groups adopt to address their low-income water problems. Figure 3.1

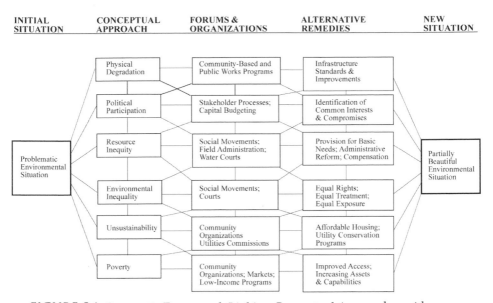

FIGURE 3.1. Pragmatic Framework Linking Conceptual Approaches with Forums and Remedies.

presents a simplified view of these chains of inquiry and some of the interactions among them. A more realistic diagram would link each chain with every other chain. Here, we briefly describe each chain to show how conceptual distinctions shape the range of potential remedies for low-income water problems. That range of remedies includes—but also extends beyond—those remedies conventionally associated with environmental justice. An expanded definition of environmental justice would certainly encompass a larger subset of remedies, but it would probably still fall short of the full range of choice encompassed by multiple conceptual approaches.

In the pragmatic tradition, inquiry arises from an initial problematic situation, and it seeks to resolve or transform that situation. Figure 3.1 describes that resolution as a "partially beautiful situation"- "beautiful" because the solution produces the aesthetic satisfaction associated with making and doing, and "partial" because each resolution, no matter how inspired, neglects some problems, aggravates others, and creates still more problems, which gives rise to new "problematic situations," new chains of inquiry, and further actions. In the sections that follow, we describe the remedies generated by different ways of conceptualizing low-income water problems.

What Problem?

For those who deny that a problem exists, there is likely to be no chain of inquiry or remedies, and thus their approach is not depicted on Figure 3.1. Such people may be receptive to "new" arguments about environmental injustice, but even if not, they may be open to recognizing the problem under one or more of the other paths described below.

From Physical Degradation to Infrastructure

If low-income water problems are defined in physical or functional terms, they may be addressed either by low-income communities themselves or by public works and public health departments. Public health concerns in the nineteenth century led to the adoption of infrastructure standards by municipal and professional organizations (for example, for drinking water protection, plumbing codes, fire codes, storm water drainage, and septic system design). These standards are closely linked with economic development plans through zoning, subdivision, and land use plans—which have had little concern for the poor. Municipal politicians, public employees, engineers, and maintenance workers are the key actors. However, these public works programs involve capital budgeting processes, in which poor areas and people rarely fare well. In Colorado, for example, the Department of Local Government creates immediate and long-term water and sewer "needs lists" prioritized by engineering and health criteria.[52] Low-income and minority communities would seem to be more likely to face health risks, but income and ethnicity are not explicit criteria for developing the water and sewer needs lists. Further research is needed on capital budgeting, health criteria, and the social distribution of water and sewer benefits.

Sometimes when public works gaps become severe, special low-income infrastructure programs are established, which provide information, financing, and technical assistance programs focused on "small systems," "rural utilities," and "affordability."[53]

To summarize, simple physical definitions of the problem lead to physical solutions, that is, infrastructure improvements. Whether the poor benefit from these programs (for example, through access to resources and improved health) or suffer (for example, through increased taxes and utilities costs) depends upon how their interests are represented and upon how they participate politically.

From Lack of Political Participation to Common Interests and Compromises

If low-income water problems are defined in terms of conflicting political interests, which are common in western water policy debates, improving political participation may be emphasized. Political participation ranges from mobilization in existing public forums to the creation of new organizations to civil disobedience. Competition for budget resources and public works are everyday examples; mobilization of resistance to noxious facilities siting and reclamation of brownfields are increasingly common.

Defining the problem in terms of political participation seems to lead, increasingly, to stakeholder processes that include representation of the water interests of low-income groups. When conducted in good faith (that is, not designed to co-opt or wear out community groups), they strive to secure the common interest, however it is defined, or an acceptable compromise.

Once again, the improvement of basic urban water supplies and sanitation in the early twentieth century provides some useful examples. Urban historians interpret the development of cheap, clean, and abundant public water supplies in U.S. cities in the early twentieth century as the joint product of muckraking activism and recognition of the common interests of rich and poor in controlling urban fires and infectious diseases.[54] In many of those early instances, low-income groups were represented by activist and reform organizations rather than by themselves. The middle of the twentieth century witnessed increasing institutionalization of public participation (mainly public comment) processes. By the 1990s, participation implied expanded stakeholder processes on issues ranging from dam operations to watershed protection. However, even when stakeholder processes are designed to be procedurally fair and inclusive, low-income groups have fewer assets available for participation and may not be equitably represented (see Sheila Foster's discussion of this problem in Chapter 6). Thus, the third chain of inquiry and remedy involves claims for equity.

From Inequity to Compensation, Administration, and Basic Needs

Equity—commonly defined as fairness—is an increasing concern in western water policy. Western water rights allocations are unequal but are still regarded by many as fair, provided they are administered fairly. If water rights transfers injure third parties, those parties are entitled to compensation as a matter of fairness. Even the most junior water rights holders are entitled to the conditions that existed at the time they appropriated water (that is, to no worsening of a weak position). The doctrine of equitable apportionment applies to interstate water disputes. It implies that each state is entitled to a fair share: not an equal share, nor a rationally calculated share, but rather a share negotiated by parties that have inherently unequal political and economic power.[55] Interstate case law involves a balancing of the equities, which tends to privilege the needs of many over injuries to the few. Thus, remedies for water inequity include some provisions for the basic needs (for example, of states), compensation for injuries, and procedural fairness.

Some inequities and minimum standards remain neglected, however. Farm workers are not compensated if they lose their jobs as the result of a water rights transfer. The homeless have no claim for basic drinking water and sanitation needs.

The equitable remedies described above may begin with social or political movements, but they more commonly gain recognition in field administration of water rights or, if local negotiations fail, in water courts and state legislatures. But it should be emphasized that equity claims are not always progressive. On the one hand, equity may require that third-party impacts of long-distance water diversions be compensated. On the other hand, it may bar differential water utility rates for low-income groups—on grounds of equity.[56] Some state courts and regulatory commissions have decided that it is not fair to make wealthier customers subsidize the utilities costs of poorer ones.[57]

Thus, equity-driven approaches may secure remedies that are deemed fair by many but not equal for all. When low-income groups shift from claims for equity to equality, they embark on a line of inquiry and a set of remedies that are central in environmental justice movements.

From Inequality to Equal Rights and Protection

If low-income water problems are defined as unjust because they are unequal, or racist, the forums and remedies take a different path.[58] While some of the inequalities mentioned above may be deemed fair, others are increasingly judged unjust and illegal. Environmental justice advocates have persuaded the courts and U.S. presidency that inequalities based on race are manifestly unjust.[59] Although narrower than Rawls's theoretical definition of "justice as fairness," environmental justice movements are more likely to adopt a forceful definition of "justice as equality"—*equal* rights to environmental safety, *equal* exposure to toxic hazards, and *equal* treatment under the law. In the water resources field, water quality regulations and lawsuits are crucial forums for asserting and remedying environmental injustices, but they only occasionally employ strict principles of equality.

Claims for equality are less well recognized in water resources policies and are thus pursued in multiple forums, from community activism and direct action to lobbying and lawsuits. Pursuit of environmental justice must begin in grassroots social movements but ultimately be secured in repeated legal declarations of equality in legislation, regulation, executive orders, case laws, and damage awards. The emphasis on legal rights, constitutional equality, and equal protection under the law is evident in environmental justice documents, including the "Principles of Environmental Justice."[60] Of the seventeen principles, eleven refer to legal rights regarding antidiscrimination, compensation, accountability, and legal relations.

Thus, the aim of environmental justice research is often to document inequalities and to secure remedies that, in principle, equalize the situation. These aims have contributed in part to an emphasis on quantitative analysis of relative exposure and spatial proximity to environmental risks. The quest for evidence of inequality also leads to historical analyses that seek to explain the origins of inequality and determine intentional wrongdoing. Pulido criticizes these approaches as focusing on a narrow set of adverse racial outcomes rather than on the pervasive white privilege and racism that have shaped and reproduced those outcomes.[61] She goes further by arguing that while race is prevalent in environmental justice movements, the movements should encompass all subaltern and subordinated social groups.

Environmental justice movements have made less progress in claiming that natural resources inequalities based on class are unjust or illegal. In the "Principles of Environmental Justice," only one principle calls for "fair access for all to the full range of resources." Perhaps because resource inequalities affect livelihood more than survival and have a direct bearing on resource allocation and property rights, they are more commonly framed as problems of infrastructure, political participation, or equity—rather than inequality.

From Unsustainability to Economic Affordability and Environmental Harmony

If low-income water problems are defined in terms of economic sustainability, which they rarely are, the socioeconomic remedies are generally framed in terms of "affordability," for example, affordable housing and affordable utility rates policies. Links between economic and environmental sustainability have rarely involved low-income water problems in the United States. Although sometimes secured through lawsuits, affordability policies are more commonly sought through political lobbying, charitable programs, administrative proceedings of utilities regulatory commissions, and social services organizations. Affordability programs are sometimes linked with broader policies of "smart growth," but they have not fully engaged with issues of environmental harmony and sustainable livelihood or with their nemesis poverty.

From Poverty to Social and Environmental Capitals and Capabilities

It seems odd that low-income water problems are rarely defined explicitly in terms of the processes of poverty that cause them.[62] However, the 1990s witnessed important changes in the U.S. poverty and welfare situation. On the one hand, economic growth reduced unemployment rates, and welfare reform policies dramatically reduced the number of persons receiving public benefits.[63] On the other hand, it was not clear which low-income people were better or worse off, as housing costs rose, food stamp programs were underutilized, and utility bills increased in many metropolitan areas.[64]

As Bebbington and others have pointed out, in less-developed countries low-income groups pursue complex livelihood strategies through a range of public, private, and nongovernmental institutions.[65] These strategies aim to build assets (for example, improved household water systems) and capabilities (for example, environmental monitoring). If, as we suspect, the complex strategies observed in Latin America have parallels in the United States, the range of potential remedies for low-income water problems is far larger and more challenging than the foregoing survey of government programs would suggest, for it points toward the need for water specialists to engage more fundamental debates and alternatives for poverty reduction. It is time, once again, for U.S. water researchers to think across resource sectors, social policies, and international boundaries.

Summary

This chapter mapped different approaches to low-income water problems, including approaches currently pursued by environmental justice activists and scholars. It clarified the key conceptual differences among those approaches and sought to show how those conceptual differences lead to different chains of inquiry, public forums, and potential remedies. We showed that environmental justice is rarely invoked in water resources management in states like Colorado. We acknowledged that environmental justice could expand, and in other fields has expanded, its scope to encompass natural resources injustices and remedies to them. But rather than leap in that direction, with its uncertain prospects and outcomes, this chapter surveyed the broad range of actual and potential approaches and remedies to low-income water problems. It purposely maintained the currently narrow connotation of environmental injustice as inequality. It chose not to conflate norms of infrastructure standards, equitable access, and equal exposure.

Of the alternatives considered, we conclude that environmental justice, when narrowly defined, demands the highest standard of justice and provides the greatest remedies for injustices based on inequality. However, we also conclude that some alternative definitions of the problem (for example, ones based on infrastructure standards, political participation, and fairness) may offer a more immediately and pervasively available set of remedies to some low-income water problems. In this chapter, we showed that two other conceptual approaches, those aimed at sustainability and poverty reduction, could further broaden the range of potential remedies. Although environmental justice movements have greater force and salience than these alternative approaches do, their appeal to equality may be more relevant and fruitful in some geographic situations and water resources problems than in others. Environmental justice claims are essential, for example, to attain equal water quality standards and to eliminate racially based infrastructure inequalities. Mainstream approaches in water resources management have failed to invoke environmental justice claims to redress these inequalities, except in situations of severe water quality degradation (such as in the Denver metropolitan area). They have thereby failed to secure equal access to safe and adequate water supplies (for example, on Indian reservations).

In other situations, accusations of environmental racism may be so provocative that they stimulate more inquiry and litigation than remedies, and impede simpler low-income water programs aimed at infrastructure upgrading, common public interests, and fairness. The latter approaches, for example, might be fruitful for improving stormwater drainage and sewer systems in drinking water quality in housing for migrant workers as well as compensation for laborers injured by water rights transfers. Indeed, it is the persistent and intentional failure to use those other approaches to secure the well-being of low-income groups that leads to and justifies environmental justice claims.

We suspect that the current gaps between equity and equality-based approaches will likely persist for two reasons. First, environmental justice claims will rightly continue to focus on racial inequalities covered by the Civil Rights Act as well as the Environmental

Justice Executive Order. They will rightly seek remedies for water problems that have intentionally not been addressed by incremental infrastructure improvements, political participation processes, and capital accumulation policies. As Bullard has argued, the black and Hispanic middle class can still not fully "vote with their feet."[66] Second, the current conceptual distinction between resource equity and environmental justice may be strategically useful for activist groups. The former currently connotes fair access to water resources, compensation for injury, a minimum supply, and procedural justice. The latter connotes equal access to water (for example, waterfront parks, public fountains, and rest rooms), uniform national water quality standards, and equal protection from water-related hazards for all economic and ethnic groups. Environmental injustices are those that are remedied by social equalization, while inequities are those remedied by actions that are fair but not necessarily equal.

These distinctions between justice as equity and justice as equality may be more deeply rooted than we think, for they recall the ancient separation between English courts of law and equity. Courts of law handled cases in which established laws were at issue. Courts of equity, by contrast, handled cases that the law did not address but that involved fundamental issues of fairness. This ancient distinction had its own problems (exemplified in Dickens's parody of the chancery courts) and has been abolished in many jurisdictions, including the United States, so we do not want to push the analogy too far. However, it is tempting to consider that divergent patterns of academic inquiry and activism today may reflect deeper tensions in struggles for justice and fairness.

Finally, we showed that approaches to natural resources equity and environmental justice both fail to draw upon research on poverty and the sustainability of low-income groups.[67] They thus fail to envision how the broad suite of remedies surveyed above, ranging from public works to expanded environmental rights, might move beyond beleaguered welfare programs to more promising paths to sustainability for low-income groups and the environments we inhabit.

Acknowledgments

We are grateful to Gary Bryner, Kathryn Mutz, David Pellow, and Laura Pulido for offering constructive criticisms on an earlier draft of this chapter, to the National Science Foundation (grant no. 9905293) for supporting the "Water, Poverty, and Sustainable Livelihoods in Colorado" project, and to the NOAA-CIRES Western Western Water Assessment for its support.

Notes

1. Katherine Berry, "Values, Ideologies, and Equity in Water Distribution: Historical Perspectives from Coastal California, United States," in *Searching for Equity: Conceptions of Justice and Equity in Peasant Irrigation*, ed. Rutgerd Bolenes and Gloria Davila (Assen, The Netherlands: Van Gorcum Press, 1998); F. Lee Brown and Helen Ingram, *Water and Poverty in the Southwest* (Tucson: University of Arizona Press, 1987); C. W. Howe, J. K. Lazo, and K. R. Weber, "The Economic Impacts of Agriculture-to-Urban Water Transfers on the Area of Origin: A Case Study of the Arkansas River Valley in Colorado," *American Journal of Agricultural Economics* (December 1990): 1200–1204; Meg Huby, "Water, Poverty and Social Policy: A Review of Issues for Research," *Journal of Social Policy* 24 (1995): 219–36; Kenneth R. Weber, "Necessary but Insufficient: Land, Water and Economic Development in Hispanic Southern Colorado," *Journal of Ethnic Studies* 19 (1991): 127–42.

2. Bunyan Bryant, ed., *Environmental Justice: Issues, Policies, and Solutions* (Washington, D.C.: Island Press, 1995).

3. James L. Wescoat Jr., "Common Themes in the Work of Gilbert White and John Dewey: A Pragmatic Appraisal," *Annals of the Association of American Geographers* 82 (1992): 587–607.

4. Exceptions in the United States include urban water utility publications on water affordability and disconnections, for example, the American Water Works Association, *Alternative Rates. Manual of Water Supply Practices*, M34 (Denver: American Water Works Association, 1992); Margot Saunders, Phyllis Kimmel, Maggie Spade, and Nancy Brockway, *Water Affordability Programs* (Denver: American Water Works Association Research Foundation, 1996).

5. Geographic research on poverty, for example, concentrates on socioeconomic correlates, such as race, gender, age, and occupation. See Janet E. Kodras, "The Changing Map of American Poverty in an Era of Economic Restructuring and Political Realignment," *Economic Geography* 73 (1997): 67–93; Wendy Shaw, *The Geography of United States Poverty: Patterns of Deprivation, 1980–1990* (New York: Garland, 1996); and Lakshman Yapa, "What Causes Poverty? A Postmodern View," *Annals of the Association of American Geographers* 86 (1996): 707–28—none of which mention water. But see Patrick West et al., "Minorities and Toxic Fish Consumption: Implications for Point Discharge Policy in Michigan," in Bryant, ed., *Environmental Justice*, 124–37.

6. Source: LEXIS/NEXIS, Academic Universe, Legal Research, March 18, 2000.

7. See, for example, Susan L. Cutter, "Race, Class and Environmental Justice," *Progress in Human Geography* 19 (1995): 111–22; and Laura Pulido, "A Critical Review of the Methodology of Environmental Racism Research," *Antipode* 28, 2 (1996): 142–59.

8. Brown and Ingram, *Water and Poverty in the Southwest*, 1.

9. Helen Ingram, personal communication (July 27, 2000), suggests that the

gaps between rural and urban concern, on the one hand, and resource supply and environmental quality, on the other, may explain the lack of contact between the two movements.

10. For example, Robert D. Bullard, *Dumping in Dixie: Race, Class and Environmental Quality*, 2nd ed. (Boulder, Colo.: Westview Press, 1994), 78, lists water pollution relative to other community concerns.

11. Western Water Policy Review Advisory Commission (WWPRAC), *Water in the West: Challenge for the Next Century* (Denver: Western Water Policy Review Advisory Commission, 1998).

12. Dan McCool, *Command of the Waters: Iron Triangles, Federal Water Development, and Indian Water* (Tucson: University of Arizona Press, 1994); Jose Rivera, *Acequia Culture: Water, Land and Community in the Southwest* (Albuquerque: University of New Mexico Press, 1998).

13. Christopher Brown, "A Watershed and Bio-Regional Approach to Transboundary Wastewater Management in the Tijuana River Watershed" (Ph.D. diss., San Diego State University, 1998); Pamela S. Doughman, "Discourse, Sustainable Development, Mexico, and Water" (Ph.D. diss., University of California, Irvine, 1999); David R. Ellis, "Socioeconomic Differentials among Selected Colonia and Non-Colonia Populations on the Texas-Mexico Border" (Ph.D. diss., Texas A&M University, 1995); Helen Ingram, Nancy K. Laney, and David M. Gillilan, *Divided Waters: Bridging the U.S.-Mexico Border* (Tucson: University of Arizona Press, 1995); Suzanne Michel, "Place, Power, and Water Pollution in the Californias: A Geographic Analysis of Water Quality Politics in the Tijuana–San Diego Metropolitan Region" (Ph.D. diss., University of Colorado, 2000). In addition, special issues of *Natural Resources Journal* on this topic include "Water Issues in the U.S.-Mexico Borderlands," 40:4 (2000), and "The La Paz Symposium on Transboundary Groundwater Management on the U.S.-Mexico Border," 40:2 (2000).

14. WWPRAC, *Water in the West*, 6-3.

15. Todd Olinger, *Indian Water 1997, Trends and Directions in Federal Water Policy; A Summary of the Conference Proceedings* (Denver: Western Water Policy Review Advisory Commission, 1997).

16. WWPRAC, *Water in the West*, 6-4.

17. WWPRAC, *Water in the West*, 4-22.

18. WWPRAC, *Water in the West*, 5-19.

19. Patrick O'Toole, "A Blueprint for Effective Water Policy in the West," printed in WWPRAC, *Water in the West*, app. B, 3.

20. WWPRAC, *Water in the West*, 4.

21. Pamela Case and Gregory Alward, *Patterns of Demographic, Economic and Value Change in the Western United States: Implications for Water Use and Management* (Denver: Western Water Policy Review Advisory Commission, 1998), 34.

22. A point made in Helen Ingram, "Reason and Rationality in Water Politics," *Water Resources Update* (March 2000), 50-3.

23. Important exceptions for other resources—for example, forests—include

Craig R. Humphrey et al., "Poverty and Natural Resources in the United States," *Society and Natural Resources* 7–8 (1994–1995).

24. Michael Brint and William Weaver, eds., *Pragmatism in Law and Society* (Boulder, Colo.: Westview Press, 1991).

25. John Rawls, *A Theory of Justice* (Cambridge: Harvard University Press, 1971), 11.

26. John Dewey, *The Logic of Inquiry* (New York: H. Holt, 1938).

27. Child welfare changes the situation dramatically and invokes a strong response from the state that reportedly inhibits requests for assistance by low-income families who fear the loss of their children.

28. Important exceptions include environmental justice organizations such as COPEEN (Colorado People's Environmental and Economic Network), which mobilizes community groups in the northeast Denver metropolitan area.

29. See also the analysis by Dorceta Taylor, "Blacks and the Environment: Toward an Explanation of the Concern and Action Gap between Blacks and Whites," *Environment and Behavior* 21 (1989): 175–205.

30. James N. Corbridge and Theresa A. Rice, *Vranesh's Colorado Water Law*, rev. ed. (Boulder: University Press of Colorado, 1999), 205.

31. *Farmers Highline Canal and Reservoir Co. v City of Golden*, 129 Colo. 575, 272 P.2d 629 (Colo. 1954).

32. *Kansas v Colorado*, 206 U.S. 46, 27 S. Ct. 655, 51 L. Ed. 956 (1907); and *New Jersey v New York*, 283 U.S. 336, 51 S. Ct. 478, 75 L. Ed. 1104 (1931). Equitable apportionment takes many factors into account and does not imply an equal or exactly proportionate allocation.

33. Bullard, *Dumping in Dixie*, 126.

34. Peter Gleick, ed., *The World's Water 2000–2001* (Washington, D.C.: Island Press, 2000).

35. On the duty to provide water for animals, James L. Wescoat Jr., "The Right of Thirst for Animals in Islamic Water Law: A Comparative Approach," *Environment and Planning D: Society and Space* 13 (1995): 637–54, cites Colorado revised statutes secs. 35-44-101, 37-92-602, 18-9-201, and 35-42-105.

36. Michael Heiman, "From 'Not in My Backyard!' to 'Not in Anybody's Backyard!': Grassroots Challenge to Hazardous Waste Facility Siting," *Journal of the American Planning Association* 56 (1990): 359–62.

37. These standards should not be taken for granted, because some argue that uniform standards are not ecologically sound or economically efficient. States also vary in their implementation of water quality regulations. See Robert W. Adler, Jessica C. Landman, and Diane M. Cameron, *The Clean Water Act, 20 Years Later* (Washington, D.C.: Island Press and the Natural Resources Defense Council, 1993), for a review; see especially 36–37 and 56–59 on environmental injustices related to shellfish contamination and beach closures.

38. Source: LEXIS/NEXIS, Academic Universe, Legal Research, March 21, 2000. By contrast, a LEXIS/NEXIS search indicates that Colorado statutes

jointly mention "water" *and* "equity" (fifty-two times) *or* "justice" (forty-two times).

39. Laura Pulido, *Environmentalism and Economic Justice: Two Chicano Struggles in the Southwest* (Tucson: University of Arizona Press, 1996), 125–90.

40. Robert D. Bullard, ed., *Confronting Environmental Racism: Voices from the Grassroots* (Boston: South End Press, 1993), 195–206; Bryant, ed., *Environmental Justice*, 1–7.

41. Andrew Szasz and Michael Meuser, "Environmental Inequalities: Literature Review and Proposals for New Directions in Research and Theory," *Current Sociology* 45, 3 (1997): 99–120.

42. Colorado statutes refer only once, and case law four times, to "sustainable" resource use.

43. WWPRAC, *Water in the West*, 3-1–3-35, 6-2.

44. Lawrence MacDonnell, *From Reclamation to Sustainability: Water, Agriculture, and the Environment in the American West* (Niwot: University Press of Colorado, 1999).

45. For example, the U.S. Department of Agriculture, Rural Utilities Service, www.usda.gov/rus; U.S. Department of Agriculture, National Drinking Water Clearinghouse, www.estd.wvu.edu/ndwc; and U.S. Environmental Protection Agency, National Small Flows Clearinghouse, www.estd.wvu.edu/nsfc; U.S. Department of Health and Human Services, Indian Health Service, www.ihs.gov; and Bureau of Indian Affairs (for example, Housing Improvement Program), www.doi.gov/bia/ots/otshome.htm.

46. State of Colorado, Department of Local Government, "Colorado Water Needs Categorization List," typescript, August 4, 1999; State of Colorado, Department of Local Government, "Colorado Sewer Needs Categorization List," typescript, August 4, 1999.

47. Pulido, *Environmentalism and Economic Justice*, employs Lakshman Yapa's distinction between poverty and identity movements and creatively adapts "subaltern" approaches to the North American context.

48. Anthony J. Bebbington, "Capitals and Capabilities: A Framework for Analysing Peasant Viability, Rural Livelihoods, and Poverty," *World Development* 27, 12 (1999): 2021–44.

49. One article that does address these issues is Judith Jacobsen, "The Navajo Indian Irrigation Project and Quantification of Navajo Winters Rights," *Natural Resources Journal* 32, 4 (1992): 825–54.

50. Although one would not expect local officials responsible for administering a program to assert environmental justice claims against the constituents, governments, or water systems they manage, one would expect an increasing awareness of environmental justice issues and arguments.

51. Dewey, *The Logic of Inquiry*.

52. State of Colorado, Department of Local Government, "Colorado Water Needs Categorization List"; State of Colorado, Department of Local Government, "Colorado Sewer Needs Categorization List."

53. Margot Saunders et al., *Water Affordability Programs.*

54. H. Rosen and A. Keating, eds., *Water and the City: The Next Century* (Chicago: Public Works Historical Society, 1991). While uniform drinking water, fire, and plumbing standards tend to support these commitments, suburbanization, exurbanization, privatization, and growth of bottled water markets tend to weaken them.

55. *Kansas v Colorado*, 185 U.S. 125 (1902).

56. A. Dan Tarlock, "Growth Management and Water Resources Planning" (paper presented at the University of Illinois at Chicago, Chicago, Ill., September 1999; copy on file with author).

57. Saunders et al., *Water Affordability Programs*. International water organizations are increasingly asserting a human right to water (see, for example, Gleick, ed., *The World's Water*), as does the International Convention on the Rights of the Child of 1990, which the United States, alone with Somalia, has not ratified. However, it is not clear whether rights-based approaches are more effective in securing access to water and sanitation than approaches based on claims for an equitable share.

58. Environmental justice movements frame their claims in multiple ways. For example, they may, and often do, assert strong claims for *equal* exposure to toxic hazards and subsequently negotiate a *fair* or *equitable* remedy in the form of site remediation, compensation, or pollution reduction.

59. Bullard, ed., *Confronting Environmental Racism.*

60. "Principles of Environmental Justice," The First National People of Color Environmental Leadership Summit, October 24–27, 1991, Washington, D.C.

61. Laura Pulido, "Rethinking Environmental Racism: White Privilege and Urban Development in Southern California," *Annals of the Association of American Geographers* 90, 1 (2000): 12–40.

62. As noted earlier, there have been important studies of rural poverty in other resource sectors. See, for example, Craig R. Humphrey et al., "Poverty and Natural Resources in the United States"; and Bryant, ed., *Environmental Justice.*

63. Joseph Dalaker and B. D. Proctor, *Poverty in the United States: 1999* (Washington, D.C.: U.S. Census Bureau, 1999): 60–210; U.S. Census Bureau, "Current Population Reports" (Washington, D.C.: U.S. Census Bureau, 2000).

64. See current reports on welfare reform at the Institute for Research on Poverty at www.ssc.wisc.edu/irp/; the National Center for Poverty Law at www.povertylaw.org; and the Joint Center for Poverty Research at www.jcpr.org.

65. Bebbington, "Capitals and Capabilities."

66. Robert D. Bullard, "Anatomy of Environmental Racism and the Environmental Justice Movement," in Bullard, ed., *Confronting Environmental Racism*, 41–52; and Pulido, "Rethinking Environmental Racism."

67. The WWPRAC, *Water in the West*, and MacDonnell, *From Reclamation to Sustainability*, reflect important progress toward more encompassing visions of sustainability.

Chapter 4

INTERNATIONAL ENVIRONMENTAL PROTECTION

Human Rights and the North-South Divide

Tseming Yang

The equity, fairness, and race issues that have concerned the environmental justice movement are important not only in the domestic context but also in international environmental governance issues. In fact, one of the most salient parallels between domestic and international environmental protection issues seems to be race. For example, a number of high-profile incidents have involved hazardous waste shipments from predominately white, developed countries to predominately nonwhite, developing countries. In the infamous Koko case, hazardous waste was shipped by an Italian company to Koko, Nigeria, and dumped on the land of a Nigerian national in return for approximately one hundred dollars "rent" per month.[1] The similarities to the pattern of toxic waste flows complained of by communities of color in the United States are striking. Parallels can also be drawn with respect to the plight of the Huaorani people in Ecuador or the Ogoni people in Nigeria resulting from the havoc that oil exploration and drilling by European and U.S. oil corporations such as Texaco have wreaked on their lands and lives.[2] Finally, equity issues have also been raised in the context of "piracy" of genetic materials found only in the rain forests and other developing country ecosystems. When U.S. and European multinational pharmaceutical corporations have patented such genetic material, the profits of commercialization have rarely, if ever, returned to benefit the indigenous communities who preserved these materials in the first place.[3]

These instances make for powerful images. But they also suggest that the struggles of the domestic environmental justice movement are little different from those encountered abroad.[4] Like the problems faced by the poor and people of color in the United States, environmental injustice abroad has involved rich corporations with wealthy (and largely white) corporate executives exploiting, destroying, and polluting the environments of poor and disenfranchised nonwhite natives. As in the United States, government officials have failed to take protective actions.

A parallel argument can be made about international, government-dominated efforts to address global environmental problems. There, developing countries have complained that the primary responsibility for global environmental problems, such as ozone depletion and climate change, should fall on developed nations. They reason that financial and other resource constraints, as well as such important competing domestic priorities as poverty and public health problems, make it difficult for them to undertake many of the environmental protection efforts called for by developed nations. They also claim that they are not responsible for the problems. Again, the dynamics pit predominately white, developed nations against developing countries that are overwhelmingly nonwhite.

Later in this chapter, I will explore the parallels between environmental justice domestically and internationally in the context of natural resources management activities and the lessons that one might derive from them. I should note here that I use the term *international environmental issue* quite broadly to mean any environmental issue that is not wholly confined to the United States. That includes matters occurring wholly within other countries, dealings of individuals and businesses between different countries, and intergovernmental relationships.

A close examination reveals that the race and wealth dynamics involved in both the United States and the rest of the world are not merely the result of coincidence but have similar roots. At the same time, the autonomy and control that developing countries have achieved through decolonization are among the very goals that are sought by environmental justice activists through community empowerment and control over local environmental decisions. How these ideals have been translated into practice by developing nations exposes some of the potential difficulties that arise with regard to the long-term consequences of such remedies.

A comparative examination also provides some important suggestions for resolving environmental justice problems. For instance, creating greater international linkages can serve as an important means of addressing the export of environmental harms to developing countries—what in economic parlance is called the externalization of environmental burdens. Greater international linkage is not unlike enhanced political inclusion of minorities and poor people in domestic environmental decision making—it increases political accountability to such communities. International linkage can thus reduce marginalization of the disenfranchised and improve accountability of multinational corporations for their environmentally harmful activities abroad. Conversely, the increased focus on cultural diversity in approaches to international environmental protection shows the importance of community-based approaches and community knowledge in achieving effective environmental protection.

The Difficulties of Comparing the Domestic to the International

Two significant difficulties present themselves to this inquiry. First, equating the international with the domestic arguably oversimplifies the relationship between domestic and international efforts to protect the environment. After all, our understanding of justice and equity under our domestic legal and moral norms is not necessarily shared by those in other nations, societies, and cultures. Consider the protestations not too long ago by leaders of some Asian countries claiming that Western notions of individual rights simply did not apply in many of the developing nations of Asia.[5] U.S. notions of justice simply may not be applicable elsewhere.

Second, even in the United States, disagreement exists among domestic activists, regulators, scholars, and critics as to what the concept of environmental justice entails.[6] There is a fundamental difficulty in trying to define *environmental justice*. *Justice* is a term that is used in a variety of contexts, ranging from notions of procedural justice to substantive ones, and which has different meanings to different people.[7]

Of course, the meaning of *environmental justice* is not entirely unconstrained. It is a term coined by U.S. domestic environmental justice activists. Attempting to study the concept divorced from the cultural context in which it was born is of questionable value in seeking to better understand its concerns and underpinnings. In fact, doing so runs the risk of losing important aspects of or adding unintended ones to the movement's concept. The result may be to turn such an inquiry into the study of some other notion of justice.

This definitional issue is not only an academic and theoretical curiosity but has important practical implications. A particular conception of environmental justice not only delineates the problem itself but also suggests the range of appropriate solutions. In a sense, a definition provides a blueprint for finding an operational remedy. In order to sidestep some of the definitional difficulties of whether environmental injustice exists in other nations, I have instead chosen to frame the inquiry into the role of environmental justice in international environmental issues by examining features of environmental protection, race, and wealth that appear to run parallel to the issues that concern the environmental justice movement.

Putting aside definitional issues, the difficulties of comparing different cultures and value systems and correlating instances of human rights abuses and environmental destruction in foreign countries to the domestic environmental justice struggles raises the question of how we can compare these concepts. Not only are the normative systems different, but the cultural and legal structures and institutions are as well. After all, in legal systems where public participation rights—such as notice and comment before administrative regulatory actions—are not generally provided for or where an equal protection provision similar to that in the U.S. Constitution simply does not exist, claims about the failure to provide such rights to particular groups or individuals must be viewed in a considerably different light. In short, one might argue that the noted instances of environmental and human rights abuses are simply nothing like the environmental justice struggles faced by communities of color and poor communities here in the United States.

Such a criticism, however, misses the point of the inquiry here. Just because the legal and cultural systems are not identical does not mean that the same type of concerns—for instance, the need to address the concerns of minorities and local populations—are not relevant. Even if the analyses might not provide for directly applicable how-to prescriptions, my analysis suggests alternatives and difficulties that might otherwise not be readily apparent.

Race, Wealth, and International Environmental Protection

As noted previously, one of the most striking characteristics of many international and foreign environmental problems is that they appear to exhibit many of the same wealth and race characteristics that environmental justice activists have complained about in the domestic context. The human rights and environmental struggles of local and indigenous communities in such developing countries as Ecuador, Indonesia,[8] and Nigeria[9] against the environmentally destructive consequences of natural resources exploitation by multinational corporations are analogous to both the wealth and the race discrimination strands of the domestic environmental justice movement. At the same time, rural native and indigenous people in developing countries have little input into the environmental decision-making processes of their governments.

And as in the United States, environmental justice activists in other countries complain that mainstream U.S. and European environmental advocacy groups ignore the special burdens of pollution on racial minority groups and poor communities. In the context of a long history of paternalism and chauvinistic ignorance toward natives and local communities, such Western attitudes have, at best, failed to appreciate the relationship between native populations and nature and, at worst, have been condescending and dismissive.[10] For instance, famous gorilla advocate Dian Fossey's almost outright hostility to native Africans and her descriptions of them as "wogs" or "apes" would strike most as rather shocking.[11] This attitude was also apparent in the statements of well-known German conservationist Bernhard Grzimek. Talking about the decolonization of African countries:

> Grzimek insisted that he was not prejudiced against [Africans]; he just did not think these brothers were ready for independence. [It was the] responsibility of the colonial governments . . . to educate the Africans so that they would be able to live democratically. The white man's burden extended to teaching the Africans about wildlife and conservation [in order to keep them from repeating] *our mistakes and our sins.*"[12]

Even in disclaiming racial prejudice in his views of Africans, Grzimek's statement at once exhibits underlying assumptions of cultural superiority and condescension toward native and indigenous views of and approaches to managing natural resources. Despite protestations denying Western superiority, the paternalistic roots of Western intervention—that colonial rulers just knew better than the local people—is patent.

But the work of Western conservationists and the application of Western wildlife conservation approaches in Africa has had much farther reaching impacts. The vestiges of Western methods of natural resources management imposed by colonial rulers and the attendant displacement of native cultures and sustainable resource uses can still be seen in the difficulties that native communities face as a result of wildlife conservation efforts in East Africa. Initial conservation efforts by the colonial ruling powers relied primarily on the American model of establishing parks as a primary means of nature preservation.

Even if the application of such a model of wildlife conservation was motivated by genuine concern for the value and preservation of wildlife, it was also based on notions that conservation of nature required separation of humans from nature—an approach that was greatly at odds with the relationship that humans had had with nature in that ecological system for a long time. For example, the creation of Serengeti National Park in Tanzania ultimately resulted in the displacement of the native pastoral Maasai people from the park area.

Reminiscent of the past treatment by the United States of Native Americans and their removal to reservation lands, so too the removal of native Maasai communities from their traditional subsistence areas in the Serengeti had profoundly destructive impacts on these communities. In fact, most of the costs and burdens associated with conservation, such as property damage and injuries to human life caused by elephants straying outside of park boundaries, have been borne primarily by those least able to shoulder it—the local communities. In the end, such conservation efforts were primarily designed to benefit Western tourists and conservationists rather than local and native populations. For example, Serengeti National Park was first created in 1919 at the behest of big-game hunters.

Later recognition of the need for full local support of wildlife conservation efforts led to programs such as the Communal Areas Management Programme for Indigenous Resources (CAMPFIRE). CAMPFIRE has sought to return some of the financial benefits of conservation to local communities. However, criticisms persist that even such local community benefits have failed to be real and substantial.[13] And Western conservationists have continued to support international measures, such as the CITES ban on elephant ivory trade, that prevent such countries as Botswana and Zimbabwe from realizing significant economic rewards from successful wildlife restoration efforts.[14]

Government-led efforts to address global and transnational problems, such as global warming, biodiversity conservation, and international hazardous waste flows, also raise parallel race and wealth dynamics. In addition to substantive distributional issues regarding heavy burdens of pollution and environmental degradation, developing countries have also complained of exclusion from environmental decision-making processes. Such claims ring similar to those of people of color and poor people with respect to domestic environmental decision-making processes. In particular, the unsatisfactory influence that developing countries have had on decision making about the funding of environmental projects by institutions such as the World Bank has been a significant target of criticism. Developed countries effectively control such institutions.[15]

Much of this may be attributed to differences in wealth and its attendant effects. In fact, that has frequently been the explanation for domestic environmental justice problems. According to this argument, unfairness in how adverse environmental impacts are distributed results from economic considerations. Thus, it is argued, disproportionate environmental burdens are not the result of race discrimination at all, but rather due to economic status. For instance, corporations seeking to lower their costs of disposing of industrial wastes simply divert waste from places where disposal is expensive to places where it is cheap. Similarly, resource extraction methods frequently proceed by methods that are least costly, but which may also be quite environmentally destructive. Poor and racial minority communities in the United States, like developing countries abroad, tend to be precisely those places where wastes are disposed of or environmentally destructive resource extraction methods are used. Poverty and economic development needs allow and attract such activities.

In the specific context of domestic hazardous waste facility siting, empirical studies, while not uncontroversial, have shown that the location of such waste sites is more closely correlated to the race of a community than to its socioeconomic status.[16] However, this type of connection is more difficult to make in the international environmental context. For instance, most of what is known about waste flows being directed at developing countries or other inequities with regard to resource exploitation harms has been anecdotal. Statistical studies similar to those done in the domestic hazardous waste siting context are not available.[17] The close correlation between the wealth and race of nations compounds these difficulties. After all, if the developing countries are exclusively nonwhite and the overwhelming majority of developed nations, with a few exceptions in Asia such as Japan and Singapore, are white, then it is difficult to distinguish the effects of race from those of wealth.

The Colonial Legacy

However, if race and wealth are so closely related internationally, these questions arise: What is the reason for the close association? Is it relevant to our understanding of why pollution and other environmental burdens tend to disparately impact developing countries?

The answer to the first question comes from the history of colonialism. Within the context of colonialism, colonial possessions were made up of nonwhite countries, while the ruling powers were, with the exception of Japan, exclusively white and located in North America or Europe. Since the overwhelming majority of present developing countries were formerly poor colonies that have only recently embarked on a path toward a modern industrialized market economy, the high correlation between race and wealth is not surprising. However, to answer how this correlation is relevant to our inquiry here, the justifications for the colonial system must be examined more closely.

Much of colonialism was based on economic and other considerations of naked self-interest. Colonial rule, however, also had a philosophical foundation that sought to excuse and justify such endeavors through an ideology of racial and cultural superiority, as expressed by the civilizing mission of European nations. Under this ideology, Europeans were justified in colonizing and subjugating nonwhites by white racial and cultural superiority over non-European "savages." Under the mantle of the civilizing mission of the colonial powers, it was the "civilized" European's perceived moral duty, the "White Man's Burden," to subjugate the nonwhite "savages" in order to enlighten, educate, and convert them to Christianity.[18] Such notions of racial superiority were scarcely different from those that motivated slavery and subsequently segregation: the assertion of the "manifest destiny" of American Anglo-Saxons to conquer and dominate the American continent and other parts of the world and the various forms of discrimination against people of color in the United States.[19]

Of course, beginning at the turn of the twentieth century and accelerating after World War II, many former colonies did eventually acquire independence. Nevertheless, national independence for former colonies did not equalize the relationship between former colonies and their colonial masters. One important reason was that during colonial times, native development and education within the colonies frequently was not encouraged, in order to maintain and facilitate colonial rule. Natural resources in the colonies were usually siphoned off for use by the colonial ruling power.[20] As a result, former colonies largely started off into independence with little in the way of governmental institutions, societal resources, and economic resources—a handicap that profoundly retarded their development as nations and placed them at a disadvantage as competitors in the marketplace.[21]

The result has been that the race, power, and wealth dynamics of colonialism continue to be replicated at the intergovernmental level in international treaty negotiations, environmental project funding, and other decisions, where the greater influence of developed countries is readily apparent.[22] However, while some countries—especially in Asia and South America—have made enormous strides toward overcoming the handicaps of their colonial past, such accomplishments should not diminish the reality that poverty is still correlated with former colonial status. At the same time, feelings of racial and cultural superiority continue to exist even today in unspoken beliefs about the superiority of social and cultural practices in developed nations over those in developing nations. In fact, belittling or ignoring the importance of subsistence or barter economies has played an important role in justifying current economic development efforts and foreign aid that have displaced local culture in developing countries in favor of culture from the developed nations.[23]

In contrast, the local human rights and environmental struggles against the natural resources exploitation activities of multinational corporate interests do not seem to be easily explainable in this fashion. While the past behavior of some U.S. companies abroad toward natives has had direct parallels in the discriminatory treatment accorded to racial minorities in the United States,[24] one might argue that race is of little relevance these days. After all, such corporations seem to act almost exclusively with economic interests and goals in mind rather than in pursuit of racial discrimination per se. Thus, environmental destruction by multinational corporations is not motivated by racial considerations but, rather, is simply the by-product of the pursuit of profits and minimization of costs.

Lawrence Summers, then–chief economist of the World Bank, posed precisely this economic rationale in a controversial internal World Bank memo. Summers expressed this reasoning as a justification for exporting to and disposing of more industrial wastes and other forms of pollution in developing countries: the economic costs of doing so were so much lower there due to poverty and lesser economic development.[25]

This simple reductionist explanation, however, begs the central question. Attributing disparate environmental burdens to wealth dynamics avoids the question of whether race plays a role. It is a rationale similar to that advanced in the hazardous waste facilities siting debate, in which racial disparities have been explained as being the result of wealth dynamics. Yet, if a decision maker knows that the poor communities that are adversely impacted are disproportionately made up of people of color and that the individuals who benefit are largely white, is such knowledge irrelevant? Many would say no and argue that actions taken with such knowledge and resulting in disparate impacts are a form of racial discrimination.[26]

But there are also considerations that connect the impoverishment of many in developing countries directly with discriminatory colonial policies. In particular, stark wealth divisions between nonwhite natives and white expatriate immigrants in the colonies can, in part, be traced to the economic effects of dispossession of land and resources and the forceful relocation of natives from their traditional lands. For instance, colonial land dispossession of native Africans in Zimbabwe resulted in a 2-percent-white minority controlling more than half of the country's fertile farmland. As one of the most visible manifestations of the colonial legacy, this control has been blamed as the cause of upheavals in Zimbabwe involving occupations of white farms by Africans.[27] Corporations that have knowingly perpetuated harms and disadvantages to such nonwhite, native populations and have indirectly benefited from the economic wealth of the former colonial masters cannot simply disclaim responsibility for the racist overtones of such actions.

There are important responses to such claims, of course. One could argue that the suffering of natives and indigenous people in developing countries from resource exploitation activities by multinational corporations has nothing to do whatsoever with race, even if the economic connection to past discrimination is considered. Rather, too much time has elapsed since the independence of many such states, and current inequities are primarily the result of present-day problems. Arguably then, environmental and social inequities are symptoms of the lack of robust democratic structures in those countries. Human rights abuses that appear to occur in such instances are simply manifestations of corruption and internal competition for wealth and resources, processes in which poor and disenfranchised populations, such as indigenous people, simply lose out.[28] After all, none of the multinational companies, such as Texaco, Shell, and Freeport McMoRan, could operate in its respective host country without the consent of the particular national government.

The invariable complicity of developing country governments with the foreign corporation, frequently rising to active involvement in environmentally destructive resource extraction, seems to underscore the importance of the internal dynamics of exploitation. For example, after Texaco gave up its oil production facilities in Ecuador, the Ecuadorean government took over the destructive oil-drilling activities in the Amazon forest.[29] That might lead one to conclude that such cases are arguably better characterized as an instance of a government sacrificing local communities for the greater national good or, in what may be frequently the case, for corrupt purposes. Casting such issues purely as outsiders exploiting and taking advantage of local people may cause us to miss a significant part of what causes these occurrences.

To go further along this line of reasoning, even the North-South divide arguably misapprehends the environmental positions of developed and developing countries. Developed countries may have acted environmentally irresponsibly in the past in bringing about much of the current global environmental degradation, such as ozone depletion and climate change. Such a focus, however, ignores the environmentally harmful activities that developing countries are engaged in now and the current restorative activities that developed nations are undertaking to remedy past environmental degradation. In fact, developing countries frequently appear to take antienvironmental positions, demanding what in essence amounts to a concession that they be permitted to destroy the environment to the same extent as developed countries in order to achieve a comparable level of wealth.[30] At the same time, their human rights records and concern for local and indigenous communities are frequently not particularly stellar.

Of course, the arguments are more complicated than stated here. There has been corresponding criticism, much of it well-founded, that U.S. solicitude for environmental issues and human rights reaches only as far as its own economic or political interests.[31] I also have knowingly oversimplified important fairness concerns related to poverty and historical contributions to many global environmental problems. Nevertheless, the concern about the commitment of developing countries to international environmental protection efforts remains the same in light of their apparent willingness to sacrifice environmental protection goals for economic development. In the end, their position stands in stark contrast to the philosophy of prominent grass-roots environmental justice activists who have sought to achieve justice and fairness and who have distinguished themselves from NIMBY ("not in my backyard") activists by promoting more effective environmental protection rather than opposing it.

One could attribute this profound difference simply to differences in shortsighted self-interest and unwillingness to take responsibility for environmentally harmful actions and unfair burdens on local populations. Or, one could equate the actions of national governments of developing countries with the actions of the federal, state, and local governments here in the United States that have resulted in the very problems that the domestic environmental justice advocates complain about. After all, within domestic poor and racial minority communities, decisions about land use, pollution permitting, or resource exploitation are vested in governmental authorities beyond that community, a problem similar to that encountered in developing nations.

But what of the differences? While developing countries and their residents may suffer similar problems of environmental degradation and resource exploitations, control over such matters rests with the government of those who previously, under the colonial system, were subject to the will of outsiders. Should it matter that, in a sense, the outsiders have become insiders? The answer to this question not only bears on the legitimacy of developed countries coercing developing countries into taking more responsibility for environmentally harmful actions that adversely affect local and indigenous populations but also is relevant to the attempts by domestic environmental justice advocates to achieve a greater measure of local and community control over environmental decision making.

The Dilemma of Local Control and International Concern

The autonomy and control that national sovereignty promotes are among the very goals sought by environmental justice activists through community empowerment and community control over local environmental decisions and impacts. It appears that environmental justice activists seek to achieve domestically what developing countries, through the decolonization process, have already achieved internationally: autonomy and control. Because of the prominence of this issue within the environmental justice movement, a close examination of this goal and what has to be reckoned with if it is taken to its logical end may be significant.

National sovereignty has given developing countries a semblance of equality internationally that has been largely missing from the domestic environmental justice struggles. Similar to protections that tribal sovereignty accords to federally recognized tribes within the United States,[32] national sovereignty assures the political autonomy and independence of a country's people and its choices. Because national sovereignty of developing countries is not subject to the limitations that tribal sovereignty is subject to, however, its benefits and difficulties for achieving environmental and equity goals are put into sharper relief.

Sovereignty can give developing countries significant leverage to achieve equity while also protecting differing cultural values and relationships to the environment. However, it can also serve as a means of escaping accountability when, at the best, internal disagreement or, at the worst, corruption and exploitation by elites lead to decisions that are patently shortsighted and exploitative of the environment and local or indigenous communities, situations that have plagued many developing countries. In fact, much environmental degradation and associated human rights violations might be explained in this fashion. The high-profile execution by the Nigerian military rulers of Ken Saro Wiwa, who had spoken out about the environmental destruction caused by oil drilling activities of Royal Dutch Shell and Chevron in Nigeria, is just one example.[33] While such human rights violations concern many environmentalists as well as Western governments, national sovereignty makes it virtually impossible in such an instance to hold the political decision makers accountable for their misdeed.

Such lack of accountability may be especially alarming when it shields broad governmental corruption or uses of governmental power to one-sidedly advance the private interests of the ruling elite as opposed to the interests of the broader nation. However, the actual adverse environmental consequences may not be much different from instances where legitimate internal political disagreements lead to the economic development interests winning out over environmental protection. Even when the economically benefited group is able to defeat the conservation interests through legitimate political processes and by legitimate means, the harm to the environment or the burdens on local populations are the same, regardless of how leaders make their decisions. Nevertheless, as a theoretical matter, when such decisions are controlled by domestic democratic political processes, they have a legitimacy that is otherwise lacking.[34]

At the same time, decisions involving, for instance, the destruction of globally unique natural resources, the extinction of species by economic development projects, or the forcible displacement of indigenous people, may also raise important international concerns.

Such conflicts go to the heart of the doctrine of sovereignty. They raise the question of what priority national control over national resources should have over important concerns by the global community regarding the scarcity and uniqueness of such resources. What is the legitimacy of the global community's interests in such local resources? And what is a legitimate reaction by the international community when a developing country chooses to sell its resources to the highest bidder in the international market rather than to conserve and share in "less-impressive conservation profits?"[35] In the end, the question that local autonomy and control over resources raises is the fundamental one of the larger community's interest in such local matters and the confidence that one should have in local communities acting as stewards and trustees of the interests of the larger community. And finally, it also raises the question of whether and when the legitimate interest of local control in itself ought to outweigh the interests of the larger community.

There are also converse issues that autonomy and independence raise. Even if political sovereignty or community control changes the environmental decision maker and turns the disenfranchised from political outsiders into insiders, it cannot fundamentally alter the unfair choices that people of color and poor people are frequently forced to make when presented with the economic development versus environmental protection alternatives. This is the infamous "jobs versus environment/health" choice put forward at times by those pushing economic development projects and polluting industries. Of course, this set of alternatives is frequently a false choice because it presupposes that environmental justice communities are not entitled to more and that any gains in jobs can only be made in exchange for degradation of the community's environment or its residents' health. Nevertheless, these options are frequently put forth in just this form.

From these observations, one thing is clear: national sovereignty, even if all the warts and blemishes of undemocratic governance are ignored, can be a double-edged sword that may also be an impediment to improving environmental protection and lead to the oppression of small dissenting communities within the larger group.[36] After all, the positions of developing countries on environmental protection issues have at times been decidedly unenvironmental, and their actions have, in many instances, sacrificed the interests of local and indigenous communities for the greater good. Moreover, even if such instances have frequently occurred in the context of tensions between the need to address poverty and economic development within such countries, they still raise troubling questions about the ability of national processes to accommodate legitimate international interests, such as in unique or shared global commons resources.[37]

Learning from International and Domestic Environmental Governance

What kinds of lessons can we then draw from these experiences and the issues they have raised?

The Difficulties of Community Control

One obvious lesson of sovereignty suggests that community empowerment in the domestic environmental justice context, if taken to the extreme of absolute local community control, may create difficult problems of reconciling national and international interests with those of the local community. This obvious tension has plagued efforts to achieve environmental justice goals in the Native American tribal context for some time.

However, in drawing comparisons between environmental justice communities and developing countries, it is also apparent that the two are not alike in all respects. The environmental justice movement has been marked by great idealism, goals of inclusion, and ecological consciousness, as compared to the more pragmatic approaches and trade-offs that developing countries have sought to make with development goals. And, given the failure of the existing domestic environmental regulatory scheme to integrate local community and racial minority concerns into environmental decision making for the most part, as a currently practical matter, any amount of additional local community participation can only be helpful to resolving such trade-offs.

But if we see the developing countries' experience as relevant to the environmental justice movement, it seems unlikely that the idealism can ultimately be maintained. In the end, the environmental justice community will be faced with the same problem that developing countries have faced, and the same choices that environmental regulators here in the United States have been presented with: what trade-offs between environmental quality and health risks are appropriate in light of the attendant benefits, and what to do with internally dissenting interests.[38]

The Significance of Cultural Diversity

There are some additional lessons we may draw from these observations. Current research appears to indicate that contrary to the implications of Garrett Hardin's "The Tragedy of the Commons,"[39] traditional, community-based natural resources management approaches can be very helpful in conserving common-pool natural resources.[40]

The utility of such locally diverse and appropriate strategies for resource conservation has, for example, been explored by others in the context of cultural "taboo" systems that have successfully limited and regulated natural resources exploitation at sustainable levels through informal, culturally based restrictions on the use and exploitation of resources.[41] Such restrictions on resource use can range from limiting the method of use to limiting the taking of resources during vulnerable life history stages of a species to restricting access to resources in time and space.

The importance of local and community-based resource management has been recognized in the Convention on Biological Diversity. The convention encourages its parties to ensure that the benefits from the use of biodiversity, such as commercial pharmaceutical exploitation, will flow back to local and indigenous communities responsible for the preservation of biological diversity. In this way, it has sought to preserve community-based approaches to conserving biodiversity.[42]

That linkage is based in large part on the recognition that cultural diversity is often part and parcel of biological diversity because it is representative of the many differing relationships that humans can have with the rest of nature.[43] Cultural diversity can be instrumental in promoting conservation of biological diversity at three different levels. First, it can serve as a repository of different approaches and systems for managing the environment that can be tapped at appropriate times, just as biological diversity preserves the ability of ecological systems to respond to changes introduced into a system. Furthermore, cultural diversity can preserve local approaches to conservation and environmental protection that have been successful through past experience with specific local conditions. Finally, traditional and indigenous cultures can contribute to biodiversity protection precisely because their approaches utilize natural resources at lower levels, are purposefully less intense, and are more sustainable than modern, superefficient resource exploitation methods. Therefore, considering cultural diversity in approaches to conservation is not only an inadvertent outgrowth of ecologically diverse systems, but also a necessity for the appropriate management of resources in a variety of local conditions and local societies.

The failure to appreciate the importance of local approaches is exemplified by the misguided effort to apply American and Western European approaches to wildlife conservation in East Africa. In fact, the ability of preexisting local culture and traditional local governance to address potentially environmentally harmful activities refutes the assumption of Garrett Hardin that local communities engage in mindless exploitation of natural resources without concern for the future and the remaining community.[44] While such traditional approaches cannot always succeed in the modern world, they do illustrate their continuing importance.

There are obvious parallels that one can draw to the domestic environmental justice movement, most notably in the activities of American Indian tribes to obtain greater regulatory control and autonomy over the use and exploitation of resources within tribal jurisdiction. There, just as in the international context, increased tribal control, combined with adequate financial resources to implement tribal environmental regulations, arguably can help preserve locally appropriate approaches to resource management that are consistent with traditional Native American culture.

There are also less obvious implications. An emphasis on culturally diverse approaches to natural resource management emphasizes that a one-size-fits-all approach to environmental protection is not appropriate. In fact, effective environmental regulation and natural resources management approaches must be contingent on locally specific circumstances, including the presence of diverse local cultures. This means that the sustainable use of natural resources cannot proceed under the traditional economic paradigm, which depends in many respects on economies of scale to ever improve the efficiency and effectiveness of resource exploitation. In fact, the importance of culturally diverse approaches to natural resources management implies that uniformity in environmental regulation, even though desired in many regulatory contexts as promoting economic efficiency, is not necessarily the best approach to environmental protection. Such problems cannot be solved only at the global or national level or in the abstract. Rather, local communities really do count and are important in efforts to protect the environment.

This does not mean that local governments ought to be able to do whatever they want, if doing so includes setting environmental standards that are less protective of the environment and human health than national ones. This is not because local interests are less important than national ones. Rather, it is because national interests, such as in unique or commons resources as well as individual human rights, are important even in the local context. My analysis does not indicate in particular how such interests are to be accommodated, except to say that national interests should be important even at the local level. Likewise, a limit on local government decision making is required by the market-failure problems that lack of national regulation invites. Lack of limits plays right into economic competitive pressures and the "race to the bottom" that federal environmental statues have sought to prevent.

Finally, the importance of cultural diversity in resource management and environmental protection also emphasizes the importance of community knowledge. In order to fashion locally appropriate approaches to environmental protection, community and local knowledge about the locally specific issues and circumstances is crucial. The domestic environmental justice struggle has manifested itself in calls for greater incorporation of community knowledge into studies on the environmental and health effects of pollution, and the particular importance of greater incorporation of community-based health surveys into epidemiological studies. After all, who knows better the distribution and incidence of disease and adverse health effects than the community residents who suffer from those very pollution impacts.

"Internalizing" the Environmental Burdens on Foreign Native Populations

Aside from implications for the domestic environmental justice movement, this analysis also has implications for the role of autonomy and self-determination internationally. Autonomy and self-determination do not necessarily address one of the fundamental problems of environmental protection and of political participation. This problem, which finds a special application in the environmental justice context, is the shifting of the costs and burdens of environmental degradation to those groups who cannot refuse. Under traditional economic efficiency views, federal environmental regulation arises as the result of the failure of pollution-generating industries to fully internalize the pollution harms of their activities into the cost of doing business. Instead, pollution harms are externalized. Unburdened by the costs of pollution harms to the environment, industrial facilities degrade the environment at unsustainable and economically inefficient levels.

In the context of the domestic environmental justice movement, the pollution externalization theory finds its analogy in the complaints of environmental justice activists that environmental justice communities are forced to bear a disproportionate share of pollution burdens without adequate compensation. The disenfranchised status and lack of political power of communities of color and poor communities allow industry and others to externalize and shift pollution burdens onto environmental justice communities without suffering the economic and political consequences of such actions. Of course, within the U.S. domestic legal system, a remedy to such situations, even if largely ineffective, exists within the Constitution's Fourteenth Amendment equal protection clause.

A similar analogy can be drawn with respect to the environmental harms and burdens borne internationally by those living in developing countries. Traditional notions about the benefits of self-determination and autonomy suggest that national sovereignty, and the control over a nation's own affairs that it provides, increases the ability of developing countries to address environmental problems. However, examining the environmental externalities that are associated with the activities of multinationals leads to a different conclusion. In fact, focusing on the political boundaries that national sovereignty creates, autonomy and political independence have served to divorce the political interests of those in the developed countries from those in the developing countries. Political separation through national borders thus cuts off the political responsibility of government officials, corporations, and citizens in developed countries from those living in developing countries. Yet, the economic realities of the desire and need by developing countries for foreign investment and technology leave these countries exposed to the economic demands and pressures of multinational corporations and developed countries. The misdeeds and environmentally irresponsible acts of Texaco, Shell, and Freeport McMoRan, for example, in various developing countries are simply reflections of the ability of multinational corporations and the citizens and governments of developed countries to externalize the costs of industrial development and unsustainable consumption patterns to those living in developing countries.

What this suggests is that fairly allocating resources and pollution burdens and improving international environmental governance is not necessarily accomplished through greater independence and promotion of local control,[45] but may be accomplished through greater incorporation of citizens of developing countries into what has been called a transnational society.[46] *Transnational society* as a term has a utopian sound to it and in that sense might seem unachievable. Whether that ultimately proves so is not my concern here. Rather, one can see *transnational society* as representing the end goal of a more important process. Such a process would increase the integration of the concerns of those living in developing countries into the political and legal responsibilities of those living in developed countries. Seeking greater integration into our political system and concern for those from countries with traditionally little influence in environmental and other global governance is actually little different from the endeavor that racial minorities have engaged in here in the United States—that is, to move from the margins of society to the center. It is the quest of racial minorities to change their status from outsiders to full members of the political and cultural community of our nation.

Thus, the answer to injustice is not necessarily political separation and independence of communities from one another, especially in a global economy, where political separation and independence inevitably result in decreased accountability and concern of citizens, corporations, and governments for one another. Rather, the solution must lie in the task of taking more—and even full—responsibility for the consequences and impacts on others of our own actions, a goal that the political and legal integration aspects of a transnational society would strive for.

Such concern and responsibility may sound inconsequential in our domestic political system, where equality is one of our core constitutional values. However, it is not at all obvious that it should be so internationally. After all, in a system without an overarching authority and where the rule of the strong frequently still prevails, the notion that we should take the interests of our cousins or neighbors across the border just as seriously as our own is still anathema. A quick look into international news sections of the newspapers and the political rhetoric frequently espoused about protection of the national interests and economic interests at the expense of other nations should easily confirm this state of affairs.

Yet, despite the utopian sound of the proposed remedy—a transnational society and the increased integration of political, legal, and economic responsibility—some simple, though not necessarily politically easy, tools already exist to promote such integration goals. One such tool can be found in self-executing treaty provisions.

Unlike most international treaty provisions, self-executing treaty provisions need no further domestic implementing legislation following U.S. Senate advice and consent to become effective domestic law and to create judicially enforceable rights and obligations under U.S.

law. While it would take too long to go through any detailed discussion of such treaty provisions, it should suffice to say here that self-executing treaty provisions have played an important part in U.S. law throughout our nations' history.[47] In this respect, their significance arises because unlike non-self-executing treaties, no congressional implementing legislation is required for the international treaty obligations to enter into effect as a matter of domestic U.S. law. Thus, internationally reached decisions can enter directly into effect without the additional political review that congressional legislation would demand. Of course, creation of self-executing treaty law is not left in the hands of the Executive Branch alone through the negotiation of such international treaties. Congress, through the Senate's advice and consent requirement, retains a crucial role in such lawmaking, and thus such law does not escape domestic political review altogether. Nevertheless, it significantly simplifies the process of political review of such treaties and congressional involvement in incorporating such treaties into U.S. law.

As a result, self-executing treaties do not eliminate the opportunity for domestic interest groups to influence the lawmaking process. In fact, the willingness of individual senators to block approval of treaties for political reasons bears plenty of testimony to this.[48] However, the key virtue of this method of lawmaking, for purposes of this analysis, is the explicit linkage of international and foreign interests to the national and domestic interests here in the United States that self-executing treaties forge. Just as congressional statutes constitute a fusion of various domestic interests into one set of norms and rules, so international treaties constitute a fusion of various international and domestic interests into one system of norms and rules. The result is that the exclusion of interests of those living in developing countries, which arguably has led to the political and legal externalization of global environmental and human rights interests in the U.S. legal system, is significantly ameliorated. Conversely, stronger linkage of such issues also forces greater incorporation of domestic interests into the foreign policy-making process.

Self-executing treaties will not be appropriate for all contexts, and I cannot offer a complete analysis of the advantages and disadvantages of such an approach in this short chapter. In fact, one important problem is that political realities leave traditional non-self-executing treaties as the only alternative to no-agreement outcomes of international negotiations. Nevertheless, even at this rough level of analysis, it should be evident that self-executing treaties bear significant potential to address issues of environmental justice at the international level.

Conclusion

While the context and specific manifestations of struggles of poor and disenfranchised communities against the effects of environmental degradation and resource exploitation are not the same in the United States as they are in developing countries, they can be traced to similar roots. As a result, the experiences in the international and the domestic area have implications for each other. The international experience suggests that the tension between national control and international concerns over natural resources conservation and environmental protection will continue to arise in domestic environmental justice struggles and cannot easily be resolved. However, it also suggests that community control can promote cultural diversity in environmental protection, which is increasingly being seen as an important part of global environmental protection. At the same time, the national experience suggests that international inequities are as much a form of "market failure" and externalization of environmental harm as they are in the domestic context, and resolving them will require more accountability and linkage rather than less.

Acknowledgments

Helpful comments were provided the editors and contributors to this book as well as by Keith Aoki. Research assistance was provided by Michael O'Brien.

Notes

1. See James Brooke, "Waste Dumpers Turning to West Africa," *New York Times,* July 17, 1988, 1; Mark Schleifstein, "Protest to Meet La. Chemicals in South Africa Shipments Will Go On, Firm Says," *New Orleans Times-Picayune,* February 17, 1994, 3; and Paisley Dodds, "South African Leaders at Odds Over Environmental Policies," *Los Angeles Times,* June 11, 1995.
2. See, e.g., James Brooke, "New Effort Would Test Possible Coexistence Of Oil and Rain Forest," *New York Times,* February 26, 1991, 4; and Paul Lewis, "Blood and Oil," *New York Times,* February 13, 1996, 1.
3. Keith Aoki, "Neocolonialism, Anticommons Property, and Biopiracy in the (Not-So-Brave) New World Order of International Intellectual Property Protection," *Indiana Journal of Global Legal Studies* 6 (1998): 11.
4. See Francis O. Adeola, "Cross-National Environmental Justice and Human Rights Issues," *American Behavioral Scientist* 43 (2000): 686; and Jeffrey L. Dunoff, "From Green to Global: Toward the Transformation of

International Environmental Law," *Harvard Environmental Law Review* 19 (1995): 241, 292–95.

5. See, e.g., Surya P. Subedi, "Are the Principles of Human Rights 'Western' Ideas? An Analysis of the Claim of the 'Asian' Concept of Human Rights from the Perspectives of Hinduism," *California Western International Law Journal* 30 (1999): 45; and Matthew A. Ritter, "Human Rights: The Universalist Controversy. A Response to 'Are The Principles of Human Rights "Western" Ideas? An Analysis of the Claim of the "Asian" Concept of Human Rights from the Perspectives of Hinduism,' by Dr. Surya P. Subedi," *California Western International Law Journal* 30 (1999): 45.

6. See, e.g., Vicki Been, "What's Fairness Got to Do with It? Environmental Justice and the Siting of Locally Undesirable Land Uses," *Cornell Law Review* 78 (1993): 1001; and Andrew Dobson, *Justice and the Environment: Conceptions of Environmental Sustainability and Dimensions of Social Justice* (New York: Oxford University Press, 1998). See also the discussion by David Getches and David Pellow in Chapter 1.

7. See Gary Bryner's discussion in Chapter 2.

8. In Indonesia, Louisiana-based Freeport McMoRan has ignored the rights of indigenous people while operating the "world's largest gold mine and third-largest copper mine on the western half of the island of New Guinea." Eyal Press, "Jim Bob's Indonesian Misadventure," *Progressive* 32 (June 1996): 32–35. There are numerous other instances of European and American corporate involvement in destroying the environment in other countries. See, e.g., Dara O'Rourke, "Oil in Burma: Fueling Oppression," *Multinational Monitor* (October 1992): 7–11.

9. See Roger Cohen, "Oil Rich, Oil Poor," *New York Times*, September 20, 1998, 1.

10. See Jonathan S. Adams and Thomas O. McShane, *The Myth of Wild Africa: Conservation without Illusion* (New York: Norton, 1992), 227–31.

11. See Adams and McShane, *The Myth of Wild Africa*, 194.

12. Raymond Bonner, *At the Hand of Man: Peril and Hope for Africa's Wildlife* (New York: dist. Random House, 1993), 176 (emphasis in original). For a more extensive discussion, see 167–203.

13. See Bill Derman, "Environmental NGOs, Dispossession, and the State: The Ideology and Praxis of African Nature and Development," *Human Ecology* 23 (1995): 199, 205–13; and Adams and McShane, *The Myth of Wild Africa*, 180; but also see Bonner, *At the Hand of Man*, 271–78.

14. See Alexander Stille, "In the 'Greened' World, It Isn't Easy to Be Human," *New York Times*, July 15, 2000, B9; and Thaddeus McBride, "The Dangers of Liberal Neo-Colonialism: Elephants, Ivory and the CITES Treaty," *Boston College Third World Law Journal* 19 (1999): 733.

15. See, e.g., Joyeeta Gupta, *The Climate Change Convention and Developing Countries: From Conflict to Consensus?* (Dordrecht: Kluver Academic, 1997), 101–10, 111–14, which details the disenchantment of developing countries with the decision making of the Global Environmental Facility,

the financial mechanism administered by the World Bank for the Climate Change Convention, Biodiversity Convention, and Montreal Protocol.

16. Robert D. Bullard, "Solid Waste Sites and the Black Houston Community," *Sociological Inquiry* 53 (1983): 273; U.S. General Accounting Office, "Siting of Hazardous Waste Landfills and Their Correlation with Racial and Economic Status of Surrounding Communities" (1983); Commission for Racial Justice, United Church of Christ, "Toxic Wastes and Race" (1987); Vicki Been and Francis Gupta, "Coming to the Nuisance or Going to the Barrios? A Longitudinal Analysis of Environmental Justice Claims," *Ecology Law Quarterly* 24 (1997): 1. There have also been other studies that have sought to disprove such a correlation. See, e.g., Thomas Lambert and Christopher Boerner, "Environmental Inequity: Economic Causes, Economic Solutions," *Yale Journal on Regulation* 14 (1997): 195; and Douglas Anderton et al., "Hazardous Waste Facilities: 'Environmental Equity' Issues in Metropolitan Areas," *Evaluation Review* 18 (1994): 123.

17. See generally Adeola, "Cross-National Environmental Justice and Human Rights Issues."

18. See Rudyard Kipling, *The White Man's Burden* (1899). See generally Ruth Gordon, "Saving Failed States: Sometimes a Neocolonialist Notion," *American University Journal of International Law and Policy* 12 (1997): 903, 930–47; and Robert A. Williams Jr., *The American Indian in Western Legal Thought: The Discourses of Conquest* (New York: Oxford University Press, 1990).

19. See, e.g., Tayyab Mahmud, "Colonialism and Modern Constructions of Race: A Preliminary Inquiry," *University of Miami Law Review* 53 (1999): 1219; Antony Anghie, "'The Heart of My Home': Colonialism, Environmental Damage, and the Nauru Case," *Harvard International Law Journal* 34 (1993): 445; Reginald Horsman, *Race and Manifest Destiny* (Cambridge: Harvard University Press, 1981), 208; and Benjamin B. Ringer and Elinor R. Lawless, *Race—Ethnicity and Society* (New York: Routledge, 1989), 87–118. See also Tseming Yang, "Race, Religion and Cultural Identity: Reconciling the Jurisprudence of Race and Religion," *Indiana Law Journal* 73 (1997): 119, 135 and n. 79.

20. See, e.g., Anghie, "'The Heart of My Home.'"

21. Not surprisingly, the one nonwhite country that has been just as successful economically as European and American nations—Japan—is one of the few nonwhite nations that have never been a colony.

22. See, e.g., Melvin L. Oliver and Thomas M. Shapiro, *Black Wealth/White Wealth: A New Perspective on Racial Inequality* (New York: Routledge, 1995), considering racial inequality and intergenerational transmission of wealth. Compare with Christopher Chase-Dunn, "The Effects of International Economic Dependence on Development and Inequality: A Cross-National Study," *American Sociology Review* 40 (1975): 720, finding that economic assistance and investment by developed countries have fostered continued dependence of the former colonies on their former colonial masters. But also see William H. Meyer, "Human Rights and MNCs:

Theory Versus Quantitative Analysis," *Human Rights Quarterly* 18 (1996): 368, finding no adverse effects.

23. See Barbara Rose Johnston, "Human Rights and the Environment," *Human Ecology* 23 (1995): 111.

24. See Stephen Schlesinger and Stephen Kinzer, *Bitter Fruit: The Untold Story of the American Coup in Guatemala* (Cambridge: Harvard University Press, 1982), 71, 82, which states: "Most of the [United Fruit Company's] American overseers . . . were from the deep South and brought their racial attitudes with them; company policy required 'all persons of color to give right of way to whites and remove their hats while talking to them.'"

25. See "Let Them Eat Pollution," *Economist* 66 (February 8, 1992), excerpting the memo by Lawrence Summers, then–chief economist of the World Bank.

26. See Gerald Torres, "Understanding Environmental Racism," *University of Colorado Law Review* 63 (1992): 839.

27. Rachel L. Swarns, "As Zimbabwe Falters, Doubts About Who Is Really to Blame," *New York Times*, April 8, 2000, 1. See generally Jeffrey Herbst, *State Politics in Zimbabwe* (Berkeley: University of California Press, 1990), 13–62; and Robin Palmer, *Land and Racial Domination in Rhodesia* (London: Heinemann Educational, 1977). Compare with Rennard Strickland et al., eds., *Felix Cohen's Handbook of Federal Indian Law* (Charlottesville, Va.: Michie Press, 1982), 78–92, regarding the dispossession of Native American aboriginal lands by the U.S. federal government.

28. See, e.g., Ibrahim J. Wani, "Poverty, Governance, the Rule of Law, and International Environmentalism: A Critique of the Basel Convention on Hazardous Wastes," *Kansas Journal of Law and Public Policy* 1 (1991): 37.

29. See generally Victoria C. Arthaud, "Environmental Destruction in the Amazon: Can U.S. Courts Provide a Forum for the Claims of Indigenous Peoples?" *Georgetown International Environmental Law Review* 7 (1994): 195.

30. See, e.g., "General Agreement on Tariffs and Trade: Dispute Settlement Panel Report on United States Restrictions on Imports of Tuna," *International Legal Materials* 30 (1991): 1594, regarding the Mexican challenge to U.S. tuna import restrictions; and "World Trade Organization: United States—Import Prohibition of Certain Shrimp and Shrimp Products," *International Legal Materials* 38 (1998): 113, regarding the challenge by India, Malaysia, Pakistan, and Thailand to U.S. shrimp import restrictions.

31. For example, the desire to create or preserve economic advantage is easily apparent in the U.S. Senate's unwillingness to approve any agreement on greenhouse gas reductions that does not impose binding commitments on developing countries. Based on a desire not to put U.S. industries at a significant competitive disadvantage over industries in developing countries, it reflects in many respects a profound sense of self-interest and unwillingness to take responsibility for the United States' historical contributions to climate change. See, e.g., S. Res. 98, 143 *Congressional Record*, secs. 8113-05 and 8138-39 (July 25, 1997).

32. See the discussions by Dean Suagee in Chapter 10 and Sarah Krakoff in Chapter 7.

33. See Howard W. French, "Nigeria Executes Critic of Regime; Nations Protest," *New York Times,* November 11, 1995, 1. In another well-known instance, rain forest activist Chico Mendes was killed by ranchers in retaliation for Mendes's activism seeking to protect rain forest resources and the use of the forest by individual rubber tappers. See generally Andrew Revkin, *The Burning Season: The Murder of Chico Mendes and the Fight for the Amazon Rain Forest* (Boston: Houghton Mifflin, 1990).

34. The problem of racial minorities creates additional problems like in the United States.

35. See Donald Hornstein, "Environmental Sustainability and Environmental Justice at the International Level: Traces of Tension and Traces of Synergy," *Duke Environmental Law and Policy Forum* 9 (1999): 291, 301.

36. Some have seen environmentalism and human rights as mutually supportive of each other; see James W. Nickel and Eduardo Viola, "Integrating Environmentalism and Human Rights," *Environmental Ethics* 16 (1994): 265. Others have disagreed; see Dobson, *Justice and the Environment.*

37. See generally David Hunter et al., *International Environmental Law and Policy* (New York: Foundation Press, 1998), 335–45. See also "U.N. Pleads with Taliban Not to Destroy Buddha Statues,"*New York Times,* March 3, 2001. Within the United States, the demands for local control of national resources managed by federal agencies raises just such issues. See, e.g., Erik Larson, "Unrest in the West," *Time,* October 23, 1995, 52.

38. See Tseming Yang, "Balancing Interests and Maximizing Rights in Environmental Justice," *Vermont Law Review* 23 (1999): 529, 533.

39. Garret Hardin, "The Tragedy of the Commons," *Science* 162 (1968): 1243.

40. Martin S. Weinstein, "Pieces of the Puzzle: Solutions for Community-Based Fisheries Management from Native Canadians, Japanese Cooperatives, and Common Property Researchers," *Georgetown International Environmental Law Review* 12 (2000): 375, 378.

41. Johan Colding and Carl Folke, "The Taboo System: Lessons about Informal Institutions for Nature Management," *Georgetown International Environmental Law Review* 12 (2000): 413.

42. Article 8(j), "United Nations Conference on Environment and Development: Convention on Biological Diversity," 31 *International Legal Materials* 818 (1992): "Each country shall, as far as possible and as appropriate . . . Subject to its national legislation, respect, preserve, and maintain knowledge, innovations and practices of indigenous and local communities embodying traditional lifestyles relevant for the conservation and sustainable use of biological diversity and promote their wider application with the approval and involvement of the holders of such knowledge, innovations and practices and encourage the equitable sharing of the benefits arising from the utilization of such knowledge, innovations and practices."

43. In its use here, the term *cultural diversity* is not confined to diverse traditional approaches to resource management. Rather, it is to be seen here as serving the same function as biodiversity itself, as a means of adaptation for new and different circumstances.

44. Adams and McShane, *The Myth of Wild Africa,* 152.

45. See, e.g., A. Dan Tarlock, "Exclusive Sovereignty Versus Sustainable Development of a Shared Resource: The Dilemma of Latin American Rainforest Management," *Texas International Law Journal* 32 (1997): 37.

46. See, e.g., David Hunter, "Toward Global Citizenship in International Environmental Law," *Willamette Law Review* 28 (1992): 547.

47. See, e.g., Jordan J. Paust, "Self-Executing Treaties," *American Journal of International Law* 82 (1988): 760.

48. See, e.g., Thomas W. Lippman, "Seeking Liberation of Treaties in Limbo; Sen. Helms Wants Bipartisan Deal to Ratify or Scrap Shelved Accords That Date to 1949," *Washington Post,* February 15, 1999, A27.

Part Two
CONCEPTS

Chapter 5

THE COINCIDENTAL ORDER OF ENVIRONMENTAL INJUSTICE

Jeff Romm

To the real question, How does it feel to be a problem?
I answer seldom a word.
—W.E.B. Du Bois, *The Souls of Black Folks,*1903

I ain't got nothing, I heard no good news
I fill my pockets with those reservation blues . . .
And if you ain't got choices
What else do you choose?
—Sherman Alexie, *Reservation Blues*, 1995

Environmental injustice is often treated as a problem that enlightened public policy can correct. That is, regulations, subsidies, taxes, and participatory requirements can be used to reduce the disproportionate share of environmental ills that people of color absorb.[1] But such measures primarily address the consequences rather than the causes of environmental injustice. The causes are embedded in the social order of environmental governance itself, and the usual correctives merely reinforce them by sustaining the prevailing inequality and exclusiveness of control. A just environment requires, instead, rather different social and ecological relations that equalize opportunities for benefit and influence among all groups of people.

The problem can be framed as follows: societal restraints on access to natural resources and racial restraints on access to opportunity together force people of color toward the ills and edges of environmental opportunity; racial minorities occupy the worst environmental conditions in America while doing most of the work of the nation's "environmental" or natural resources occupations; environmental institutions (cultural, legal, political, financial) typically try to reduce human opportunities rather than distribute opportunities toward those whose livelihoods depend on sustaining them; environmental governance is so overwhelmingly white although "environment" is common property. Without equalizing opportunity, tightened restraints exacerbate this effect.

This chapter explores America's synchronous use—but segregated discussion—of policies for the territorial protection of natural resources and the race-based limitations of social opportunity. It does so through examination of California forest policy, the lessons from which I then apply to suggest socially just forms of forest governance. In that process, forests as hinterland enclaves are transformed into contemporary forests as metropolitan processes that engage, reflect, and need everyone.

Mobility, Restraint, and Race-Based Resource Distribution

Environmental governance in America relies upon restraints on spatial and social mobility to prevent excessive and unwanted uses of nature. These restraints include, for example, the fences of rules around national forests and parks and the standards that protect air and water quality. They include screens of procedure—for example, the twelve or fifteen or twenty-two timed steps to legitimate participation in public environmental and forest planning processes. They include the boundaries around arenas of public engagement—in community resource management, for example—that encourage cooperative activities among some while discouraging participation by others.

These restraints embed the power and interests of those in positions to define them, and discourage those who do not share the same values, identities, resources, and rhythms. An environmental standard redistributes enterprise, well-being, and the relative strengths of constituencies. A harvest rule changes the social and economic as well as ecological qualities of a forest. A participatory procedure empowers and benefits those who can use and control it relative to those who cannot.

Although convention identifies such restraints as "environmental," they are in the larger social order a structure of inclusions and exclusions that distribute the relative control of privilege, powers and opportunity among groups. These restraints stop, elect, screen, and otherwise channel streams of relative human opportunity. They express a nation's tendency to protect its stability and cohesion—social, environmental, economic—through restraints on the spatial and social mobility of people.

Restraints on social mobility—on where people can go, what they can do, and who they can be—operate like spatial restraints, confining certain opportunities so as to expand others. Restraints, deliberate or implicit, restrict access to opportunities for some racial groups to the benefit of others. If, for example, some racial groups can own or use land and others cannot, the diminished opportunities for those discriminated against expand the scope for others. If race is used to differentially organize and pay workers, then the low-wage condition of those discriminated against expands possibilities for others. If some groups govern while others are excluded, dominant interests are expressed at the expense of others. Indeed, the most pernicious discrimination occurs not through overt personal or aberrant racism but through public processes and controls that are believed to be fair, beneficent, legitimate, virtuous, and even morally necessary for our success as a national community. Nowhere has this discrimination been both so visible and so unseen as in the environmental order of America.

Resource restraints and discriminatory restraints on racial groups together force racial minorities toward the margins of environmental opportunity. This is because the diminished opportunities created by resource restraints are then distributed in a manner that favors people who face no racial restraints relative to those who do.[2] The combination of restraints concentrates social control of the environment in dominant groups and transfers the consequent problems toward those who lack access to the means to compensate for them. Barriers to resource use and barriers to racial mobility operate together to shape a distribution of environmental conditions and social opportunities that typically needs, perpetuates, and even creates racial inequality.

Race and Resource Policy: The Invisible Coincidence

Although racial restraints and resource restraints together shape the relationships between people and their environment, the United States has segregated their treatment throughout its history. The segregation has been sustained despite synchronous formations of racial and resource policies and despite accessible explanations of their interactive effects. Scholars have treated the two realms of history and politics as if totally unrelated to each other.[3] The distinction is so pervasive and runs so sharply against normal logic and experience that it constitutes a fundamental feature of American society. A few examples illustrate its power and begin to reveal features of the environmental order that sustain it.

In the first years of post–Civil War Reconstruction, the United States initiated massive homesteading of the West, issued huge land grants for the extension of railways to the Pacific, and purchased Alaska for its potential role in transpacific expansion.[4] Approximately 300 million acres were allotted to homesteaders. The railways received more than 100 million acres in land grants. Scientists like John Wesley Powell inventoried, classified, and organized western resources in ways that continue to exert a profound influence on environmental concepts and policies. These events are duly regarded as grand formations of the American environment.

Simultaneously, the nation stopped land reform of the plantation South, revoking it where freed slaves had done it themselves. Instead, it returned land to the planters and installed sharecropping as the basis for the free, southern agrarian economy, immobilizing the once-slaves without awarding land ownership. Although emancipation had brought widespread expectation of "forty acres and a mule,"[5] land distribution to former slaves was, in contrast to homesteads, said to be paternalistic and therefore to encourage "a life of indolence."[6]

Agents of the Freedman's Bureau, the federal agency responsible for the confiscated lands of a defeated South, confirmed plantation owners' land rights in Alabama and Mississippi as follows: "The government owns no land in this State. It therefore can give away none. Freedmen can obtain farms with the money that they have earned by their labor. Everyone, therefore, shall work diligently, and carefully save his wages, till he may be able to buy land and possess his own home."[7] Roger Ransom and Richard Sutch estimate that by 1880, former slaves had been able to purchase ownership of 7.3 percent of the farms and 6.7 percent of the land of the Cotton South, which contained almost half of the Confederacy.[8]

The contrast is stark. Freed slaves bought about 5.5 million acres of former slave-worked plantation in the South with their own earnings, while western lands were given away free to whites on a vast scale.[9] The processes were simultaneous and displayed hints of common origin—Senator Andrew Johnson led passage of the Homestead Act; President Andrew Johnson blocked southern land reform. Together, they determined the race/resource distribution of the nation, and it seems reasonable to suggest that immobilization of the black South was no less environmentally or socially formative than the storied white opening of the West, and that interactions between the two regions shaped the environment and society of the nation as a whole. In terms of their relations and their effects, racial and resource policies were inseparable.

Segregating people of color within spatial and social barriers reserved the wealth of the West and the South for whites. It also secured nonwhite reserves of cheap labor for the agricultural and natural resources economies of the two regions. African Americans, half of the prewar southern population, became the region's dominant source of workers as white southerners moved westward.[10] In prewar California, the *California Farmer* of May 26, 1854, had written: "The Chinese . . . are to be to California what the African has been to the South. This is the decree of the Almighty, and man cannot stop it."[11] Chinese workers, while denied the rights to citizenship and to land ownership, developed California's structure of water control, transport, and agriculture, and were significant forces in mining and forestry as well.[12] By the mid-1870s, a time of emerging paradox between the natural bounty and the human poverty of California, issues of race and resources that had played out between regions of the United States converged sharply in California. There, they made enduring marks on the nation as a whole.

White workers in California blamed the depressed 1870s on Chinese workers. The Anti-Chinese Movement, based on the argument of unfair labor competition, fermented in a soup of racist attitudes that became pervasive features of California politics and policies.[13] Meanwhile, the San Francisco journalist Henry George, in his classic book *Progress and Poverty*, instead explained the California paradox as a consequence of the monopoly concentration of land ownership, the *latifundiazation* of California, without even mentioning Chinese workers.[14] (One imagines anti-Chinese riots in the streets of San Francisco while, upstairs, the conceptually color-blind antimonopolist George toils over his tract.) Then, cataclysmic floods hit the Central Valley, forging a propertied constituency, smallholders as well as large, for government water control and watershed protection that presaged the rise of the technocratic state.[15]

Although California's Progressive Constitution of 1879, the first of its kind in the nation, included liberal protections for (white) workers, women, and children, aggressive public education, (nonland) monopoly control, and the governmental authorities to regulate watershed, forest, flood, and drainage conditions, it perpetuated discriminatory patterns of resource governance.[16] The constitution also prohibited further Chinese immigration, which the Chinese Exclusion Act of 1882 put into national effect.[17] Subsequent renewals and expansions barred citizenship and land ownership among Chinese, Filipino, and Japanese residents until after World War II and were augmented by harsh and ubiquitous nonlegal restraints.[18] California's Progressive racial policy structured a working underclass of color and secured a white reservation of private property, while its resource policy prescribed the most advanced concepts of watershed and river basin management of the times. The link between the two—a racialized low-wage-dependent system of agricultural, forest, and water management—continues to prevail to this day.

The coincidence of race and resource policies was not peculiar to relations between the South and the West and within California. The California convergence previewed the national scene. In the Progressive Era of the latter 1890s, Congress created the national forest reservations of public land through historic acts that we herald as the first major accomplishments of the conservation movement.[19] These reservations now contain several hundreds of millions of acres, a fair share of which otherwise would have been privately settled. The reservations stopped homesteading, started to control logging and grazing, and slowed degradation of the nation's public forests. They increased the value of privately held lands and forests outside the reservation lines, not a small part of the motivation to create them,[20] and dampened wages by concentrating the growing population in a fraction of the territory previously open for settlement.[21]

At the very time that Congress imposed reservation boundaries around forests to conserve them, boundaries of social reservations based on race stiffened. The Supreme Court's "separate but equal" doctrine of its *Plessy v Ferguson* decision legitimized racial segregation in the United States for the next seventy years, further confining the opportunities for occupancy and occupation for people of color.[22] Nor was *Plessy* an aberration: Rayford Logan describes it as "the nadir" of brutal racial repression in America; Robert and Pamela Allen record its pervasiveness and intensity.[23] Meanwhile, American Indian reservations were formed and racially based immigration controls were imposed explicitly to secure pools of low-wage labor for local farms and fisheries in the West.[24] Together with Jim Crow codes and their violence, these measures immobilized Native, black, and Asian Americans in certain locations and occupations. While the forest reservations reduced people's access to land, racial segregation reserved ownership of the remaining private land for whites.

The coincidences between racial and resource policies—the former restraining specific groups; the latter restraining people's access to specific resources—have continued. New Deal protections of workers and of resource industries, through the growth of production, conservation and fair-labor restraints, for example, were not extended to agricultural and forestry workers of color.[25] While the Civil Rights Act of 1964 eliminated legal race-based barriers to full citizenship and opportunity, that decade's various environmental acts restrained human access to resources and resource qualities that otherwise would have enlarged the pool of environmental opportunities available to those newly free to take or influence them.

Today, endangered species restraints or logging bans are debated as if established interests are the stakeholders, although the consequent burdens pass to those whose confined opportunities make them least able to avoid, bear, or compensate for them. See, for example, Henry Carey's discussion of forest management in northern New Mexico in Chapter 9. Wilderness reserves and inner-city ghettos form opposite poles of the same range of restraints on mobility, the one bounded territorially to keep people out, the other bounded socially to keep them in.

Amid population growth, tightening environmental restraints squeeze the scope of opportunity while tilting the burden of scarcity toward those who face racial restraints as well. "White flight" intensifies America's racial chromatograph from city to countryside. Expanding open space and greenbelt reserves increase land and housing costs, further diffusing suburban sprawl into cheaper farmlands while concentrating people of color in the urban core and in underclass settlements of the agricultural fringe. In California's Sierra foothills, the most rapidly urbanizing region of the state, homogeneous white urbanization is spreading along the whole western edge of the national forest reserve, obliterating remnants of unremembered Chinese settlements, tribal harvest sites, and black-worked timber mills transplanted from the South.[26] Meanwhile, environmental cleanup of the once-industrial San Francisco Bay shoreline is leading quickly to white displacement of people of color, often the very communities whose appeals for environmental justice initiated the restoration.[27]

Reservations of nature and reservations of people (social controls of the relative availability, distribution, and value of resources and people) are simultaneous choices whether conscious or not. Together, they have expressed and shaped an environmental order that persists to this day in the whiteness of property ownership, of the public processes that regulate property-based actions and impacts, and of the social organization of common property interests.[28] But despite the synchrony of their formation and the synergy of their effects, racial policy and resource policy in America continue to be treated as if they are "separate but equal" themes of national life. I have come to conclude that the racial inequality of the United States and the U.S. "environment" are kept separate because they are so tightly bound together. Their separation has the force of collective denial. In these circumstances, justice is not a matter of building bridges but of healing chasms.

The Social Order of California Forests

The governance of California's forests offers an opportunity to explore the value of considering racial policy and resource policy as one. The pattern of governance emerged a century ago when the state's population was roughly 2 million people. The political arena was white and male,[29] and the power over forests was concentrated in the hands of a small elite of people who—whether as owners, influentials, or public agents—shared the entitlement to control forested property. The majority of today's population of 35 million are people of color who no longer face bars to the vote, yet the racial structure of forest power remains virtually unchanged. Despite its massive demographic and political diversification, California has maintained an exclusive, elite white order of forest governance. The very way that the term *forest* has been defined expresses and sustains the power of the order, risking the sustainability of the forest itself.

At the beginning of the twentieth century, when California held center stage in the drama of the nation's conservation movement, racial feeling was unambiguous. Speaking of Asians, James Phelan, the mayor of San Francisco and a central figure in the Progressive development of San Francisco's Hetch Hetchy Reservoir in Yosemite National Park, said: "California is white man's country, and the two races cannot live side by side in peace."[30] Phelan campaigned for reelection to the U.S. Senate in 1920 on the slogan "Keep California White." As Carey McWilliams shows, Phelan's views typified those of California's leaders, including Hiram Johnson, the noted Progressive governor of the state.[31] When Frederick Roberts became the first

African American to be elected to the state assembly in 1919, his opponent had distributed buttons declaring "My Opponent is a Nigger," presumably in the belief that these helped his candidacy.[32]

Progressive forest policy belonged to a small elite group, which has come to be symbolized by the larger-than-life triad of John Muir, the Timber Barons, and Gifford Pinchot, the first chief of the U.S. Forest Service.[33] Muir, the founder of the Sierra Club, represented a strong moral position and elite urban constituency for pure forest preservation. The Timber Barons, whose private holdings would have been devalued by unrestrained logging and settlement of public lands, favored controlled exploitation to stabilize markets for timber, land, and labor. Pinchot, a pervasive influence in Theodore Roosevelt's administration, represented the scientific-utilitarian rationality of Progressive governance. The essence of their policy was the formation of forest ownership and control: the division of territory between public and private ownership, between federal and state jurisdictions, between scientific, wild, and commercial regimes, and, by default, between genders and races.

Much is made of the differences among Muir, Pinchot, and the Barons—or the interests they symbolize—in part because their story continues to choreograph disputes between environment, government, and industry to this day. They disagreed about the appropriate degree of forest use relative to preservation, and of public relative to private control. But what they shared was stronger than their differences, strong enough to keep their circle virtually closed for a century. They shared opposition to forest control by others. They shared a view of forests as the hinterland beyond cities and farms, as resources kept separate from people for the forests' own good. They accepted and represented an elite social order, defined variously in moral, financial, and scientific terms, that sought to secure the best for the nation, and for themselves, by blocking the urges of the masses through a system of forest ownership that excluded them. Even more significant for our purpose, their "masses" did not include people of color, who were totally beyond the social pale.

The elite social order of Muir, Pinchot, and the Barons is embedded in the forest maps and authorities of California. Approximately 30 million acres of public domain (the territory of California is 100 million acres) were reserved in federal ownership for public management as national forests and national parks by, according to one caustic observer, Pinchot's "scientific gentlemen."[34] Equivalent areas of forest, predominantly in corporate aggregations of railway grants and forest variants of homesteads, were held in private hands under state jurisdiction.[35] Apart from the Native American reservations, these vast forest territories were white domain.[36]

The elite social order is rooted as well in the mid-twentieth-century procedural innovations that opened the regulation of private property to public participation and influence. The tale of Muir, Pinchot, and the Barons continues to organize the processes of engagement among industrial, environmental, and scientific-governmental interests, and to legitimize by omission the absence of others in the management of private lands. It appears in disputes over logging, endangered species, watersheds, fire, and land conversion. It is retold at meetings of federal and state forestry officials, industry representatives, resource management professionals, and environmentalists, as if to reaffirm the group's shared commitment and identity. It is taught in universities as the structure of thought. It is the underlying assumption of all institutions and participants in organized forestry debates. It is the script of "standing," as socially territorial as any property line. It codifies a shared subliminal view about who belongs in the circle and who does not.

In meetings of the State Board of Forestry, people debate the kind and degree of restraint on private forest ownership with language that lifts directly from debates generations old. Forest policy is treated as belonging to those who own land that is isolated from cities and farms, and that, although it involves work, does not seem to involve workers. People of color are not in the room. They are not in professional and owner associations. They are not in most environmental organizations. They are not in federal forest policy hearings or in state and federal forestry agencies. They are treated as problems of compliance with civil rights laws rather than as entitled participants in the processes of forest governance.

While few today would claim that such racial exclusion should continue, the absence is the fact. It is rationalized as "others' racial choice" rather than exclusion. It is said, for example, that people of color have other better opportunities or are not interested in forests and forestry. This claim is ironic in California, where people of color do virtually all of the forest planting, thinning, nontimber harvesting, pruning, fire fighting, pest protection, and wood processing; many grew up in forest-dependent communities of the reservations, the South, Southeast Asia, Mexico, and Central America; all have their own, different forest stories.[37] The rationalization protects the forest order from the social learning and reform through which other parts of society have passed.

Thus, the racial selectivity of forest governance procedures remains unexamined. People who are screened by color throughout their lives are less likely than others to embrace "science-based resource management," "public participation," and other contemporary codes for procedural barbed wire that screens who can be in an organization and which citizens can have access to it. Procedural experts interrupt meetings with "But what about process?" when a rare unscripted or arhythmic intervention is raised, as it is if a Native American or Mexican American wishes to speak.

The patterns of selection are too consistent with racial lines to support claims of intended equality of the process. Thus, an agency's environmental justice objectives may encourage the recruitment of people of color, if they qualify; or the solution of racially based injustices, unless, like prohibitions on fuelwood harvest in northern New Mexico, solutions run counter to established-order privilege; or the holding of community meetings, as long as people stay on time, follow the rules, and stick to the point. The justifications for exclusivity, the fundamental reflexes of restraint, continue to legitimize boundaries of the white/forest reserve.

The Just Forest

Despite a century of ratification, the forest order of Muir, Pinchot, and the Timber Barons is obviously at odds with an expanding, diversified, and democratized citizenry and the forests they value. The forest as a hinterland enclave has disappeared. A metropolitan system of roads, settlements, influences, and needs extends to virtually every acre of forest in California state, and forests penetrate the cities as riparian and wildlife corridors, parks, and the forest aggregations of home and street trees. People in cities know well that forests store the water they drink, clean the air, moderate climate, pose fire dangers, stabilize streams and fisheries, protect wildlife, and create natural beauty and diversity, as well as provide wood and energy. Millions of urban people live in the smoke of forest fires each year. Ten million Californians live in counties we think of as "rural," exceeding the populations of forty states.[38] The forests of California no longer are physically separate hinterlands, and only through an extraordinary exercise of will can they be thought to lack people or to be white. They have become integral features of a vast, racially diverse state metropolis.

The extension of the environmental justice movement to forest issues is one indicator of a disconnect between viewing forests as hinterlands and the reality of forest use and values. So, too, are the movements for community and metropolitan resource management, multiracial organization of forest workers, cooperative forestry endeavors among Native American tribes, partnerships and steward-ship agreements, and the community organization of forests, forest restoration, and forest services in urban areas. Thus far, these find no place or support in established structures, authorities, science, and education; nor are they as yet immune from abrupt dismissal in a racialized social order.

Governance of forests as hinterland enclaves no longer even serves the interests of those who control it. Contextual "static" over-whelms their efforts, for example, to support and achieve sustainable regimes for timber production, riparian management, or species preservation. Members of the forest elite tear one another apart over these issues, while the real challenges are the metropolitan processes that swamp the boundaries of their shared interests and privilege. The tension is clear in a cursory comparison between a map of forest own-ership and a visualization of proliferating social forest classes—water forests, riparian forests, habitat forests, timberlands and timber regions, agroforests and plantation forests, carbon and biodiversity banks, research forests, energy forests, and community, school, and neighborhood forests—each representing new combinations of forest characteristics that express the interests of new constituencies. The once-dominant control of forests through the sharply congruent boundaries of hinterland territory and owners are increasingly over-whelmed by transboundary relations that engage the interests of every citizen of the state.

What would be "just" forest governance in this context? Pursuit of the answer may begin with speculation about the nature of forest organization and governance if the principal goal were to equalize sustainable opportunities for benefit, influence, and responsibility among all groups. One can imagine, for example, a pluralization of systems, and competition among them for public support, to replace hinterland governance that has become unsustainable. One can imag-ine as well the formation of these systems in consonance with metro-politan processes of forests that link everyone in the state, stimulating the capacity, accessibility, and representative power that vigorous sus-taining governance requires. In other words, the forest order would evolve over time to mesh with the social diversity of California, simultaneously transforming the very nature of forests and the capac-ities—political, financial, scientific, educational—that are needed to sustain them.

Three schematic examples suggest the plausibility and value of such future developments.

The Production Forest. Metropolitan society shapes and relies upon a system of timber forests and agroforests, workers, mills, communities, markets, retailers, home builders, furniture makers, and consumers. Governance of this system has viewed treatment of forest production as a hinterland ownership battle between industrial and environmental elites rather than as a system of relations that profoundly affects the material and social well-being of all people. In the just forest, people who lack adequate housing or who work in the forest or who sell paper, for example, would have the same opportunity for influence in the management of production as those who own the timber or manage its public trust values.

The Stabilization Forest. Metropolitan society relies upon a system of strategic exclusions and inclusions to protect species, cultures, habitats, climate, ecosystems, nature, and open space. These simultaneously regulate the value and use of resources outside their fences, channeling patterns of settlement, controlling resource and labor markets, and guiding the distribution of residential, agricultural, and work opportunities—and thus the interests of all citizens. In the just forest, for example, urban planners and workers, suburban developers, and valley farmers would have the same opportunity for influence as those who preserve and use forest enclaves directly.

The Water Forest. The hydrologic and aquatic flows of forests—from high-elevation snows through riparian zones and electricity generators to farm fields and orchards, households, schools, and factories to the sea—involve a wholly different configuration of metropolitan interests, issues, and capacities than do the forests of production and stabilization functions. Just governance of the forest infrastructure of water storage, flows, fisheries, allocations, uses, qualities, and human and ecological health would require the same opportunity for benefit, influence, and responsibility among, for example, creekside urban schools and neighborhoods, valley farm workers, fishers, and forest owners as is currently available to public utilities and water districts, farmers, and environmentalists.

The hinterland governance model that lumps these different systems within one exclusive structure of governance disembodies forests from their nonhinterland functions and constituencies, with a consequent decline in the legitimacy, capacity, and effectiveness of forest governance. But even changes in the governance of forests to recognize the diversity of interests will not achieve social justice if racial discrimination continues to exclude people of color from influence. There is need as well to replace the Muir-Pinchot-Barons myth with new stories that include, legitimize, and empower diverse visions and that begin to guide the processes through which people engage one another. The dominant idea that people are ignorant of forests because they live in urban areas misses the fact that many, if not most, city people of color grew up, work, have their ancestral homes, or have their primary residence and relatives in forest regions. Most adults in the industrial city of Richmond, California, for example, have migrated during their lifetimes from forest-dependent areas of Louisiana and Arkansas, Laos and Cambodia, and Mexico, where they continue to maintain familial ties. It is the dominating convention of "forest," the racial definition of people's legitimate roles in forests, or the concept of urban-rural relations as among places rather than within and among people that sets them apart.

Just Environmental Orders

Racial discrimination structures environmental opportunity in America as surely as do restraints on the uses of forests, lands, air, and water. American history is a remarkable display of "separate but equal" segregation of its culture of racial protection and its policies of environmental discrimination. Both restrain the mobility of people and together squeeze opportunities in a manner that hurts those least in a position to claim them. Our concepts and governance of "environment" have formed in this process of segregation and, consequently, express the interests of those who dominate the nation's property, power, and privilege.

If California forests are illustrative, one possible remedy is to identify inclusive social patterns of environmental relations, then form processes of governance that justly include those who are engaged in these relations. Imagine, for example, an urban system designed primarily to equalize the well-being and influence of its residents. What would "environment" mean then, and how would it be governed? Imagine the planning of metropolitan greenspace preserves that include as equivalent commitments the impacts on homelessness, urban congestion, and suburban conversion of farmlands. "Environment" would come to be systems of relations among interdependent groups and actions rather than a series of topical problems, such as "pollution" or "forest degradation."

If discrimination in housing, education, employment, and wealth forces disproportionate shares of racial minorities into inner-city ghettos and the invisible shacks and trailer camps of the Central Valley, it controls the relation between land and people as surely as do policies for the reservation of parks, forests, farms, and water qualities. The social and spatial restraints on mobility interact; the interests in both belong in an "environment" that treats ecological integrity and human dignity together.

If farm workers absorb the harm of agricultural chemicals, and the cost of producing cheap food, because racial discrimination undercuts protections of their health, then discrimination determines the pattern of land use and human health as surely as do the land and crop markets and water quality regulations. If people of color suffer disproportionately from industrial pollution and also lack access to influence in pollution governance, then one must surmise that the regulatory system embodies, as if one, the privileges of industrial ownership and the discriminatory customs of the society. If the water rights of an American Indian reservation are officially and publicly declared "irrelevant" in California water hearings,[39] then the choice of "relevant constituencies" has racial content and environmental definition together, as well as risks for the effectiveness of a plan that ignores key participants out of racial habit.

If that is unacceptable, reform of terms, rules, and circles must change the environment from a system of property to a system of human health and habitat. The order of environmental justice is not token admission to the circle or due consideration for "their" problem but, rather, is respectful, full, and fair control of the basic terms, rules, standards, and processes of governance.

Acknowledgments

Students of my graduate and undergraduate courses in resource policy at Berkeley over the past five years or so have used, challenged, and sharpened the ideas presented in this paper. My colleagues and friends in the National Network of Forest Practitioners, the Round Valley Reservation, and the Alliance of Forest Workers and Harvesters have forged the need and the passion for the pursuit. I wish to express my special appreciation to Gene Ray, Gus Townes, Steve Cohn, Geoff Mann, Victor Benevides, and Bev Brown, and to Carl Anthony and Amahra Hicks, for their profound insights into the processes through which our society and its governance of natural resources preserve racial inequality.

Notes

1. *Integrated Federal Interagency Environmental Justice Action Agenda*, EPA 300-R-00-008 (Washington, D.C.: Office of Environmental Justice, 2000), summarizes federal responses to the 1994 Executive Order 12898 on environmental justice, which established mechanisms for interagency assessment, action, and accountability in easing the weight of environmental harms on disadvantaged groups.
2. Several examples illustrate how the burdens of scarcities created by resource reservation transfer primarily to groups facing racial discrimination. By the 1880s in California, massive federal and corporate concentration of land ownership and control, estimated as at least 70 percent of the land, had confined the scope for family-scale farms and ranches. See W. W. Robinson, *Land in California* (Berkeley: University of California Press, 1948). Racial discrimination emerged, explicitly or not, to alleviate the competition. See Andrew Gyory, *Closing the Gate* (Chapel Hill: University of North Carolina Press, 1998), 169–84. The California Constitution of 1879, while preventing foreclosure on small farms, banned Chinese ownership of land and Chinese employment in corporations and public works. It permitted the legislature to zone neighborhoods as Chinese and to exclude Chinese residence within cities and towns. Subsequent developments applied to Japanese, Filipino, and black settlers until well after World War II. One consequence was the deprivation of inheritance for people of color in the intergenerational transfer of land and derivative equity, reproducing the radicalization of land and capital ownership to this day. Another was to concentrate people of color in less desirable employments and locations and to justify weaker educational commitments that are consistent with these opportunities, diminishing the mobility that higher incomes and education provide. Analogous processes can be observed today in the simultaneous preservation of open space, its upward pressure on land values, and the concentration of people of color in low-value industrial belts and edges of agricultural towns.
3. The separateness of racial policy and resource policy possibly relates to their primary development in different regions. Issues of the American West, or constructions of the West in different periods, color the literature on U.S. natural resources policy, as if policy developed were free of ties to the East, and as if it were a kind of mapping problem, federal or corporate or scientific or religious or indigenous, each embodying an ideology that is presumed to be the primary policy. In Wallace Stegner's *Beyond the 100th Meridian* (New York: Houghton Mifflin, 1954), John Wesley Powell, losing an arm in the Civil War, proceeds westward as if he and the West have no history. The slate is fresh; there is no need to "negotiate" a relationship, except with nature, of which Native Americans are part. It is as if the West is a state of mind that, above all, divorces eastern preoccupations with the past and with people, producing an intellectual as well as

physical divide, one side honed by history, the other by nature. The West's fights are over which group's lines in the landscape have the might to prevail, not about the processes of relationships among groups. Today, a New Western History has emerged to record the lives and legitimize the claims of those who have been held invisible to work beneath a steep and racialized social hierarchy. Compare Patricia Limerick, *The Legacy of Conquest* (New York: Norton, 1987); Tomas Almaguer, *Racial Fault Lines: The Historical Origins of White Supremacy in California* (Berkeley: University of California Press, 1994); Devra Weber, *Dark Sweat, White Gold* (Berkeley: University of California Press, 1996); and Carl Anthony, "Integrating the Vision," *Terrain* (Winter 1998): 27. Although deeply enriching, it affirms the pattern of debating the ownership of nature rather than forming relations that will improve the qualities of social life.

4. George Coggins and Charles Wilkinson, *Federal Public Land and Resources Law* (Mineola, N.Y.: Foundation Press, 1981 and 1987), provides an excellent summary of federal land policy, law, and commentary. Steven Cohn's *Federal Reserves and the Politics of Alaskan State and Native Sovereignty* (master's thesis in Wildland Resource Science, University of California–Berkeley, 1998), 29–45, discusses motivations for the Alaska Purchase and, more importantly, the forceful use of interactions between racial and resource policies at the core of relations between federal, state, and tribal sovereignties.

5. Leon Litwack, *Been in the Storm So Long* (New York: Vintage, 1980), 399–408.

6. Eric Foner, *Reconstruction: America's Unfinished Revolution* (New York: Harper and Row, 1988), 248.

7. Litwack, *Been in the Storm So Long*, 403.

8. Roger Ransom and Richard Sutch, *One Kind of Freedom* (Cambridge: Cambridge University Press, 1977), 86–87, 281, show the strong white resistance to the sale of land to blacks, including the use of violence as well as social sanction toward those who would sell. Among other things, this meant that land purchase prices were higher for blacks, to compensate for white risks.

9. The 5.5-million-acre estimate derives from Ransom and Sutch data on the share of Cotton State land that transferred into black ownership.

10. I have not located quantitative records of the southern white westward migration. In his classic *California* (New York: Pantheon, 1948), 178–82), Josiah Royce describes the dominance of southern culture in the politics and styles of the new state. Weber reports the legislature-assisted movement of southern cotton planters to the San Joaquin Valley during and after the Civil War. See Weber, *Dark Sweat, White Gold*, 17–20. Ransom and Sutch (*One Kind of Freedom*, 266–67) argue that westward migrations were of sufficient scale to increase per capita incomes in the South, and Gavin Wright, in *Old South, New South* (Baton Rouge: Louisiana State University Press, 1986) implies this process while suggesting a consequence that bears interesting analogy to the vertical versus horizontal, or intensive

versus extensive, subdivisions of today's relations between inner-city black ghettos of tenements and cheap-land-nourished white sprawl. The separate scholarly treatment of black southern labor and white western migration seems part of the larger intellectual segregation this article addresses.

11. Donald Worster, *Rivers of Empire* (New York: Pantheon, 1985), 219.

12. See, e.g., Charles Nordhoff and Jules Remy, *Northern California, Oregon and the Sandwich Islands* (1874; reprint, Berkeley: Ten Speed Press, 1980), 127–34 and 141–48; Gyory, *Closing the Gate;* Almaguer, *Racial Fault Lines,* 153–204; and Worster, *Rivers of Empire.*

13. Gyory, *Closing the Gate,* 169–70; Robert Kelley, *Battling the Inland Sea* (Berkeley: University of California Press, 1998), 179–81 and 195–96.

14. Henry George, *Progress and Poverty* (New York: Robert Schalkenbach Foundation, 1956).

15. Kelley, *Battling the Inland Sea,* 177–96.

16. Kelley, *Battling the Inland Sea,* 177–96.

17. Gyory, *Closing the Gate.*

18. See, e.g., Carey McWilliams, *Prejudice* (New York: Little, Brown, 1944); Carlos Bulosan, *America Is in the Heart* (Seattle: University of Washington Press, 1973); Ronald Takaki, *A Different Mirror* (Boston: Little, Brown, 1993); and Almaguer, *Racial Fault Lines.*

19. Robert Wiebe, *The Search for Order, 1877–1920* (New York: Hill and Wang, 1967), and Richard Hofstadter, *The Age of Reform* (New York: Vintage, 1955), provide exceptional background about the character of the times. Samuel Hays, *Conservation and the Gospel of Efficiency* (Cambridge: Harvard University Press, 1959); Gifford Pinchot, *Breaking New Ground* (New York: Harcourt Brace, 1946); and Carl Schurz, *The Reminiscences of Carl Schurz* (New York: McClure, 1908), present Progressive conceptions of rationally ordered and scientific governance. Samuel Dana, *Forest and Range Policy* (New York: McGraw-Hill, 1956); Norman Wengert and A. A. Dyer, *The "Purposes" of the National Forests: A Historical Re-Interpretation of Policy Development* (Ft. Collins: Colorado State University Press, 1979); and William Robbins, *Lumberjacks and Legislators: Political Economy of the U.S. Lumber Industry, 1890–1941* (College Station: Texas A&M University Press, 1982), illuminate the processes through which the national forest reserves were created. Coggins and Wilkinson, *Federal Public Land and Resources Law,* and Roderick Nash, *Wilderness and the American Mind* (New Haven, Conn.: Yale University Press, 1967), offer samples of narrative and court decisions of the times.

20. Robbins, *Lumberjacks and Legislators,* records the support of large land and timber corporations for public forest and park reservation, despite rhetoric to the contrary. Reservation promised a measure of market control that an open frontier prevented. A Progressive government might achieve by forest reservation in the West what it sought to undermine by trust-busting in the timber industry of the South.

21. These statements draw from the Ricardian theory that open frontiers in

populated resource-abundant conditions diffuse settlement, raise returns to labor, and depress resource prices. Closing boundaries contract labor opportunities and wages, reduce resource flows, and increase the value of resources to those who own them. Within this framework, further confining the opportunities for some groups' ownership reduces the effects on others. The social and resource restraints operate together to distribute work, property, income, and wealth among people and over space. The influence of these restraints declines to the extent that commerce and industry develop alternative opportunities relative to population growth. Their influence increases to the extent that technological change displaces labor or that nonagricultural uses of land expand.

22. C. Vann Woodward, *American Counterpoint* (New York: Oxford University Press, 1971), 212–33.

23. Rayford Logan, *The Negro in American Life and Thought: The Nadir, 1877–1901* (New York: Dial Press, 1954); Robert Allen and Pamela Allen, *Reluctant Reformers* (Washington, D.C.: Howard University Press, 1974), 92–94.

24. Samuel Cohn, *Federal Reserves and the Politics of Alaskan State and Native Sovereignty*; John Walton, *Western Times and Water Wars* (Berkeley: University of California Press, 1992).

25. See, e.g., McWilliams, *Prejudice*; Bulosan, *America Is in the Heart*; Wright, *Old South, New South*; and Weber, *Dark Sweat, White Gold*.

26. U.S. Census Bureau, State Population Estimates, *U.S. Statistical Abstract 1999*, available at www.census.gov/prod/99pubs/99statab/sec01.pdf. According to an unpublished spatiodemographic analysis by Karen DeGannes of Urban Habitat, they are also the whitest (about 95 percent) counties of the state.

27. See, e.g., Cameron Yee et al., *There Goes the Neighborhood: A Regional Analysis of Gentrification and Community Stability in the San Francisco Bay Area* (San Francisco: Urban Habitat Program, 1999).

28. An alternative hypothesis is that people of color own and control environmental resources no less than their share of the more general distribution of wealth in America. This alternative has basis. In 1989, whites held 95 percent of America's financial wealth (excluding home equity), while blacks held 1.3 percent. Melvin Oliver and Thomas Shapiro, *Black Wealth/White Wealth* (New York: Routledge, 1995), 91–125. The same distribution held in 1995. Edward Wolff, "Recent Trends in the Size Distribution of Household Wealth," *Journal of Economic Perspectives* 1 (1998): 131–50. One percent of American households owned almost half of the nation's financial wealth. Blacks and Hispanics were 0.7 percent of the households in this 1 percent. Ten percent of households held 78.7 percent of nonhome real estate assets, a somewhat more equitable distribution than the 90 percent of other forms of wealth, but the real estate estimates do not appear to include the value of equity in corporate land ownerships, such as timber corporations.

29. Women and Asians were ineligible to vote (the Nineteenth Amendment

wasn't ratified until several decades later), and not until 1924 were all Native Americans granted citizenship. Francis Paul Prucha, *Documents of United States Indian Policy* (Lincoln: University of Nebraska Press, 1975), 171–74, 199, 207, 215, 218. Voting was difficult for other minorities in a state that did not ratify the Fifteenth Amendment until 1962. Two out of three Hispanic residents did not seek citizenship and therefore did not vote. Harry Pachon, "U.S. Citizenship and Latino Participation in California Politics," in *Racial and Ethnic Politics in California,* ed. Bryan Jackson and Michael Preston (Berkeley: University of California Institute of Governmental Studies, 1991), 71–88.

30. *San Francisco Chronicle,* November 7, 2000, from a 1919 Phelan interview in the *Boston Herald.*

31. McWilliams, *Prejudice.*

32. Susan Anderson, "Rivers of Water in a Dry Place—Early Black Participation in California Politics," in *Racial and Ethnic Politics in California,* ed. Bryan Jackson and Michael Preston (Berkeley: University of California Institute of Governmental Studies, 1991), 69.

33. Pinchot, *Breaking New Ground;* John Muir, *The Yosemite* (New York: Century, 1912); and Robbins, *Lumberjacks and Legislators,* humanize what has become a mythical drama. Several works on California water form a helpful contextual vision. The first of these is Robert Kelley's *Battling the Inland Sea,* which frames the political dynamics of drainage and flood control to which forest politics were substantially tributary. William Kahrl's *Water and Power* (Berkeley: University of California Press, 1982), and John Walton's *Western Times and Water Wars* (Berkeley: University of California Press, 1992), together provide a comprehensive view of the social relations in and around one of the Progressive Era's formative classics, the development of the Owens Valley, including Pinchot's creation of a treeless national forest to protect water rights for Los Angeles. Walton and Devra Weber, whose *Dark Sweat, White Gold* focuses on the development of Central Valley cotton, illuminate the interactions between government resource policies and agencies, agricultural producers and markets, and the racial-minority tillers of the land. These stories are consistent with—albeit more developed than—observable patterns in forestry.

34. Kahrl, *Water and Power,* 213.

35. California Department of Forestry, *California's Forests and Rangelands: Growing Conflict over Changing Uses* (Sacramento: State of California, 1989), 59–64.

36. Omer Stewart, in *Handbook of North American Indians—California,* ed. Robert Heizer (Washington, D.C.: Smithsonian Institution Press, 1978), 705–12. According to Stewart, there are 116 reservations in California. These total 612,530 acres, including 130,922 acres of public domain allotment. About three-fourths of the reservation land is in 13 reservations. Such numbers do not reflect the boundary fluctuations that have

occurred, and continue to occur, through changing legal commitments and interpretations, incursions, and expansions.

37. See, e.g., Beverly Brown and Agueda Marin-Hernandez, eds., *Voices from the Woods* (Wolf Creek, Oreg.: Jefferson Center, 2000); Carl Anthony, *The National Park Service Needs a New Story* (San Francisco: Urban Habitat Program, 1999); Sherman Alexie, *Reservation Blues* (New York: Warner, 1995); Louise Erdrich, *Tracks* (New York: Harper, 1989); Toni Morrison, *Song of Solomon* (New York: Plume, 1987); H. Gates, *Colored People* (New York: Vintage, 1995); Barbara Kingsolver, *Pigs in Heaven* (New York: Harper, 1993); and John Nichols, *The Milagro Beanfield War* (New York: Ballantine, 1976).

38. William A. V. Clark, "Immigration, High Fertility Fuel State's Population Growth," *California Agriculture* 54 (January/February 2000): 11–18; U.S. Census Bureau, State Population Estimates, *U.S. Statistical Abstract 1999*, available at www.census.gov/prod/99pubs/99statab/sec01.pdf.

39. For example, CALFED public meeting, Burbank Center, Santa Rosa, Calif., September 9, 1999.

Chapter 6

ENVIRONMENTAL JUSTICE IN AN ERA OF DEVOLVED COLLABORATION

Sheila Foster

Environmental decision making is undergoing a profound shift. Traditional forums and processes of decision making are increasingly being displaced by mechanisms emphasizing local, place-based decision making. These emerging mechanisms are orchestrated through collaborative processes featuring stakeholders from both the public and the private sectors.[1] This transformation is evident in a number of recent governmental initiatives, including those by the U.S. Environmental Protection Agency (EPA), most notably its Community-Based Environmental Protection (CBEP) Program.[2] Other federal agencies, particularly those with land or species management responsibilities like the U.S. Forest Service, have similarly advocated a desire to promote a greater role for local decision makers and collaborative problem solving. Many nonadministrative and nongovernmental entities have also joined the growing chorus of support for collaborative approaches to environmental decision making.

The emphasis on community-based decision making in the environmental context is, to be sure, a clear paradigm shift away from the traditional "command-and-control" regulatory approach, which embraces top-down, national, uniform environmental standards. It is also a move away from the "announce-and-defend" method of administrative decision making, whereby crucial decisions are made by government agencies at junctures when the public is not involved, followed by the agency announcing and defending its decisions to the public. Similarly, community-based decision making is a rejection of interest group politics and related processes of decision making where private preferences are too often elevated above public interests and the common good. Rather, the shift toward a "devolve-and-collaborate" model is more closely associated with the emergence of alternative dispute resolution processes in public decision making and is married to ideas of regionalism, which permeate the science and theory of natural resources management.

The current impulse to rethink the appropriate scale (administratively and geographically) of decision making power needed to tackle our thorniest environmental problems is strong and pervasive—for good reason. The need for more practical and creative solutions to environmental problems is widely acknowledged, as is the need for improved decision making processes for identifying and equitably distributing the costs and benefits of resources management. Devolved collaboration promises to fulfill these needs, yet the ability of this decision making model to produce these outcomes has appropriately been called into question. Indeed, there is some danger that devolved collaboration may simply reproduce many of the deeper and troublesome aspects of current decision making processes. In some contexts, the use of devolved collaboration may add renewed legitimacy to decisions made on the backs of these problems, further entrenching them in the landscape of environmental decision making. Perhaps more importantly, devolved collaboration may introduce new equity problems in decision making by modifying current patterns of participation and representation in unforeseen ways. Until devolved collaboration is viewed through the lens of environmental justice, the full implications of this new decision making paradigm cannot be fully understood.

Critiques of the Traditional System

The shift toward CBEP protection arises, particularly, out of various critiques of environmental decision making processes that question the substantive focus of environmental decisions and the processes by which those decisions are made. Traditional top-down, command-and-control strategies have failed to adequately address the current generation of environmental problems. Moreover, the administrative decision-making processes through which much of environmental law is enforced too often subordinates the concerns and values of less powerful (and, in many instances, local) interests to those of more powerful interests. These critiques—regulatory ineffectiveness and inequity—are nested within a larger debate and agenda of governmental reform challenging many facets of public decision making structures and processes. The emergence of a devolve-and- collaborate model of environmental decision making can thus be seen as responsive both to the shortcomings of our current environmental protection regime and to a larger project of rethinking the ways in which decisions about public goods get made.

A variety of both substantive and procedural criticisms surround traditional processes of environmental decision making. Existing programs, particularly those reliant upon command-and-control mandates, are widely considered to be too rigid, complex, and fragmented to deal with modern environmental problems, such as nonpoint source pollution, pollution prevention, and management of complex ecosystems.[3] Not only are permitting requirements fashioned under the single-agency, single-media regulatory framework frequently viewed as ineffective and even counterproductive, they are challenged as being unduly burdensome upon industry and for promoting a highly adversarial relationship pitting the agency and applicant against each other, and often the public against both of them. Similar complaints abound in the natural resources arena, where environmentalists lament the ineffectiveness of laws designed to protect fragile ecosystems, while landowners in rural and western areas protest laws that limit their property rights.[4]

Underlying these regulatory deficiencies is a host of technical and scientific tools and norms built upon utilitarian principles of welfare economics. Under this philosophy, rational policy making requires decisions that produce "the greatest good, to the greatest number, for the longest time."[5] This philosophy supports the widespread use of scientific and technical decision-making techniques that distill environmental impacts and values to a common metric and that direct decision making to those options that minimize aggregated costs and maximize aggregated benefits. One such tool is comparative risk assessment, which is at the core of many pollution control programs, including the cleanup of contaminated land under the Superfund program and the regulation of drinking water, air pollution, pesticides, and waste disposal. The corollary in the natural resources domain is cost-benefit analysis, a tool derived from the water development arena that suggests that society is best served by those projects that produce the highest net benefits (benefits minus costs). This model of technocratic utilitarianism, and the complex mathematics associated with quantifying and measuring the recognized variables, presumes that environmental decision making "is a technical task and that our goals and objectives can be met through the application of experts' specialized tools."[6] See Henry Carey's discussion of northern New Mexico forestry issues in Chapter 9 for a different perspective.

This tradition, so entrenched in law and agency culture, raises several equity-related issues.[7] Two issues are of primary concern. First is the observation that the utilitarianism–social welfare model does not account for distributional impacts. Part of the logic of converting costs, benefits, and risks into a common metric is the assumption that each is "sufficiently fungible as to be compared, traded off, or otherwise aggregated by analysts."[8] Although considering net benefits (or risks) in isolation of their *distribution* may satisfy the standard of efficiency, separating consideration of costs and benefits from their distribution surely violates most notions of equity and justice. Many environmental issues, such as siting decisions, entail clear separations between benefits and costs (or risks), often along lines of geography, income, political power, and race. A similar lack of congruence can be associated with programs reliant upon uniform regulatory standards that may impose social and economic costs on certain populations that may be unnecessary, excessive, or disproportionate in relation to the benefits obtained by those populations. See Gary Bryner's discussion of these various frameworks for understanding "justice" in Chapter 2.

The other equity concern raised by the existing reliance on technocratic decision making is its failure to recognize the complex social, political, and ethical concerns embedded in many environmental and natural resources issues. Technically trained decision makers often lack either the skills or the legitimacy (or both) to make decisions that have ethical and value dimensions. Reliance upon technical decision-making techniques allows environmental decision makers to argue that difficult social and political questions are being resolved "scientifically." However, most environmental decisions do not simply reduce themselves to matters of impartial judgment embodied in "a concrete problem-solving calculus," but are instead "inherently infused with value judgments."[9] To the extent that different perceptions about risk or the comparison of incommensurable values come into play in environmental decisions, they cannot simply be reduced to a single utility metric, be it scientific or otherwise, without significant loss to those values. Public values, such as those of Carey's land grant communities in northern New Mexico (see Chapter 9), demand consideration and weight in some way.

It has proven to be exceedingly difficult to accommodate values and public input in forums emphasizing autonomous technical decision making guided by principles of utilitarianism and welfare economics. In theory, this challenge is at least partially addressed by the requirement that environmental and natural resources decision making follows a tightly structured and open public process, consistent with the tenets of the Administrative Procedures Act of 1946.[10] In practice, however, this requirement is frequently manipulated into announce-and-defend decision making, in which meaningful outside input is effectively stillborn. Equally problematic in many policy areas is the near erosion of deliberative agency decision making under the pressures of interest group politics (or pluralism). Functioning much like a market, the pluralist model of administrative decision making aggregates the preferences of all interest groups to reflect, on balance, a mix of predominating preferences.[11] However, in doing so, it generates outcomes that are frequently suspect, especially where complex environmental problems are concerned.

Perhaps the most troubling aspect of pluralism involves the manner in which preferences are inequitably aggregated. Political power and economic power, as well as technical ability, are the currencies of pluralism; parties lacking these resources lack access and influence, and they can expect to have their preferences systematically devalued or completely excluded. For instance, many disadvantaged (economically, socially, or politically) communities complain of being excluded from environmental land use and natural resources planning processes because they are often not aware that a decision-making process is under way or because the logistics of the process effectively exclude them from participating in the process. (See Jan Buhrmann's discussion in Chapter 11 and Sarah Krakoff's discussion in Chapter 7.) Even when disadvantaged communities are formally included early on in the process, they tend to be limited in their ability to meaningfully participate, based on the lack of expertise, information, and resources (time and money). (See Dean Suagee's discussion of Native Americans' participation in National Environmental Policy Act processes in Chapter 10.) In this way, certain preexisting social disadvantages can interact with pluralistic decision-making processes to produce even more severe material inequalities.

It is widely recognized that pluralism is not an ideal model for resolving highly contentious public issues in ways that lend legitimacy to the ultimate decision. A better approach would be one that provides more "meaningful" participation, a requirement likely defined to mean a deliberative process whereby stakeholders engage in rational discourse about what outcome(s) best serve the common good of the affected community.[12] Such a process would not simply equate the "public interest" with the aggregate self-interested, private preferences of its participants. Nor would such an approach naively assume that a simple tallying of benefits and costs would, by itself, be sufficient. Rather, the ideal process would seek to bring together citizens to *create* the common good, as opposed to *discovering* it through preexisting preferences. Participants would be expected to set aside, and revise, their own preferences in the interest of finding shared values. While participants would be expected to, and would, express private preferences, these preferences would be subjected to critical examination and reasoned debate. Such debate hopefully would move participants beyond their own self-interests toward consensus or, at the least, bring forth alternative perspectives, additional information, and better decisions.

Devolved Collaboration in Theory and Practice

Devolved collaboration, in theory and practice, holds out the promise of bringing together diverse interests in a cooperative spirit to craft creative solutions to difficult environmental concerns that have gone unresolved by traditional regulatory approaches. Devolved collaboration allows stakeholders within a community to specifically address environmental or resource problems at a geographically focused scale, thus ensuring that community values, as well as a range of environmental, social, and economic goals, are accommodated by the solutions. Existing examples of collaborative processes in the natural resources and environmental context illustrate that efforts to realize these promises are well under way.

The Promise

The current enthusiasm for collaborative decision making builds upon recent positive experiences with alternative dispute resolution (ADR) techniques and, more specifically, environmental dispute resolution (EDR). Tools such as mediation have been successfully employed to resolve a wide variety of disputes, from the siting of waste disposal facilities to managing natural resources valued by both industry and environmentalists.[13] Mediation and negotiation are now widely accepted methods for resolving disputes and for building consensus around both policy and site-specific environmental and natural resources issues. In the context of CBEP, collaboration requires enhanced dialogue and shared power between governmental decision makers, organized stakeholder groups and, perhaps most importantly, ordinary citizens and other parties frequently disenfranchised through traditional decision-making mechanisms. This collaborative ideal is clearly articulated in the EPA's CBEP initiative, which promises an explicitly "holistic and collaborative" process designed to allow public and private stakeholders to actively deliberate about not only environmental protection issues but also "human social needs," focusing on achieving "long-term ecosystem health" and fostering linkages between economic prosperity and environmental well-being.[14]

Advocates of the collaborative decision-making process invariably cite its normative appeal—namely, its promise of democratic legitimacy.[15] Central to this normative claim is the requirement of consensus—getting diverse interested parties to agree with one another on solutions to their disputes or common problems. Real consensus building requires taking into account all of the affected interests (representation), creating a communicatively rational process (deliberation), and giving everyone the same information and resources (equity). Consensus building is said to be superior to conventional decision-making methods for many reasons, including its ability to produce more stable decisions. Once a consensus is reached among all interested parties, it becomes very difficult for participants to reject the collective result. These qualities are notably lacking in more paternalistic processes, such as announce-and-defend decision making, and in the pseudo-market framework of pluralism.

Collaboration promises many other benefits. Whether as part of a formal process, such as negotiated rulemaking, or of a more broadly focused or ad hoc planning effort, ideal collaborative efforts can provide public and private stakeholders with opportunities to explore differences of opinion and shared interests, to collectively gather and analyze data, and to evaluate bargains and trades. Additional benefits, according to proponents, include saving the public money, producing quicker results than conventional dispute resolution methods (such as litigation), and helping to free up the heavily burdened dockets of the nation's judges.[16] A final benefit of devolved collaboration pertains to the geographic locus of decision making, particularly the recognition that many problems are uniquely regional and therefore require novel mechanisms for linking the activities of different agencies, governments, and private stakeholders.

By focusing decisions at geographic scales consistent with ecosystem complexity and the relationship of communities to resources, devolved collaboration promises improved outcomes. These improved outcomes flow, in part, from the promises of deeper representation of local communities, shared information and resources among stakeholders, and the concomitant expansion of the range of values and expertise in the decision-making process. Moreover, the iterative nature of collaboration is said to be the mechanism by which diverse stakeholders will not only reach consensus on questions of the common good but also act on it in ways that bring about better, and more legitimate, outcomes. For example, recent years have seen an increasing use of regional collaborative efforts among local governments to address certain economic, social, and ecological issues—including land use, sprawl, and transportation—which transcend local borders.[17] This New Regionalism supports limited-purpose, regional governance structures that do not completely supplant local governments but, instead, allow for the management of mutual regional concerns in a more efficient manner than if these concerns were left up to the fragmented local governments that make up a particular region. Similarly, regionalism has also made steady, if not spectacular, progress as an organizing principle in many federal and state natural resources agencies.[18] Rather than formal consolidations or reorganization of agencies, reform often focuses on finding novel and frequently informal means of interagency and interjurisdictional cooperation. Such regional mechanisms promise more efficient and effective resource management and, largely due to the emphasis on collaborative decision making, require minimal restructuring of formal authorities, responsibilities, and budgetary arrangements.

Modern Examples

There are several recognizable strands of devolved collaboration, two of which are described below. The first involves mostly ad hoc groups that are concerned with diverse issues in natural resources planning and management, while the second features greater formality and a focus on environmental land use and pollution control decisions.

AD HOC COLLABORATIVE PROCESSES: WATERSHED INITIATIVES AND FORESTRY PARTNERSHIPS

Recent years have seen a proliferation of collaborative ad hoc groups, such as "watershed initiatives" and "forestry partnerships." These initiatives and partnerships are groups of self-directed public interests (governments and natural resources agencies) and private stakeholders (local residents, landowners, and interest groups) assembled to address mutual natural resources concerns (for example, water quality, biological restoration, and forest health) at physically relevant geographic scales (for example, watersheds).[19] Many of these groups have successfully developed, and in some cases implemented, detailed plans both to protect vulnerable natural resources, such as watersheds and forests, and to allow local interests to use those resources in ways that promote the economic and social sustainability of the surrounding communities. In bringing together traditional adversaries—such as landowners, resource extractors, environmentalists, and federal agencies—to seek solutions of mutual benefit, these ad hoc collaborative partnerships strive to elevate the pursuit of practical, multistakeholder plans above the conflict, delays, and administrative red tape so characteristic of mandated planning processes and regulatory programs.

Many of these efforts are found in the West, particularly in communities where the ties between economies and landscapes remain strong and where an abundance of federal public land ensures a complex resource management environment. Watershed initiatives, for example, frequently focus on the desire to accommodate local water use practices with environmental protection values and, more directly, federal environmental regulations associated with the Endangered Species Act and the Clean Water Act. The decline of salmon fisheries and the subsequent listing of many runs as endangered have made the Pacific Northwest, in particular, an extremely active laboratory in devolved collaboration. Among the best-known western watershed initiatives are the Henry's Fork Watershed Council (Idaho), the Upper Clark Fork River Basin Steering Committee (Montana), and the Coquille Watershed Association (Oregon).

Forestry partnerships, meanwhile, are particularly common in regions where economic and social forces encouraging timber harvesting conflict with environmental values. One example is the Applegate Partnership in southern Oregon, a collaborative group working to move beyond the polarizing conflict between environmentalists and the timber industry concerning the use of old growth forests. Other examples of devolved collaboration with a predominantly land use focus include the development of the Inimim Forest management plan within the Yuba River Watershed (northern California) and the work of the Malpai Borderlands Group, a collaborative group concerned with an ecosystem straddling the southern Arizona–New Mexico border. The Inimim Forest effort involves public lands where traditional resource management practices conflict with emerging community and social values; similarly, the Malpai effort is an attempt to integrate sustainable ranching practices into the larger social and economic context of the community.

Perhaps the best-known and most controversial experiment in devolved collaboration is a forestry partnership called the Quincy Library Group (QLG).[20] The QLG comprises approximately thirty local civic, business, and environmental leaders from Quincy, California, who have been meeting since 1993 in the local library to discuss solutions to the "timber wars" in the nearby Plumas National Forest. The group has worked for several years to devise and implement a management plan promising to protect environmental resources, sustain the local timber industry, and reduce the threat of a catastrophic forest fire. In many respects, the QLG is highly atypical of other community-based collaborative groups in its ambition and influence; however, that is what makes it so useful as a case study. Whether or not the QLG represents the future of devolved collaboration and whether or not it *should* be the future are both questions of considerable importance (which will be revisited later in this chapter).

The QLG was founded upon the premise that the region needed to move beyond divisive conflict, undue outside control (by federal agencies, federal laws, and national interest groups), and narrow problem-solving strategies. Rather, the situation called for a locally generated forest management plan that was comprehensive in scope and design. The QLG developed such a plan but found the plan impossible to enact through the national forest planning process outlined in the National Forest Management Act and administered by the U.S. Forest Service. Consequently, the group took the unusual step of introducing the proposal as a bill in Congress and, after a turbulent struggle, was rewarded by passage of the Herger-Feinstein Quincy Library Forest Recovery Act of 1998.[21]

STRUCTURED/REGULATED COLLABORATIVE PROCESSES: LOCAL ADVISORY COMMITTEES

The second strand of devolved collaboration reflects a more structured type of collaborative decision making: community "working" or "advisory" committees or boards. Increasingly, but not exclusively, used as part of pollution control and environmental land management disputes, these committees are generally set up by statutory or regulatory mandate to bring together public and private interests to deliberate on such issues as the siting of hazardous waste facilities and the cleanup and redevelopment of contaminated land.[22] These local, site-specific committees are an outgrowth of regulatory negotiation and policy-level advisory committees, which have been used at the national level for years. In contrast to the "consultative" function of expert advisory committees and some policy advisory committees, the "collaborative" function of local advisory committees involves "active deliberation" and "an emphasis on consensus among members." More than an exchange of ideas and information between governmental officials and nongovernmental stakeholders, these consensus-based processes involve "finding areas of common ground and shared understanding among stakeholders that form the foundation of out-comes to which all stakeholders can agree."[23]

Site-specific advisory boards and committees have several fea-tures in common.[24] First, they are appointed to address environmen-tal, social, or economic issues (or all three) pertaining to a particular site. In the siting context, an advisory committee may be directed to ascertain the environmental, social, and economic impact a particular facility will have on the host community, to negotiate compensation for the host community, or to develop permit conditions and moni-toring requirements. Rarely do such committees have the authority to decide whether or not to grant the permit, an issue the permitting agency retains in its jurisdiction. In the cleanup and redevelopment context, an advisory board might be directed to develop recommen-dations for reuse of the contaminated land, to prepare an environ-mental impact report for the reuse plan, and to propose cleanup stan-dards consistent with the planned reuse of the land.

Second, the breadth and depth of representation on these commit-tees is tightly regulated. Advisory committees seek consensus among a diverse membership of representatives from all, or at least most, potential stakeholders. Thus, such a committee might include a spe-cific number of representatives from federal, state, and local agencies, environmentalists concerned with quality of life issues, conservation proponents, local businesses, property owners, and environmental justice advocates.

Third, most advisory committees are eligible to receive technical assistance, usually in the form of grants for hiring consultants, lawyers, and other necessary personnel. All advisory committee members have access to the same information and documents, ideally in a form accessible and understandable to all members. Technical assistance provisions exist out of recognition that local citizens might not always possess the knowledge and expertise to deliberate effec-tively with other interests on the committee. Having information and technical resources at their disposal makes it possible for a group of otherwise unsophisticated citizens to influence environmental deci-sions, in part, by signaling errors made by technical experts or politi-cal leaders, or by demonstrating that substantial public opposition exists.

Local advisory boards generally embrace a deliberative ideal, "meaning that essential activities are learning about the issues, can-didly discussing reasons for and against various alternative solutions, and striving to reach a consensus resolution."[25] Ideally, advisory com-mittee discussions result in a consensus recommendation to the sponsoring agency about the outcome that is in the best interest of the community. However, "even if consensus cannot be reached, a successful citizens advisory board can narrow areas of disagreement, help affected parties recognize others' concerns and their bona fides, bring forward alternatives that had not previously been considered, and (if nothing else) elucidate issues that remain to be resolved."[26]

Equity Implications of Devolved Collaboration

Achieving the full promise of collaborative decision making is highly dependent on a number of factors.[27] Collaborative decision making is most apt to work only in those situations where all parties have strong incentives to reach a collective decision, where fundamental value-based conflicts do not divide participants, and where resources (that is, time, money, and expertise) are adequate to support the frequently lengthy process. The existence of some of these factors will depend upon the scale, or physical qualities, of the on-the-ground problem, while others may depend upon the degree of social capital between the participants. Even in the absence of some of these factors, collaboration may still help improve understanding and further delineate issues. For example, a skilled facilitator is often highly useful in distinguishing true value conflicts, which are rarely negotiable, from those built upon differences in preferences, misperceptions about costs and benefits, or simple miscommunications.

There is nothing inherent in collaboration, however, either as a norm or a practice, that promises a resolution to the problems of unequal representation and influence that underlie conventional decision-making processes, and which are central to environmental justice critiques of those processes. In fact, there is reason to believe that many collaborative efforts simply replicate, and perhaps even exacerbate, these problems in new decision-making structures. Additionally, devolving or decentralizing decision-making influence can render these problems less visible or subject to scrutiny because the further the process is removed from a centralized decision maker, the less accountability there will be for the legitimacy of the process. Failure to address these democratic process problems inevitably derails the promise of devolved collaboration to achieve its substantive promises. That is, much of the promise of this approach to yield better, and more legitimate, environmental decisions depends so crucially on who is included in the process and the corresponding values, norms, and influence they bring with them. If inadequate attention is given to these process concerns, then devolved collaboration can have significant environmental justice implications.

The Tension between Representational Equity and Geographic Scale

If collaboration is to achieve its substantive and normative promise, it must strive for a quality and balance of representation. This can be a formidable challenge. In collaborative processes, governmental regulators and decision makers are crucial participants, as are representatives of interests who have different relationships to the environmental conflict, concern, or issue. Other stakeholders may be more difficult to identify and involve (for example, future generations), but nonetheless they demand some form of representation. Ideal representatives are those empowered to speak for or to bind a particular constituency or interest group. This desire for inclusion, however, must be balanced by the practical requirements of deliberation and decision making. Consensus decision making is extremely dependent upon finding mutually beneficial, or win-win, solutions. This provides a strong group incentive for limiting the total number of participants, particularly in a way that excludes those representatives likely to express values inconsistent with those of other participants, or for demonizing such participants within the collaborative process.

Devolution can be the tool used by a collaborative group to exclude legitimate interests and to produce a disingenuous consensus. This aim may be further aided by processes that are largely unstructured and opaque, conditions that can encourage "capture" of the process by a group of local stakeholders who achieve consensus through exclusion, intimidation, or coercion. This is the charge leveled by critics of the QLG, which allegedly achieved local consensus only through the exclusion of legitimate "outside" interests.[28] Chief among those excluded was the U.S. Forest Service, the systematic demonization of which accounted for, in some minds, much of the QLG's legitimacy and strength in reaching a local consensus. Also notably absent from deliberations were representatives of national environmental groups. This exclusion was evident from the coalition of 140 forest protection organizations that organized to block the QLG bill in the Senate, forcing proponents to secure passage of the proposal by attaching it as a rider on an appropriations bill.

The exclusion of national stakeholders in collaborative efforts is particularly troublesome in the natural resources context, where national interests are almost always implicated in local efforts. These

interests are easily excluded, particularly in informal, ad hoc collaborative processes where representatives from national environmental
groups may not reside in the locality or may lack the ability or legitimacy to speak for national interests or future generations.[29] These
observations lead to a troubling conclusion: if devolved collaboration
achieves a greater involvement of local interests only at the expense of
a reduced presence of national interests, then the problem of inadequate representation in natural resources management has not been
resolved, but only modified.

Localizing Unequal Influence

Beyond the potential for exclusion of certain interests, devolved collaboration fails to escape another trap that haunts current environmental decision making, and one that more potently involves environmental justice concerns. That is, environmental decision-making
processes may suffer from an inequitable distribution of influence,
more often than not along lines of race or class. Many of the representation problems associated with devolved collaboration can presumably be minimized through the use of more structured, or regulated, processes. This approach is frequently seen, for example, in
rules establishing site-specific citizen advisory boards and committees. Generally, these rules provide for a specific number of representatives from various stakeholder groups as well as from federal, state,
and local agencies. Advisory committees are also apt to make their
deliberations transparent, unlike some ad hoc collaborative groups,
which helps to ensure appropriate and adequate representation.

Even where formal representation is regulated, however, the
assurance of deliberative and egalitarian decision making can remain
elusive. Collaborative processes depend upon some degree of social
capital between and among various participants, particularly at the
local level. In general, the term *social capital* refers, by analogy to physical capital and human capital, to the "norms and networks of civil
society that lubricate cooperative action among both citizens and their
institutions."[30] Those norms—such as mutual trust, reciprocity, credi-
bility, and respect—are necessary to solve common problems through
collaborative processes. These qualities, unfortunately, are in short
supply in many local communities and among various communities
impacted by a particular environmental or natural resources decision.
Social theorists have come to understand social capital as having both
horizontal and vertical aspects. In general, "horizontal" social capital
refers to those social networks that bring together agents of *equivalent*

status and power. "Vertical" social capital refers to those social networks that link *unequal* agents in asymmetric relations of hierarchy and dependence. The existence of both horizontal social capital and vertical social capital is crucial to the ability of collaborative processes to overcome the exclusionary tendencies of current pluralistic processes.

For instance, horizontal social capital is important where a community has a history of strong associations or networks in which its members have made common decisions together, developed trust, and formed bonds of solidarity and respect. Horizontal social capital is particularly important for collaborative processes that involve multiple or dispersed communities which would be significantly impacted by a particular environmental or resource decision. For instance, nontimber forest workers (such as wild mushroom pickers) are typically composed of various immigrant or other disadvantaged groups (for example, Southeast Asians, Native Americans, Mexicans, Guatemalans, Salvadorans, low-income Europeans). These groups tend not to be a part of any dense social network; in fact, they tend to be politically disorganized and geographically mobile. As such, they have a history of exclusion from traditional natural resources decision-making processes that fundamentally affect their lives and livelihoods.[31] Without a tradition of civic engagement within these types of communities, or extraordinary efforts by government agencies or nonprofit groups to help establish networks for such groups, it will be quite difficult to assemble a broadly representative decision-making process in the face of multiple, and dispersed, communities. Even in geographically compact and homogenous communities, horizontal capital is crucial to the ability of different constituencies in a community, or different affected communities, to appoint or empower appropriate representatives, to "speak" for certain groups within a community and to bring community values to the process.

Vertical social capital will be implicated between stakeholders who possess different social, economic, or political status. This is particularly true when there are many types of communities at issue—whether defined by geographic place, common ethnic or economic identity, or common interests. Collaborative processes are likely to be problematic in communities with insufficient vertical social capital between and among different interests or stakeholders. Without sufficient vertical capital, certain groups or interests might be disenfranchised from local officials running the process, or traditionally underrepresented groups or interests may be subject to further exclusion on the basis of prejudice or lack of respect. Imbalance in political power or social influence can skew the representation of any collaborative group of individuals and ultimately the legitimacy of any consensus solution.

For example, in his study of the use of advisory committees in three California communities, Luke Cole attributes the successful use of a committee in one community, and the failed use of committees in two other communities, partly to power struggles among interests differently situated in terms of social capital.[32] Under the California act mandating the use of "local assessment committees" in toxic waste facility siting decisions, the local agency or body (for example, city council) appoints three representatives of the community at large (out of seven total appointees). However, often there is no easy answer to who adequately represents the "community" among the limited number of "local" representatives on a citizen advisory committee.[33] Moreover, as Cole has demonstrated, since local officials usually appoint members on advisory committees, representation can easily become an issue of the relative power of those choosing the representatives and the influence of powerful interests on that official.

In both communities where the advisory committees were deemed "unsuccessful," the committee was widely considered as unrepresentative (both geographically and demographically) of the community where the proposed facility was to be located. In one case, local elected officials (county supervisors) appointed primarily individuals from the surrounding county (with token representation from the host city), with a preference shown for individuals in favor of the facility being sited. The meetings were also held forty miles from the host city, making even informal representation of that city difficult, particularly for the low-income minority population.

In contrast, in the case of the one "successful" use of a committee, local officials (city council) drew committee members from a "local" area that was more geographically compact and demographically homogenous. The interests of the officials who appointed the committee and the members of the committee happened to be identical (both were against the facility siting). This homogeneity, Cole notes, not only made achieving broad representation easier but also likely increased the committee's effectiveness in reaching consensus and responsiveness to public input. The effectiveness of mechanisms designed to give power to the local level depends upon both the decision makers and the participating public having a commitment to the qualities that a good process comprises, including broad representation. The failure of local officials in the two "unsuccessful" communities to set up representative processes "points to a central flaw" in devolved efforts, concludes Cole, even the most structured ones like the California act mandating local assessment committees. That is, there is no guarantee that officials responsible for convening these committees will follow the mandate to set up transparent, representative, and equitable processes.

Beyond Devolved Collaboration

The ideal of devolved collaboration expresses quite well the democratic wish of those who desire more inclusive, representative, creative, and effective environmental decision making. The "democratic wish"—the imagery of a single, united people bound together by consensus over the public good, which is discerned through direct citizen participation in community settings—has a long tradition in America.[34] It is, as James Morone has emphasized, a legitimate populist counter to the liberal status quo that various social movements have seized upon at critical moments throughout American history.

Ultimately, however, the democratic wish is utopian in its imagery of a "people" coming together to deliberate, unite around conceptions of the common good, and restore community among and across broad interests groups. The trouble with participatory yearning, explains Morone, is "its innocence of organizational dynamics" and the constraints that new forms of participatory arenas can place on the very fundamental changes taking place. These constraints tend to "limit the oppressed at the same time as it legitimates them," in part because the democratic urge and its new forms of participation tend to "leav[e] behind the underlying conditions it found: a political economy of self-seeking interests pushing ahead within a complex welter of political rules that advantage some citizens, disadvantage others, and seem almost invisible to all."[35]

The search for better and more legitimate decision making will require more than crafting a stronger participatory norm and shifting decision-making power to the local "people" affected by decisions about social goods such as the environment. Any decision-making process that hopes to improve upon the current, pluralist model of participation must pay sufficient attention to the political economy and the resulting social relations of constituencies in a participatory process. Disparities in representation and influence among interests in collaborative processes are inextricably linked to the same set of social relations that make pluralistic decision-making processes problematic. Without attention to these issues, the entire participatory process is placed into jeopardy: it will be difficult to attain broad participation, meaningful deliberation, and a legitimate consensus.[36]

The debate surrounding the appropriate scale of decision making in the local government arena illustrates the type of normative coherence, and focus, that can aid efforts to reform decision-making processes about public goods.[37] In this context, it is the so-called "regionalists" who worry about the inequities that can result from highly decentralized decision making, and the self-maximizing ways in which decision-making powers are exercised. For instance, given the uneven distribution of property wealth and service needs, affluent localities benefit the most under "localism," while poorer ones suffer. "Localists" counter that decentralized decision making, in general, promotes the efficient provision of public goods and services, provides local citizens with more meaningful opportunities for participation in government decisions, and gives citizens the power to shape their communities. Both sides agree that decision-making arrangements should seek to satisfy norms of efficiency, democracy, community, and equity, but they disagree about which form of governance will best advance these goals.

As the debate about New Regionalism in local government law suggests, perhaps we should be paying more attention to the normative goals we want to achieve in our decision-making processes than to trying to craft new decision-making structures or processes that will achieve those goals in every instance. That is, the proper locus of, and the most appropriate structure for, decision making that effectively manages complex decisions about social goods is not likely a question subject to a universal answer. Rather, calls for decentralized, collaborative decision making should be viewed as a collective demand for a shared set of normative goals. Those goals include deeper public participation by those most affected by environmental decisions, accountability of decision makers (both public and private) to those they represent, incorporation of community values and local expertise in environmental decisions, and equity among all interests and participants (vis-à-vis resources, influence, and representation).

How one achieves these goals in a particular decision will depend upon a close examination of the context in which such a decision is to be made. One key contextual element is the ecological nature of the problem. Devolved collaboration may not be appropriate for many public natural resources decisions because of potential underrepresentation of national, diffuse, and public interests. Devolved collaboration likely gives greater weight to the economic interests of citizens near the natural resources than to the noneconomic interests of more distant, and often urban, stakeholders who use and appreciate resources on public lands. The result is the triumph of local values over those held by more widespread and dispersed constituencies. Arguably, this outcome is much more defensible in the context of pollution control decisions, particularly those where the populations most impacted are geographically compact and readily identifiable. Examples include the cleanup, redevelopment, and reuse of land and the siting of hazardous facilities. These are decisions that involve a very limited and manageable class of interests—that is, those populations that are likely to bear the social, economic, and health impacts of the proposed decision.

The social, political, and economic context of a community is also crucial in deciding the appropriateness of, and potential for, devolved collaboration. Collaborative processes, as explained above, are likely to be problematic in communities with insufficient amounts of social capital between and among different interests and stakeholders.

Conclusion

The move toward a devolve-and-collaborate approach in environmental and natural resources decision making certainly expresses some core values, or norms, necessary for more equitable, and better, decision-making outcomes. However, like its preceding decision-making approaches, this evolving approach is indifferent to (or innocent about) the ecological, social, and political conditions necessary to realize its own promise. Rather, devolved collaboration may in fact further solidify some of the very problems that its ascendancy is theoretically designed to address. Hence, simply devolving decision-making influence and embracing a collaborative decision-making norm does not specify the means of achieving the promise of this model, including its aspiration of more equitable decisions. The contextual approach hinted at above recognizes that no one approach, or model, of decision making will be sufficiently attentive to the various contexts and normative goals that are embedded in our most difficult environmental challenges, including environmental justice. Instead, using the aspirations expressed through new decision-making approaches like devolved collaboration, perhaps we can best address our current environmental and natural resources problems by identifying the normative goals underlying these approaches and then tailoring appropriate decision-making mechanisms to specific environmental problems in particular contexts (ecological, social, economic, and political) to achieve those goals.

Acknowledgments

The author wishes to thank Doug Kenney for his invaluable feedback and tireless editing of this chapter.

Notes

1. See generally Julia M. Wondolleck and Steven L. Yaffee, *Making Collaboration Work: Lessons from Innovation in Natural Resources Management* (Washington, D.Č.: Island Press, 2000). See also DeWitt John, *Civic Environmentalism: Alternatives to Regulation in States and Communities* (Washington, D.C.: CQ Press, 1994).
2. U.S. Environmental Protection Agency, Office of Sustainable Ecosystems and Communities, "Framework for Community-Based Environmental Protection," August 27, 1998, available at http://yosemite.epa.gov/osec/osechome.nsf/all/d-cbep.html.
3. See generally J. Clarence Davies and Jan Mazurek, *Regulating Pollution: Does the U.S. System Work?* (Washington, D.C.: Resources for the Future, 1997); National Academy of Public Administration, *Resolving the Paradox of Environmental Protection* (Washington, D.C.: National Academy of Public Administration, 1997); Jody Freeman, "Collaborative Governance in the Administrative State," *UCLA Law Review* 1 (1997): 14–16; David Zaring, "NonPoint Source Pollution and Regulatory Control: The Clean Water Act's Bleak Present and Future," *Harvard Environmental Law Review* (1996): 515, 516–518.
4. Stephen M. Nickelsburg, "Mere Volunteers?: The Promise and Limits of Community-Based Environmental Protection," *Virginia Law Review* (1998): 1371, 1374.
5. Wondelleck and Yaffee, *Making Collaboration Work,* 11, quoting the first chief of the U.S. Forest Service. More generally, see Samuel P. Hays, *Conservation and the Gospel of Efficiency* (Cambridge: Harvard University Press, 1959).
6. Timothy P. Duane, "Community Participation in Ecosystem Management," *Ecology Law Quarterly* 24 (1997): 771, 772.
7. See, e.g., Robert H. Nelson, *Public Lands and Private Rights: The Failure of Scientific Management* (Lanham, Md.: Rowman and Littlefield, 1995); Donald T. Hornstein, "Reclaiming Environmental Law: A Normative Critique of Comparative Risk Assessment," *Columbia Law Review* 92 (1992): 562, 577–79.
8. Hornstein, "Reclaiming Environmental Law," 576–77.
9. Jim Rossi, "Participation Run Amok: The Costs of Mass Participation for Deliberative Agency Decision Making," *Northwestern Law Review* 92 (1997): 173, 198.
10. 60 Stat. 237 (codified as amended at 5 U.S.C., secs. 551–559, 701–706) (1994).

11. See, e.g., Eileen Gauna, "The Environmental Justice Misfit: Public Participation and the Paradigm Paradox," *Stanford Environmental Law Journal* 17 (1998): 3; and Jonathan Poisner, "A Civil Republican Perspective on the National Environmental Policy Act's Process for Citizen Participation," *Environmental Law Journal* 26 (1996): 53.

12. See, e.g., Gauna, "The Environmental Justice Misfit."

13. See, e.g., Walton J. Blackburn and Willa Marie Bruce, *Mediating Environmental Conflicts: Theory and Practice* (Westport, Conn.: Quorum Books, 1995); and Lawrence S. Bacow and Michael Wheeler, *Environmental Dispute Resolution* (New York: Plenum Press, 1984).

14. For a full discussion of the CBEP philosophy, see the EPA's CBEP initiative home page at www.epa.gov/ecocommunity.

15. See, e.g., Judith E. Innes, "Planning through Consensus Building: A New View of the Comprehensive Planning Ideal," *Journal of the American Planning Association* 62 (1996): 460; Ortwin Renn, Thomas Weber, and Peter Wiedemann, *Fairness and Competence in Citizen Participation: Evaluating Models for Public Discourse,* (Dordrecht: Kluwer Academic, 1995); and Jody Freeman and Laura Langbein, "Regulatory Negotiation and the Legitimacy Benefit," *New York University Environmental Law Journal* 60 (2000).

16. Several authors critically review these claims. See, e.g., Douglas Amy, *The Politics of Environmental Mediation* (New York: Columbia University Press, 1987); Gail Bingham, *Resolving Environmental Disputes: A Decade of Experience* (Washington, D.C.: Conservation Foundation, 1985); Douglas Kenney, *Arguing about Consensus* (Boulder, Colo.: Natural Resources Law Center, 2000); and Cary Coglianese, "Assessing Consensus: The Promise and Performance of Negotiated Rulemaking," *Duke Law Journal* 46 (1997): 1255.

17. Sheryll D. Cashin, "Localism, Self-Interest and the Tyranny of the Favored Quarter: Addressing the Barriers to New Regionalism," *Georgetown Law Review* 88 (2000): 1985, 2028.

18. Several of the more notable efforts are described by the Interagency Ecosystem Management Task Force, *The Ecosystem Approach: Healthy Ecosystems and Sustainable Economies,* vol. 2, *Case Studies* (Washington, D.C.: U.S. Government Printing Office, 1996).

19. Detailed inventories have been produced by several authors, including Douglas Kenney et al., *The New Watershed Source Book* (Boulder, Colo.: Natural Resources Law Center, 2000); and Yaffee et al., *Ecosystem Management in the United States* (Washington, D.C.: Island Press, 1996). This discussion primarily draws from Kenney et al. and from Duane, "Community Participation in Ecosystem Management"; Nickelsburg, "Mere Volunteers?" and the EPA's CBEP initiative, available at www.epa.gov/ecocommunity.

20. One of the most comprehensive case studies of the Quincy Library Group is by Duane, "Community Participation in Ecosystem Management."

Also useful is Lawrence Ruth, "Conservation on the Cusp: Reformation of National Forest Policy in the Sierra Nevada," *UCLA Journal of Environmental Law and Policy* 18 (1999/2000): 1.

21. The act is buried in the hodgepodge of legislation known as the Omnibus Consolidated and Emergency Supplemental Appropriations Act of 1998, Public Law 105-277, available at http://thomas.loc.gov/.

22. Sheila Foster, "Public Participation," in *The Law of Environmental Justice: Theories and Procedures to Address Disproportionate Risks,* ed. Michael B. Gerrard (New York: American Bar Association, 1999), 205–6.

23. Thomas C. Beierle and Rebecca J. Long, "Chilling Collaboration: The Federal Advisory Committee Act and Stakeholder Involvement in Environmental Decision Making," *Environmental Law Reporter* 29 (July 1999): 10399.

24. John S. Applegate, "Beyond the Usual Suspects: The Use of Citizen Advisory Boards in Environmental Decision Making," *Indiana Law Journal* 73 (1998): 903.

25. Applegate, "Beyond the Usual Suspects," 921.

26. Applegate, "Beyond the Usual Suspects," 921.

27. For a general review of these issues, see Wondelleck and Yaffee, *Making Collaboration Work.*

28. Duane, "Community Participation in Ecosystem Management."

29. Michael McCloskey, "Problems with Using Collaboration to Shape Environmental Public Policy," *Valparaiso University Law Review* 34 (2000): 423, 431.

30. Robert Putnam, "Forward," *Housing Policy Debate* 9 (1998): 1, 4.

31. Rebecca McLain, "Controlling the Forest Understory: Wild Mushroom Politics in Central Oregon" (Ph.D. diss., University of Washington, College of Forest Resources, Seattle, Wash., 2000).

32. Luke Cole, "The Theory and Reality of Community-Based Environmental Decisionmaking: The Failure of California's Tanner Act and Its Implications for Environmental Justice," *Ecology Law Quarterly* 25 (1999): 733.

33. See, e.g., Kris Wernstedt, "Terra Firma or Terra Incognita? Western Land Use, Hazardous Waste, and the Devolution of U.S. Federal Environmental Programs," *Natural Resources Journal* 40 (2000): 157.

34. James A. Morone, *The Democratic Wish: Public Participation and the Limits of American Government* (New York: Basic Books, 1991).

35. Morone, *The Democratic Wish,* 323 and 335.

36. Lynn M. Sanders, "Against Deliberation," *Political Theory* 25 (June 1997): 347, 353, 367–69.

37. See, e.g., Gerald Frug, "Decentering Decentralization," *University of Chicago Law Review* 60 (1993): 253; and Richard Briffault, "The Local Government Boundary Problem in Metropolitan Areas," *Stanford Law Review* 48 (1996): 115.

Chapter 7

TRIBAL SOVEREIGNTY AND ENVIRONMENTAL JUSTICE

Sarah Krakoff

Diapers, lard tins, old tires, and pop cans in desert washes. Open trash heaps with medical waste, and the occasional litter of puppies. The perpetual swirl of plastic trash bags in supermarket parking lots. Alongside breathtaking vistas, the foregoing are unfortunately common sights on many American Indian reservations. As discussed by David Getches and David Pellow in Chapter 1, the environmental justice movement has focused necessary attention on the disproportionate siting of solid and hazardous waste in minority communities. But disproportionate siting does not cause the pervasive trash and litter on most Indian reservations. To understand the roots of the garbage problem on Indian reservations, one must consider the unique sovereign status of tribes. This status, combined with congressional and regulatory gaps and a history of tribal economic deprivation, prevents most reservations from maintaining adequate public sanitation systems.

Why is the reservation garbage problem not a prominent part of the environmental justice discussion, whereas the siting of solid and hazardous waste facilities is? The answers are in large part due to the fact that American Indian tribal sovereignty does not map well onto conventional understandings of justice—environmental or otherwise. Lack of knowledge and stereotypes about tribes exacerbate the problem. Yet, Indian people and tribes are often lumped in with those groups that are subject to disproportionately negative environmental impacts.[1] Thus, information about tribes being targeted by waste companies makes its way into much of environmental justice scholarship, but many problems that are more universal among tribes and more central to tribal life are glaringly absent from this literature.[2] As

161

long as we are going to include tribes in the analysis at all, we must do so with a full sense of what tribal life is about, what tribes are, and what we think the future ought to hold for tribes.

If Indian tribal sovereignty complicates the environmental justice analysis, some might question including tribes in the framework at all. But there are two compelling reasons to do so. First, virtually all Indian tribes clearly fit into Getches and Pellow's definition of groups who come to the table with "palpable and endemic disadvantage," stemming from a long history of discrimination, exclusion, and deliberate attempts to destroy their cultural and political communities. Second, the obvious disproportionate environmental harms borne by Native peoples have meant that they are *already* a part of the discussion—to let them continue to be so without a conscious articulation of the role of tribal sovereignty would be counterproductive to determining appropriate remedial strategies.

To ensure that these issues are being considered from within the environmental justice movement, this chapter reframes the environmental justice discussion in the Indian context to include explicit consideration of tribal sovereignty. First, this chapter will briefly outline the unique legal status of tribes and make the case for expanding the environmental justice umbrella to include support for tribal environmental self-governance. Next, it will examine exercises of tribal sovereignty within the environmental context, analyzing what kinds of procedural practices and substantive outcomes constitute environmental injustice. Finally, using the garbage problem described above, the chapter will explore remedies for ongoing environmental injustices and means for preventing future ones.

Tribal Sovereignty and Tribal Survival: Justice for Tribal People Requires the Existence of Tribes

Native Americans are classified as a racial group for the purposes of antidiscrimination law,[3] but most Native Americans are also members of Indian tribes. Indian tribes are sovereign nations, not merely political or social clubs.[4] The United States Supreme Court has defined Indian tribes as "dependent sovereigns," meaning, in short, that their sovereignty predates that of the United States, but that it is nonetheless internal to, and dependent upon, the federal government. Tribes therefore have the authority to govern their members and their territory (with various complicated exceptions), but they cannot engage in diplomatic relations with other countries.[5]

The Supreme Court has also found that only Congress can diminish tribal sovereignty or abrogate treaties with tribes.[6] Despite this seemingly bright line, federal courts often determine the contours of tribal sovereignty in the context of litigation. Thus, while Indian tribes predate the U.S. Constitution—and therefore their sovereignty does not derive from that document nor from any other enactment of the U.S. government—tribes are nonetheless constantly negotiating the terms of their sovereignty in Congress and the federal courts. As a consequence of legislative and judicial action, tribes have been stripped of some attributes of self-governance. For example, Indian tribes do not have criminal jurisdiction over non-Indians. Nor can tribes imprison anyone, Indian or not, for a period longer than one year. In the civil context, tribes have jurisdiction over non-Indians within their reservations, but this rule is subject to myriad and needlessly complex exceptions.[7] Tribal sovereignty is thus a paradox. It transcends, and therefore requires no validation from, the U.S. government. At the same time, tribal sovereignty is vulnerable and requires vigilant and constant defense in our legal and political forums.

While scholars have provided important critiques of the "dependent sovereign" notion,[8] it is essential to recognize that, however flawed, the framework provides a protective shell for the survival of tribal ways of life. Indian people have fared far worse during historical periods when the United States has tried to eliminate tribes as sovereigns than when the federal government has tried, albeit in misguided and sometimes paternalistic ways, to support tribes.[9] Moreover, American Indians themselves have struggled long and hard to ensure that they continue to exist as distinct and separate peoples, both as a political and a cultural matter.[10] If we support the survival of tribal ways of life, we must support the existence of tribes as political entities. Therefore, any kind of justice for tribes, including environmental justice, must include the norm of supporting tribal sovereignty.

That said, we can now home in on our concept of environmental justice in the Indian context. Environmental justice for tribes must be consistent with the promotion of tribal self-governance. Environmental injustice occurs when tribes fail to receive support in their efforts to control and improve their reservation environment. A preliminary definition of the term *environmental justice* for tribes might be the achievement of tribal authority to control and improve the reservation environment.

Toward an Environmental Justice Framework for Tribes

Using this preliminary definition of environmental justice for tribes—the achievement of tribal authority to control and improve the reservation environment—we can explore particular examples that fill out the contours of environmental injustice in Indian country. Because tribes, unlike other minority groups, are separate political entities, their sovereignty is crucial to their ability to control their environment. Attacks on tribal sovereignty may therefore have environmental justice implications. Of course, not all attacks on tribal sovereignty are environmental justice issues. Most such attacks are matters that have more to do with commerce, taxation, and control of people than with environmental quality per se.

Less obvious, however, may be the conclusion that not all acts that contribute to the degradation of the reservation environment are environmental justice issues. According to the proposed definition, only acts that both challenge a tribe's ability to control the tribal environment and degrade the environment are environmentally unjust. Some might contend that a community's right to make environmental decisions is itself an environmental justice issue. I think that it is important, in the environmental justice context, to distinguish between the norm of self-determination, at the community or tribal level, and the norm of preventing environmental degradation. Environmental injustices involve *both* environmental degradation and the undermining of self-determination. Thus, when a tribe is prevented, by means that undermine tribal sovereignty, from taking steps to *degrade* the environment, there is a justice issue for the tribe, but not necessarily an environmental justice issue. In other words, not all exercises of tribal sovereignty in the environmental context should be labeled matters of environmental justice. The following examples explore and apply this understanding of environmental justice for tribes.

Easy Cases: Attacks on Tribal Authority to Regulate Water Quality

Since the 1980s, tribes have been belatedly included in various federal programs aimed at cleaning up the environment.[11] Under the Clean Water Act (CWA), for example, tribes may be designated by the Environmental Protection Agency (EPA) as having "treatment as a state" (TAS) status. According to the EPA, tribes with TAS status may set water quality standards and impose them upon water users within the boundaries approved by the EPA. Tribes with TAS designations are therefore empowered to require nontribal members to comply with tribal water quality regulations. Because the Supreme Court has woven a tangled web in Indian country jurisdiction, this capability is a significant and contested one for tribes.

Two cases from the 1990s illustrate the challenges tribal governments face when they assume TAS status. The first case, *Albuquerque v Browner,* involves the Isleta Pueblos' adoption of stringent water quality standards to comport with their religious ceremonial needs. The second case, *Montana v EPA,* concerns the Confederated Salish and Kootenai Tribe's ability to impose its water quality standards on non-Indian landowners within the boundaries of the Flathead Reservation.

Albuquerque v Browner

The Pueblo of Isleta, like many southwestern tribes, has retained both its homelands and its traditions. Thus, the governing structure of the Pueblo still embodies many aspects of its pre-Columbian form. As for all Indian tribes, however, survival, including survival of tradition, has also meant adaptation. So after tribes became eligible for TAS status under the CWA, Isleta Pueblo undertook the steps necessary to qualify for TAS and then applied to the EPA.

The EPA recognized Isleta Pueblo as a state for purposes of the CWA on October 12, 1992. The Pueblo adopted water quality standards for Rio Grande water flowing through the tribal reservation, which were approved by the EPA on December 24, 1992. The Isleta Pueblos' water quality standards were more stringent than the State of New Mexico's standards so that the water would be safe for use in tribal religious ceremonies, which may involve dunking and incidental drinking.

The City of Albuquerque operates a waste treatment plant that discharges into the Rio Grande approximately five miles upstream from Isleta Pueblo. The EPA issues National Pollutant Discharge Elimination System (NPDES) permits to waste treatment facilities. To comply with Isletas' more stringent water quality standards, the EPA had to revise the permit requirements under which Albuquerque could operate its plant. The City of Albuquerque, wanting to avoid compliance with Isleta Pueblos' standards, filed suit against the EPA. The lawsuit challenged the EPA's approval of Isleta Pueblos' water quality standards and their application to an off-reservation entity.[12]

While some aspects of Albuquerque's claim were procedural, the main thrust of the lawsuit attacked Isleta Pueblo's ability to set its own standards for water flowing through its reservation. Albuquerque argued that the Pueblo could not set standards higher than those required by federal law, and that those standards could not apply to an upstream user that was outside of the tribal reservation boundaries. These questions had been settled in favor of the downstream entity with respect to states and upstream users, and so in essence Albuquerque was arguing that tribal inherent authority to determine reservation water quality was less than that of states.[13] The lawsuit named the EPA because the EPA designates tribes as states under the CWA and tribes themselves are immune from suit, but the essence of the claims attempted to undermine a crucial aspect of sovereignty: the ability to determine minimum standards for the reservation environment. The Tenth Circuit ruled in favor of the EPA on all issues, thereby affirming the Pueblos' sovereignty in this respect.

Montana v EPA

As in *Albuquerque v Browner*, this case involves the EPA's decision to grant TAS status to a tribe. Here, the objection to tribal authority to regulate water quality came from on-reservation non-Indian landowners.[14]

In 1992, the Confederated Salish and Kootenai Tribes applied for TAS status to regulate water quality within the boundaries of the Flathead Reservation. As the federal appellate court put it, the Flathead Reservation is notable for two reasons: the presence of Flathead Lake and the large amount of non-Indian-owned land within reservation boundaries (referred to as "non-Indian fee land").[15] The State of Montana and several counties and municipalities (hereafter "Montana et al.") are among the non-Indians who own fee land within the Flathead Reservation. Montana et al. have NPDES permits to discharge waste into Flathead Lake and other waterways within the reservation. If the Tribes established more stringent water quality standards through their TAS status, the requirements of these NPDES permits would be altered.

Montana et al. opposed the granting of TAS status to the Tribes. The EPA nonetheless granted that status to the Tribes, including recognizing the Tribes' inherent power to regulate non-Indian landowners. Montana et al. then filed suit in federal district court, challenging the EPA's TAS designation and contending that the Tribes lack the authority to regulate non-Indian landowners. The plaintiffs based their arguments on a previous case arising out of a conflict between non-Indian landowners and a Montana Indian tribe, *Montana v United States (Montana I)*.[16] In that case, the U.S. Supreme Court held that

Indian tribes lack the inherent power to regulate non-Indians on non-Indian fee land within the boundaries of a reservation, unless the non-Indian has a consensual relationship with the tribe or the non-Indian behavior threatens or has a direct effect upon tribal health or welfare. Operating in the shadow of the Supreme Court's *Montana I* opinion, the EPA conducts its own review of whether a tribe can demonstrate that the regulated activity meets the *Montana I* tribal health and welfare exception. Indeed, as the Ninth Circuit determined in *Montana v EPA*, the EPA's review is more exacting than the Supreme Court's opinion requires.[17] The EPA requires a showing that the "impairment of waters would have a serious and substantial effect on the health and welfare of the tribe."[18] Based on this review, the Ninth Circuit upheld the Salish and Kootenai Tribes' TAS designation, including the finding by the EPA that the Tribes have inherent authority to regulate non-Indian owners of fee land within the reservation.

ENVIRONMENTAL JUSTICE ASSESSMENT

Fortunately for both the Pueblo of Isleta and the Confederated Salish and Kootenai Tribes, the federal courts determined that the EPA did not exceed its authority in approving TAS status in either case. But the challenges posed by the City of Albuquerque and Montana et al. were potent ones, going to the very heart of tribal self-governance. In addition, in both cases the tribes were attempting to heighten environmental quality. Thus, these are easy cases, not in the legal sense but in the sense that they are easy to describe as examples of attempts to perpetrate environmental injustice in Indian country. They involve attacks on tribal sovereignty in the context of environmental regulation—in particular, regulation that is more stringent than that of the surrounding non-Indian lands. Had the plaintiffs in these cases succeeded, tribes would be deprived of the sovereign authority to improve their reservation environments.

While these cases may seem far afield from the discriminatory siting cases that ignited the environmental justice movement, they should be recognized as environmental injustices on a par with placing a hazardous waste dump in an African American community. Indian tribes fought for a long time to be included in the environmental regulatory scheme. Now that they are exercising their sovereign powers under environmental statutes, they must often undergo a second struggle litigating against hostile landowners and upstream polluters. Indian tribes must be permitted to get on with the business of cleaning up the (often desecrated) lands that they have been granted, either by treaty or statute. To prohibit them from doing so by attacking their status as sovereigns is to perpetrate environmental injustice.

Harder Cases: Tribal Land Use Decisions

Environmental justice concerns lurk in tribal land use decisions, but they are not the obvious ones. As noted earlier, some articles cite disparate siting of waste dumps as an environmental justice problem in Indian country, but the situations vary a great deal and, depending on the facts, may or may not present environmental justice issues according to the definition proposed in this chapter. Below, I discuss two well-known examples of tribal attempts to site unpopular projects on tribal lands. The first is a landfill proposed by the Campo Band of Mission Indians. The second is the Rosebud Sioux Tribe's contract with a factory hog farm.

Campo Band of Mission Indians' Proposed Landfill

The Campo Band resides on a small reservation in eastern California. The reservation, which is not the Campos' traditional homeland, is devoid of any features that would make it attractive for agriculture, gaming, or tourism—economic development that other tribes have engaged in successfully.[19] The Campos undertook to contract with a solid waste disposal company to site a landfill on their reservation. The proposal received unanimous support from tribal members but drew vehement opposition from the Band's mostly white neighbors, who formed the opposition group Backcountry Citizens Against Dumps (BAD).

As with the TAS cases discussed earlier, when the opponents of the Campo project got into high gear, they attacked not just the project itself but the tribe's sovereign authority. BAD enlisted a state assembly member to push through legislation that would subject the Campo landfill to state regulation. The legislators knew that it would be difficult, if not impossible, to draft a law subjecting the Tribe's dump to state regulation that would withstand federal court scrutiny, but they persisted nonetheless. The legislative battle cost all sides enormous amounts of time and money. Ultimately, the factions reached a compromise that required tribes to enter into cooperative agreements with the state regarding regulation and oversight of landfills. Indeed, all along, the Campos intended to regulate their proposed dump in a manner consistent with, or more stringent than, California requirements.[20]

The battle regarding the landfill did not stop with the legislative compromise, however. BAD continued to fight the landfill at every possible turn. They were joined by San Diego County, which had an interest in limiting competition in the solid waste disposal business.[21] The county filed a lawsuit in federal court, alleging violations of the National Environmental Policy Act (NEPA), which was unsuccessful.[22] BAD lobbied Secretary of the Interior Bruce Babbitt not to approve the lease for the landfill. This too was unsuccessful. BAD also filed a lawsuit alleging that the EPA lacks the authority under the Resource Conservation and Recovery Act (RCRA)[23] to issue permits to tribes for their solid waste plans.[24] BAD prevailed on this issue, but the result for the Tribe was not adverse in terms of its impact on tribal sovereignty. The court found that while the EPA lacks authority under RCRA to treat tribes as states for permitting purposes, tribes retain their own sovereign authority to authorize and regulate landfills in tribal territory.[25]

Despite winning many of the skirmishes, the Campos still face a number of challenges. The original corporation that sought to site the landfill, Mid-American, withdrew from the project. Meanwhile, as required by the Clean Air Act, the Tribe has received an air permit from the EPA and has been given a one-year extension by the agency to find a new vendor.[26] While no other regulatory hurdles stand in the way of the landfill, the non-Indian neighbors may still have won a war of attrition.

ENVIRONMENTAL JUSTICE ASSESSMENT

It is very tempting to label the general phenomenon of waste companies approaching Indian tribes as an environmental justice problem. There is no doubt that these companies seek out places where they think there will be little opposition and where they hope there will be minimal environmental regulation.[27] The waste companies could be described as perpetually attempting to *perpetrate* an environmental injustice. But the Campo example teaches that each case involving a tribal decision must be assessed individually to determine if an environmental injustice in fact occurs. The Campos were well informed. They made a decision to regulate the landfill with operating and monitoring requirements that would be more stringent than those that would have been required by the state. The Campos were not, by the unanimous consent of their members, being duped by the waste industry, and the Campos' stringent regulations ensured that the waste industry was not permitted to exploit a regulatory loophole. Thus, there does not appear to be an environmental justice issue with respect to the Campos' decision to attempt to site a landfill on their reservation. Some might argue that there is an environmental justice issue with respect to the impacts of the proposed landfill on the non-Indian neighbors, who contend that their groundwater is at risk and whose interests were not represented. But the members of BAD were predominately white ranchers, who do not belong to a disempowered group. As explained by Getches and Pellow in Chapter 1, there are dangers to defining environmental justice too broadly, as might be the case if the ranchers were included here.

There is a justice issue here, however. As discussed earlier, justice for tribes requires the protection of tribal sovereignty. In opposing the landfill, BAD attacked the Campo Band's sovereignty by attempting to get the California legislature to pass a law subjecting tribes involuntarily to state regulation. The Campo case exemplifies tribal vulnerability in the environmental context—whether tribes are elevating environmental standards, as in the TAS cases, or attempting to engage in economic development that has the potential to degrade the environment, non-Indian opponents resort to the tactic of stripping tribes of their powers of self-governance.

The tendency of non-Indian opponents of tribal projects to fight the projects by attacking tribal self-governance underscores the need to define environmental justice problems carefully in Indian country. If the very fact that a tribe is considering an undesirable land use constitutes an environmental justice issue for the tribe, then non-Indians may feel justified in attacking tribal self-governance "for the tribe's own good." While the non-Indian community may attack the project or the tribe, or both, regardless, they should not be able to convince themselves that undermining sovereignty is in the tribe's best interests. To allow them to do so only obscures their objectives, which are to halt the project irrespective of tribal interests.

More constructively, if non-Indian opponents of tribal projects are sensitized to the importance of tribal sovereignty, they may fight undesirable land uses in more fruitful ways. Several participants in, and observers of, the Campo situation speculate that BAD could have influenced the tribal decision had they not started by assuming the incompetence of the Tribe.[28] Indeed, several groups who work nationally to oppose the siting of locally undesirable land uses (LULUs) on Indian reservations recognize the importance of supporting tribal sovereignty, and therefore they support only tactics that either work within the tribe's democratic process or invoke the federal judiciary without making sovereignty an issue.[29]

In sum, the Campo case highlights the need for a nuanced environmental justice analysis in Indian country. What at first appears to be an environmental justice issue, because it involves potential degradation of tribal lands, may not be one, because tribal self-determination remains intact. Casting such a tribal decision as an environmental injustice obscures the nature of the battle and may open the door to attacks on tribal sovereignty.

Rosebud Sioux Tribe's Proposed Hog Farm

The Rosebud Sioux Tribe, like the Campo Band, is located in a remote, arid region that is devoid of most forms of economic development. Bell Farms, a North Dakota corporation, approached the Tribe and proposed to contract with them to run a factory-style hog farm on tribal land. The proposed site was to be located outside of the current reservation boundaries, and most, though not all, of the neighbors were non-Indian ranchers.

As proposed, the hog farm would eventually house up to 895,000 pigs, making it the third largest hog farm in the world. The NEPA applies to any major project on tribal lands that may have significant environmental effects, and the statute requires federal agencies to disclose to the public the possible environmental impacts of such projects. Often, the first step in the NEPA process is for the lead agency to conduct an environmental assessment. If the environmental assessment yields a "finding of no significant impact," then the NEPA process is complete. If the lead agency determines that there may be significant impacts, then the agency must prepare an environmental impact statement, which requires more detail, scientific evaluation, and a consideration of less environmentally harmful alternatives. An environmental impact statement also requires the opportunity for public comment.

As discussed in detail by Dean Suagee in Chapter 10, the lead agency for NEPA implementation when a project is on tribal lands is the Interior Department's Bureau of Indian Affairs (BIA). The BIA conducted an environmental assessment concerning the proposed hog farm and, despite concerns about potential groundwater contamination, air pollution, and desecration of historic and sacred sites, made a finding of no significant impact.[30] A significant number of tribal members opposed the project, but the 1998 tribal council nonetheless voted to approve the lease to Sun Prairie, a subsidiary of Bell Farms. Before the hog farm opponents could file suit or seek further administrative review, Sun Prairie began construction and completed the first phase of the hog facility, which was roughly one-third of the total project.

Shortly thereafter, several groups, one including some tribal members, filed suit in federal district court in the District of Columbia against Secretary of the Interior Bruce Babbitt and Assistant Secretary for Indian Affairs Kevin Gover alleging procedural and substantive inadequacies in the environmental assessment.[31] They requested a temporary restraining order and permanent injunction to halt the construction of the hog facility, arguing that the BIA's approval of the lease violated the NEPA.

Before the D.C. lawsuit was resolved on the merits, Gover voided the lease for lack of environmental compliance. Gover conceded that the BIA had failed to consider the environmental, cultural, and historic impacts. Then, in a twist imaginable only in the context of American Indian litigation, a federal district court judge in South Dakota determined that Gover's actions exceeded his authority and enjoined the assistant secretary from invalidating the lease. In his decision, Judge Charles Kornmann accused Gover and the BIA of undermining tribal sovereignty by making it impossible for businesses to rely upon tribal agreements.[32]

Tribal members who opposed the hog farm made it an issue in the ensuing tribal elections, voting in a new tribal chairman, William Kindle, who promised to put the issue to tribal voters in a referendum. Kindle promised that if the referendum showed overwhelming opposition, the tribe would consider canceling the lease.[33] Kindle acknowledged that cancellation could be very costly financially to the Rosebud Sioux Tribe, but he did not rule it out on those grounds. Kindle also voiced disappointment that Bell Farms's promise of bringing 240 jobs to the reservation went unfulfilled. He estimated that only ten out of approximately thirty employees at the partially constructed facility were tribal members.[34]

ENVIRONMENTAL JUSTICE ASSESSMENT

In this example, the predominant barrier to the Rosebud Sioux Tribe's ability to control the reservation environment was the BIA. The BIA's skimpy environmental assessment and finding of no significant impact failed to adequately inform the Tribe and its members about the potential consequences of siting the third largest hog farm in the country on tribal lands. The fact that several states have recently passed initiatives requiring heightened regulation of factory-style hog farms precisely due to their enormous potential for air and water contamination highlights the BIA's laxity in this area.[35] Thus, the environmental justice issue here is not the probable impacts on the community surrounding the hog farm, most of whom are non-Indian ranchers. For those neighbors, there is certainly a potent *environmen-*

tal issue. The environmental *justice* issue here is the BIA's failure to carry out its responsibilities to the Tribe under the NEPA, thereby undermining the Tribe's ability to govern itself or regulate its own environment in an informed manner. This failure set in motion an eventual no-win situation, resulting in the bizarre scenario of Kevin Gover's unilateral cancellation of the lease while Justice Department lawyers representing Gover's department defended the BIA's actions in court.[36]

Another factor raising environmental justice concerns is the disparity between what Bell Farms promised the Rosebud Sioux Tribe in terms of employment opportunities and the apparent reality. As noted in the Campo example, it is not helpful to generalize about the inability of tribes to make informed decisions simply because they are hard-pressed economically. But if non-Indian businesses are dealing dishonestly with tribes in an attempt to persuade them to site environmentally questionable projects on tribal lands, then tribes are not able to consider all of the factors relevant to a jobs-environment trade-off. Tribal self-determination could therefore be undermined in a context that could result in the degradation of environmental quality. According to this chapter's proposed definition, corporate deception could lead to environmental injustice.

Like the Campo case, the Rosebud example highlights the importance of examining the details of proposed facility sitings in order to determine whether such sitings implicate environmental justice concerns. Here, the impacts of the proposed hog farm are salient, but they become an environmental justice issue only by virtue of the BIA's failure to convey them to the Tribe. As Suagee points out in Chapter 10, the failure to enforce the NEPA in Indian country is an environmental justice problem of proportions even larger than the third largest hog farm. The inadequacy of the BIA's environmental review process fails to assist tribes in acquiring the information necessary to make informed decisions about the reservation environment. This constitutes an environmental injustice, albeit a very bureaucratic one.

The Rule That Swallows the Exceptions?

Having discussed several cases at a microlevel, it is now important to step back and look at environmental justice in Indian country from a broader perspective. If environmental justice for tribes involves the ability to control and improve the tribal environment, then we need to look at the context in which tribes exercise that control. That context is very constrained. Tribes are not arms-length transactors in a free market. To the contrary, their market has been diminished and their arms have been twisted by a history of colonialism and broken treaties. Lands that were promised were taken away.[37] The government has failed, repeatedly, to exercise its trust responsibility to manage and oversee Indian lands and resources.[38] In sum, many Indian tribes lack the land, infrastructure, and resources to make unfettered choices about economic development.

From this perspective, it might be impossible to say that Indian tribes ever actually control the reservation environment. Consequently, any decision that tribes make that degrades the environment might be described as an environmental justice issue because, in some sense, tribes do not have control. When they "choose" to undertake economic development that pollutes their land, water, and air, they are not choosing freely. They are constrained by a history of disenfranchisement and a present economic system based on excessive consumption.

But Indian tribes might respond in the following ways. They might argue that this view leads to paternalism, in that every tribal land use decision could be subject to environmental review by non-Indians who claim to know better. Tribes might also respond that such a view is borne of theoretical or academic perfectionism at the expense of sovereignty in the imperfect here and now. While it is true, as a matter of historical and political record, that tribes operate in a very constrained environment, focusing on those constraints alone does not alleviate the problem. If we accept the norm of promoting tribal existence, then we need to find ways to assist tribes as they eke out greater degrees of environmental control. Otherwise, the norm of environmental protection would always trump the norm of tribal sovereignty, even in the environmental justice context. The self-determination component of environmental justice would evaporate, and environmental justice would be just another way of promoting environmentalism.

Furthermore, to focus on the ways in which tribes are exercising their sovereignty to degrade the environment is to misconceive the bulk of what goes on in Indian country. The Mescalero Apaches consider siting a nuclear waste facility, and newspapers leap on the story. The Campo Band and the Rosebud Sioux Tribe consider dumps and hog farms, and scholars (now including myself among the guilty) fly to their keyboards. But many attempts to site environmentally questionable projects on Indian reservations have been successfully opposed by grass-roots groups of tribal members, working from within their tribal governments.[39] Moreover, many tribes are also getting down to the serious, tedious, not particularly headline-getting business of creating their own environmental protection agencies. Tribes are also taking care of the environment in ways that build upon their cultural and religious traditions.[40] Focusing on the environmentally problematic choices some tribes make might cause one to miss the ways in which tribes are seizing control of their reservation environments in order to make improvements, and are, according to the definition proposed here, therefore operationalizing environmental justice in Indian country.

At the same time, it would be naïve to ignore the constraints within which tribes operate. The tension tribes presently face between viable economic development opportunities and sound environmental practices is a product of those constraints. But the solution is not to subsume all exercises of tribal authority that are inconsistent with environmental protection goals into the category of environmental injustice. Such a response would lead too easily to actions that would undermine tribal sovereignty, which would undermine justice for tribal members. Environmentalists should not necessarily shy away from condemning antienvironmental actions by Indian tribes. It could, in fact, be a sign of respect for tribes as governments to level the same kinds of criticisms at them as one levels at county, state, and federal governments. But criticizing tribal governments and attempting to remove from them their governmental status are two distinct actions. The environmental justice framework, with its emphasis on self-determination, cannot be used to justify the latter.

The Garbage Problem

Let us return to the hospital refuse, swirling plastic bags, leaking oil cans, and decaying mattresses that despoil so many otherwise breathtaking reservation landscapes. This problem captures the complex nature of environmental injustice in Indian country. It is a product of the unique jurisdictional status that tribes occupy. But it is also a function of the constraints placed on tribal life that were discussed in the previous section. And only an environmental justice solution—the strengthening of tribal authority over the reservation such that tribes can improve the environment—can solve the problem.

RCRA establishes the framework for the disposal of hazardous and solid waste. With respect to hazardous waste, RCRA creates a comprehensive federal program for all aspects of handling and disposal. The EPA administers the hazardous waste program, although it can delegate the responsibility to states. With respect to solid waste,

RCRA gives states the main regulatory role. States develop their own solid waste plans, consistent with federal guidelines, and the EPA provides financial assistance. The EPA does not administer federal permits for solid waste disposal, nor does the EPA have any direct enforcement authority unless there is an imminent threat to health or the environment.[41]

Indian tribes are defined as "municipalities" under RCRA, leaving them in a regulatory void when it comes to establishing their own solid waste disposal programs.[42] If tribes were defined as states, they would be eligible for the same economic assistance as states. As "municipalities," they can apply for federal funding, but the reality is that the EPA lacks the resources and the staff to assist tribes. Most tribes that have developed comprehensive waste management plans have done so without federal financial or technical assistance.[43]

The EPA began to address this problem, issuing proposed rules that would allow tribes to apply to the EPA for approval of solid waste programs. The Campo Band was one of two tribes to apply for such approval.[44] One of the court decisions that emerged from the Campo landfill battle, however, invalidated EPA approval of tribal solid waste plans. The federal appellate court for the District of Columbia determined that the EPA had exceeded its authority under RCRA when it treated the Campo Band as a state. Federal agencies are generally given deference to interpret statutes in accordance with their purposes. But the court determined that, on its face, RCRA prohibited defining tribes as states because they were already defined as municipalities.[45]

The court also noted, however, that tribes retain inherent sovereignty to establish and maintain their own solid waste management plans. The court minimized the importance of TAS status under RCRA, contending that the operators of landfills in Indian country remain subject to RCRA's criteria for solid waste facilities in that they are subject to citizen suits under the statute if they are out of compliance.[46] Furthermore, tribes themselves are subject to citizen suits under RCRA.[47] The court is correct in these observations, but the reality is that until tribes can be treated as states under RCRA, there will continue to be a regulatory void as a practical matter. Most tribes will be unable, financially and technically, to create adequate solid waste disposal systems for their reservation lands without assistance from the federal government.

Moreover, tribes will be likely to encounter inherent conflicts of interest in establishing their regulatory programs until they receive EPA funding. The Campo case provides another object lesson in this regard. The Campos had the funding and technical assistance necessary to establish their environmental programs by virtue of their contract with the solid waste disposal company that intended to establish the landfill. With no disparagement to the tribal leaders who implemented the program, it would be impossible for them to avoid at least the specter of undue influence under those circumstances.[48]

Tribes are thus hampered in their efforts to control the reservation environment due to legislative language that results in a regulatory void. It is an environmental justice issue for tribes and tribal members that Congress contributes to the garbage problem in this way. The garbage problem on reservations is further compounded by historical and economic circumstances. Only recently has the EPA been available, even in the very limited way described above, to provide any assistance to tribes with respect to solid waste disposal.[49] For decades, the regulatory vacuum was unmitigated. Any entity operating on the reservation, including the Indian Health Service, had no incentive to clean up its own waste. In addition, as reservations became barraged with consumer products, tribes themselves had no money or infrastructure to create adequate disposal systems. The problem is further compounded by the very rural nature of most reservations and the poverty levels of tribal members. Even if there were private commercial waste disposal companies operating on reservations, most tribal members could not afford them. Due to these factors, most reservations are pockmarked by open dumps, official and unofficial.[50]

The solution to this environmental injustice involves strengthening tribal governments so that they can control and improve their reservation environments. One solution would be to amend RCRA so that tribes are eligible for treatment as states. Another approach would be to create a division within the EPA's tribal programs office that deals exclusively with providing technical and financial support to tribes interested in developing comprehensive waste management plans. A third approach is for grass-roots groups on reservations to organize and demand that their tribal governments prioritize the problem of solid waste disposal.[51] Whichever avenue is pursued, it must be one that provides tribes with the means and incentives to address this problem themselves, without being dependent upon the opportunistic largesse of private industry or the wavering, and often unwilling, commitments of states. In sum, the garbage problem, which embodies the nature of environmental justice in Indian country, can only be solved by recognizing and promoting tribal self-governance in the broadest sense.

Conclusion

Any account of environmental injustice in Indian country must confront the complex nature of tribal sovereignty. Because justice for tribal peoples requires support for tribes as distinct political entities, any definition of environmental justice must include the norm of tribal sovereignty. This is particularly important because of the paradoxical nature of tribal sovereignty: on the one hand, tribal sovereignty predates that of the federal or state governments and therefore requires no validation; on the other hand, as a practical matter the contours of tribal sovereignty are constantly being negotiated in this country's courts and legislatures. In other words, tribal sovereignty is sacrosanct yet entirely vulnerable. Its vulnerability calls for vigilant defense.

The cases discussed in this chapter provide examples of tribal vulnerability in the environmental context. A close examination of these cases, in light of the environmental justice principles discussed in Chapter 1, allows us to develop the contours of environmental justice in the tribal setting.

The *Browner* and *Montana* cases highlight the obstacles tribes face when they attempt to use their sovereign powers to improve their reservation environments. When tribes attempt to raise the standards for reservation water quality, opponents attack not just the standards themselves but the tribes' rights to set and enforce them. These are clear examples of environmental injustice in the tribal setting.

When tribes engage in the decision-making process over when and whether to site environmentally problematic projects on reservation lands, the analysis is more complicated. Such cases must be examined carefully in order to identify whether there are any environmental justice concerns for tribes. I conclude, for example, that the Campo case does not present an environmental justice issue at all. There are, in the Campo case, issues concerning whether non-Indians should attack tribal sovereignty (justice issues for the Tribe) and issues concerning the problem of siting waste facilities generally (environmental issues for the non-Indian neighbors), but there is no combination of the two. The factors leading to this conclusion include (1) the absence of any evidence that the Campo Band was misled or ill informed; and (2) the absence of any evidence, due to the Band's proposed stringent environmental regulation of the landfill, of the waste company taking advantage of a regulatory loophole. In the Rosebud example, the environmental justice issue consists of the BIA's inadequate environmental assessment and its consequent failure to inform the tribe of potential environmental hazards. Another issue raising environmental justice concerns is the possibility that the corporate hog farm misled tribal leaders about economic benefits. Both of these actions may have prevented the tribe from making a fully informed decision about how and whether to make a jobs-environment trade-off.

The garbage problem provides a useful example of the pervasiveness (literally) of the unique brand of environmental injustice for tribes and tribal peoples. A complex combination of legislative oversight, regulatory insufficiency, and historic and economic deprivation contributes to this environmental hazard for tribes. There is no single evil actor, and the solution therefore does not lie in sanctioning or scaring off one entity. Rather, the solution lies in supporting tribes to overcome both the historical and present causes of their deprivation.

The problems discussed herein are not the only examples of the unique nature of environmental justice in Indian Country. The depletion of natural resources, such as salmon in the Northwest, has singular effects on tribes whose cultures and livelihood depend upon them. Mining has ravaged reservation lands, and cleanup has often been delayed due to the unique sovereign status of tribes. The space permitted by this chapter is insufficient to account for all of the ways in which tribes face environmental challenges that affect their self-determination.

What the examples discussed herein share with those omitted is the broad nature of the environmental justice solution for tribes. This includes strengthening tribes' abilities to address their own environmental problems. In some instances, as in the garbage example, federal assistance or statutory amendments may be required. In others, as in the CWA examples, the federal government must be prepared to defend vigorously the environmental self-determination that tribes already have. In many cases, tribes and tribal members must struggle with prioritizing environmental health over pressing needs for economic development. In this way, environmental justice for tribes dovetails with the larger goal of sustainability that Gary Bryner discusses in Chapter 2. But, to be consistent with environmental justice norms as herein defined, those struggles must remain within Indian country communities. They should not be short-circuited by non-Indians who attempt to strip tribes of their powers of self-government. The solutions, in other words, are varied and complex. Nevertheless, they all share the simple and long-held American norm of respecting pluralism in a deep sense—a sense that allows distinct and ancient cultures to flourish and adapt simultaneously, so that they may retain their past without sacrificing their futures, environmentally or otherwise.

Acknowledgments

I am grateful to the Natural Resources Law Center for sponsoring this project. Kathryn Mutz deserves particular recognition for riding herd on all of us, providing useful edits, and maintaining good humor throughout. Thanks also to Jennifer Kemp for excellent research assistance.

Notes

1. See, e.g., Olga L. Moya, "Adopting an Environmental Justice Ethic," *Dickinson Journal of Environmental Law and Policy* (1996): 215, 225–26, listing proposed waste sitings on two Indian reservations as instances of environmental injustice; Adam Swartz, "Environment Justice: A Survey of the Ailments of Environmental Racism," *Howard Scripps Social Justice Review* 2 (1993): 35, 39; and Robert D. Bullard, "Environmental Justice for All: It's the Right Thing to Do," *Journal of Environmental Law* 9 (1994): 281, 302, describing targeting of tribes by solid and hazardous companies as environmental injustices.
2. Dean Suagee's scholarship is a prominent exception to this rule. See, e.g., Dean B. Suagee, "The Indian Country Environmental Justice Clinic: From Vision to Reality," *Vermont Law Review* 23 (1999): 567; and Dean B. Suagee, "Turtle's War Party: An Indian Allegory on Environmental Justice," *Journal of Environmental Law and Litigation* 9 (1994): 461.
3. See *Meyers v Board of Educ. of San Juan School Dist.*, 905 F. Supp. 1544 (D. Utah 1995).
4. *United States v Mazurie*, 419 U.S. 544 (1975).
5. See *Johnson v McIntosh*, 21 U.S. (8 Wheat) 543 (1823); *Cherokee Nation v Georgia*, 30 U.S. (5 Pet.) 1 (1831); *Worcester v Georgia*, 31 U.S. (6 Pet.) 515 (1832); and *Williams v Lee*, 358 U.S. 217 (1959).
6. *Worcester v Georgia; Lone Wolf v Hitchcock*, 187 U.S. 553 (1903).
7. See *Oliphant v Suquamish Indian Tribe*, 435 U.S. 191 (1978) (criminal jurisdiction over non-Indians is inconsistent with tribes' dependent status); *Montana v United States*, 450 U.S. 544 (1981) (no tribal civil jurisdiction over non-Indians on non-Indian fee land within reservation boundaries, unless direct threat to tribal welfare or consensual relationship with tribe); *Strate v A-1 Contractors*, 519 U.S. 1038 (1996) (extending *Montana v United States* to state right of ways within reservations); and *Nevada v Hicks*, 121 S.Ct. 2304 (2001) (extending *Montana* to tribal trust land).
8. See, e.g., Robert Williams, *The American Indian in Western Legal Thought: The Discourses of Conquest* (New York: Oxford University Press, 1990), which describes and critiques the colonialist origins of federal Indian law.

9. John Fredericks, "America's First Nations: The Origins, History and Future of American Indian Sovereignty," *Journal of Law and Policy* 7 (1999): 347.

10. Vine Deloria Jr., *Custer Died for Your Sins: An Indian Manifesto* (New York: Macmillan, 1969); Vine Deloria Jr., *American Indians, American Justice* (Austin: University of Texas Press, 1983).

11. See, e.g., Clean Air Act, U.S.C., sec. 1377; Clean Water Act, 42 U.S.C., sec. 7410(o); and Comprehensive Environmental Response, Compensation and Liability Act, 42 U.S.C., sec. 9607(a)(4)(A); see also David F. Coursen, "Tribes as States: Indian Tribal Authority to Regulate and Enforce Federal Environmental Law and Regulations," *Environmental Law Reporter* 23 (1993): 10579, reviewing environmental statutes authorizing the EPA to treat tribes as states.

12. *Albuquerque v Browner*, 97 F.3d 415 (10th Cir. 1996).

13. *Albuquerque v Browner*, 424. See also *Arkansas v Oklahoma*, 503 U.S. 91, 102 (1992).

14. *Montana v Environmental Protection Agency*, 137 F.3d 1135 (9th Cir. 1998).

15. *Montana v EPA*, 1139.

16. 450 U.S. 544 (1981).

17. See *Montana v EPA*.

18. Environmental Protection Agency, "Final Rule, Amendments to the Water Quality Standards Regulation That Pertain to Standards on Indian Reservations," 56 *Federal Register* 64879 (1991).

19. See Dan McGovern, *The Campo Indian Landfill War: The Fight for Gold in California's Garbage* (Norman: University of Oklahoma Press, 1995), 105–10, reporting that in 1987, when the Campos first began to consider the landfill, the tribal unemployment rate was 79 percent and the tribal budget was fifteen thousand dollars, derived mostly from sand mining and leases for cattle grazing.

20. See McGovern, *The Campo Indian Landfill War*, 120–66, for a detailed account of the legislative battle and ultimate compromise, and 179–84, for a discussion of proposed dump regulations.

21. McGovern, *The Campo Indian Landfill War*, 112–19.

22. 42 U.S.C., sec. 4332.

23. 42 U.S.C., secs. 6901–6992k.

24. *Backcountry Against Dumps v EPA*, 100 F.3d 147 (D.C. Cir. 1996).

25. *Backcountry Against Dumps v EPA*.

26. Phone Conversation with Brian Conley, Campo EPA, July 5, 2000.

27. See McGovern, *The Campo Indian Landfill War*, 27–54.

28. See McGovern, *The Campo Indian Landfill War*, 240–46.

29. See McGovern, *The Campo Indian Landfill War*, 240–46 (Sierra Club's national policy is to support tribal sovereignty; Greenpeace provides support only to tribal members opposing tribal projects) and 52–53 (quoting Tom Goldtooth, chair of the Indigenous Environmental Network, as being in full support of tribal member opposition to LULUs but nonetheless respectful of tribal sovereignty.)

30. See RESPEC, *Environmental Assessment for Proposed Pork Production Facility*, prepared for the Rosebud Sioux Tribe and the BIA (August 1998); and "Judge Says Hog Farm Can Proceed," *Omaha World-Herald*, April 5, 1999, available in 1999 WL 4494327.

31. Concerned Rosebud Area Citizens v Babbitt, 34 F. Supp. 2d 775 (D.D.C. 1999).

32. "Judge Says Hog Farm Can Proceed"; Rosebud Sioux Tribe v Gover, 104 F. Supp. 2d 1194 (D. S.D., February 3, 2000).

33. "Rosebud, S.D. Council Considers Referendum on Hog Farm," *Indian Country Today*, March 31, 2000, available at 2000 WL 17762296. The election took place on May 25, 2000, and tribal members voted not to expand the lease. The council has not yet decided how to respond. "Rosebud Hog Farm Under Fire," *Associated Press Newswires*, June 21, 2000, available in 6/21/00 APWIRES 16:58:00.

34. "Rosebud, S.D. Council Considers Referendum on Hog Farm."

35. See, e.g., Colorado Revised Statutes, secs. 25-7-138, 25-8-501.1, 25-8-504 (1998); Iowa Code Annotated, sec. 455B.161 et seq. (West 1995); N.C. General Statutes, sec. 106-800 et seq. See also Peter T. Kilborn, "N. Carolina Awash in Animal Waste After Hurricane Floyd," *Plain Dealer*, October 17, 1999, available in 1999 WL 2387622; "Animal Waste Threatens N.C. Water, Hurricane Floyd Reveals Flaws in State's Environmental Laws," *Star-Tribune*, November 25, 1999, available at 1999 WL 7519514 (describing water contamination in North Carolina after hurricanes caused factory hog farms' lagoons to overflow into water supplies).

36. "Judge Says Hog Farm Can Proceed."

37. See, e.g., Edward Lazarus, *Black Hills, White Justice: The Sioux Nation versus the United States, 1775 to the Present* (New York: Harper Collins, 1991).

38. See Nell Jessup Newton, "Indian Claims in the Courts of the Conqueror," *American University Law Review* 41 (1992): 753; and *Cobell v Babbitt*, 91 F. Supp. 2d 1 (D. D.C. 1999) (Indian plaintiffs allege century of mismanagement of Indian trust funds by BIA, resulting in multimillion-dollar losses).

39. McGovern, *The Campo Indian Landfill War*, 51–53.

40. See Rebecca Tsosie, "Tribal Environmental Policy in an Era of Self-Determination," *Vermont Law Review* 21 (1996): 225, 287–301.

41. 42 U.S.C., secs. 6901–6992k.

42. 42 U.S.C., sec. 6903 (13).

43. Suagee, *Turtle's War Party*, 477, citing to Indian Lands Open Dump Cleanup Act of 1994, H.R. Rep. No. 783, 103rd Cong., 2nd sess. 8 (1994).

44. "Campo Band of Mission Indians; Tentative Adequacy Determination of Tribal Municipal Solid Waste Permit Program," 59 *Federal Register* 24422 (1994); "Cheyenne River Sioux Tribe; Tentative Adequacy Determination of Tribal Municipal Solid Waste Permit Program," 59 *Federal Register* 16642 (1994); "Campo Band of Mission Indians Final Determination of Adequacy," 60 *Federal Register* 21191 (1995).

45. *Backcountry Against Dumps v EPA*.

46. *Backcountry Against Dumps v EPA*, 152, citing to 42 U.S.C., sec. 6972.

47. *Backcountry Against Dumps v EPA*, citing to *Blue Legs v U.S. Bureau of Indian Affairs*, 867 F.2d 1094 (8th Cir. 1989).

48. See McGovern, *The Campo Indian Landfill War*, 36–38, in which a Greenpeace leader labels the problem an "on-its-face" conflict and assumes that the tribal EPA will provide no enforcement.

49. See Barry Hill and Nicholas Targ's discussion of equal treatment and opportunity for benefits under environmental laws in Chapter 12.

50. Suagee, *Turtle's War Party*, 477–78, discussing problem of open dumps on reservations and citing the Indian Lands Open Dump Cleanup Act of 1994 as a recent attempt to address the problem. Legislative history to the act indicates that there are anywhere from 600 to 1,500 open dumps on reservations. Suagee, *Turtle's War Party*, n. 53, citing to H.R. Rep. No. 783, 103rd Cong., 2nd Sess. 6–7 (1994). That estimate is probably quite low. On most reservations, there are many unofficial dumps that do not receive any monitoring at all. See, e.g., *Chischiligi v Jones*, Navajo Nation District Court, Window Rock District, a lawsuit against the Navajo Nation alleging violations of Navajo common law for the Nation's failure to address solid waste disposal problems throughout the reservation, citing numerous unofficial open dumps as part of the problem.

51. The *Chischiligi* case provides an example of such intratribal activism. Navajo plaintiffs, represented by DNA-People's Legal Services, are suing the Navajo Nation in Navajo tribal courts, basing their arguments on breaches of Navajo common law. They are therefore holding their government accountable without attacking their government's sovereign status.

Part Three

STRATEGIES AND APPLICATIONS

Chapter 8

EXPANDING CIVIL RIGHTS PROTECTIONS IN CONTESTED TERRAIN

Using Title VI of the Civil Rights Act of 1964

Luke W. Cole

In the past twenty years, the intersection between civil rights violations and environmental degradation has become both clearer and more contested. It has been unequivocally demonstrated, in dozens of empirical studies, that certain environmental hazards are inequitably distributed by race—some locally, some regionally, and some nationally.[1] As people of color have come to understand this disparate impact, they have increasingly described it as a civil rights violation and sought to invoke civil rights laws to challenge it.[2]

As the intersection between civil rights and the environment has become clearer, however, the stakes have grown higher for those interests potentially affected by the application of civil rights laws to environmental disputes—people of color, industry, and state and local governments. As people of color affected by environmental hazards allege civil rights violations, government agencies and industry have responded by aggressively lobbying for rollback of civil rights laws in the environmental context, or a narrowing of the coverage of such laws to exclude most complained-of situations.[3] Civil rights complainants have, not surprisingly, argued for expansive readings of civil rights laws.[4] This contested ground is the subject of lawsuits, administrative actions, regulatory rumblings, and congressional machinations.

Emerging out of the clarity, and contestation, are new civil rights theories for protecting people of color from the degradation of their environments. These theories, often centered on Title VI of the Civil Rights Act of 1964,[5] have been expressed in lawsuits in state and federal court, and in administrative complaints before federal agencies, as well as in the literature.

The theories have addressed not only the disparate impact of particular environmental hazards (which remains the most popular topic) but also disparate enforcement of environmental laws, discriminatory treatment of participants in permitting processes, and disparate spending on environmental benefits.

This chapter explores another civil rights theory, examining the potential for using Title VI and its implementing regulations to address damage to natural and cultural resources. Title VI bars discrimination on the basis of race, color, and national origin by entities that receive federal financial assistance. In keeping with the ambition of this book to examine new approaches, the use of Title VI that I explore here would be an expansion from the historical application of this civil rights statute, but an expansion that is already being tried out on the ground in several civil rights complaints. For example, in *The Mattaponi Indian Tribe v Commonwealth of Virginia*, the Mattaponi Tribe alleged violations of Title VI because a reservoir constructed by Virginia would flood the Tribe's cultural and natural resources.[6]

The new Title VI approach differs in scope and coverage from the more traditional environmental justice cases in which Title VI has been invoked, but is comfortably within the judicially and administratively defined boundaries of the law. Several authors in this volume make compelling cases for a "big tent" to encompass broad definitions of the terms *environment* and *justice,* and I join them in pushing the boundaries of environmental justice to include cultural and natural resources damages; on the other hand, because I am examining a civil rights statute, part of my analysis is narrowly focused on impacts to people of color.

The second part of this chapter examines definitions of the term *impact* under federal case law and federal agency guidances to discern whether they are pliable enough to include cultural and natural resources damages. The third part then uses a Native American Nation's challenge to a proposed freeway through sacred petroglyphs to illustrate the potential application of Title VI to address natural and cultural resources damages. First, however, I explain what I mean by cultural and natural resources and why we should be looking to civil rights law at all.

Some Definitions

A starting point in the inquiry would be to define the terms *natural resources* and *cultural resources* as well as to discuss some of the damages to them that might implicate Title VI. The term *natural resources* is defined in several federal laws as

> land, fish, wildlife, biota, air, water, ground water, drinking water supplies, and other such resources belonging to, managed by, held in trust by, appertaining to, or otherwise controlled by the United States . . . any State or local government or Indian tribe, or any foreign government.[7]

In crafting this definition, the U.S. Congress consciously excluded most private property, unless substantially controlled by government.[8] Even with this limitation, the definition still provides the foundation for a working definition in "land, fish, wildlife, biota, air, water, ground water, and drinking water supplies." This definition, applied to private and public property, is what I mean when I refer to "natural resources."

The damages to natural resources to which Title VI might apply include air and water pollution, habitat destruction, forest harvesting, killing wildlife, and grazing on grasslands, to name a few. As I discuss later in this chapter, the challenge would be documenting how such resource damage had a disparate impact on an identifiable population on the basis of race, color, or national origin as Title VI of the Civil Rights Act requires.

The term *cultural resources* I define broadly to mean resources of historical or present interest to people for historical, religious, or spiritual reasons. My definition is similar to that of UNESCO, which includes the human-built environment, including monuments and sites. UNESCO defines "monuments" as "architectural works, works of monumental sculpture and painting, elements or structures of an archaeological nature, inscriptions, cave dwellings and combination of features, which are of outstanding universal value from the point of view of history, art or science." It defines "sites" as "works of man or the combined works of nature and man, and areas including archaeological sites which are of outstanding universal value from the historical, aesthetic, ethnological or anthropological point of view."[9] In many statutes, cultural resources older than a certain age—usually fifty to one hundred years old—are called "archaeological resources," but for the purposes of this chapter, my definition of "cultural resources" includes those otherwise classified as "archaeological."

The term *cultural resources* has a life in American law primarily related to Native Americans, but here I use it broadly. My definitional tent, to continue David Getches and David Pellow's metaphor from Chapter 1, includes murals painted at Chicano Park in San Diego's Barrio Logan, the route of the Selma-to-Montgomery Civil Rights March, Stonehenge, a Marc Chagall painting, and folk art environments, such as Howard Finster's Paradise Garden, Grandma Prisbrey's Bottle House, and the Dickeyville Grotto, as cultural resources.[10]

The damage to cultural resources takes at least two forms: intentional and incidental. Intentional damage may come from either benign interest or malicious activity. In the American Indian context, as Constance Callahan points out, "Domestic interest and foreign demand for Native American contemporary art and antiquities has fueled an epidemic of pothunting, or looting, of ancient habitation sites and Native American burial grounds."[11] Other cultural resources, such as Stonehenge and the caves of Lascaux, France, are defaced, graffitied, or "loved to death"—damaged or destroyed by repeated visits from admirers. Of greater consequence, perhaps, is the incidental damage to cultural resources during the exploitation of natural resources—for example, the destruction of archaeological sites or burial sites during mining operations or the desecration of worship areas by road building and timber harvesting.

The terms *cultural resources* and *natural resources* are often found in tandem, particularly when talking about the rights and resources of Native Americans. To blur the definitional boundaries, in some cases, natural resources *are* cultural resources. The Warm Springs Tribal Code (sec. 490.010 [4]), for example, defines "cultural materials" to include such things as "eagle feathers, fish, game, roots, berries, cedar bark, Indian medicines and water having special significance." In the famous G-O Road case, *Lyng v Northwest Indian Cemetery Protective Association*, the Indian plaintiffs argued that a particular section of a national forest was a cultural resource "that disruption of the natural environment caused by the G-O road will diminish the sacredness of the area in question," and that "[s]carred hills and mountains, and disturbed rocks destroy the purity of the sacred areas."[12] The Supreme Court ruled against them, however, holding that the free exercise clause of the First Amendment did not forbid timber harvesting in or construction of roads through portions of national forests traditionally used for religious purposes by Indian tribes.

Why Civil Rights Law?

There are dozens of state and federal laws that protect natural and cultural resources.[13] Why, then, should we look to the unlikely area of federal civil rights law? Put simply, Title VI has the potential to offer protection in the interstices of the loosely knit, and often tattered, fabric of existing legal protections for natural and cultural resources.[14]

The protection of natural resources under existing laws is spotty at best. Indeed, most laws are set up to encourage and facilitate the exploitation of natural resources. As Oliver Houck observes, the "bedrock principle of natural resources management for much of this century has been 'multiple use.' . . . The failure of this principle to provide even for the bare survival of natural resources—something far short of their perpetuation in a sustainable state—has become one of the better known lessons of environmental law."[15] Some laws, such as the Comprehensive Environmental Response, Compensation, and Liability Act (CERCLA, also known as Superfund), make provisions for natural resources damages.[16] There are two significant limitations that preclude the use of CERCLA and similar statutes in environmental justice disputes: first, because natural resources are defined as only those resources under public control, natural resources damage claims under CERCLA can only be brought by state or federal trustees of those resources or by trustees of Indian tribes.[17] Private entities, and the tribes themselves, cannot bring such claims. Second, such damages are only available retrospectively—the damage must have occurred—and thus the claims are little help in *preventing* such damage.[18] Title VI avoids both limitations, providing a private right of action (or the ability to file an administrative complaint) to any affected person and offering prospective, injunctive relief.

Cultural resources have more protection, at the federal, state, and tribal levels, but coverage is still uneven. Because most federal laws cover only federal or tribal lands, and state laws generally cover only public or tribal lands, cultural resources generally are not protected on private property. As Callahan notes: "Because private lands make up most of the property in this country, a large proportion of the archaeological sites in the nation are still unprotected from looting by the owners of the property."[19]

Laws that protect archaeological sites often do so only from those who are intentionally exploiting the site, not those who incidentally damage it. An example illustrates the shortcomings of such laws. The Inyo County Code in California (sec. 9.52.010) is typical of statutes protecting cultural resources. It states that "excavation or exploration for archaeological, educational, or artifact collection purposes of any

Native California Indian burial site shall not be permitted." The Timbisha Shoshone Tribe of Death Valley unsuccessfully sought to use this section of the code to block a massive cyanide heap leach gold mine proposed on their ancestral homeland. Tribal elders who claimed the mine would destroy tribal burial sites were rebuffed by county officials, who explained that the ambition of the mining project was not to excavate for archaeological purposes but to mine for gold, and thus the code did not apply. A Title VI theory could address such damages on private land if the other elements of a Title VI claim were met. Those elements are set forth below.

Defining "Impact" under Title VI

At the heart of any inquiry into the use of Title VI to address impacts to natural and cultural resources is discerning how court and federal agencies have defined the term *impact*—that is, could natural and cultural resource impacts be considered under Title VI? The short answer is yes, although such attempts may fare better in court than before the one administrative agency to specifically define "impact" in the Title VI context, the U.S. Environmental Protection Agency (EPA). After a short primer on Title VI, this section examines the broad (and multiple) definitions fashioned by federal courts for "impact," the narrow definition articulated by the EPA in its civil rights guidance, and the broader working definitions used by other agencies.

Title VI in a Nutshell

Title VI of the Civil Rights Act of 1964 was Congress's attempt, at the height of the civil rights movement, to bar state-sponsored discrimination. Title VI prohibits discrimination on the basis of race, color, or national origin in programs or activities receiving federal financial assistance.[20] Title VI itself has been construed by federal courts to bar actions taken with discriminatory intent,[21] an almost insurmountable hurdle for the civil rights plaintiff. Almost every federal agency has implemented Title VI through regulations that bar discriminatory *impact*, however, and the Supreme Court endorsed this approach,[22] making Title VI regulations an attractive tool for civil rights advocates.[23] Such regulations must be enforced through 42 U.S.C., sec. 1983, because the Supreme Court recently ruled that there is no private right of action under these regulations.[24]

Title VI does not provide compensation unless a plaintiff proves discriminatory intent, but it does allow declaratory and injunctive

relief, which are generally what plaintiffs trying to block environmental degradation seek.[25]

The Elements of a Title VI Action

Title VI prohibits discrimination by an entity that gets federal financial assistance, so the first element is showing the receipt of federal
assistance by the defendant. A plaintiff in a Title VI disparate impact
lawsuit or administrative complaint bears the initial burden of establishing a prima facie case that a facially neutral practice or decision
has resulted in a racial disparity. Courts have fashioned three elements that plaintiffs must prove in disparate impact cases under Title
VII of the Civil Rights Act, which is often used as a benchmark in Title
VI actions. First, a plaintiff must identify with particularity the decision or practice that is being challenged. Second, the plaintiff must
demonstrate that the decision or practice has a disparate impact on a
protected class based on race, color, or national origin. Finally, the
plaintiff must show that the decision or practice is in fact the cause of
the alleged discriminatory impact.[26]

If the plaintiff meets that burden, the burden then shifts to the
defendant to rebut the prima facie case. To do this, the defendant has
two options: first, a defendant can establish a "substantial legitimate
justification" for the decision or practice. Or, alternatively, a defendant can articulate a legitimate, nondiscriminatory reason for the
decision or practice.[27] It is important to note that Title VI does not prohibit discriminatory impact, only *unjustified* discriminatory impact.
As a district court held in one case challenging the alignment of a
highway, defendants "are not *per se* prohibited from locating a highway where it will have differential impacts upon minorities. Rather,
Title VI prohibits taking actions with differential impacts without adequate justification."[28] Even "unfortunate and insensitive" siting decisions are not necessarily discriminatory.[29] If the defendant is able to
meet its rebuttal burden, it is then up to the plaintiff to determine if
there are less discriminatory alternatives to the action that achieve the
same goals, or if the "proffered justification is no more than a pretext
for racial discrimination."[30] In the context of an administrative complaint, the burden here shifts to the *investigating agency,* rather than
the complainant, because the government stands in the stead of the
complainant in an administrative action.[31]

At trial, a Title VI disparate impact plaintiff must prove actual disparate impact. Whether or not cultural and natural resources can be
protected using Title VI depends on whether or not impacts to those

resources would be considered "impacts" under Title VI. Under judicial constructions of the term *impact*, it is likely that Title VI could be used to reach cultural and natural resources impacts, as is explained below. Under federal agencies' definitions, it is a slightly murkier picture, with a very narrow definition of "impact" by the EPA most likely precluding such coverage, but a broader working conception of "impact" at the U.S. Department of Transportation allowing such impacts to be addressed. These agency definitions are explored in the next section.

A Broad Reading: The Case Law

There is no accepted judicial definition of the term *impact* in the civil rights context. Indeed, courts have been reluctant to set forth specific definitions of concepts like impact in civil rights cases. This is particularly problematic in the environmental arena because there are so few reported environmental civil rights cases. Thus, to come up with a definition of "impact," one has to analogize from other areas of civil rights laws, particularly Title VII employment discrimination cases, which courts have read as instructive in the Title VI context. While the connection between Title VII definitions and Title VI impacts may seem strained at first, ultimately Title VII offers a path to arguing for cultural and natural resources protections under Title VI.

Title VII cases have defined the term *adverse effect* in the context of disparate treatment cases, and their holdings are instructive. Courts have held that an adverse effect (in this context, sexual harassment) must be sufficiently severe or pervasive as to alter the conditions of the victim's employment and create an abusive work environment.[32] To constitute an actionable adverse employment action, the action must have a material impact on a term, condition, or privilege of employment, not just a tangential one, and mere inconvenience is not enough.[33] So where does this leave the Title VI plaintiff? In my conception, an impact to cultural or natural resources must be sufficiently severe as to alter the environment. The alteration must be material, not simply tangential or causing inconvenience. Thus, damages to natural or cultural resources must have a material impact on a member of a protected class (on the basis of race, color, or national origin). An action that destroyed a Native American sacred site would clearly be material and would qualify as an impact, while an action that made it inconvenient to visit such a site, without damaging the site itself, might not meet this standard. An action that caused air pollution that was merely an irritant might not be material, but air pollution with demonstrable health impacts would be material.

This "material impact" standard would be relatively easy for plaintiffs in cultural and natural resources Title VI cases to meet. While the Supreme Court has read Title VII to require an objective approach, it has also left room for some subjectivity, including asking questions such as "Do members of the protected population perceive the effect to be adverse?"[34] This idea of impact, or effect, is favorable to the civil rights complainant.

Administrative Constructions of "Impact": From the Ridiculous to the Workable

Agency interpretations of "impact" range from narrow (EPA) to broad (Department of Transportation). EPA's narrow construction appears to be a result of political pressure, while other federal agencies, out of the Title VI spotlight, more closely track the expansiveness of federal case law.

A NARROW READING: EPA'S TITLE VI GUIDANCE

Unlike the federal courts, which have yet to adopt a uniform, specific definition of impact, the EPA has actually defined the concept of impact in the Title VI context. After seven years of receiving Title VI complaints from affected communities, and six years of pressure from those communities, the EPA in March 2000 issued a guidance intended to help its staff resolve Title VI complaints. The *Draft Revised Guidance for Investigating Title VI Administrative Complaints Challenging Permits* defines "impact" in the health and environmental context as a "negative or harmful effect on a receptor resulting from exposure to a stressor (e.g., a case of disease)."[35]

Determining exactly what the EPA means by this definition of "impact" is not entirely straightforward, however, and requires a scavenger hunt through the glossary in the Title VI guidance. What emerges is a meaning that markedly contrasts with the expansive idea of impact drawn from federal court rulings. Parsing the definition reveals the EPA's constriction of the concept of impact. A "receptor" is separately defined as "an individual or group that may be exposed to stressors." The EPA defines "exposure" as "contact with, or being subject to the action or influence of, environmental stressors, usually through ingestion, inhalation, or dermal contact." The EPA then defines "stressor" as

> any factor that may adversely affect receptors, including chemical (e.g., criteria pollutants, toxic contaminants), physical (e.g., noise, extreme temperatures, fire) and bio-

logical (e.g., disease pathogens or parasites). Generally, any substance introduced into the environment that adversely affects the health of humans, animals, or ecosystems. Airborne stressors may fall into two main groups: (1) those emitted directly from identifiable sources and (2) those produced in the air by interaction between chemicals (e.g., most ozone).[36]

Teasing apart these definitions, a stressor is something (chemical, physical, or biological) that "adversely affects the health of humans, animals, or ecosystems." Exposure is contact with a stressor, and a receptor is a human being. Thus, under the EPA's definition, impact is a negative or harmful effect on a human being from contact with something that adversely affects human health. Contrast this with the definition of "impact" drawn from federal precedent, above, and one could easily draw the conclusion that federal courts, rather than the EPA, are where one should turn to use Title VI to address impacts to cultural and natural resources.

While the EPA hedges with the qualifier "in the health and environmental context" in its definition of "impact," it does not appear that impacts to cultural or natural resources that do not also have a physical impact on a human being would be recognized as impacts under Title VI by the EPA. This appears to have been a conscious policy choice by the EPA, which was presented by its own Title VI Implementation Federal Advisory Committee with two very different conceptions of impact to choose between.

Although the EPA's definition appears on its face to exclude an action for cultural or natural resources damages (and the EPA, in adopting this definition, appears hostile to such a reading of Title VI), careful crafting of a complaint could creatively push the boundaries of the EPA's definition. One could make the argument that cultural or natural resources damages caused emotional or mental harm to a person, which is an impact as defined by the EPA. Take, for example, damage to petroglyphs held sacred by a particular tribe (an example that, as we shall see in a later section, is not wholly unlikely). Building a road through (and thus destroying) the petroglyphs could be considered a stressor under the EPA's definition, because a road is something physical that "adversely affects the health of humans, animals, or ecosystems." Exposure is contact with a stressor, and members of the tribe would have contact with the road. Because the road destroyed sacred tribal resources, members of the tribe might sustain emotional or mental "damage," or illness. Thus, the impact complained of is a negative or harmful effect on a human (tribal member) from contact with the road, which adversely affects the person's (mental or emotional) health. There are, however, no current Title VI claims (out of the more than one hundred filed with the EPA thus far) that allege such emotional or mental harm, and given the EPA's narrow construction of the statute, such claims may not be successful.[37]

AN EXPANSIVE AGENCY INTERPRETATION:
THE DEPARTMENT OF TRANSPORTATION

Other federal agencies use definitions of "impact" that are substantially broader than that employed by the EPA. Among them is the U.S. Department of Transportation (DOT). Although DOT does not have an "official" definition of "impact," its civil rights investigators use an informal working definition that would clearly encompass cultural and natural resources.[38] A DOT guidance document (which I call the Brenman Guidance after its principal author, Marc Brenman) answers the question, "What is an adverse effect?" with the following definition:

> A statistical disproportion between the effect of an allegedly discriminatory act or acts on the general or comparison population and on the protected population, which shows a harmful effect on the protected population.[39]

The Brenman Guidance instructs DOT's investigators to ask, "Does [the impact] limit the protected population's ability to participate in or benefit from some aspect of their environment?" It then lists a variety of ways this might occur: mobility; access; community cohesion; employment; displacement of people, businesses, farms, housing; tax and property value losses; aesthetic impacts and loss of recreational sites; lack of water hookups, storm-sewer capacity, street paving, curbs; groundwater contamination; odors; and lessened enjoyment. Another criteria for measuring adversity is the question, "Must the protected population incur economic or monetary costs to cope with the adverse impact, compared to little or no cost to the general population?"

The Brenman Guidance also asks the question posed by *Harris v Forklift Systems, Inc.*: "Do members of the protected population perceive the effect to be adverse?"[40] The final question is, "Would a 'reasonable person' judge the effect to be adverse?"

Each of these questions indicates a broad definition of "impact" or "adverse effect" by DOT civil rights investigators. Looking at the petroglyph hypothetical, it would be simple to allege that damage to petroglyphs (1) limited the ability of the protected population (here, Native Americans) to participate in or benefit from several aspects of their environment, including effects on access to the petroglyphs, community cohesion from interruption of spiritual practices, and aesthetic impacts and loss of recreational sites; (2) could cause Native Americans to incur economic costs not borne by the general population; (3) would be perceived by Native Americans as adverse; and (4) would be deemed adverse by a reasonable person. Thus, such a claim would likely succeed before DOT, or at least warrant an investigation.

A NOTE ON THE USE OF TITLE VI

It would be irresponsible to set forth a theory of addressing natural and cultural resources impacts under Title VI without, at least in passing, discussing the potential fluidity of Title VI's coverage. For the past three years, there has been an ongoing debate, played out in various federal courts, as to whether or not there is a private right of action under federal agencies' Title VI regulations. States and industry, and their academic proponents, have argued that although Title VI itself can be enforced by individuals, through the courts, the regulations promulgated by federal agencies can only be enforced by those agencies. Civil rights plaintiffs, and their academic defenders, have argued that they can bring suit under both Title VI and the agency regulations.[41]

Can private citizens enforce agency regulations promulgated under Title VI? The stakes in the answer to this question are significant. If so, then states (and other recipients of federal financial assistance) are vulnerable to court challenges based on disparate impact. If not, then states are liable only for intentional discrimination, a court-devised hurdle so high that few civil rights plaintiffs are able to surmount it. The Supreme Court introduced yet another hurdle to civil rights plaintiffs in early 2001 when it overturned thirty years of federal precedent and ruled that plaintiffs could no longer enforce Title VI regulations' disparate impact standard by suing under the regulations themselves.[42] Civil rights litigators have since used 42 U.S.C., sec. 1983, to enforce the Title VI regulations,[43] but the Supreme Court, openly hostile to civil rights, may soon eliminate that avenue to redressing discrimination as well. If so, then the arguments developed here would be relevant only to administrative complaints to federal agencies.

Title VI in Action: The Petroglyphs Dispute

To illustrate how one might make a Title VI claim for natural or cultural resources damages and the difficulties with administrative complaints, this section analyzes the invocation of Title VI by a Native American Nation in an environmental justice struggle.[44] In choosing the example of the Petroglyph struggle in New Mexico, I realize that it involves not natural resources but cultural resources; nonetheless, the theories explored would be relevant in a natural resources case as well.[45] This case is an administrative complaint that has not yet been resolved, so the discussion here is about the theories proposed, not the ultimate resolution by the administrative agency.

Just to the west of downtown Albuquerque is a remarkable park, Petroglyph National Monument. The monument is a dramatic series of cliffs and canyons of black volcanic rock, a winding, seventeen-mile escarpment inscribed with more than fifteen thousand petroglyphs, or rock carvings, depicting animals, birds, people, stars, crosses, spirals, and spirits. Some of the petroglyphs are thought to be up to three thousand years old, although most date from 1300 to 1650 A.D.[46] It is not known what their exact meanings are, but archaeologists say that some represent spirits associated with the rain. What is remarkable about the monument goes beyond the rock carvings, however: it is bordered, for almost ten miles, by a rapidly expanding city. The suburban sprawl of Albuquerque has led to more than a decade of tension and conflict between advocates of growth and those trying to preserve the petroglyphs. The conflict has also led to one of the first exercises of Title VI to attempt to preserve cultural resources, a complaint filed by the Pueblo of Sandia in 1997.[47]

The Context and Conflict

Petroglyph National Monument was established by Congress in June 1990, the result of years of lobbying by Native American tribes and preservationists.[48] Its 7,244 acres were set aside "to preserve, for the benefit and enjoyment of present and future generations . . . the nationally significant West Mesa Escarpment, the Las Imagines National Archaeological District . . . and other significant natural and cultural resources, and to facilitate research activities associated with the resources."[49] Before the monument was established, the lands— sacred to the Pueblo Indians—were most recently "used as dumping grounds, and its rock carvings were pockmarked by vandalism and marred with graffiti."[50]

The area that is now the monument at one time stood as the west edge of Albuquerque; today, the city is expanding to surround the petroglyphs. Albuquerque grew by 15 percent from 1990 to 1998, and the West Mesa, bordering the monument, is the city's most rapidly developing area.[51] In twenty-five years, the city's population of seven hundred thousand is expected to increase 50 percent, and there are already-planned subdivisions for sixty thousand residents on the west side of the monument. Suburban sprawl laps at the edge of the petroglyphs, with one advertisement for a new subdivision reading "Beautiful Courtyard Homes—Next to the Petroglyph National Monument."[52]

These development pressures have led to conflict over the monument. The chief battleground has been roads: the expansion of Unser Boulevard, a north-south arterial along the east edge of the monument (which actually crosses the monument going north to south), and the extension of Paseo del Norte, which currently runs west from the Rio Grande River and dead-ends near the eastern border of the monument. The fight over Unser Boulevard has been ongoing since the late 1980s, but the main battle has been over Paseo del Norte, which would cut across the monument.

On one side of the battle are developers and their political allies, including Senator Pete Domenici and most of the state's congressional delegation. In 1993, the pro-highway forces appeared to have won the day when Albuquerque officials voted to extend Paseo del Norte through the monument. They chose the narrowest point of the monument, a quarter mile wide and covering 8.5 acres—about one-tenth of 1 percent of the monument's area—but the road would divide the monument in half. The highway proponents noted that the highway would require only a dozen of the petroglyphs to be relocated. The highway is slated to ultimately carry eighty thousand people a day, roughly as many people as visit the monument in a year.

The proposal has been stymied for years, however, by the vocal protests of highway opponents. The Pueblo Tribes and Indian groups have been joined by environmentalists, preservationists, the National Park Service, and an antisprawl, smart-growth group. They also have the support of some local politicians, including Albuquerque's mayor, Jim Baca, who was elected in 1997 after being the only one of seven candidates to oppose the highway extension. The highway opponents have ridiculed Paseo del Norte as the "road to nowhere," as the planned development slated for the west side of the Monument has not taken place.

The Petroglyphs' Significance

The conflict over Paseo del Norte illustrates two widely differing views of Petroglyph National Monument's significance. The Pueblo Indians see the area as a church. The site is used for spiritual practices by the Pueblo and by other Indians from across the Southwest as far as California, including Zunis from western New Mexico and Hopis from Arizona. It is not coincidental that the petroglyphs are carved at the base of five ancient volcanoes; the volcanoes are seen as links to the spirit world.[53]

The Pueblo creation stories feature their ancestors emerging from the earth, and the Pueblo strongly rejected a proposal made by Martin Chavez, Baca's predecessor as mayor, to dig a highway tunnel below the park. As Chavez put it, "This is not Indian land, this is public land. . . . They say it's a 17-mile-long church. Well, the Vatican has a road going through it."[54] The Pueblo say Chavez missed the point: "The monument is like a snake," said Sonny Weahkee, a leader of the Petroglyph National Monument Protection Coalition, which represents five Pueblo tribes. "Could a snake be a snake without a tail?"[55]

As Raymond Apodaca of the National Congress of American Indians succinctly summarized the Native American perspective: "Indians would like to see Bear Butte in South Dakota's Black Hills, Mt. Graham in Arizona, and the petroglyphs in New Mexico thought of with the same reverence as St. Patrick's Cathedral in New York City."[56] Highway proponents have questioned the religious significance of the monument and the Indians' spiritual use of the area. "A lot of politicians in this area are questioning our religion's legitimacy," said Sonny Weahkee. "Would you ask a Christian to prove his religion is real?"[57]

Indians were incensed when one proposed alternative route was dropped because it would cut through a few holes on a golf course in Paradise Hills, north of the monument. As William F. Weahkee, a Cochiti Indian who led the opposition to the highway until his death in 2000, told a reporter, "In Albuquerque, major roads stop at golf courses. Are those sacred sites to you guys?"[58] As James Brooke observes, "On one level, the debate is over what modern America holds more sacred: Commuting times or religious practices? Ancient rock carvings or golf courses?"[59]

The Complaint

The Pueblo of Sandia and twenty-two individual tribal members filed a complaint with DOT and the Department of the Interior (DOI) under Title VI and the agencies' implementing regulations on August 14, 1997. The Pueblo of Sandia, a federally recognized Indian tribe, alleged that the City of Albuquerque's proposals to "site, construct and operate" a freeway, trails for horseback and mountain bike riding, and new visitor centers in the Petroglyph National Monument "would adversely affect the Pueblos, including the Pueblo of Sandia, differently than it would impact others without any justification for so doing and, by so doing, subject the Pueblos to discriminatory effects." The complaint also named other agencies responsible for parts of the highway proposal.[60]

The complaint alleged violations of both DOT's and DOI's Title VI disparate impact regulations. In particular, the complaint alleged that the construction and operation of Unser Boulevard and Paseo del Norte through the monument "would physically separate the now contiguous escarpment into distinct parts."[61] It also noted that construction and operation of the horse and mountain bike trails, as well as new visitor centers, would "disturb the sanctity of the Monument, which is essential to the Pueblos' practice of their religion in the Monument."[62] According to the complaint, "the Pueblos view the Monument area as a whole, not as a group of discrete cultural resources."[63] Dividing up the monument would have a significant, negative impact: the Pueblos believe that the petroglyphs along the escarpment, the five volcanoes to the west of the escarpment, and the spirit trails to the west of the escarpment are physically and spiritually interrelated, forming a communication nexus to the spirit world that can be used by living people to assist in their prayers and medicine in this world. The roads, trails, and visitor centers would increase noise and light from vehicles traveling through the monument and could alter water flow patterns, causing erosion, while the construction of the roads would destroy petroglyphs and thus interfere with the Pueblos' religious practices. Because no other groups except Native Americans use the monument for religious purposes, the actions have a disparate impact on the basis of race.

The complaint sets forth several "viable, non-discriminatory alternatives,"[64] including improving and widening existing roadways and three alternate highway routing configurations. It concludes by requesting that DOT and DOI prevent Albuquerque from constructing the roads and other improvements in the monument, or in the alternative, perform an environmental impact statement to analyze whether the alternatives to the roads and trails would have the same disparate impact.

The complaint is a nice illustration of how Title VI could be invoked to protect cultural and natural resources. The petroglyphs are clearly cultural resources; indeed, the area that comprises the entire monument is within the Las Imagines Historic District, which was placed on the New Mexico State Register of Cultural Properties in 1986. The complaint set forth all the elements of a violation under the agencies' Title VI regulations: action by a recipient of federal financial assistance that had disparate impact on the basis of race. All this said, did it work?

DOI accepted the complaint for investigation and within three months of the complaint had dispatched an investigator to work on the case.[65] DOT ceded investigatory responsibilities to DOI.[66] After DOI's investigator spent a week in Albuquerque interviewing local and state officials, the Pueblo did not push the investigation, fearing that to do so would displease New Mexico's senior senator, Pete Domenici (Republican) and thus imperil a major land claim lawsuit the Pueblo was pursuing in federal court. The Pueblo did not press the claim, and it appears to have languished at DOI since that time.

The Petroglyphs Dispute: An Epilogue

The Title VI complaint has not led to major action by either DOI or DOT, illustrating one of the central weaknesses of the administrative complaint route: federal agencies may choose to do nothing.[67] The tribe's attorney, Charles Miller, still likes the strategic quality of the Title VI complaint, which shifts the focus off environmental impacts: "It changes the dynamics of a case—now it's a matter of discrimination."[68]

The freeway struggle is far from over, however. In 1998, freeway supporters scored a major victory when Senator Domenici attached a rider to a relief bill for Persian Gulf War veterans that deleted the land needed for the six-lane highway from the monument, and President Clinton signed the bill.[69] The road project is still stalled, however: the bill gave the City of Albuquerque the authority to decide whether to extend the highway through the monument, and thus far the City has not taken that step.

Conclusion

An examination of federal statutes, regulations, and case law indicates that affected people should be able to invoke Title VI (and federal agencies' implementing regulations) to address damage to cultural and natural resources if that damage has a disparate impact on the basis of race, color, or national origin. The use of Title VI and its implementing regulations may help stitch up some of the holes in the fabric of protection of natural and cultural resources, specifically those resources important to people of color.

As the Sandia Pueblo case illustrates, this strategy is already in use. The analysis here, though, indicates that a Title VI argument could be even more broadly construed to include not only cultural resources but also natural resources. The federally subsidized cutting of timber that causes erosion in Indian communities but not in white communities and the damming by a state of a stream used primarily by African American subsistence fishers are two scenarios that come to mind; there are countless others, I am sure. The increased use of Title VI will expand protections in the contested terrain of cultural and natural resource preservation.

Acknowledgments

I thank Gary Bryner and Kathryn Mutz for their insightful comments on earlier drafts. For their expert research assistance, I thank Martina Barash, Gene Yee, and particularly Adrienne Bloch. I thank the University of Colorado Natural Resources Law Center and Leo Martinez and the University of California–Hastings College of the Law for the resources to complete this chapter. I also thank Charles Miller and Marc Brenman for their assistance.

Notes

1. Luke W. Cole and Sheila R. Foster, *From the Ground Up: Environmental Racism and the Rise of the Environment Justice Movement* (New York: New York University Press, 2001), 167–83, listing sixty-eight studies documenting racial disparity in proximity and exposure to environmental hazards. See generally David Getches and David Pellow's discussion in Chapter 1.
2. See James H. Colopy, "The Road Less Traveled: Pursuing Environmental Justice through Title VI of the Civil Rights Act of 1964," *Stanford Environmental Law Journal* 13 (1994): 125; and Richard Moore, "EPA's Lack of Commitment to Civil Rights," *Environmental Forum* 17 (September/October 2000): 52 (fifty environmental justice civil rights complaints awaiting investigation by EPA).
3. See, e.g., Keith McCoy, "A Tilt toward Encouraging Complaints," *Environmental Forum* 17 (September/October 2000): 51.
4. See, e.g., Moore, "EPA's Lack of Commitment to Civil Rights."
5. 42 U.S.C., sec. 2000d.
6. 31 Va. App. 472 (2000).

7. 33 U.S.C., sec. 2701(20) (Oil Pollution Act of 1990); see also 42 U.S.C., sec. 9601(16)(Comprehensive Environmental Response, Compensation, and Liability Act of 1980 [CERCLA]).

8. *Ohio v Dept. of Interior*, 880 F.2d 432, 460 (D.C. Cir. 1989).

9. United Nations Educational, Scientific and Cultural Organization, World Heritage Convention (1972), section I, article 1. Available on-line at www.unesco.org/whc/world_he.htm.

10. Joseph L. Sax, "Is Anyone Minding Stonehenge? The Origins of Cultural Property Protection in England," *California Law Review* 78 (1990): 1543; John F. Turner, *Howard Finster: Man of Visions* (New York: Knopf, 1989); Santa Barbara Contemporary Arts Forum, *Visions from the Left Coast: California Self-Taught Artists* 54 (1995).

11. Constance M. Callahan, "Warp and Weft: Weaving a Blanket of Protection for Cultural Resources on Private Property," *Environmental Law* 23 (1993): 1323–24.

12. 485 U.S. 439, 447–448 (1988).

13. Callahan, "Warp and Weft," 66–107.

14. I owe the analogy to Callahan, "Warp and Weft."

15. Oliver Houck, "Are Humans Part of Ecosystems?" *Environmental Law* 28 (1998): 1, 7.

16. 42 U.S.C., sec. 9607(a)(4)(C).

17. 42 U.S.C., sec. 9607(16).

18. 42 U.S.C., sec. 9607(a)(4)(c).

19. Callahan, "Warp and Weft," 1324.

20. 42 U.S.C., sec. 2000d (1988).

21. *Guardians Ass'n v Civil Service Comm'n of City of New York*, 463 U.S. 582, 591–596 (1983).

22. A divided Supreme Court issued a multipart opinion in *Guardians Assn. v Civil Service Comm'n*, 584, in which a majority of five justices held that under Title VI federal agencies could promulgate regulations barring discriminatory impact.

23. See Luke W. Cole, "Civil Rights, Environmental Justice and the EPA: The Brief History of Administrative Complaints under Title VI of the Civil Rights Act of 1964," *Journal of Environmental Law and Litigation* 9 (1994): 309, 313.

24. *Alexander v Sandoval*, 121 S.Ct. 1511 (2001).

25. *Guardians Ass'n v Civil Service Comm'n*, 612. See also *Eastman v Virginia Polytechnic Institute*, 939 F.2d 204, 206–207 (4th Cir. 1991), reading *Guardians* to hold that "intentional discrimination is a prerequisite to an award of any sort of 'compensatory damages' to a private litigant in a Title VI case."

26. *EEOC v Steamship Clerks Union, Local 1066*, 48 F.3d 594, 601 (1st Cir. 1995).

27. *Powell v Ridge*, 189 F.3d 387, 393–94 (3rd Cir. 1999); *New York Urban League*,

Inc. v New York, 71 F.3d 1031, 1036 (2nd Cir. 1995).

28. *Coalition of Concerned Citizens Against I-670 v Damian*, 608 F. Supp. 110, 127 (S.D. Ohio 1984).

29. *Bean v Southwestern Waste Management Corp.*, 482 F. Supp. 673, 679–80 (S.D. Tex. 1979).

30. *Powell v Ridge*, 394.

31. Marc Brenman, Investigating Environmental Justice (EJ) Complaints (October 1999), 26–27, on file with author.

32. *Meritor Savings Bank v Vinson*, 477 U.S. 57, 67 (1985).

33. *Lederberger v Stangler*, 122 F.3d 1142 (8th Cir. 1997); *Rabinovitz v Pena*, 89 F.3d 482, 488 (7th Cir. 1996).

34. See, e.g., *Harris v Forklift Systems, Inc.*, 510 U.S. 17, 21–22 (1993).

35. U.S. Environmental Protection Agency, *Draft Revised Guidance for Investigating Title VI Administrative Complaints Challenging Permits* (2000), app. A: Glossary of Terms, 65 *Federal Register*, 39667, 39685.

36. 65 *Federal Register*, 39667, 39684–86.

37. The concept of psychological harm comes up often in Title VII employment discrimination cases and may be useful to import into this type of Title VI case. See, e.g., *Harris v Forklift Systems*.

38. Telephone interview with Marc Brenman, senior policy advisor for civil rights, Office of the Secretary, U.S. Department of Transportation, November 20, 2000 (hereafter, "Brenman interview").

39. Brenman, Investigating Environmental Justice Complaints, 26–28.

40. *Harris v Forklift Systems*, 21–22.

41. See *Chester Residents Concerned for Quality Living v Seif*, 132 F.3d 925, 936–37 (3rd Cir. 1997), vacated as moot, 524 U.S. 974 (1998).

42. *Alexander v Sandoval*.

43. *South Camden Citizens in Action v New Jersey Department of Environmental Protection*, 145 F. Supp. 2d 505 (D. N.J. 2001).

44. There is an unsettled question as to whether, and how much, Title VI covers Native Americans. My friend and colleague Richard Monette argues, not unconvincingly, that Indians are not covered by Title VI, particularly when they are in Indian country. Richard Monette, "Environmental Justice and Indian Tribes: The Double-Edged Tomahawk of Applying Civil Rights Laws in Indian Country," *University of Detroit Mercy Law Review* 76 (1999): 721, 744. I disagree with this conclusion on grounds that I will explore in a forthcoming article. Because Native American Nations such as the Pueblo of Sandia are using Title VI, as discussed below, the question may ultimately be academic. See also Colopy, "The Road Less Traveled," 125, 153 n. 124 (Title VI does not cover aid extended to Native Americans located on reservations, with few exceptions).

45. Such cases might include the harvesting of timber that causes erosion or siltation which has a disproportionate impact on the environment of a nearby Indian reservation, or the building of a dam that dramatically affects fish stocks used by African American and Latino subsistence fish-

ers, for example. In each case, the impact to the natural resource must be both definable and disparate on the basis of race, color, or national origin to come within Title VI's ambit.

46. The description of this conflict is drawn primarily from several articles, including Jeremy Pawloski, "Domenici Aims to Fill Out Monument," *Albuquerque Journal,* March 31, 2000, 1, available at 2000 WL 17137474; and John McQuaid, "Standing Their Ground," *New Orleans Times-Picayune,* May 24, 2000, A6, available at 2000 WL 21259411.

47. *Pueblo of Sandia, et al. v City of Albuquerque, et al.,* filed with the U.S. Department of the Interior and the U.S. Department of Transportation on August 14, 1997 (hereafter, "Pueblo of Sandia complaint").

48. Petroglyph National Monument Establishment Act of 1990, Pub. L. No. 101-313, sec. 108, 104 Stat. 272, 276 (1990) (codified as amended at 16 U.S.C., sec. 431 et seq.).

49. 16 U.S.C., sec. 432(a).

50. Pawloski, "Domenici Aims To Fill Out Monument," 1.

51. Anita P. Miller and John B. Wright, "Report of the Subcommittee on Innovative Growth Management Measures: Preservation of Agricultural Land and Open Space," *Urban Lawyer* 23 (1991): 821, 831.

52. McQuaid, "Standing Their Ground," A6.

53. Pueblo of Sandia complaint.

54. Tim Korte, "Petroglyph Monument at Center of Road Battle," *Philadelphia Inquirer,* March 5, 1995, A5; Anastasia P. Winslow, "Sacred Standards: Honoring the Establishment Clause in Protecting Native American Sacred Sites," *Arizona Law Review* 38 (1996): 1291–292.

55. McQuaid, "Standing Their Ground," A6.

56. As quoted by Katie Davis, National Public Radio, *All Things Considered* (March 13, 1994), transcript 1420-6.

57. McQuaid, "Standing Their Ground," A6.

58. James Brooke, "Highway Plans a Monument to Suburban Sprawl," *Chicago Tribune,* May 17, 1998, 1, available at 1998 WL 2856833.

59. Brooke, "Highway Plans," 1.

60. Pueblo of Sandia complaint, 1.

61. Pueblo of Sandia complaint, 13.

62. Pueblo of Sandia complaint, 12.

63. Pueblo of Sandia complaint, 13.

64. Pueblo of Sandia complaint, 16–17.

65. Telephone interview with Charles Miller, Oakland, Calif., November 17, 2000 (hereafter, "Miller interview"). Mr. Miller represented the Pueblo of Sandia in this matter and filed the Title VI complaint.

66. Brenman interview.

67. See, e.g., *Cannon v University of Chicago,* 441 U.S. 677, 707 n. 41: "Furthermore, the agency may simply decide not to investigate—a decision that often will be based on a lack of enforcement resources, rather than any conclusion on the merits of the complaint." See also Cole, "Civil Rights,

Environmental Justice and the EPA," 309, 318, 321.

68. Miller interview; compare Luke W. Cole, "Environmental Justice Litigation: Another Stone in David's Sling," *Fordham Urban Law Journal* 21 (1994): 523, 541–44, outlining the political benefits of civil rights cases.

69. Gregory S. Wetstone, Sharon Buccino, and Nathan Daschle, "Damage Report: Environment and the 105th Congress," American Law Institute—American Bar Association (February 10, 1999).

Chapter 9

FOREST MANAGEMENT AND ENVIRONMENTAL JUSTICE IN NORTHERN NEW MEXICO

Henry H. Carey

Several years ago, in a remote village in the Rocky Mountains, I saw a woman break down, quietly crying at her kitchen table as she spoke of the complete cessation of logging on the national forests surrounding her home. She told us of her husband's long absences, working as a logger in an adjacent state, of her loneliness, and of the uncomprehending faces of her children. A week later, I passed through Hayfork, California, and saw the remains of the great sawmill there, recently closed, already dismembered and looted. Two hundred fifty jobs evaporated with the closing of the mill, which had been an island of employment in a sea of public lands.

The logger had been put out of work and the mill closed for many reasons. Maintaining large manufacturing facilities at a long distance from transportation networks defied the logic of modern business practice. The surrounding forests had been cut beyond the limits of sustainability. Lawsuits brought by environmental organizations were perhaps the final blow in a complex social, economic, and ecological drama.

Acknowledging that only a fragment of America's native forests are left uncut, society has placed a priority on preserving what remains. At the same time, much of the burden of environmental protection has fallen on rural communities. Our institutions have also largely denied these communities a place at the table in determining their own future. Sheila Foster's discussion of public participation and collaboration in Chapter 6 and Jeff Romm's discussion of forestry institutions in Chapter 5 explore this.

In Chapter 1, David Getches and David Pellow comment that the environmental justice movement has focused historically on the suffering caused by waste facility siting in disadvantaged and minority communities. Thus, the origin of the movement lies in a concern for the quality of the environment surrounding disadvantaged people. Getches and Pellow suggest that the realm of environmental justice should be expanded to include "concerns in which natural resources are developed, managed, and used in ways that exacerbate social injustice." This suggestion fits with Gary Bryner's system for organizing an inquiry into environmental justice presented in Chapter 2. Bryner discusses two categories relevant to this discussion: (1) distributive justice—the way in which we allocate benefits and burdens related to natural resources; and (2) procedural justice—the process by which decisions are made, including how those affected by the decisions participate.

While distributive justice and procedural justice are relevant to Getches and Pellow's broadened definition, I suggest the continued need to differentiate concerns for the use and distribution of natural resources from concerns relating specifically to environmental quality. Whereas distributive issues address conservation—that is, the flows of timber or grass that are made available to local communities—the term *environmental justice* also raises a separate set of questions. These questions relate to the right of rural communities to a quality forest environment and to their access to the decision process affecting that environment.

The terms *resource conservation* and *environmental protection* have related, but vitally different, meanings. Conservation was defined by Gifford Pinchot, Theodore Roosevelt, and other important thinkers in the early 1900s as "the wise use of resources."[1] The goal of conservation is to perpetuate resource supplies. Conservation is marginally concerned with resource quality, focusing instead on the quantity of natural resources stocks. Sustained-yield timber production and big game management are examples of conservation policies that emphasize quantitative outputs.

By contrast, the environmental movement is built upon concerns for habitat. Environmental interests focus on the quality or condition of natural resources as a home for humankind and other species. These concerns are characterized in qualitative terms and only secondarily involve quantitative measures. Initiatives addressing air and water quality and wildlife habitat are familiar features of the environmental emphasis of the 1980s and 1990s.

In her biography of Aldo Leopold, Susan Flader describes the early stages in the transition from conservation to the environment as a dominant theme in natural resources policy:

> The purpose of environmental management in the broadest sense, as distinguished from management of deer herds or deer ranges, was not so much to increase productivity of or carrying capacity for a single species as to rebuild a diverse, healthy environment. . . . Thus did Leopold express the transition from conservation as a preoccupation with supply and demand to conservation as a state of land health.[2]

In sum, assurances of the sustainability of timber supplies are no longer adequate to address public concerns regarding forest management. Environmental concerns include the quality of the forest, the distribution of old growth, biological diversity, wildlife habitat, watershed condition, and the forest's health and resilience.

This chapter focuses on issues of environmental justice raised by forest management in the remote mountains of northern New Mexico. I suggest that many of the environmental concerns, including those described above, are shared by the Hispanic residents of northern New Mexico and that environmental justice requires that the quality of the forest be maintained in a manner that meets the cultural priorities of this population. I show that the residents of the northern villages have suffered both distributive injustice relating to timber supplies and procedural injustices in connection with road policies and the preservation of desired forest conditions. Finally, I suggest the introduction of community forestry as a means of correcting these inequities.

Northern New Mexico

The Hispanic villages of northern New Mexico have a long history of close association with the surrounding forests and grasslands. The mountains rising high above the semiarid plains capture moisture from air masses flowing from the Pacific and Gulf Coasts and thereby support a rich abundance of life. Much human settlement has concentrated in the high valleys. The inhabitants of the small, scattered villages are predominantly Spanish American peoples, having an ancient tradition of rural pastoralism.

The early Spanish settlers of these valleys were descendants of the colonists who had followed Don Diego de Vargas after his reconquest of New Mexico in 1692.[3] Early colonization of northern New Mexico was confined to the Rio Grande Valley due to heavy raiding by American Indian tribes. The Indians' depredations began in 1740 and put such heavy stress on the early Spanish colony that many villages which had sprung up in the reaches of the Rio Grande Valley had to be abandoned. A successful military campaign in 1779 reduced the threat to life and property and again opened the prospect of Hispanic colonization of the mountains.

For military and political reasons, the Spanish authorities had closed their northern boundaries to all commerce and travel. Trappers and traders coming from the eastern United States were often detained and occasionally imprisoned. The settlers' loyalties were closely tied to Spain. Long after Mexico's declaration of independence, and even after the acquisition of the colony by the United States, many residents of northern New Mexico still considered themselves subjects of Spain.

Due to the extreme remoteness of the area and to the great poverty of the residents, barter was the primary form of commerce. Subsistence farming and grazing were the only means of livelihood. There was a near-complete absence of manufactured goods. Weapons for defense frequently consisted of bows, arrows, and spears. Iron was so rare and expensive as to be prohibitive for use in farm implements. The limited metal available was cast and recast for knives, axes, and arrowheads until all the temper had left the metal, at which time it was used to make decorative ornaments. Almost all the materials of life were derived from the mountains and forests. Houses were built from mud bricks. Windows were made from hides that were scraped thin. Floors were made from packed earth. The residents depended for survival upon their self-reliance, ingenuity, and the land. Their material lifestyle differed very little from that of the settled Pueblo Indians who practiced agriculture along the Rio Grande Valley.

In 1821, Mexico declared its independence from Spain. This event reopened old trading routes to the United States. The isolated, insular existence changed with the arrival of traders coming down the Santa Fe Trail from Missouri. In August 1846, General Kearny claimed northern New Mexico as a territory of the United States. With this event, the social and economic life in northern New Mexico began to change in earnest, in time becoming closely linked to external events occurring far beyond its borders.

At this point in the history of northern New Mexico, the stage was set for a period of prosperity and development. This period was sparked by the arrival of the railroad in 1879. The railroad immediately created new opportunities and markets and drew in large receipts from both shippers and passengers, affecting all sectors of the local economy. Although the boom in the rail centers had a relatively dramatic effect on the lives of all inhabitants of northern New Mexico, life in the remote villages changed remarkably slowly. The material life of the villagers included new elements, such as metal farm implements. However, the people still depended upon subsistence agriculture and grazing for the majority of their needs. In rural areas, this tradition has largely continued to the present.

Simple Justice and Land Grant Claims

The Hispanic villages were often created amid large grants of land made by the Spanish or Mexican governments. Such land grants were generally made to further colonization of the new frontier. Grants were made either to a group of petitioners—the community land grant—or to prominent individuals who then took charge of distributing building sites and founding a village. In either case, members of the grant were accorded the right to graze livestock and cut timber for building materials and firewood.

During the early historical period, the forests and rangelands served as a commons that supported the needs of villagers for forage, hunting, fuelwood, and building materials. At the close of the Mexican-American War in 1848, the Treaty of Guadalupe Hildalgo was signed, providing protection to the nearly 8 million acres of Spanish land grants. According to the treaty, the United States was to accord the same rights of ownership to Hispanic heirs of the land grants as it would to its own citizens.[4]

At the turn of the twentieth century, however, many of the common lands were alienated from the village populations by Anglo-American attorneys utilizing a legal code that was unfamiliar to the local people. Several grants were acquired by private logging companies and were later sold to the federal government. Since 1854, more than 2 million acres of land have been alienated from Spanish American ownership.[5] Through a series of subsequent transactions, many of these lands came under the jurisdiction of the U.S. Forest Service.[6]

Descendants of the original grantees have not forgotten that the grant lands once belonged to their ancestors. Over the past fifty years, efforts of land grant heirs to regain title to their lands have increased in both magnitude and sophistication. As recently as February 2, 2000, land grant activists took their claims based on the Treaty of Guadalupe Hidalgo to the New Mexico State Legislature.[7] Senators Pete Domenici and Jeff Bingaman have asked the controller general to review land grant issues, and Congressperson Tom Udall has introduced legislation to investigate these claims in the U.S. House of Representatives.[8]

The underlying land claims both cloud and clarify questions of environmental justice on the national forests. Although the alienation of the land grants from their original owners raises serious questions of equity vis-à-vis a minority population, this event does not invoke distributive or procedural questions pertaining to the use and development of natural resources or to the maintenance of a quality forest environment. In addition, remedies for the land grant dispute do not necessarily require the application of environmental justice. Thus, the land claims appear to raise issues of simple legal justice—not environmental justice per se.[9]

Nonetheless, these ownership issues underlie almost every discussion of the forests. Recently, Jesse Romero of the village of Truchas pointed out a newly burned section of trees on a far ridge. The Forest Service had attempted a cool understory burn to reduce forest fuels, but the fire had climbed into the canopy and burned fifty acres before being put out. "Look at that," he said. "Look at what they did. That's not right. They don't know anything." He turned to me and said, "That's our land."[10] In this statement, Mr. Romero based his criticism of Forest Service management on a judgment as to true ownership.

Distributive Injustice: Access to Timber Supplies

Although almost all disputes in the northern mountains over natural resources loop back to the fundamental issue of land ownership, questions of distributive justice abound. Since the early 1900s, Forest Service management of the grant lands reflected an Anglo-American perspective with origins far from northern New Mexico. Forest managers perceived the land as needing to meet national objectives and did not recognize a need to tailor programs to the unique cultural context of northern New Mexico. Decades of local disaffection of Forest Service policies came to a head in the 1960s with several demonstrations of social unrest that sent shock waves through the federal bureaucracy.

These feelings were expressed most acutely in Vallecitos and the other villages surrounded by the Vallecitos Federal Sustained Yield Unit (hereafter, Vallecitos Unit) in north-central New Mexico. The Vallecitos Unit is located north of Española and west of Taos and comprises 73,400 acres that once were part of a land grant. The Vallecitos Unit was created in 1948 as part of a national program to pool public and private timber resources to provide steady supplies of timber products to specific local communities. Five sustained yield units were created around the country, combining overharvested private lands with essentially virgin national forest lands, under the assumption that the public timber could be harvested while allowing the private forests to regrow.[11] This initiative grew out of the Forest Service's obsession with timber flows as a primary instrument of social utility. On the Vallecitos Unit, the Forest Service searched for a single "designated operator" to harvest and mill timber.[12] The timber was required to be milled locally, and the agency felt that the resulting jobs would adequately provide for the needs of the nearby communities. The agency also felt that working with more than a single, large mill would be inefficient.

Over the next forty years, the Forest Service designated three non-Hispanic operators from outside the community, with mixed results. Neither of the first two operators, having a combined tenure of five and one-half years over a twenty-four-year period, complied with the terms of their contracts requiring the use of local labor. The third operator remained in place for twenty-two years but was absorbed by a multinational holding company and became embroiled in repeated labor disputes with local residents.

Between 1948 and the late 1980s, local Hispanic businesses repeatedly petitioned the Forest Service for the right to be selected as designated operators. Even though the Vallecitos Unit was inactive for up to fifteen years for lack of an operator, the Forest Service turned down these requests. The reason given was that the local businesses were too small to achieve the industrial-scale management envisioned by the Forest Service.

Finally, in 1990, as a result of community opposition to proposals for management of the unit presented in the draft Carson National Forest Land and Resource Management Plan, the Forest Service made a commitment to offer 1 million board feet of commercial timber and 1.1 million board feet of small forest products each year directly to local businesses.[13] However, between 1990 and 1993, the Forest Service did not provide any of the promised volume for local loggers, citing a wide variety of reasons.[14] Thus, well into the 1990s, although local community members were offered occasional employment at the sawmill, they were not allowed direct access to timber resources.

Doug Henderson and Lane Krahl reflect on this history: "In spite of chronic failures, [the Forest Service] has held steadfast to a strategy—dominated by a concern for establishing forest regulation—in which sustained timber flows to a single operator employing local people are foreseen to produce community satisfaction."[15] This tendency extended as late as 1997, when the district ranger for the unit expressed a fond desire to work with a single, large operator.[16]

The situation changed dramatically in 1994 when local logger and land grant activist Antonio ("Ike") DeVargas initiated a lawsuit against the Forest Service with the assistance of a civil rights attorney, Richard Rosenstock, in Santa Fe. The lawsuit resulted in the first meaningful concessions from the Forest Service. As a result of an out-of-court settlement, several current and upcoming sales have been designated exclusively for small, local businesses. Although lawsuits brought by environmentalists have interrupted logging several times, direct economic benefits have begun to flow to local businesses for the first time in the fifty-year history of the unit.[17]

Procedural Injustice: Forest Roads

Residents of the Vallecitos Unit frequently raise issues of procedural injustice. These people have been given little say in the management of the lands surrounding their communities. An example is provided by the recent focus of the Forest Service on road closures.

Roads are a hot issue on national forests around the country. Responding to assessments that paint the road system as overbuilt and undermaintained, the Clinton administration initiated a program that might close many of these roads to control erosion and impacts on wildlife while reducing costs to the government.[18] Many western representatives, spearheaded by Representative Helen Chenowith, a Republican from Idaho, quickly voiced strident opposition to the Clinton plan.

The Forest Service proposal for the Agua Caballo timber sale on the Vallecitos Unit produced a similar response in the community by suggesting the closure of forty-six miles of existing road after harvest.[19] Feelings ran high at a community meeting held on April 8, 1999, to discuss the proposal. Initially, many people opposed all road closures. As the evening progressed, a tongue-in-cheek suggestion that the primary tourist road through the community be closed provoked a more thoughtful discussion. Finally, the idea of decommissioning many of the badly eroded, redundant travel ways began to appeal to the group.

Following this meeting, the Forest Trust commissioned a series of interviews with community members, undertaken by a local high school intern.[20] The intern sought specific information on which roads should be recommended for closure and what guidelines should be applied for new road construction. In general, interviewees felt that Forest Service standards for road construction and maintenance are too high and that narrow roads are serviceable and easier to maintain. Interviewees reaffirmed the view that the unit contains too many roads. One logger and community leader felt that most, if not all, of the roads should be closed.[21]

In sum, it appears that rural community leaders in the Vallecitos Unit have widely different attitudes toward road closures, depending on who makes the final decision. Not surprisingly, if the decision is made by the local Forest Service or in Washington, D.C., the community is opposed to all closures. If the community is allowed full engagement in the decision process, substantial road closures appear appropriate and even desirable. Unfortunately, the process envisioned for the national review of roads allows only for "public involvement," as opposed to a full collaborative process.[22]

Environmental Injustice and Forest Condition

I suggested above that the environmental justice movement originated in a concern for the quality of the environment surrounding disadvantaged communities. In forested areas, the condition of the forest, as measured by crown cover and age class distribution, provides the principal measure of environmental quality. In the Vallecitos Unit, community concerns over the impact of logging on the condition of the forest provides an excellent example of the interplay of forces contributing to environmental injustice.

Although some urban activists have characterized rural people as devoid of environmental sensitivities, members of the Vallecitos communities have taken strong proenvironment positions over many years. DeVargas describes his personal environmental epiphany after returning from Vietnam: "I couldn't relate to city life. Finally, I went into the woods, and there was peace. I felt like I had finally come home." In the same article, county commissioner Moises Morales asserts, "We [rural people] are environmentalists."[23]

Manifestations of this environmental ethic are evident in several controversies in northern New Mexico. One example emerged from the La Jarita timber sale. Forest Service policy changed in the early 1980s, favoring heavier logging that resembled clear-cutting. The La Jarita sale was one of the first, heavily destructive logging operations emerging from this policy. At the time, the Vallecitos Unit represented a remote corner of the national forest system, little known to the outside world. Ike DeVargas brought the timber sale into the public eye: "I blew the whistle on [that sale]. I lost my job over [it]."[24]

In another example, in 1985, the Forest Service proposed to double the annual timber harvest for the Vallecitos Unit to 8 million board feet. Many community members expressed dismay that this harvest was not sustainable and would have serious impacts on the watershed. Rudy Jaramillo, a local logger and president of the Vallecitos Sustained Yield Unit Association, "called the proposed increase 'devastating' and [recommended] . . . that the USFS protect the environment in the Unit by not increasing the allowable annual cut and not building any more roads."[25]

A third example of community leaders' concern over the impact of logging on the forest environment emerged in 1998. Heavy logging on private land on the outskirts of the county seat, Tierra Amarilla, generated significant citizen concern for downstream watercourses and irrigation systems. County commissioner Moises Morales and the Rio Arriba County Planning Department responded by developing the first, strict county ordinance in New Mexico relating specifically to timber harvesting.[26] The planning department enlisted technical assistance from the Forest Trust and the Western Environmental Law Center and based the rule on guidelines developed by the Forest Stewardship Council, an organization that promotes third-party certification of sustainable forestry operations internationally. Despite significant opposition from the timber industry, the commission passed this ordinance in 1998. The ordinance provides a higher level of environmental protection than state forest practices regulations and has provided an effective planning tool for the county.

Individual or community objections to destructive forest management prescriptions have surfaced in other situations as well. At a public meeting in April 1999, Ike DeVargas spoke out on a proposed timber sale: "We do not want the Forest Service to turn this area into a tree farm." This statement raises specific issues relating to the condition of the forest. DeVargas is suggesting that the Forest Service move to silvicultural techniques that do not produce an industrial forest.

DeVargas has also been concerned about the end result of Forest Service management on forest conditions in the La Manga timber sale area, a sale that his company won the right to harvest after bitter battles with the Forest Service and environmentalists. Initial harvesting by DeVargas's company left the forest in an exemplary condition. However, the Forest Service planned to make several other entries into the sale area for additional "thinning." DeVargas feared that the forest would be overharvested and that his work would be compromised, but he felt powerless to discourage these activities.[27] Other efforts by northern New Mexico communities to encourage the Forest Service to use a less heavy hand in thinning operations have also met with resistance from the agency.[28]

Conflicts reached a feverish pitch in the 1990s when the U.S. Fish and Wildlife Service listed the Mexican spotted owl as an endangered species and required that logging activities be suspended until biological assessments could be completed. Lorenzo Valdez, Rio Arriba county commissioner, decried "the ongoing campaign of public misrepresentation [that] helps the Forest Guardians to hide and legitimize their economic warfare against and harassment of New Mexico's indigenous peoples."[29] The environmental community responded in a similar vein, castigating Ike DeVargas as having "a long and well-documented history of violence against citizens trying to protect national forests" and also asserting that "much of the destruction [to the forests] has been caused by so-called 'small scale' logging companies such as [DeVargas's company]."[30]

In sum, members of rural communities surrounding the Vallecitos Unit have expressed strong environmental values and have taken strong positions—not to stop logging altogether but to restrict timber harvesting to specific silvicultural methods and to certain locations in order to protect the forest. These efforts reveal an appreciation of natural values in the context of the working landscape. The community's environmental sensitivities are rooted in rural culture and are distinct from the values expressed by urban activists in their search for a static state in the forest.[31] However, these efforts to preserve the forest environment have been overridden consistently by both the Forest Service and conservation organizations. The Forest Service has rejected local residents' goals for the landscape in favor of an industrial forest structure developed in the context of mainstream Anglo-American culture. The environmental community has similarly rejected the Hispanic vision of a natural-appearing working landscape in favor of a concept of nature "untrammeled by man, where man himself is a visitor who does not remain."[32]

The foregoing discussion suggests that a challenge underlying any discussion of environmental justice is that the concept of environmental quality varies from culture to culture. In fact, the term *environmental protection* may only be relevant in an urban, Anglo-American context and not to describe a reverence for the earth and a desire to care for its landscapes, vegetation, and creatures as expressed by rural people and other cultures.

This notion is supported by the positions of two leaders of Diné CARE, a Navajo organization. Ernie Atencio describes Earl Tulley, the president of Diné CARE, as "distanc[ing] himself from the Anglo environmental movement."[33] Adella Begaye, an activist with the organization, follows in the same article: "As Native people we can't really separate our environment from us, so it's hard to call us environmentalists. We stress cultural values, the natural laws learned from the creator."

In the case of Vallecitos, the disadvantaged community is suffering harm, in part from being deprived of the benefits of environmental protection policies that are consistent with the community's vision for the forest, and in part from the overzealous application of policies developed in an alien cultural context. Indeed, Getches and Pellow foreshadow this problem in Chapter 1, suggesting that some communities may be disadvantaged by strong application of environmental laws.

Conclusion

The communities surrounding the Vallecitos Unit are besieged from multiple perspectives. The federal agencies are unwilling to recognize the unique cultural requirements of the villages, to provide appropriate supplies of timber, to welcome residents into decision making, and to accede to the residents' vision for the forest environment. On the other hand, the urban environmental community is pressing for standards of forest protection that do not accommodate a working landscape or the cultural values of northern New Mexicans.

The animosity that has emerged between environmentalists and rural community leaders, despite the fact that they appear to hold similar values, suggests that more is going on than meets the eye. Ben Twight and J. J. Paterson characterize similar behavior in several case studies of national forest public participation as a "power strategy": "[A] power strategy involves exaggerating the differences between rivals in order to build cohesion, identity and commitment within a group. By maximizing its power, the group can strengthen itself."[34]

The impression that such power strategies are at work in northern New Mexico is strengthened by the words of Michael McClosky, chairman of the Sierra Club, who counseled environmentalists to mistrust creating partnerships with rural communities and declared that there are "Limits of Collaboration." The reasons McClosky gave for his suspicion of these efforts have to do with power—preserving the power of the national environmental organizations: "Collaboration would have the effect of transferring influence to the very communities where we are least organized and least potent. [T]his redistribution of power disenfranchises our constituency."[35]

McClosky's statements suggest that his caution about engaging in collaborative efforts has less to do with protecting the environment than with maintaining the political power of his constituency. While a powerful environmental organization may be important to McClosky's mission of environmental protection, certainly there is a strong possibility that activists in northern New Mexico could have achieved greater environmental gains by collaborating with local communities. In a similar fashion, the Forest Service could have achieved the terms of its goal statement, "caring for the land and serving people," if it were willing to depart from dated and outworn policies. In each of these cases, the cause of environmental justice—distributive, procedural, and substantive—would have been well served.

In contrast to a strategy of power that depends on limiting collaboration, the new discipline of community forestry offers a method for resolving conflicts and ensuring social justice. Community forestry, as defined by Thomas Brendler and Henry Carey, is an approach to forestry that helps rural people gain access to a portion of the benefits flowing from nearby forests. Community forestry also provides local people with a meaningful role in decision making. Finally, community forestry represents a learning process by which society can engage the knowledge of those living closest to the land in developing a sustainable relationship with our forests.[36]

Rural communities have much to teach. The ancestors of today's inhabitants of the mountain villages learned to survive in the arid deserts over many hundreds of years. In partnership with these communities, some environmentalists are learning a philosophy of resource use, a system of social and cultural restraints, that is relevant to the demands imposed by today's technologies, population growth, and global economy. In this context, community forestry offers a promising approach for both activists and professionals in their search for ways to sustain our forests.

These efforts must be based, however, on the recognition that the struggle to protect the environment is more than simply about power; it is also about fairness and civility. As we work to challenge society to cherish and protect the natural world, we must base our efforts on the sensitivity and courtesy we extend to one another.

Notes

1. Samuel Hays, *Conservation and the Gospel of Efficiency: The Progressive Conservation Movement, 1890–1920* (Cambridge: Harvard University Press, 1959).
2. Susan Flader, *Thinking Like a Mountain* (Lincoln: University of Nebraska Press, 1974).

3. Much of the material for this section was drawn from William de Buys, *Enchantment and Exploitation* (Albuquerque: University of New Mexico Press, 1985).

4. John B. Wright, "Hispano Forestry, Land Grants and the U.S. Forest Service in Northern New Mexico," *Focus, a Journal of the American Geographical Society* 44 (1997): 10–14; Treaty of Guadalupe Hidalgo, Treaty of Peace, Friendship, Limits, and Settlement with the Republic of Mexico, February 2, 1848, United States–Mexico, 9 Stat. 922.

5. Clark S. Knowlton, *Causes of Land Loss among the Spanish Americans in Northern New Mexico* (s.l.: s.n., n.d).

6. de Buys, *Enchantment and Exploitation.*

7. Kay Matthews and Mark Schiller, "Land Grant Forum Celebrates the Treaty of Guadalupe Hidalgo," *La Jicarita Newsletter* (March 2000): 1.

8. New Mexico Community Land Grant Review Act, S. 2022, 106th Cong., sess. 2, February 2, 2000; Guadalupe-Hidalgo Treaty Land Claims Act of 1999, H.R. 505, 106th Cong., sess. 1, February 2, 1999.

9. Other authors in this volume—for example, Jeff Romm in Chapter 5 and Jan Buhrmann in Chapter 11—might argue that because the communities of northern New Mexico are primarily people of color who apparently lack the political power to force compliance with the Treaty of Guadalupe Hidalgo that the land claims are, indeed, per se questions of environmental injustice.

10. Jesse Romero, personal communication with the author (2000).

11. Keith Easthouse, "A Failed Experiment," *Inner Voice* (July/August 1999): 11–16; Federal Sustained Yield Management Act of 1944, March 29, 1944, c. 146, sec. 1, 58 Stat. 132; 16 U.S.C., sec. 583 (1994).

12. Much of the following discussion on timber is based on the work of Lane Krahl and Doug Henderson. See Lane Krahl and Doug Henderson, "Uncertain Steps toward Community Forestry: A Case Study in Northern New Mexico," *Natural Resources Journal* 38 (winter 1998): 53–84; and Doug Henderson and Lane Krahl, "Public Management of Federal Forest Land in the United States," *Unasylva* 47 (1996/1): 55–61.

13. USDA Forest Service, Carson National Forest, "Carson Forest Plan Amendment No. 8, Timber-13" (1990).

14. *La Compania Ocho, Inc. v U.S. Forest Service et al.,* 874 F. Supp. 1242 (D. N.M. 1995).

15. Henderson and Krahl, "Public Management of Federal Forest Land"; see box titled "The Vallecitos Federal Sustained Yield Unit."

16. Kurt Winchester, personal communication with the author (June 18, 1997).

17. Issues underlying the lawsuits filed by environmentalists are described later in this chapter.

18. USDA Forest Service, "National Forest System Road Management Strategy Environmental Impact Statement and Civil Rights Impact Analysis" (2000).

19. USDA Forest Service, Southwestern Region, "Supplemental Draft Environmental Impact Statement for the Proposed Agua/Caballos Projects. Carson National Forest, El Rito Ranger District" (2000).
20. The Forest Trust, a forest conservation organization based in Santa Fe, New Mexico, works closely with rural Hispanic communities to identify preferred resource management strategies.
21. M. Peña, "Rural Residents Speak Out about Forest Service Roads," *Forest Trust Quarterly Report* 22 (August 2000): 9.
22. Laura F. McCarthy, "New Strategy for Managing Roads," *Forest Trust Quarterly Report* 22 (August 2000): 8.
23. J. Goldberg, "La Manga: Finding the People among the Trees," *Santa Fe Reporter,* October 15–21, 1997, 17–23.
24. Goldberg, "La Manga."
25. Krahl and Henderson, "Uncertain Steps toward Community Forestry," 53–84.
26. Steve A. Harrington, "Who's Watching Private Forests? A New Mexico County Tackles Timber Regulation," *Forest Trust Quarterly Report* 19 (November 1998): 1–2, 10.
27. Ike DeVargas, personal communication with the author (1998).
28. David Cordova et al., letter to district ranger Crockett Dumas (1998).
29. Lorenzo Valdez, letter to Ms. Katherine Roberts of the *New York Times* (August 12, 1997).
30. Chad T. Hanson, letter to the Earth Island Institute board of directors (October 10, 1997).
31. Carl Wilmsen, "Fighting for the Forest: Sustainability and Social Justice in Vallecitos, New Mexico" (Ph.D. diss., Clark University, Worcester, Mass., 1998).
32. Wilderness Act of 1964, Pub. L. 88-577, September 3, 1964, 78 Stat. 790; 16 U.S.C., sec. 131(c).
33. Ernie Atencio, "'People of the Earth' Stress 'Natural Laws'," *High Country News,* October 31, 1994, 4.
34. Ben W. Twight and J. J. Paterson, "Conflict and Public Involvement: Measuring Consensus," *Journal of Forestry* 77 (December 1979): 771–76.
35. Michael McClosky, "The Limits of Collaboration," *Harper's* (November 1996): 34–36.
36. Thomas Brendler and Henry Carey, "Community Forestry, Defined," *Journal of Forestry* 96 (1998): 21–23.

Chapter 10

NEPA IN INDIAN COUNTRY

Compliance Requirement to Decision-Making Tool

Dean B. Suagee

American Indian and Alaska Native tribes face a wide variety of issues relating to natural resources. Tribal cultural practices and religious beliefs are deeply rooted in the land, woven into the web of life. Decimation of wildlife and destruction of wildlife habitat have inflicted suffering on tribal cultures. Buffalo and salmon are two prominent examples, and there are many others. Many tribal cultures bear scars of the allotment era of federal Indian policy, when federal laws were used to force Indians to stop hunting and fishing and gathering wild plants and to become farmers. Largely agrarian tribal cultures have also suffered from changes in the environment brought about by the dominant American society. For example, they have had their water sources diverted or their bottomlands flooded by reservoirs. Many reservations bear scars from the extraction of minerals and from industrial forestry and agriculture. Alaska Native tribes face variations on these themes, such as crashing populations of fish and wildlife species on which they have depended for countless generations. But Alaskan tribes lack reservation-based territorial sovereignty and must confront these threats to their survival without that defining feature common to tribes in the lower forty-eight states.

While the roots of tribal cultures reach back into mythic time, tribal communities exist in present-day America, and they face many of the same kinds of environmental issues that non-Indian communities face, such as where to put the trash. In some fundamental ways, though, Indian country is different. As Sarah Krakoff explains in Chapter 7, the problem of what to do with trash is a classic example of how environmental law is different in Indian country.[1]

Looking at natural resources issues in Indian country through an environmental justice lens could help people in the larger society understand why tribes struggle to preserve their right to be different. An environmental justice lens might help the larger American society understand the legal principles that apply exclusively in Indian country at least well enough that we can find ways to ensure that tribes are treated fairly while honoring their right to be different. An environmental justice lens might also help people understand why Alaska Native tribes have sought to have their homelands considered "Indian country," which would make their tribal territories more like reservations.[2]

Of course, more understanding on the part of people in the larger society will not by itself help the people and the tribal governments of Indian country deal with natural resources and environmental issues. We will have to move beyond mere understanding and on to informed action. But tribal communities do need support from the larger society, and to be useful, such support must be informed. The environmental justice movement can help to inform the non-Indian public and to mobilize support for tribal efforts to protect the environment.

Furthermore, the environmental justice movement and the mainstream environmental movement need Indian people within their ranks, maybe more than Indian people need either movement. People of the tribal cultures rooted in this continent can speak the truth to both movements, the truth that human societies are, and must understand themselves to be, part of the web of life.

Environmental Justice in Indian Country

Some of the other chapters in this book have discussed the meaning of the term *environmental justice* and have commented on the lack of consensus. One of the definitions used by the U.S. Environmental Protection Agency (EPA) defines environmental justice as "the fair treatment and meaningful involvement of all people regardless of race, color, national origin, or income with respect to the development and enforcement of environmental laws, regulations, and policies."[3] "Fair treatment," in turn, "means that no group of people, including racial, ethnic, or socioeconomic group should bear a disproportionate share of the negative consequences resulting from industrial, municipal, and commercial operations or the execution of federal, state, local, and tribal programs and policies."[4]

For the purposes of this chapter, I assume that Indian communities generally do fit within one or more of the list of characteristics with which David Getches and David Pellow (in Chapter 1) and others identify the kinds of groups that environmental justice seeks to protect. The race-ethnicity dimension, however, is only part of the picture. For most purposes, the key factor in being Indian is membership in a tribe that has federally recognized status, a government-to-government relationship with the United States. Based on this factor, the Supreme Court has said that being Indian is a "political classification" rather than a racial one.[5] This "political" status sets Indian tribes apart from other minorities. Over the course of American history, while other minorities have struggled for equal treatment under the law, Indian tribes have bargained and fought and litigated and lobbied to preserve their right to be different, their right to "measured separatism."[6] This political status also makes it constitutionally permissible for Congress to enact statutes that treat Indians differently from other citizens.

Although Indian people have suffered much discriminatory treatment from people who apparently define Indian identity in primarily racial-ethnic terms, the fact that tribes are sovereign governments is a significant distinction between them and other kinds of minorities. This distinction is especially relevant in the environmental justice context, as I have discussed in other works[7] and as Krakoff discusses in Chapter 7. As the EPA uses the term *environmental justice community*, one of the four defining characteristics is having been "excluded from the environmental policy setting and/or decision-making process."[8] Indian tribes have the sovereign authority to make and enforce laws to govern their reservations. In theory then, if environmental impacts result from policies set for, or decisions made on, their reservations, tribes might not qualify as environmental justice communities. In actual practice, however, the dominant American society, through its institutions of government, has imposed some rather substantial limits on tribal sovereignty. Of the three kinds of sovereigns in our federal system, tribal governments are the only ones that have to deal with the judge-made rule that certain aspects of their sovereignty have been divested by implication.[9]

In conjunction with limits on tribal sovereignty, the dominant American society also has imposed many of its laws on tribes and tribal homelands, including federal environmental laws, pursuant to the doctrine known as the plenary power of Congress. Unfortunately, in the 1970s, when Congress enacted the first generation of federal environmental laws, it did not give much thought to how these laws would be carried out in Indian country. Moreover, the general approach of cooperative federalism, in which states perform major roles, had the practical effect of creating a regulatory system in which the environmental concerns of tribal communities were largely ignored. Beginning in the mid-1980s, Congress began to rectify this oversight by enacting tribal amendments to some of the federal environmental statutes, and now tribes can use these laws to develop environmental protection programs. The basic approach offered by many of the federal statutes is for a tribe to apply to the EPA for treatment in the same manner as a state.[10] There is more to this, however, than a tribal government simply deciding that it needs a law to protect its environment and then enacting and enforcing such a law. This is especially true for tribes whose reservations contain substantial amounts of land that is not in federal trust (or restricted) status (a widespread feature of the legacy of the allotment era). The lingering practical effect of the original congressional neglect of Indian country is that the environmental regulatory infrastructure on most reservations is simply not comparable to that of the rest of the country.

The extent to which any particular tribal government has effective control over the environmental policy-setting or decision-making process—and, thus, whether this dimension of the term *environmental justice community* applies—can be examined on a case-by-case basis. Sometimes tribes have effective control; sometimes they do not. In many cases, decisions made by federal agencies, and by state or local governments, regarding activities outside reservation boundaries cause environmental impacts to occur within reservations or cause impacts on off-reservation resources in which tribes have rights supposedly protected by treaty or statute.

Sometimes, even when the activity occurs within a reservation and even though a tribe makes the decision, the information available is so sketchy that it is not really accurate to say that the tribe has effective control. This is illustrated by the commercial hog farm development discussed later in this chapter. The hog farm is an example of how the approach taken by the Bureau of Indian Affairs (BIA) for compliance with the National Environmental Policy Act (NEPA)[11] often ensures that tribal officials will be called upon to make decisions without enough information to fully appreciate, let alone give careful consideration to, the environmental impacts of their decisions.

Much of the literature on environmental justice has emphasized the "disproportionate impacts" aspect of the concept. If we take this as the defining characteristic of environmental justice as applied to Indian country, then we can describe just about any environmental issue as an environmental justice issue. The relative lack of environmental regulatory infrastructure results in what might be described as structural disproportionate impacts.[12] At another level, for tribal cultures that still find sustenance and identity in the natural world, environmental impacts affect them disproportionately almost by definition. And then when tribes do step up and try to exercise their sovereign powers to protect the environment, they have to contend with "predatory" judge-made doctrines that apply only to tribal governments, such as implicit divestiture.[13]

Is it at all useful to view all environmental issues in Indian country as environmental justice issues? Does the label "environmental justice" help us to understand what should be done to make things right? Using Gary Bryner's theoretical frameworks in Chapter 2, an emphasis on disproportionate impacts could be described as an example of the "distributive justice" framework.[14] For the case study examined in this chapter, however, I think it will prove more constructive to place it within Bryner's "public participation" framework, which corresponds to the category that Professor Robert Kuehn describes as "procedural justice."[15] Accordingly, in this chapter, I focus on procedural justice in making decisions that will result in environmental impacts affecting Indian country. My focus is limited to a subset of such decisions, those in which the proposed action would take place on Indian trust land and in which both the BIA and a tribal government have authority to deny permission or to impose conditions if permission is granted.

Sarah Krakoff argues in Chapter 7 that environmental justice for tribes should be understood to mean ensuring respect for tribal authority to control and improve reservation environments, and that any notion of environmental justice should include protecting tribal sovereignty. I agree. People in the environmental justice movement need to understand and respect tribal sovereignty. This does not mean, however, that the movement should never challenge a tribal government decision but, rather, that the movement should not challenge the tribe's right to make such decisions. I have no objection to environmental justice groups trying to influence such tribal decisions using whatever procedural opportunities exist under tribal law. When federal law establishes procedural requirements that apply to projects that tribes are considering, environmental justice groups may find these federal requirements useful in making their views known before decisions are made. Through attention to procedure, we may find ways to satisfy expectations of justice on the part of people affected by tribal government decisions while maintaining respect for tribal sovereignty.

NEPA as the De Facto Permitting Process

NEPA has become a de facto permitting process for "development" proposals in Indian country. NEPA applies to federal agency actions. In Indian country, NEPA may apply because the BIA or another federal agency proposes to take an action affecting the environment. More commonly, in this era of self-determination, NEPA applies to a proposed development project because a federal agency has provided funding to a tribal government. NEPA may also apply because a tribe or tribal enterprise has arranged for private financing but still needs BIA approval for a transaction involving trust land. A number of tribes have enacted their own legislation establishing an environmental review process; such a tribal law is sometimes generically known as a "tribal environmental policy act," or a TEPA. If a tribe has a TEPA, it may facilitate compliance with NEPA, but it does not render NEPA inapplicable.

The Basics

The following sections briefly explain what NEPA requires and how this requirement has been implemented through regulations and agency policies. Although NEPA was enacted more than three decades ago, even federal employees whose jobs include responsibility for NEPA compliance sometimes have misconceptions. In Indian country such misconceptions may result from the fact that training in NEPA has never been a priority for the BIA.

What NEPA Requires

Section 102(2)(c) of NEPA requires that before any federal agency takes an action "significantly affecting the quality of the human environment," the agency must prepare an environmental impact statement (EIS).[16] This requirement has been implemented through regulations issued by the President's Council on Environmental Quality (CEQ).[17] The CEQ regulations, which are binding on all federal agencies, govern the process for preparing an EIS, including the requirements for allowing the public to become involved in the preparation and review of an EIS. The CEQ regulations also establish procedural requirements for consultation with governmental entities (federal, state, local, tribal) other than the federal agency that is considering the proposed action. In many cases, other governmental agencies have jurisdiction over a proposed action or have relevant expertise.

Under the CEQ regulations, the preparation of an EIS includes the following steps: (1) a notice of intent to prepare an EIS; (2) a "scoping process," in which interested persons, organizations, and governmental entities discuss the kinds of environmental impacts that might result from the proposed action and ways to avoid or mitigate the adverse impacts, including alternatives to the proposed action; (3) the actual writing of the draft EIS, including any studies that must be done to gather information or to analyze particular issues; (4) the distribution of a draft EIS for public review and comment; (5) a public comment period, which may include hearings; (6) the preparation of a final EIS, including responses to comments received on the draft EIS; (7) the distribution of the final EIS; (8) a thirty-day waiting period, in which other federal agencies can express their concerns; and (9) a decision—that is, whether to go ahead with the proposed action or to choose one of the alternatives considered in the final EIS.

The minimum time in which an EIS can be completed—from the decision to prepare an EIS to a decision based on the EIS—is about six months. Typically, however, an EIS takes longer, often a year or more. Because of the time required and the cost, federal agencies—and the proponents of development projects that require federal approval—typically try to avoid having to do an EIS.

The Threshold Question: Is an EIS Required?

The key question in determining whether NEPA requires an EIS for a proposed federal action is whether the proposed action may "significantly" affect the "quality of the human environment." The CEQ regulations establish a kind of screening procedure to determine if an EIS is required. Those regulations require each federal agency to make a list of the kinds of actions it takes and to sort these actions into three categories: (1) those that normally have significant environmental impacts and thus require an EIS; (2) those that normally do not have significant environmental impacts and thus do not require an EIS ("categorical exclusions"); and (3) those that the agency must consider on a case-by-case basis and decide whether an EIS will be required.[18] For proposed actions in the third category—the case-by-case category—the federal agency must prepare an environmental review document known as an environmental assessment (EA).[19] The basic purpose of an EA is to determine whether the impacts of the proposed action will be significant. If so, then an EIS must be prepared. If the federal official responsible for NEPA compliance determines, based on an EA, that the impacts will not be significant, then she signs a document known as a finding of no significant impact (FONSI). The EA and a FONSI fulfill the requirements of NEPA, unless a higher level federal official reverses the decision or unless someone files an administrative appeal or sues the federal agency and obtains an order from an appeals board or a federal court directing the agency to prepare an EIS. If the federal official determines that the impacts will or may be significant, then an EIS is required.

In actual practice, when faced with an EA that does not support a FONSI, most agency officials do not decide to proceed directly to the preparation of an EIS. Rather, they tend to decide that more work must be done on the EA—more analysis and the development of additional measures to mitigate environmental impacts so that the EA will support a FONSI. In any case in which NEPA compliance requires an EA, if it becomes apparent that an EA will not support a FONSI, the responsible federal official can decide to skip the EA step, but this rarely happens.

Agency Implementing Procedures

Under the CEQ regulations, each federal agency is required to adopt procedures to carry out its NEPA responsibilities. In 1978, when the CEQ regulations were issued in final form, the Department of the Interior (DOI) decided to have one set of NEPA implementing procedures for the entire DOI rather than have each bureau within DOI adopt its own procedures. The DOI's procedures were published as part of the Departmental Manual.[20] Each bureau, including the BIA, was required to develop a list of the types of actions it takes and then sort these actions according to the categories listed above.

In order to apply the NEPA screening process to any proposed project involving a BIA action, we must look in the BIA's lists in the Departmental Manual.[21] For "development" projects initiated by a tribe or an enterprise doing business with a tribe, the BIA action is typically approval of a land transaction that is a legal necessity before the project can proceed. The question is whether the proposed BIA action is the kind of action that would normally require an EIS or whether it is the kind of action that fits within a categorical exclusion.

The answer, almost always, is that it does not fit into either of these categories, so NEPA compliance requires an EA to determine whether an EIS is required. The categorical exclusion that typically comes close to applying is one for "approvals or grants of conveyances and other transfers in land where no change in land use is planned."[22] Of course, a change in land use is almost always planned, even if the plans are not well enough developed to evaluate their environmental impacts.

Writing the EA

The information contained in the DOI implementing procedures is not really enough for those outside DOI, including the tribes, who need to deal with the BIA on NEPA matters. Most "development" projects in Indian country are "externally initiated proposals," and the proponents are tribal governments, tribal enterprises, private businesses, or some combination of such entities, rather than the BIA. According to the BIA's internal guidance document for its staff, the BIA NEPA Handbook, the proponent of an "externally initiated" action is generally responsible for preparing the EA.[23] The BIA is responsible for the content of EAs prepared by tribes and other external applicants, and the BIA is also responsible for determinations of significance, that is, deciding whether NEPA requires an EIS. But the applicant is responsible for writing the EA or for otherwise making arrangements to have an EA written by a contractor. Unfortunately, since the BIA has never issued any guidance for the public on NEPA, it may not be easy for applicants to learn this seemingly critical piece of information.

Guidance to the public on how to write an EA for an Indian country development project is also limited. The CEQ regulations do not provide any guidance on preparing an EA beyond that contained in the definition in 40 C.F.R., sec. 1508.9: an EA is supposed to be a "concise public document" that contains sufficient information to determine whether to prepare an EIS. This section of the regulations also says that an EA must include "brief discussions of the need for the proposal, of alternatives as required by section 102(2)(E) [of NEPA], of the environmental impacts of the proposed action and alternatives, and a listing of agencies and persons consulted." The Departmental Manual adds a little to this, but not much, suggesting that applicants should contact BIA for assistance. In the absence of any guidance developed specifically for use by the public, applicants can use the BIA NEPA Handbook for guidance, assuming that they can obtain a copy from the agency.[24]

How It Works in Practice: The Mitigated FONSI

Despite the intent and procedures of NEPA, decision makers in BIA, as in many other federal agencies, show great reluctance to decide that an EIS is required. The depth of analysis in an EA is supposed to be limited to "that needed to determine whether there are significant environmental effects."[25] In practice, however, when an EA identifies significant impacts, the next step is to rewrite the EA and add mitigation measures to reduce the severity of the impacts. An EA may be rewritten several times before the decision maker is satisfied that enough mitigation measures have been added so that the EA supports a FONSI. An EA that has been prepared to support such a "mitigated FONSI" may approach the length of an EIS, which is supposed to be no longer than 150 pages.[26]

This practice is driven, in large part, by the private partners who bring financing to development projects. Private partners generally regard NEPA as a compliance requirement, and they do not want to pay for, or take the time for, any more than necessary to get through the process. Because of the time and expense involved in doing an EIS, private partners may say that if an EIS is required, the deal is off, or they may set project development deadlines that would preclude an EIS. If the tribal governing body has expressed support for a project, BIA officials tend to be reluctant to insist on an EIS.

If the mitigation required in a mitigated FONSI really does reduce the severity of impacts, then what's wrong with this approach to NEPA compliance? Often what's wrong is a lack of public involvement. The CEQ regulations do not specify any particular process for seeking public involvement in the preparation of an EA, nor do the regulations even require that an EA be made available to the public before the responsible federal official determines whether or not the EA supports a FONSI. Rather, the CEQ regulations require only that a notice be published after that decision is made, and that the notice tell people that the EA is available to the public.[27] An agency is not required to prepare a draft EA and circulate it for comments before deciding whether the EA supports a FONSI.

One reason that the CEQ regulations provide so little guidance on the preparation of EAs is that the CEQ intended for the EA process to be a threshold inquiry—agencies would quickly decide whether or not to prepare an EIS, using an EA as a tool for making that decision. In practice, agencies and outside applicants tend to invest substantial resources in the preparation of EAs in order to be able to conclude that an EIS is not required, that is, by preparing an EA that supports a mitigated FONSI. The CEQ did not anticipate the development of this practice and even issued guidance saying that it is not authorized by the regulations.[28] The federal courts, however, have sustained this practice.[29]

In practice, an EA may be circulated as a draft and comments solicited. Sometimes public meetings are held.[30] On the other hand, the process of writing and rewriting the EA may go on for six months or more before any document is made available to the public. Even if this approach leads to a thorough EA, it may not be an acceptable substitute for community involvement. Sometimes, neither tribal nor BIA officials anticipate the depth of community opposition to a project that has been approved based on an EA and a FONSI. Sometimes the practice of relying on an EA and a FONSI serves to catalyze community opposition, because people assume that information is being kept from them and that environmental impacts are being down-played. By omitting public participation, a project can become a case of environmental injustice whether or not its environmental impacts are "significant."

One True Story: The Rosebud Hog Farm

In late September 1998, construction commenced on what was planned as a very large confined animal feeding operation (CAFO) on trust land owned by the Rosebud Sioux Tribe. The facility was designed to produce more than 850,000 hogs per year, although it now appears unlikely that it will be completed as planned. In August 1998, the BIA had issued a final environmental assessment for a pro-posed pork production facility. The proponent of the project was Sun Prairie, a partnership that would build and operate the facility in a joint venture with the Rosebud Sioux Tribe.

Before issuing the final EA, the BIA had gone beyond the bare minimum requirements for public involvement by making a draft EA available to the public and soliciting comments before making the determination of significance.[31] A public meeting was held on June 15, 1998, the draft EA was released in late June, and comments were accepted until July 29.[32] Regardless of whether or not the BIA and Tribe did more than the minimum, the process failed.

In her brief account of the Rosebud hog farm in Chapter 7, Sarah Krakoff emphasizes the BIA's failure to ensure that important infor-mation was available to the Tribal Council before it made its decision. Concerned members of the reservation community found the process of seeking public input on the EA to be confusing. They were trying to figure out the process at the same time that they were trying to comprehend the scope of the project and its environmental impacts.[33] The reservation community's inability to understand and participate in the NEPA process was partly due to the inadequacy of the process and partly a function of the BIA's failure to follow its own proce-dures.

The EA—Content Issues

The Sun Prairie EA is a seventy-six-page document that presents a substantial amount of descriptive information about the environment that would be affected by the project, a fairly extensive listing of the kinds of impacts that could occur (some of which are discussed in a rather superficial way), and a section on mitigation measures. Despite its length, in my view, the EA had several major flaws in content, including a failure to adequately (1) consider alternatives and (2) incorporate other applicable review and consultation requirements. These flaws might have been corrected if citizens and government agencies had been given more time to review and comment on the draft EA. The flaws could have been avoided altogether if the responsible BIA officials, tribal officials, or even the project sponsors had just decided to prepare an EIS.

Since the emphasis in this chapter is on the procedural dimension of environmental justice, my substantive critique of the EA is brief, and I am not particularly concerned with whether the decision by the BIA area director not to do an EIS is ultimately sustained in federal court. Given the amount of water that this project would use if built as planned (1.6 million gallons per day) and the amount of animal waste that would be produced and processed in lagoons (the waste of more than 850,000 hogs, comparable to the waste of a major city without a wastewater treatment plant), my opinion is that this is a project for which the BIA should have immediately decided that an EIS should be done.

Of course, under the CEQ regulations, "significance" is a judgment call. The definition of the term *significantly* takes up nearly a full page in the Code of Federal Regulations.[34] This definition sets out some ten kinds of factors that the responsible federal official must consider, but there are no hard and fast rules. In part, it is a judgment regarding the environmental impacts of a proposed project; in part, it is a judgment of whether or not opponents of the project will take the agency to court.[35] In this case, after the opponents went to court, the assistant secretary of the interior for Indian affairs overruled the judgment of the area director and, finding that the EA did not support the FONSI, declared the lease void. The proponents of the project then filed suit in a different federal district court, and that court disagreed with the assistant secretary. Regardless of who was right on this point, this was a case in which reliance on an EA and a FONSI led to a decision that many members of the Tribe found so objectionable that they ultimately used the political process to reverse it.

DISCUSSION OF ALTERNATIVES

When an EIS is prepared for a proposed action, the CEQ regulations require the lead federal agency to "rigorously explore all reasonable alternatives," including "reasonable alternatives not within the jurisdiction of the agency."[36] This requirement does not apply to an EA. The purpose of an EA, after all, is to determine whether the impacts will be significant.

The Sun Prairie EA considered only two alternatives: (1) build the project as described in the EA; or (2) do not build it. The federal district court found this analysis to be sufficient for the EA.[37]

Regardless of whether the court was right on this issue, if an EIS had been prepared, a wider range of alternatives would have been required. The extent of the analysis would have depended, at least to a large extent, on the people who would have participated in the process. The preparation of an EIS begins with a process known as "scoping."[38] This is an open process in which the lead federal agency, with input from affected government agencies (federal, tribal, state, and local) and interested persons, determines the "scope" of the EIS. As defined in the CEQ regulations, the term *scope* means the range of actions, alternatives, and impacts to be considered in an EIS.

In fashioning a range of alternatives an EIS should consider, we first start at the "purpose" or "need" for the proposed action. As stated in the Sun Prairie EA, the purpose of the project was "to bring economic development and opportunity to the Rosebud Sioux Tribe," and the need for the project was "to provide the opportunity for economic prosperity to the area and tribal members."[39] An open scoping process could generate a wide range of alternatives that would satisfy this purpose and need.

The court's interpretation of what was adequate for consideration of alternatives in the Sun Prairie EA illustrates one of the problems of project proponents, agencies, and the tribes treating NEPA as a compliance requirement rather than as a decision-making tool. When an EA considers only two alternatives—do the project or do not do it— and the BIA official signs a FONSI, the usefulness of the EA to tribal officials is very limited. In essence, the FONSI is some assurance that a federal official thinks that the environmental impacts of the project will not be so bad. NEPA documents can be much more useful. They can present a range of choices in which the comparison of environmental impacts can inform the decision makers.

OTHER ENVIRONMENTAL REVIEW AND CONSULTATION REQUIREMENTS

When an EIS is prepared for a proposed action, the CEQ regulations require that the EIS integrate compliance with other applicable environmental review and consultation requirements.[40] This requirement does not apply to EAs. Instead, an EA need only include a list of the agencies and persons consulted.[41] The BIA NEPA Handbook recommends dealing with any applicable environmental review and consultation requirements in the EA. If such compliance is not addressed, then the EA is at least supposed to identify any applicable requirements and say what will be done to achieve compliance.[42] Determining what requirements apply can be challenging, and some of the complications result from the nuances of federal Indian law. One approach is to circulate the EA and let other agencies say whether they think they have jurisdiction. Regardless of whether they do, the comments offered by such agencies can be useful in deciding whether or not the EA supports a FONSI.

The Sun Prairie EA's "Compliance with Environmental Statutes" section is cursory with respect to most requirements and is simply wrong with respect to others. Specifically, it appears that the EA did not resolve questions regarding the applicability of at least two federal statutes, the Clean Water Act (CWA) and the National Historic Preservation Act of 1966 (NHPA). Issues surrounding requirements of the CWA illustrate one of the problems of employing a mitigated FONSI rather than deciding that an impact may be significant and proceeding with an EIS. EPA's comment letter on the draft EA indicates that the project proponents had intended to apply to the EPA for a National Pollutant Discharge Elimination System (NPDES) permit, and the EPA advised that the issuance of such a permit would require additional NEPA analysis. The final EA suggests that the project proponents decided to try to avoid the requirement for applying to the EPA for a NPDES permit by redesigning the project so that all of the waste produced would be stored and processed on site using lagoons, evaporative ponds, and biogas digesters. The EPA's comment letter on the final EA stated that there was not enough information in the EA to assess the environmental impacts of these methods of dealing with the waste. If the project were analyzed in an EIS process, such alternative development methods and appropriate mitigation measures would have been fully analyzed.

The Sun Prairie EA also demonstrated a cursory approach to the consultation requirement established by Section 106 of the NHPA, which is intended to avoid inadvertent damage to or destruction of places that are listed on, or eligible for, the National Register of Historic Places.[43] In addition to an apparent misunderstanding of the regulatory requirements of Section 106, including the requirement to consult with the State Historic Preservation Officer, the EA failed to address the possibility of traditional cultural properties. These are places that are eligible for the National Register because of their ongoing importance in the religious and cultural practices of an Indian tribe.[44] There may be no physical evidence of such importance; rather, the only source of information about the importance of such places may be stories told by tribal elders. The EA made no attempt to find out if such places would be affected by the Sun Prairie project. It made no effort to gather information from tribal elders who might know of the significance of places in the Tribe's oral tradition, even though some of the tribal people involved in the opposition to the project had publicly said that such places did exist.

The Attempt to Appeal the FONSI—Failed Process

The final EA was released by the BIA on August 14, and that same day the BIA superintendent for the Rosebud Agency signed a FONSI. The FONSI was published in local newspapers the following week accompanied by only a statement that construction activities would not commence "until 30 days after advertisement of this finding."[45] The FONSI did not provide any information on how a person who objected to the FONSI might file an appeal. The Interior Board of Indian Appeals (IBIA) had ruled that the decision by a BIA official to sign a FONSI is subject to appeal,[46] but the BIA had issued an internal memorandum that sought to limit the applicability of this ruling.[47] This memorandum states that a FONSI is subject to appeal at the time the BIA takes final agency action based on the FONSI—for example, when a lease analyzed in an EA and FONSI is approved—and the memorandum implies that the notice of the FONSI should say this.

Despite the BIA's failure to provide proper notice, five individuals, including one tribal member who lives near the site of the proposed hog facility, attempted to follow proper procedures to protest the decision. The group sent a letter to the Aberdeen area director of the BIA asking for clarification of the procedure for objecting to the FONSI and filing an administrative appeal.[48] This letter cited the BIA regulations for administrative appeals,[49] and asserted that these appeal regulations apply to the FONSI. The letter asked for the BIA to confirm that the FONSI was subject to appeal or to inform the writers whether there was any other administrative remedy that could be exhausted prior to seeking relief in federal court.

The acting area director responded that the FONSI did not qualify for appeal.[50] This statement is contrary to the BIA memorandum because the FONSI would have been subject to appeal in the context of an appeal of the approval of the lease. In the litigation that followed, the federal district court asserted that the people challenging the Sun Prairie project should have appealed the approval of the lease for the project, not the FONSI, and the court noted that none of the letters of protest even referred to the lease.[51]

But how were the opponents of the project supposed to know that they should have appealed the lease rather than the FONSI? Part of the answer is that the BIA was legally obligated to tell them. If it was the approval of the lease that was the appealable decision, then the BIA official was required to give "all interested parties known to the decision-maker" written notice of the decision, including an explanation of the appeal process and a statement that there is a thirty-day time limit for filing a notice of appeal. Furthermore, because one of the protestors was a tribal member and was not represented by counsel, the BIA was even obligated to assist in the preparation of the appeal.[52]

From Litigation to a Political Solution?

Relying on the letter from the BIA stating that the FONSI was not subject to an administrative appeal, hog farm protestors elevated their protest to the courts. On November 23, 1998, the unincorporated association known as Concerned Rosebud Area Citizens (CRAC) sued the federal government in the District of Columbia federal district court, alleging that the BIA's approval of the lease was invalid for violations of NEPA and the NHPA, and seeking injunctive relief.[53] This complaint was not briefed or argued. Rather, on January 27, 1999, the assistant secretary for Indian affairs, Kevin Gover, issued a letter declaring that the lease was void because of the failure of the BIA to comply with NEPA.[54] In essence, the assistant secretary agreed with the basic allegation of the complaint filed by CRAC—that the EA did not support a FONSI. After the assistant secretary's decision, CRAC agreed to have its lawsuit dismissed.

Sun Prairie and the Rosebud Sioux Tribe then filed a lawsuit, in federal district court in South Dakota, against the assistant secretary alleging that the decision voiding the lease was arbitrary and capricious. Sun Prairie and the Rosebud Sioux Tribe sought a preliminary injunction to prevent the BIA from interfering with the construction of phase 1 of the project. CRAC and the other organizations that had been plaintiffs in the original lawsuit joined the second lawsuit as intervenors. Sun Prairie and the Rosebud Sioux Tribe sought to have the preliminary injunction also apply to the intervenors, to prevent them from interfering with construction of the project. In March 1999, the district court issued a preliminary injunction, as Sun Prairie and the Rosebud Sioux Tribe had sought, and then, in February 2000, the district court issued a permanent injunction.[55] This decision is currently on appeal before the Eighth Circuit.[56]

In the fall of 1999, the Rosebud Sioux Tribe held elections for the Tribal Council. Several council members who had been supporters of the Sun Prairie project lost their seats. Several people who were, and are, opponents of the project were elected. On January 5, 2000, the Tribal Council enacted a resolution calling for a full "Environmental Impact Study" (presumably meaning an EIS) of the project and expressing the council's determination that no further expansion of the project should be undertaken until the EIS is completed.[57] In July 2000, the Tribal Council decided to switch sides in the litigation and has since filed briefs supporting the assistant secretary in the case on appeal before the Eighth Circuit.

It can be argued that the tribal political process worked in this case to rectify the failure of the NEPA process. The facts remain, however, that the lease for the first phase of the Sun Prairie project was approved and that some of the phase one facilities are in operation. Moreover, the tribe's efforts to prevent further expansion of the project through action in Tribal Court have been rebuffed by the federal court.[58] If the NEPA process had worked, tribal officials would not have to contend with the ongoing operation of a project that they no longer want.

The Trust Responsibility and the NEPA Process

NEPA applies to a project such as the Sun Prairie hog farm because the land on which it is located is Indian trust land and the transaction that makes the project possible requires BIA approval. In exercising this kind of approval authority, the BIA is subject to the federal trust responsibility to Indian tribes, through which the federal government has "charged itself with the moral obligations of the highest responsibility and trust."[59]

The federal district court mentioned the trust responsibility in its opinion, in a cursory way, saying that "a significant factor that must be weighed under the particular facts of this case is the tribal trust relationship and the need for economic development on Native American reservations."[60] In this statement, the court seemed to lump the trust responsibility and the need for economic development together, as a single factor. The court then says that if it were to sustain the assistant secretary's decision:

> The logical conclusion [would be] that bureaucratic misconduct will prejudice these plaintiffs and will also prejudice other entities who might be considering contracts with Native American Tribes for the beneficial use of tribal trust land. Indeed, the failure of this project based on administrative ineptitude and procedural unfairness would absolutely deter private entities and lending insti-

tutions from pursuing economic relationships with the various tribes.[61]

The court's superficial analysis of the trust responsibility is wrong, as is its asserted "logical" conclusion as to the practical consequences of sustaining the assistant secretary's action to void the lease. Arguably, the assistant secretary did just what the federal trust responsibility required.

All three branches of the federal government recognize the doctrine of the federal trust responsibility to Indian tribes.[62] The doctrine has its roots in the treaties through which the tribes ceded vast portions of their aboriginal lands in exchange for the federal government's promise to protect the rights of tribes to continue to exist as self-governing nations within the lands that they had reserved for themselves. The doctrine is also based on the practice of the federal government of holding legal title to Indian land in trust for the beneficial use of Indian tribes and individuals, and much of the case law has arisen in the context of mismanagement of land and other trust resources by the BIA.[63] The doctrine is often described as unique. One scholar suggests the term *sovereign trusteeship* to distinguish the trust responsibility of the modern era of Indian self-determination from the historical concept of the guardian-ward relationship.[64] Congress has expressly recognized that the trust responsibility "includes the protection of the sovereignty of each tribal government."[65]

Although it is something of an oversimplification, it is nevertheless accurate to say that the trust responsibility includes at least two key facets: (1) the fiduciary obligations to manage Indian lands and other trust resources for the benefit of the Indian landowners; and (2) the duty to protect the governmental authority, the sovereignty, of the tribes. In the modern self-determination era of federal Indian policy, tensions sometimes arise between these two facets of the trust responsibility. In some instances, the obligation for the management of trust resources may appear to conflict with the duty to support a tribe's right of self-government. How can the BIA find the right balance? How can the BIA exercise its obligations as the trustee of Indian lands, including ensuring that future generations of Indian people will be able to make use of trust land, without returning to the paternalism of the guardian-ward era of federal Indian policy?[66] If the BIA simply defers to the judgment of the present tribal governing body without adequately considering the interests of future generations, it may be setting itself up for a claim for mismanagement of trust resources.

In cases in which tribal government decisions may have long-term impacts on the reservation land base, a modern conception of the trust responsibility doctrine counsels that the BIA has, at the very least, a fiduciary obligation to ensure that sufficient information is available to the tribal government so that the likely impacts on future generations are taken into consideration.[67] The NEPA process is designed to develop this kind of information and make it available to federal officials and tribal officials who are charged with making decisions.

Whether these two aspects of the trust responsibility came into conflict in this particular case is not really the issue. NEPA provides an opportunity for an informed decision. The assistant secretary determined that the EA did not support a conclusion that the environmental impacts would not be significant. He was concerned that the EA did not adequately address some of the likely impacts of the project. Regardless of whether the intensity of any one or more of the impacts was such that an EIS should have been prepared, the project called for a substantial amount of trust land, and a substantial amount of trust water, to be dedicated to this project for a substantial period of time. This is precisely the kind of BIA approval decision in which the federal trustee should have said, in effect, "Let's take a closer look before we make that decision." That, in essence, is what the assistant secretary tried to say in his letter voiding the lease, and it was the right thing to do. It was the responsible thing to do as a trustee.

The district court asserted that the logical conclusion of sustaining the assistant secretary's action would be that entrepreneurs and financial institutions will simply choose not to do business in Indian country. An alternative conclusion can be drawn: businesses and lending institutions doing business in Indian country will learn to treat the NEPA process as a decision-making tool rather than a compliance requirement. Enlightened entrepreneurs will suggest that, for any project that may cause controversial environmental impacts, a full EIS really should be done, even if the responsible BIA official says that an EA and a FONSI will suffice. Enlightened entrepreneurs will realize that it is better to have community involvement in planning a project than to face a groundswell of community opposition committed to using the tribal electoral process to reverse a tribal government decision and stop a project that the community really does not want.

Lessons and Recommendations

Environmental justice is a potent concept with many constituencies, and it may be unrealistic to seek consensus among all the people and groups with a stake in the term on all aspects of its meaning. Most will agree, though, that public participation in governmental decisions affecting the environment is an important dimension of environmental justice, especially where those decisions affect minority and low-income communities. In Indian country, it can be challenging to achieve meaningful public involvement in federal decisions while still showing deference to the authority of tribal decision makers—unless tribal officials make it clear that they value public involvement. The NEPA process can help to meet such challenges. As illustrated by the case study examined in this chapter, though, the NEPA process often falls short of its potential. Drawing on this case study, I offer some recommendations for improving the way NEPA works in Indian country.

1. The BIA should issue guidance on NEPA that is readily available to the affected public. This is particularly important in the era of self-determination when much of the actual work of NEPA compliance falls on tribal governments and the proponents of development projects.[68]

2. It would be helpful to have more objective standards for determinations of significance, but even without such standards, tribal officials should engage in these determinations and be willing to recommend that an EIS be done.

3. There should be more specific requirements for public involvement in EAs. In particular, if the decision-making official and project proponent want to avoid an EIS by developing a mitigated FONSI, the EA should be made available to the public before being reworked. EAs for controversial actions should routinely be distributed as drafts for comments before the decision maker signs a FONSI.

4. There should be better guidance on how to determine which other environmental review and consultation requirements apply and how to achieve compliance. This is particularly important given the confusion that results from the complexities of federal Indian law.

5. There should be a transparent appeal process, one that avoids environmental impacts during the period of appeal, and one that does not put tribes in the position in which they are compelled to raise sovereign immunity as a defense.

6. Tribal officials should insist that NEPA documents, and documents prepared under tribal law, be used to guide decision making, not merely to document compliance with a required process. They should also consider enacting and implementing

their own tribal environmental policy acts, to establish their own processes.

7. BIA and other federal agencies, with tribes as cooperating agencies, and other interested persons should prepare a programmatic EIS on economic development in Indian country.

My seventh recommendation leads into a more general lesson that can be drawn from the Sun Prairie project. Public participation by itself cannot ensure that governmental decisions will not cause disproportionate environmental impacts on disadvantaged communities. We need much more attention to creative ways to promote environmentally sustainable and culturally compatible economic development so that we can spend less time arguing over which communities will be forced to put up with environmental degradation. The people of tribal communities need better access to information about ways to accomplish economic development while living within the carrying capacity of the Earth's natural systems. People in the larger society who think that a large-scale confined animal feeding operation is not an ideal way for a tribe to pursue economic development could help to create other strategies. Gary Bryner addresses this dimension of environmental justice in Chapter 2 as the "ecological sustainability framework." In tribal communities, to be sustainable, economic development should also be consistent with tribal cultural values.

Over the last quarter century or so, there has been a great deal of technological development that can be used to provide for the needs of human communities while reducing the kinds of stresses that humans have been imposing on the Earth. Solar and renewable energy technologies offer some examples of this kind of development, and there are many other examples as well.[69] The people of Indian country could use some help from the people of the larger society in using such technological development to make tribal communities better places to live.

If environmentally sustainable, culturally compatible projects are included among the alternatives considered in the NEPA process, and in similar processes established under tribal law, I believe we will find that the people of Indian country routinely choose such options as their preferred alternatives. After all, Indian people can look within their cultures to find a basic truth about our existence on this Earth— that human societies are, and must understand themselves to be, part of the web of life.

Acknowledgments

Quite a few people helped me write this chapter by providing me with documents about the Rosebud confined animal feeding operation and by talking with me on the phone. I am not sure whether any of them would want to be formally acknowledged; some may prefer to remain anonymous. In any event, I am grateful to all of them.

Notes

1. See also Dean B. Suagee, "Turtle's War Party: An Indian Allegory on Environmental Justice," *Journal of Environmental Law and Litigation* 9 (1994): 461, 473–79.
2. See *Alaska v Native Village of Venetie Tribal Government*, 522 U.S. 520 (1998). See also Dean B. Suagee, "Cruel Irony in the Quest of an Alaska Native Tribe for Self-Determination," *Natural Resources and Environment* 13 (winter 1999): 495.
3. U.S. Environmental Protection Agency, *Final Guidance for Incorporating Environmental Justice Concerns in EPA's NEPA Compliance Analyses* (April 1998), 5–6, available at http://es.epa.gov/oeca/ofa/ejepa.html (visited December 19, 2000). (Note: Page citation is to the version of the document posted on the Internet.)
4. U.S. Environmental Protection Agency, *Final NEPA Compliance Analyses Guidance*, 6. This definition is also quoted in U.S. Environmental Protection Agency, *Final Guidance for Consideration of Environmental Justice in Clean Air Act 309 Reviews* (July 1999): 6, available at http://es.epa.gov/oeca/ofa/ej_nepa.html (visited December 19, 2000). Both of these documents attribute this definition to the EPA Office of Environmental Justice, but neither cites a specific source document. A 1998 memorandum from the director of the EPA Office of Environmental Justice defines the term with somewhat different wording:

    > The fair treatment of people of all races, cultures, incomes, and educational levels with respect to the development and enforcement of environmental laws, regulations, and policies. Fair treatment implies that no population should be forced to shoulder a disproportionate share of exposure to the negative effects of pollution due to lack of political or economic strength.

    Memorandum from Barry E. Hill, director, Office of Environmental Justice, EPA, to deputy regional administrators, EPA, et al. (December 16, 1998), quoted in Robert M. Kuehn, "A Taxonomy of Environmental Justice," *Environmental Law Reporter* 30 (September 2000): 10681, 10683–84.
5. See *Morton v Mancari*, 417 U.S. 535, 554 n. 24 (1974). See also David C. Williams, "The Borders of the Equal Protection Clause: Indians as Peoples," *UCLA Law Review* 38 (1991): 759; and Carole Goldberg-Ambrose,

"Not 'Strictly' Racial: A Response to 'Indians as Peoples,'" *UCLA Law Review* 39 (1991): 169.

6. Charles F. Wilkinson, *American Indians, Time and the Law* (New Haven, Conn.: Yale University Press, 1987), 32; see also Dean B. Suagee, "The Indian Country Environmental Justice Clinic: From Vision to Reality," *Vermont Law Review* 23 (1999): 567, 573–75.

7. Suagee, "Turtle's War Party"; Suagee, "The Indian Country Environmental Justice Clinic."

8. To be classified as an "environmental justice community," as the term is used by EPA, residents must be a minority or low income group; excluded from the environmental policy setting or decision-making process; subject to a disproportionate impact from one or more environmental hazards; and experience a disparate implementation of environmental regulations, requirements, practices, and activities in their communities.
   U.S. Environmental Protection Agency, "What Is Environmental Justice?" available at http://es.epa.gov/oeca/main/ej/faq.html (visited December 19, 2000), quoted in Kuehn, "A Taxonomy of Environmental Justice," 10683.

9. *Alaska v Venetie.* See Suagee, "Cruel Irony."

10. See generally David F. Coursen, "Tribes as States: Indian Tribal Authority to Regulate and Enforce Federal Environmental Law and Regulations," *Environmental Law Reporter* 23 (October 1993): 10579 ; see also Judith V. Royster, "Native American Law," in *The Law of Environmental Justice*, ed. Michael B. Gerrard (Chicago: American Bar Association, 2000).

11. 42 U.S.C., secs. 4321–47.

12. See Suagee, "The Indian Country Environmental Justice Clinic," 579–84.

13. Frank Pommersheim, "Coyote Paradox: Some Indian Law Reflections from the Edge of the Prairie," *Arizona State Law Journal* 31 (1999): 439, 463, describing the "predatory" jurisprudence of the U.S. Supreme Court, including the new doctrine of "judicial plenary power."

14. Professor Robert Kuehn also uses this term in his four-part categorization of environmental justice issues. Kuehn, "A Taxonomy of Environmental Justice," 10683–88.

15. Kuehn, "A Taxonomy of Environmental Justice," 10688–93.

16. 42 U.S.C., sec. 4332(2)(c).

17. 40 C.F.R., pts. 1500–1508. See generally Daniel L. Mandelker, *NEPA Law and Litigation*, 2nd ed. (Deerfield, Ill.: Clark Boardman Callaghan, 1992, updated annually); and Karin P. Sheldon and Mark Squillace, eds., *The NEPA Litigation Guide* (Chicago: American Bar Association, 1999). See also Gillian Mittelstaedt et al., *Participating in the National Environmental Policy Act: A Comprehensive Guide for American Indian and Alaska Native Communities* (Marysville, Wash.: Tulalip Tribes, 2000), available in the Vermont Law School First Nations Environmental Law Program Tribal Environmental Law Virtual Library at www.tribalenvironmentallaw.org under the heading, "Books, Links, and Other Resources."

18. 40 C.F.R., sec. 1507.3(b)(2).

19. 40 C.F.R., secs. 1501.3 and 1508.9. See generally James M. McElfish Jr., "The Regulations Implementing NEPA," in Sheldon and Squillace, eds., *The NEPA Litigation Guide*, 155, 173–85.

20. 516 DM, chaps. 1–6.

21. 516 DM 6, app. 4 [soon to be 516 DM 10].

22. 516 DM 6, app. 4, sec. 4.4.I., 61 *Federal Register* 67848 (December 24, 1996) (soon to be 516 DM 10.5I, 65 *Federal Register* 52229 [August 28, 2000]).

23. 30 BIAM Supp. 1, sec. 4.2B, citing 516 DM 1.4C; officials responsible for "loan, grant, contract, lease, license, permit" or other federal actions in response to such proposals "shall require applicants, to the extent necessary and practicable, to provide environmental information, analyses, and reports as an integral part of their applications."

24. 30 BIAM Supp. 1, chap. 4. The BIA NEPA Handbook was rescinded on October 14, 1998, as part of a project to reorganize the BIA's system for issuing internal directives. Memorandum from Acting Deputy Commissioner of Indian Affairs to Regional Directors and Central Office Directors (May 12, 2000). Until the process of revising and reissuing the NEPA Handbook is completed, BIA staff have been advised that they should continue to refer to the NEPA Handbook for guidance.

25. 516 DM, sec. 3.4C.

26. 40 C.F.R., sec. 1502.7.

27. 40 C.F.R., sec. 1506.6(b).

28. Council on Environmental Quality, Question 19 in "Forty Most Asked Questions Concerning CEQ's National Environmental Policy Act Regulations," 46 *Federal Register* 18026, 18031–32 (March 23, 1981), reprinted in Nicholas C. Yost, *The NEPA Deskbook*, 2nd ed. (Washington, D.C.: Environmental Law Institute, 1995): 263, 268–69.

29. *Cabinet Mountains Wilderness v Peterson*, 685 F.2d 678 (D.C. Cir. 1982), expressly refusing to follow CEQ's "Forty Most Asked Questions"; *Sierra Club v U.S. Dep't of Transportation*, 753 F.2d 120 (D.C. Cir. 1985).

30. For some kinds of BIA actions—for example, accepting land into trust for a gaming facility—the circulation of a draft EA with a draft FONSI has apparently become the standard practice, although this is not specified by a rule that someone outside the BIA could seek to have enforced if disregarded.

31. 30 BIAM Supp. 1, sec. 4.5A.

32. *Rosebud Sioux Tribe v Gover*, CIV. 99-3003 (D. S.D., February 3, 2000), slip opinion at 2.

33. This statement is based on telephone conversations between the author and members of Concerned Rosebud Area Citizens, an unincorporated association.

34. 40 C.F.R., sec. 1508.27.

35. If a decision not to prepare an EIS is challenged in court, the case law provides little guidance for predicting the outcome. Daniel Mandelker says, "The courts usually decide these cases on an ad hoc basis with no attempt to provide criteria under which environmental significance can be meas-

ured." Mandelker, *NEPA Law and Litigation*, sec. 8.03[3]. In this case, opponents of the hog farm argued in part that the EA did not even consider certain kinds of impacts, including odor from the hog farm and the possibility of disease transmission. The district court rejected these points, saying, "An agency's failure to consider an arguably relevant factor does not, by itself, establish an NEPA violation. The administrative record may reveal that the factor was not sufficiently significant to merit discussion." *Rosebud Sioux Tribe v Gover*, 22.

36. 40 C.F.R., sec. 1502.14.

37. *Rosebud Sioux Tribe v Gover*, 21–22. The court said, "Given the significant need for economic development in the region, it would not be an effective or logical public policy to require private corporations to consider various alternatives which may not be in their economic self-interest, simply for the sake of considering alternatives in the EA."

38. 40 C.F.R., sec. 1501.7.

39. Bureau of Indian Affairs, "Final Environmental Assessment for Proposed Pork Production Facility" (August 1998), 1 (on file with the author).

40. 40 C.F.R., sec. 1502.25.

41. 40 C.F.R., sec. 1508.9.

42. 30 BIAM Supp. 1, sec. 4.3G.

43. 16 U.S.C., sec. 470f.

44. See generally Dean B. Suagee, "Tribal Voices in Historic Preservation: Sacred Landscapes, Cross-Cultural Bridges, and Common Ground," *Vermont Law Review* 21 (1996): 145, 170–74.

45. Larry J. Burr, agency superintendent, Rosebud Agency, Bureau of Indian Affairs, U.S. Department of the Interior, "Finding of No Significant Impact, Pork Production Facility," Melette County, S.D. (August 14, 1998), published August 19, 1998.

46. *Friends of the Wild Swan v Portland Area Director, Bureau of Indian Affairs*, 27 IBIA 8, at 15–23, 1994 I.D. Lexis 146 (1994).

47. Memorandum from Deputy Commissioner of Indian Affairs to All Area Directors and All Central Office Directors, Subject: Appeals of National Environmental Policy Act Decisions (Nov. 6, 1995), rescinding Memorandum from Deputy Commissioner of Indian Affairs to All Area Directors and All Central Office Directors, Subject: Appeals of National Environmental Policy Act Decisions (August 14, 1995).

48. Letter from Nancy Hilding, president, Prairie Hills Audubon Society of Western South Dakota, et al., to Cora Jones, area director, BIA (September 4, 1998).

49. 25 C.F.R., pt. 2.

50. Letter from acting area director, Bureau of Indian Affairs Aberdeen Area Office, to Nancy Hilding, president, Prairie Hills Audubon Society of Western South Dakota (September 17, 1998). At the time, according to the deputy commissioner's memorandum dated November 6, 1995, the FONSI was not yet subject to appeal because the lease had not yet been approved. The lease was approved on September 18, 1998. Construction

commenced on the project "on or about September 21," although the approval of the lease had not yet become final agency action, since the time for filing a notice of appeal must expire before a decision becomes final (25 C.F.R., sec. 2.6).

51. *Rosebud Sioux Tribe v Gover*, 3, 8.
52. 25 C.F.R., secs. 2.7 and 2.9(b).
53. *Concerned Rosebud Area Citizens et al., v Babbitt*, Complaint for Declaratory and Injunctive Relief (filed November 23, 1998) (on file with the author). It took CRAC a little more than sixty days to file the action, in part because they had trouble finding an attorney who was willing to take the case, they had very limited funds to pay for legal counsel, and it took some time to find other organizations with more resources that were willing to join in the case. Some of the organizations that they approached declined because they did not want to be perceived as opposing the Tribe.
54. *Rosebud Sioux Tribe v Gover*, 2–3. One day earlier, on January 26, 1999, the Department of Justice had filed an answer denying the alleged violations of NEPA and NHPA.
55. *Rosebud Sioux Tribe v Gover*, 1.
56. *Sun Prairie v Gover*, Nos. 00-2468 and 00-2471 (8th Cir.).
57. Rosebud Sioux Tribe, Resolution No. 2000-1.
58. Kay Humphrey, "Judge OKs Hog Farm Development: Said Former Council Signed Valid Lease," *Indian Country Today*, May 23, 2001, D1 (reporting that the federal district court has prohibited the tribe from "using its tribal court to stop construction under way on a new site").
59. *Seminole Nation v United States*, 316 U.S. 286, 297 (1942).
60. *Rosebud Sioux Tribe v Gover*, 14.
61. *Rosebud Sioux Tribe v Gover*, 14–15, quoting from "Doc. 53 at 13."
62. See generally Felix S. Cohen, *Handbook of Federal Indian Law* (Charlottesville, Va.: Michie Press, 1982): 220–28.
63. See, for example, *United States v Mitchell*, 463 U.S. 206 (1983), holding BIA to fiduciary duty for management of timber resources on allotted Indian lands; *Navajo Tribe v United States*, 364 F.2d 320, 322–24 (Ct. Cl. 1966), holding federal government liable for mismanagement of helium lease on tribal lands; and *White Mountain Apache Tribe v United States*, 11 Cl. Ct. 614, 649–51 (1987), holding government liable for mismanagement of range and forest resources, aff'd, 5 F.3d 1506 (Fed. Cir.), cert. denied, 511 U.S. 1030, 114 S. Ct. 1538 (1993).
64. Mary Christina Wood, "Indian Land and the Promise of Native Sovereignty: The Trust Doctrine Revisited," *Utah Law Review* (1994): 1471, 1498.
65. 25 U.S.C., sec. 3601.
66. See Mary Christina Wood, "Protecting the Attributes of Native Sovereignty: A New Paradigm for Federal Actions Affecting Tribal Lands and Resources," *Utah Law Review* (1995): 109, 139 n. 111, explaining that a "tribe's present and future generations are similarly situated to the life

and remainder interests of a private trust, and the trustee's duty runs to both."

67. See Wood, "Indian Land and the Promise of Native Sovereignty," 1550–64; see also Wood, "Protecting the Attributes of Native Sovereignty," 126–49.

68. See Dean B. Suagee, "The Application of the National Environmental Policy Act to 'Development' in Indian Country," *American Indian Law Review* 16 (1991): 377, 464–95, offering suggested guidance for the BIA to publish in title 25 of the Code of Federal Regulations. An updated version of this guidance document is available in the Vermont Law School First Nations Environmental Law Program Tribal Environmental Law Virtual Library at www.tribalenvironmentallaw.org under the heading, "Faculty Papers."

69. See Amory Lovins, L. Hunter Lovins, and David Hawkins, *Natural Capitalism: Creating the Next Industrial Revolution* (Boston: Little, Brown, 1999). See also Andres Duany, Elizabeth Plater-Zyberk, and Jeff Speck, *Suburban Nation: The Rise of Sprawl and the Decline of the American Dream* (New York: North Point Press, 2000), explaining how communities that feature "walkable" neighborhoods not only reduce use of cars but also offer an improved quality of life in a variety of ways.

Chapter 11

A FRAMEWORK TO ASSESS ENVIRONMENTAL JUSTICE CONCERNS FOR PROPOSED FEDERAL PROJECTS

Jan Buhrmann

Since the proclamation of the Environmental Justice Executive Order, "Federal Actions to Address Environmental Justice in Minority and Low-Income Populations,"[1] federal agencies have increasingly acknowledged the importance of promoting environmental justice in environmental decision making. Federal agencies are guided by statutory authorities and specific guidance documents with regard to the potential environmental impacts of federally funded projects.[2] An important task of federal agencies is considering environmental justice when evaluating proposed projects impacting natural resources and the physical environment.

The National Environmental Policy Act (NEPA) review process plays an important role in this evaluation process. Ray Clark and Larry Canter point out that NEPA has been a principal avenue for public involvement in both the planning and the decision-making processes of federal agencies. They add that NEPA's broad mandate allows agencies to incorporate and integrate other regulatory requirements and emerging objectives, including biodiversity, conservation, environmental justice, and risk analysis.[3]

Goals of the executive order include fostering nondiscrimination in federal programs that substantially or potentially affect human health and the environment and providing communities with greater opportunities for public participation in (and access to) public information on matters relating to the environment or human health. All federal agencies are encouraged to consider environmental justice in their NEPA analysis, and the U.S. Environmental Protection Agency

(EPA) has a special role in promoting environmental justice through its role in the NEPA review process:

> Environmental Justice issues may arise at any step of the NEPA process and agencies should consider these issues at each and every step of the process, as appropriate. Environmental justice issues encompass a broad range of impacts covered by NEPA, including impacts on the natural or physical environment and interrelated social, cultural, and economic effects. In preparing an EIS or an EA, agencies must consider both impacts on the natural or physical environment and related social, cultural, and economic impacts. . . .

> The provisions of the Clean Air Act Section 309 require the Administrator of EPA to comment in writing upon the environmental impacts associated with certain proposed actions of other federal agencies; including actions subject to NEPA's EIS requirement. The comments must be made available to the public."[4]

A critical element when assessing social impacts and potential environmental justice implications is to initiate this process early in the planning phases of a project, before siting and permitting decisions are made, and before feasible alternatives are developed. If potentially impacted communities are brought to the table at the inception of project planning and development, the concerns and ideas of minority, low-income, and tribal communities can be more fully integrated into decision making at all stages of the process. Unfortunately, agencies have had difficulty identifying environmental justice situations and, therefore, incorporating this kind of analysis into their NEPA documents.

This chapter presents a four-point framework, previously developed by EPA Region 8, for identifying situations in which low-income and minority communities are at risk of being disproportionately burdened with the negative impact of projects, and for incorporating their concerns into NEPA impact analysis. The case study presented here applies the concept of environmental justice, as defined in the executive order and as described in the NEPA guidance documents. The case study applies the EPA's framework to a flood control project for which the U.S. Army Corps of Engineers (hereafter, the Corps) is the lead agency. The chapter also illustrates how an imbalance of benefits and burdens may result from specific natural resources management actions, potentially resulting in disproportionate impacts to low-income and tribal communities.

In its role as a cooperating agency in the NEPA process, EPA Region 8 assisted the Corps, St. Paul District, in highlighting environmental justice considerations for the proposed Devils Lake Emergency Outlet.[5] The EPA's role was to examine the potential impacts to various individuals and groups in the Devils Lake Region of North Dakota and to determine whether a potential environmental justice situation existed with regard to construction and operation of the proposed emergency outlet. The case study was designed as a qualitative examination of the potential impacts of the proposed outlet on various communities surrounding Devils Lake, taking into consideration feedback from farmers, ranchers, tribal members, and others. This chapter presents the process and findings of this study; presents a methodology for environmental justice assessment that can be adapted by other federal and state agencies, academia, and community organizations; and illustrates the role of federal agencies in ensuring that environmental justice considerations are an integral part of natural resources and land use decisions.

A Framework for Conducting Environmental Justice Analyses

The Environmental Justice Program from Region 8 of the EPA developed a four-point framework for conducting environmental justice assessments in its NEPA oversight role. This framework, which can be adapted by other government agencies and community organizations, includes analyzing *demographics, benefits and burdens, disproportionate impacts,* and *stakeholder involvement* to examine proposed projects (prior to implementation) in a way that takes into consideration potential impacts to low-income and minority communities. A brief description of these four components is presented below.

Demographics

The first element of the framework, demographics, is a threshold evaluation of whether those potentially affected by the project are within the scope of the executive order and, therefore, whether additional environmental justice analysis is needed. Section 1-101 of the executive order focuses the attention of federal agencies on the human health and environmental conditions of minority and low-income populations.[6] Low-income populations can be identified using the annual statistical poverty thresholds from the U.S. Bureau of the Census: Current

Population Reports, Series P-60 on Income and Poverty, well as Household Median Income for specific counties. Minority populations are members of the following population groups: American Indian or Alaskan Native; Asian or Pacific Islander; black, not of Hispanic origin; or Hispanic. In this chapter, the terms *low-income populations* and *minority populations* are used interchangeably with the terms *low-income communities* and *minority communities,* and with the term *environmental justice communities.* For its framework, the EPA has defined a "community" as either a group of individuals living in geographic proximity to one another or a set of dispersed individuals (such as migrant workers), in which either type of group experiences common conditions of environmental exposure or effect.

An important initial step in environmental justice analysis is to determine whether areas or groups potentially impacted by a proposed project can be classified as environmental justice communities. Factors that must be examined include the percent minority and the percent low-income within the impacted area as percentages of the state average. Although a number of criteria can be used, EPA Region 8 has generally used population concentrations of 20 percent (or greater) of the state population as a general guideline to classify a community as minority, and concentrations of 20 percent (or greater) above the state average for poverty as a guideline for designating low-income communities.[7] The existence of tribal or reservation lands within a geographic area under consideration can be used to establish the presence of a federally recognized tribe and, consequently, the presence of a potential environmental justice community.[8]

Benefits and Burdens

All segments of the society regardless of race, color, national origin, or income should share fairly in the benefits of environmental protection and in shouldering the burdens of implementation of these policies. In the second component of the four-point framework. the agency identifies the distribution of the benefits and burdens of the project and the associated implementation of federal laws, regulations, and policies. Important questions to ask in this area include the following: Which benefits (economic, social, cultural, environmental, health— direct and indirect) will result from the proposed action, and to which stakeholders?[9] What burdens (economic, social, cultural, environmental, health—both direct and indirect) will come from the proposed action, and to which stakeholders?[10]

To assess potential benefits and burdens, it is important not only to examine documents and other literature published about a proposed project but also to investigate attitudes and perceptions of the communities involved, seeking out their concerns about what impacts they may experience as a result of the proposed project (or, in the case of an existing activity or facility, are currently experiencing). Including communities' concerns and perceptions provides for a broader range of existing or potential impacts and may uncover impacts not mentioned in official project documents or by project proponents. As the range of benefits and burdens of a particular project is examined, we can begin to determine whether those impacts would be fairly distributed or would disproportionately impact specific communities.

Disproportionate Impacts

The third important step in the four-point framework—determining whether there are disproportionate impacts to environmental justice communities—begins with assessing whether there is (or will be) an impact on the natural or physical environment that significantly (as employed by NEPA) and adversely affects a minority or low-income population. Such effects may include ecological, cultural, human health, economic, or social impacts, when those impacts are interrelated with impacts to the natural or physical environment. Determining disproportionate impacts addresses the question of whether these impacts—the benefits and burdens of a proposed project—are fairly distributed or unequally distributed with a majority of benefits accruing to some communities or stakeholders while most of the burdens (or negative impacts) fall on other communities.

Initially, it is important to assess whether environmental laws are being complied with, in the case of an existing facility, or likely to be complied with, in the case of a proposed project. The answers to this question may impact the direction of the analysis. Next, an assessment must be made of whether adverse environmental effects exist (or are likely to result from a proposed action). This assessment asks if any environmental effects are significant. Then, the assessment is used to determine whether the projects have (or will have) an adverse impact on minority or low-income populations that appreciably exceeds (or is likely to appreciably exceed) those on the general population or other comparison group. Assessment in this area should also include consideration of whether the environmental effects occur (or would occur) in a minority population or low-income population already affected by cumulative or multiple adverse exposures from environmental hazards.[11]

Determining whether potential impacts disproportionately affect low-income or minority communities can be challenging. By carefully considering information and feedback from all stakeholders (including community members and groups, industry groups, interest groups, and government agencies), lead agencies on a proposed or existing project can assess the range of benefits and burdens and determine whether these impacts are fairly distributed. This determination can make a valuable contribution to the NEPA process and potentially affect permitting and project decisions.

Stakeholder Involvement

Environmental justice requires a fair process so that the actual impacts of a proposed project are objectively and accurately considered. Gary Bryner's discussion of a public participation framework (in Chapter 2) and Sheila Foster's discussion of the challenges of achieving meaningful participation in an environmental justice community (in Chapter 6) highlight this. The executive order on environmental justice directs federal agencies to allow all populations a meaningful opportunity to participate in the development of, compliance with, and enforcement of federal laws, regulations, and policies affecting human health or the environment. Federal agencies are directed to give minority communities and low-income communities greater opportunities for participation in, and access to, public information on matters relating to human health and the environment. Consequently, the EPA or a lead agency can use the fourth component of the framework to determine how well the agency is meeting (or has met) this goal as part of the decision-making process. Important questions to ask include the following:

- How has information been made available to the community (for example, use of foreign language translations; understandable and accessible materials, including clearly explained technical information; personal contact; and community-wide distribution)?
- What opportunities has the community had to participate in environmental decision making around this action?
- Were all potentially affected parties heard from?
- How was community representation selected and invited?
- What have we heard from the community?
- How satisfied was the community with its involvement in decision making around the issue?
- To what degree did the community influence the decision-making process?

It is important that active involvement by all stakeholders takes place early in a proposed project. This is particularly important for community members and groups, who are often excluded from the initial planning phases.

Integrating the Four-Point Framework

If the four components of this framework are analyzed, environmental justice communities can be identified, the distribution of benefits and burdens and the potential for disproportionate impacts can be determined, and effective stakeholder involvement can be accurately assessed. As Gloria Helfand and L. James Peyton point out: "Environmental justice is a complex concept that combines social, political, and economic factors. All these factors contribute to the identified correlation of minority/poor status with environmental risks."[12] The EPA Region 8 framework provides a tool for integrating these factors so that risks to low-income and minority communities can be accurately assessed, and mitigated or avoided where appropriate. The following case study illustrates how the four components—demographics, benefits and burdens, disproportionate impacts, and stakeholder involvement—can be used in an environmental justice assessment.

Applying the Four-Point Framework: The Proposed Emergency Outlet at Devils Lake, North Dakota

The case study used to illustrate the four-point framework centers on the Devils Lake Region of North Dakota and the proposed federal project to construct a flood control outlet on Devils Lake. The lake level has risen approximately 25 feet since 1993, to its current level of 1,446 feet.[13] What some perceive as a natural and cyclical phenomena is seen by others as unacceptable damage to houses, business, and farmlands. Proponents of the proposed outlet feel that such a control structure is necessary to permanently stabilize lake levels and minimize further damage. Opponents of the outlet cite concerns about property damage and potential noise pollution due to outlet construction and operation, as well as problems related to both water quality and quantity as water from Devils Lake is channeled downstream into the Sheyenne River. Economic, environmental, cultural, and other concerns have also been expressed by the outlet's opponents. As mentioned previously, the Corps St. Paul, Minnesota District, has been designated as the lead agency on the proposed Emergency Outlet at Devils Lake. At present, two west-end outlet routes are under consideration: (1) the Peterson-Coulee Route, and (2) the

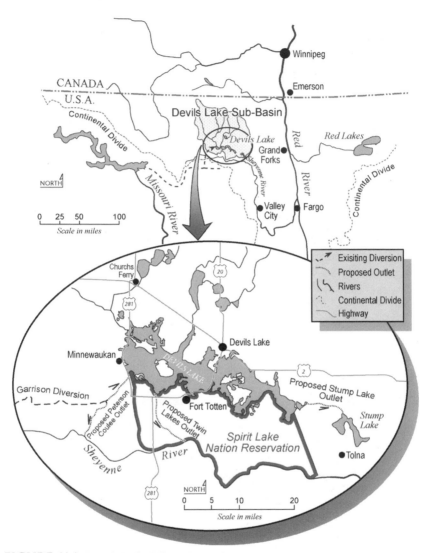

FIGURE 11.1. Devils Lake Water Diversions

Twin Lakes Route. These proposed outlet routes are illustrated in Figure 11.1. Other outlet options are currently being considered but are not the focus of this case study.[14]

This analysis was designed as a social impact assessment that emphasizes considerations of environmental justice with regard to the proposed outlet project. Section 1508.14 of the Council on Environmental Quality (CEQ) NEPA guidance states that "when an environmental impact statement is prepared and economic or social and natural or physical environmental effects are interrelated, then the environmental impact statement will discuss all of these effects on the human environment."[15] Clark and Canter refer to a consensus outlined by the Interorganizational Committee for Social Impact Assessments that includes the recommendation that social, cultural, demographic, economic, social-psychological, and political impacts need to be considered.[16] Data collected for this study emphasized these factors in order to examine the full range of potential impacts of the proposed Devils Lake emergency outlet and how perceptions of those impacts vary between groups and individuals.

Data collection efforts focused on obtaining feedback on the potential impacts of the proposed outlet from respondents in various communities of the Devils Lake Region. Public comments published in the Corps' draft scoping document on the Devils Lake outlet demonstrate that community members in the Devils Lake Region are highly educated and informed with regard to the proposed outlet project and to the potential impacts on their specific communities, homes, and farmsteads.

Many community members sought out research studies or the opinions of professionals on the potential impacts of the proposed emergency outlet. These potential impacts included the impacts of upper basin drainage on Devils Lake levels; potential water quality issues affecting the Sheyenne River; noise levels and impacts on property values that would result from outlet construction and operation on their property; and impacts to existing infrastructure, including access to grain elevators, hospitals, and emergency medical services. Some communities have formed associations to promote their views of the potential impacts and costs to their communities. Some have even become involved in litigation regarding potential impacts of the proposed outlet project and related flooding issues. Obtaining the ideas and input of these community members therefore offered an ideal opportunity to assess potential impacts of the proposed emergency outlet on Devils Lake communities and to help ensure that the views of community members were heard and considered as part of the NEPA decision-making process for this project.

Sampling and Interview Format

A purposive sample was chosen for this study since it was critical to obtain opinions and ideas from individuals who had voiced particular interest in the proposed emergency outlet or specific ideas about other water management options for the Devils Lake area.[17] For this reason, initial respondents for the study were obtained from reviewing written comments in the *Draft Scoping Document, Devils Lake Emergency Outlet Environmental Impact Statement.*[18] Initial participants were also obtained from news articles covering various aspects of Devils Lake flooding in North Dakota papers (between June and September 1998) in which specific individuals were quoted.[19] Efforts were made to obtain respondents from all communities within the Devils Lake Region, including the Spirit Lake Sioux Nation and downstream communities. Snowball sampling techniques were used to obtain additional participants, resulting in a final sample size of forty-five respondents.[20] Figure 11.2 indicates the geographic location of study participants.

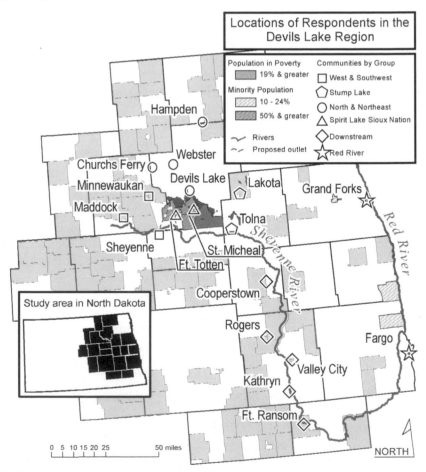

FIGURE 11.2. Geographic Location of Study Participants

Interviews were conducted by telephone (with one exception, in which a participant was interviewed in person), ranging from forty-five to ninety minutes in length. Question topics for these interviews included respondents' assessment of solutions to flooding in Devils Lake, opinions on the proposed emergency outlet, potential impacts to themselves and others of the proposed outlet, and assessments of the Corps' NEPA scoping process. Interview questions were generally open-ended, providing the opportunity for individualized responses. Follow-up interviews were conducted several months later to assess opinions and attitudes on recent developments in the Devils Lake Region.

Data Analysis Strategy

For purposes of analysis, respondents were divided into six separate communities, based on their geographic proximity to Devils Lake.[21] Geographic location of these communities is illustrated in Figure 11.2. The data were analyzed from a variety of perspectives. Relationships were examined between demographic variables (tribal membership and geographic proximity to Devils Lake—referred to as "communities" in this study) and responses to questions in the following areas:

• Opinions on flood control options
• Perceptions of upper basin drainage
• Groups or communities benefited by the proposed outlet
• Groups or communities disadvantaged by the proposed outlet
• Respondents' perceptions of impacts to themselves of the proposed outlet
• Perceived environmental impacts of the proposed outlet
• Respondents' awareness of or involvement in the scoping process
• Respondents' perception of opportunity for community involvement in the scoping process
• Respondents' perception of their views being heard.

A central goal of this analysis was to determine whether low-income communities or minority communities (in this case, primarily tribal members) would shoulder a disproportionate burden (economically, environmentally, or culturally) from the proposed outlet project. For this reason, the responses of communities in various regions of Devils Lake were examined in order to compare and contrast the potential impacts of the proposed project and other water management options.

Discussion of Findings

In this section, initial findings of the study are discussed in terms of the four components of the framework—demographics, benefits and burdens, disproportionate impacts, and stakeholder involvement—to develop a comprehensive picture of potential environmental justice considerations for the proposed Devils Lake emergency outlet. If the data suggest that minority communities or low-income communities might shoulder a disproportionate share of the environmental, economic, or social burdens from construction of the proposed emergency outlet, this information needs to be included in the environmental impact assessment process and to inform subsequent decisions on this proposed project.[22]

DEMOGRAPHICS

The Devils Lake Region encompasses a variety of communities and lifestyles. Much of the area affected by the lake is agricultural, with grain farming and cattle ranching providing a livelihood for many residents in the area. Agriculture also plays a large role in the lives of many downstream communities (areas southeast of Devils Lake on the Sheyenne River). Other residents, especially those in the town of Devils Lake, do not rely as heavily on agriculture and, instead, earn their living through small businesses or the tourist or fishing industries.

As noted earlier, the sample for this study consisted of forty-five respondents. Of this total, 20 percent identify themselves as Native American.[23] Respondents for this study are equally distributed between low-, medium-, and high-income groups, although a small number of respondents preferred not to report this information. The distribution of respondents is relatively equal among the six community groups, with the Spirit Lake Sioux Nation having the highest number of respondents. In addition, respondents are located (geographically) throughout the various communities, with the exception of the Red River communities, for which respondents are located primarily in the cities of Fargo and Grand Forks (see Figure 11.2).

At this stage in the analysis, communities whose demographics indicate the presence of a significant number of low-income or minority individuals are considered to be "potential" environmental justice communities. A more conclusive determination can be made only if the adverse impacts of a proposed or existing activity or facility are shown to disproportionately impact those communities. For this reason, the term *potential environmental justice community* is used to indicate those areas that have minority or low-income populations significantly higher than the state average.

In the Devils Lake Region, there is one federally recognized tribe, the Spirit Lake Sioux Nation, which is located south of Devils Lake. Other areas of Devils Lake do not include federally recognized tribes or significant numbers of minorities. For this study, comparisons between tribal and nontribal respondents are used to assess differences in perceptions between federally recognized tribes and other communities. Since tribal communities differ in their values, cultural traditions, and relationship to natural resources, it was important to compare their responses as a group to the collective responses of nontribal respondents, providing an opportunity to determine significant differences in perceptions and concerns about the proposed outlet between the two groups.

Based on U.S. Census data, communities west and southwest of Devils Lake (Benson County), the Spirit Lake Sioux Nation, the Stump Lake area, and the downstream community (in a five-mile zone on either side of the Sheyenne River between Cooperstown and Fort Ransom) were determined to be potential environmental justice communities. Responses from these groups were compared to those of other groups to determine the potential for benefits and burdens, disproportionate impacts, and level of stakeholder involvement. Table 11.1 presents demographics of the six communities in the Devils Lake Region defined in this study.

BENEFITS AND BURDENS

The question of who *benefits* and who shoulders the *burdens* from a specific project is the second important area of consideration in environmental justice analysis. In the case of the proposed Devils Lake outlet, it is important to examine the advantages of the proposed outlet and what the potential disadvantages would be in terms of impacts to individuals, communities, and the environment. The following sections summarize findings from the study in specific areas where positive or negative impacts from the proposed outlet were perceived.

Benefits of the Proposed Outlet

The Corps and the North Dakota State Water Commission, as well as other agencies, developed estimates measuring effects the proposed emergency outlet would have on reducing the level of Devils Lake. Estimates differ considerably, ranging from only a few inches to sev-

TABLE 11.1. Demographics of Study Communities

Communities	Median Household Income Compared to State Average of $29,321	Significant % Minority Population	Poverty Rate Compared to State Average of 11.9%
Potential EJ Communities			
West & Southwest (Benson County)	$21,021	no	28.3%[a]
Spirit Lake Reservation:			
St. Michael	$14,615[b]	yes[c]	46.0%[b]
Fort Totten	$10,833[b]	yes[c]	55.0%[b]
Stump Lake Area (Nelson County)	$23,537	no	11.4%
Downstream Community	[d]	no	15.3%[d]
Not Potential EJ Communities			
North & Northwest (Ramsey County)	$28,438	no	13.5%
Red River Area:			
Cass County	$35,953	no	8.9%
Traill County	$32,861	no	10.5%
Grand Forks County	$32,161	no	10.9%

Note: Unless otherwise indicated, figures are based on U.S. Census Bureau July 1996 estimates for specific counties and the state of North Dakota.

[a]In a separate analysis of North Dakota counties based on U.S. Census data, Benson County ranks third (out of fifty-three counties) with regard to the highest percentage of those living in poverty. U.S. Environmental Protection Agency, Region 8, "Environmental Justice: Companion Report to Maps for Region 8 States" (August 22, 1997).

[b]From 1990 U.S. Census figures. The median household income for the state of North Dakota in 1990 was $23,213.

[c]The Spirit Lake Sioux Nation is considered a federally recognized tribe, thereby falling under the executive-order definition of minority populations. Minorities compose 5.9% of the population of North Dakota compared to 38.9% in Benson County, which encompasses the towns of Ft. Totten and St. Michael on the Spirit Lake Reservation.

[d]Using a geographic information system, communities in this area were defined by creating a five-mile buffer on either side of the Sheyenne River between Cooperstown and Fort Ransom, North Dakota. This buffer encompasses only parts of Griggs, Steele, and Barnes counties. For this reason, it is not feasible to use county-level data to determine poverty levels for this community. Per capita income for this buffer in 1989 was $10,166 (compared to the 1989 state average of $11,051). The percentage of those in poverty within this buffer area is 15.3%, approximately 28% above the state average.

eral feet. Interview data indicate that reducing the lake level would be beneficial to residents living in the city of Devils Lake, since many of those residents are currently dealing with flooding of their homes and businesses. Interview data also indicated that business owners who run fishing, boating, and tourist-related industries at Devils Lake would have greater economic security if lake levels were reduced and stabilized. Farmers and ranchers just north and northwest of Devils Lake would also experience a lessening of flooding on their properties and would be able to farm a larger number of acres than in previous years, because lake levels have risen.

A large number of respondents mentioned another issue related to the potential benefits of the proposed outlet: drainage of wetlands in the upper basin of the Devils Lake Region. Some see this drainage as a significant contributor to the increase in lake levels in recent years. Potential benefits of the proposed outlet, according to some respondents, include allowing farmers and ranchers north and northwest of Devils Lake to continue upper basin drainage practices, without continuing to increase flooding on Devils Lake. Drainage of naturally occurring ponds and wetlands allows farmers in this area to maintain significantly more acres of cropland in production, which would otherwise return to their natural state. The U.S. Fish and Wildlife Service estimates the amount of wetlands currently drained in the upper basin at over 189,000 acres,[24] so it is likely that the proposed outlet could have a positive economic impact on the ability of these farmers to continue this practice.

Burdens Associated with the Proposed Devils Lake Outlet

Respondents in this study mentioned a substantial number of potential negative impacts from the proposed outlet, which ranged from endangering livelihoods to lowering property values, to having certain environmental and cultural impacts.

Currently, two west-side outlet routes are under consideration (as illustrated in Figure 11.1). Negative impacts mentioned by residents in the proposed path of the outlet include the destruction of property, a decrease in property values, and severe noise problems from outlet operation. Tribal respondents on the Fort Totten Reservation voiced additional negative impacts if the outlet were built. A number of tribal members felt strongly that constructing an outlet at Devils Lake would prevent the lake from fluctuating in its natural cycles and would not allow nature to take its own course within the lake basin. Many of these respondents felt that it was more important for *people* to modify the way they live in order to accommodate naturally occurring changes in lake levels, with some voicing the opinion that Devils Lake may not be the right place for commercial and residential development. Similarly, a number of tribal members mentioned the spiritual connection they have with the lake, noting that the construction of a man-made outlet would interfere with their responsibility of stewardship toward the lake and would negatively impact historic and sacred sites in the lake area.

Residents of downstream communities voiced other concerns about environmental impacts from the proposed outlet. Among the impacts mentioned were the potential for serious flooding of the Sheyenne River during seasonal heavy rains or rapid snowmelt, severe bank erosion, loss of trees and plants, and loss of wildlife habitat. Other negative impacts included a lack of access to roads (due to the Sheyenne River flooding or running at capacity), which would affect the economic stability of farmers in the area, bring about a loss of cropland or pastureland, and negatively impact cattle operations, as a result of impacts to both water quality and water quantity.

It is apparent from this study that construction of the proposed emergency outlet would include both positive and negative impacts. The next step in this analysis is to look at the way these benefits and burdens would be distributed, in order to determine whether this distribution would be fair or disproportionate.

DISPROPORTIONATE IMPACTS:
THE DISTRIBUTION OF BENEFITS AND BURDENS

As discussed in the previous section on demographics, communities north and northwest of Devils Lake and the Red River communities do not have significant numbers of either low-income or minority populations. For this reason, they have not been considered in this study as potential environmental justice communities. Demographic data for communities west and southwest of Devils Lake, the Spirit Lake Sioux Nation, the downstream community, and the Stump Lake area has indicated that these areas have low-income or minority populations that are significantly above the state average. For purposes of this study, therefore, these communities are considered potential environmental justice communities.

Communities North and Northwest of Devils Lake

These communities are approximately ten to thirty miles north of Devils Lake and include the towns of Churchs Ferry, Hamden, and Webster, and the city of Devils Lake. At this time, the town of Churchs Ferry has experienced heavy flooding from Devils Lake. Residents in this town could potentially benefit if the outlet reduces the lake level by a significant amount. Flooding has affected some farmers in this area. Geographically, this area includes a number of natural marshland or wetland areas. Drainage of some of these wetlands is perceived by some to be a primary contributor to extensive flooding on Devils Lake. Flooding is currently impacting some farms and residents in the north-west portion of Devils Lake and could be exacerbated by heavy sea-sonal rainfall or rapid snowmelt. Some who own property or busi-nesses directly north of Devils Lake have already lost property to rising lake levels. The Federal Emergency Management Agency has replaced a number of homes on or near Devils Lake, and a large vol-ume of (previously) lakefront property is currently underwater.

Respondents in these areas believe impacts of the proposed outlet would benefit these communities. Such impacts would include a decrease in the level of flooding of homes and farmland just north and northwest of the lake and a reclamation of vacation, residential, or commercial property located on or near the lakeshore if the outlet sig-nificantly reduces the lake level. Some residents in this area men-tioned the benefits of controlling lake levels for business owners who run tourist or fishing industries on Devils Lake. Additionally, a num-ber of respondents (from communities throughout the Devils Lake basin) felt that farmers in the upper basin area would benefit from the proposed outlet by being able to continue the drainage of ponds and wetlands in order to maximize the number of acres that can be culti-vated on their farms.[25]

Red River Communities

These communities include cities and towns along the Red River, including Fargo and Grand Forks. This area is characterized by a mix of urban and rural communities. Currently, communities along the Red River are not directly impacted by flooding from Devils Lake. No perceived impacts to their homes, livelihoods, or properties were mentioned by these respondents. The potential indirect impacts of the proposed emergency outlet to the area, as a whole, center on issues of water quality if Devils Lake water is channeled into the Red River by way of the Sheyenne River.[26] Impacts to water quality, however, appear to be of greater concern to respondents in this area who are members of the scientific community than to other respondents along the Red River.

Communities West and Southwest of Devils Lake

This area of the lake covers the western portion of Benson County and includes the towns of Maddock, Minnewaukan, and Sheyenne. This area is primarily agricultural and is characterized by small to medium-size farms and a number of small towns, ranging in population from one hundred to six hundred residents. At this point, flooding has not impacted the towns of Maddock and Sheyenne. However, these areas could be significantly impacted if either of the currently proposed outlet routes is chosen. Residents in this area would be impacted by noise problems from outlet operation, a potential decrease in property values, and the destruction of property from outlet construction. Respondents in this area are strongly against the proposed outlet routes and feel that they would not receive any benefit from the outlet, while experiencing a number of negative impacts. For these reasons, the potential for disproportionate impacts exists, and communities west and southwest of Devils Lake would be considered environmental justice communities with regard to this project.

The Spirit Lake Sioux Nation

The Fort Totten Reservation comprises the southern area of the Devils Lake Region. This eastern portion of Benson County includes the towns of Ft. Totten, St. Michael, Tokio, and Warwick. Changes in lake levels are a problem for some members of the Spirit Lake Sioux Nation. In previous years, houses and businesses have been relocated due to rising floodwaters. Some tribal members also lost cropland due to flooding. One tribal respondent was not opposed to the outlet but felt that it would be beneficial to the Tribe if control of operation and construction of the outlet were given to the Tribe. This respondent noted, however, that if the Tribe did not have control in these areas and the outlet were constructed through Tribal lands (as is currently proposed), the impacts would largely be detrimental to them.

In contrast, however, tribal members in other areas of the reservation have not been directly impacted by fluctuating lake levels but would be impacted by the Twin Lakes Route for the proposed emergency outlet. A number of tribal respondents from this study felt that construction of an outlet would negatively impact cultural resources and sacred areas around the lake. In addition, several respondents felt that an outlet would go against their spiritual connection to the lake and would interfere with the natural cycles of the larger Devils Lake basin. Impacts to the Spirit Lake Nation, therefore, would be both beneficial and detrimental. A majority of tribal respondents, however, felt that the impacts of the outlet would be largely negative, and they strongly opposed the proposed project. Since a number of potential impacts on the Tribe would be adverse, and the potential exists for disproportionate impacts as a result of the outlet, the Spirit Lake Nation would be considered an environmental justice community with regard to this project.

The Stump Lake Area

This area lies east and southeast of Devils Lake and encompasses the eastern part of Nelson County, including Stump Lake and the cities of Tolna and Lakota. Agriculture provides a livelihood for a majority of people in this area. This area houses the Stump Lake National Wildlife Refuge, one of the nation's oldest wildlife refuges, which could be impacted by a natural overflow into Stump Lake if Devils Lake continues to rise. For this reason, potential flooding is a concern for those with property close to Stump Lake. Construction and operation of the outlet would not affect residents in this area directly, but these residents could potentially derive benefits if the outlet significantly reduced the level of Devils Lake.

Demographically, the Stump Lake area could be considered a potential environmental justice community, based on U.S. Census data indicating that household median income in Nelson County is well below the state average. However, data from this study indicate that this area would not be directly impacted by the proposed emergency outlet, and that there does not appear to be the potential for disproportionate impacts. For purposes of this analysis, therefore, the area surrounding Stump Lake and parts of Nelson County are not considered to be environmental justice communities. However, the Stump Lake community should be given specific consideration when examining environmental justice considerations for other proposed outlet projects in the area.[27]

The Downstream Community

This area encompasses cities and towns near the Sheyenne River, including Valley City, Kathryn, Cooperstown, and Fort Ransom. For purposes of this analysis, a five-mile zone on either side of the river between Cooperstown and Fort Ransom was identified as the "downstream community." While some property owners in this area operate small to medium-sized cattle ranches, many others grow beans, grains, or feed. There is also a mix of small business and industry in this area, with a state university at Valley City also providing employment. Direct flooding from Devils Lake is not a problem in these areas at this time, and respondents are unable to see any direct benefits to themselves from the proposed outlet. However, the outlet could pose a number of economic and environmental problems for this community.

Potential impacts to downstream communities include direct impacts on their incomes or livelihoods as a result of the Sheyenne River running at or above capacity for a majority of the year (which is likely to result from outlet operation). Such impacts include property damage to farms and ranches along the Sheyenne River; potential tax increases (from costs to the state for outlet construction and operation or if a water quality treatment plant is required in the area); flooding of homes, farms, or ranches; flooding of roads, impacting access to cropland and pastureland; and serious negative impacts to cattle operations as a result of both water quality and water quantity. Respondents in this area note that these impacts could result in a high degree of economic instability for low-income farmers in the area.

In addition, a number of downstream respondents are concerned about the potential for serious environmental impacts in their area, including serious problems with bank erosion, a corresponding loss of trees and plants, and loss of wildlife habitat. These impacts could directly affect both property and property values, result in economic impacts to farmers and homeowners along the Sheyenne, and could negatively impact recreational areas and wildlife refuges.

Potential impacts to the downstream community appear to be largely adverse, with virtually no direct benefits from the proposed outlet. With regard to this project, therefore, the downstream community is considered an environmental justice community.

STAKEHOLDER INVOLVEMENT

Stakeholder involvement is the fourth key component in assessing whether a potential environmental justice situation exists with regard to a proposed action, and it is an important part of the NEPA decision-making process. During the course of the focused interviews, respondents were asked about their awareness of and involvement in the Corps' scoping process on the proposed emergency outlet. In addition, participants were asked about their assessment of opportunities for community involvement in the scoping process, and whether they felt their views had been heard.

A significant finding from this study was that respondents from communities west and southwest of the lake, as well as the downstream community and some respondents from the Spirit Lake Sioux Nation, felt that the Corps was not open to real input from the public during the scoping process and simply promoted the proposed west-end outlet. It is important to note that based on analysis of demographics and the potential for disproportionate impacts, these communities are all considered to be environmental justice communities in this study. It is even more critical, therefore, that in order to follow the guidance set forth in the executive order, as well as for the NEPA decision-making process, these communities are provided with opportunities to be part of the decision-making process and to voice their concerns in an open, receptive atmosphere. In contrast, respondents from communities north and northwest of Devil's Lake, Stump Lake area communities, and Red River communities rarely expressed these sentiments. These findings may indicate that the proposed outlet primarily represents the interests of communities north and northwest of the lake and either represents, or at least does not conflict with, the interests of those in the Stump Lake area and Red River communities.

Tribal respondents voiced more concern than other respondents with the lack of meetings on the proposed outlet project. Some respondents from the Spirit Lake Sioux Nation mentioned that there had been some difference of opinion within the tribal community regarding holding scoping meetings on the proposed outlet at the reservation. These findings, therefore, reflect the view of some tribal respondents that there were not enough meetings held on the Fort Totten Reservation to allow for full public participation by the tribal community.

Respondents from the environmental justice communities downstream, west and southwest of the lake, and (to some degree) the Spirit Lake Sioux Nation were most likely to voice concerns about inadequate opportunities for community input with regard to the scoping process or to feel that the Corps was not genuinely seeking input and feedback from the public on the proposed outlet. The potential environmental justice implications in this area should not be overlooked with regard to providing full opportunities for community participation in the decision-making process.

In addition to opportunities for providing input on the proposed emergency outlet, respondents were asked if they felt that their views on the proposed outlet had been heard by the Corps (as well as other decision makers). Few respondents from the entire study sample indicated that they felt their views had been heard and acted upon. A few respondents in each community felt that their views had been heard but not necessarily acted upon. A larger number of respondents (representing all communities in the lake region) felt that their views had not been heard, although respondents from Red River communities were less likely to express this view. An important dynamic observed from the study is that collective effort appears to have been an empowering factor for some groups. Over half of the respondents from communities west and southwest of the lake, and over a third of those from downstream communities, felt that the efforts of their citizens or community group had made some difference.

Overall, findings in this area are significant in that they point to the unrealized potential for the traditional scoping process to provide forums in which community members feel heard and feel a part of the decision-making process. A number of concerns raised by respondents were not addressed during either the initial scoping meetings or in subsequent meetings after they were brought to the Corps' attention. Findings in this area point to the need for outreach efforts (prior to initial scoping meetings) that can be customized to the needs and concerns of specific communities. In addition, the data indicate a need for more willingness on the part of the Corps to hear a variety of concerns during scoping meetings and throughout the scoping process.

Recommendations

Following the study, specific recommendations provided to the Corps on the proposed emergency outlet focused on four areas: (1) identifying environmental justice communities that might be impacted by the project, (2) types of impacts that should be considered in the NEPA analysis, (3) the need for providing technical information to all communities in the affected areas, and (4) improvements in scoping methods and other outreach efforts. These recommendations to the Corps were, of course, made with the benefit of hindsight. The more general value of the study is, however, in how this study on Devils Lake can help other agencies apply the EPA's four-point framework to assess environmental justice considerations for proposed projects with the goal of ensuring that environmental justice considerations are part of the various NEPA decision-making processes.

Demographics

As discussed earlier, the demographics component of the analysis provides a threshold evaluation of whether there is a potential (based on the existence of low-income or minority populations) for an environmental justice issue to require analysis in the NEPA document. The Devils Lake study demonstrates that U.S. Census data is a valuable tool for this analysis. The limitations, however, include the timeliness of census data (because populations in all areas of the United States are likely to fluctuate over a ten-year period). For this reason, U.S. Census estimates for more recent years are helpful in making more accurate determinations of low-income and minority populations. Other reliable data sources, such as state, county, and municipal data, might also be used.

Because it is a threshold issue, it is important for lead agencies to accurately assess the demographics of all communities in the project area at the *inception* of the design or scoping process. At the present time, however, not all EPA regions use demographics as a threshold issue. Some regional offices begin by determining if adverse environmental or health impacts exist, then examine the populations that would be affected. This method can be effective in determining environmental justice considerations. However, it is the view of EPA Region 8 that the more comprehensive process of determining the distribution of impacts is unnecessary if the communities in question lack significant numbers of low-income or minority populations.

The case study presented in this chapter used a relatively small sample size, although the number of respondents in this study appeared to capture the sentiments of each community with regard to the proposed emergency outlet. Constraints in time, as well as in staff and monetary resources, often present limitations for regulatory agencies in obtaining larger sample sizes or in conducting larger-scale studies. This case study used a purposive sampling technique in order to obtain respondents who were well versed in issues surrounding the proposed outlet. Other sampling techniques can also be considered for environmental justice assessments. For proposed projects that are widely publicized, or that involve large population groups or more extensive geographic areas, probability or random sampling designs may be feasible and can provide sample populations that are more statistically representative of an entire region. In contrast to a purposive sampling design, however, researchers using random samples will generally find a percentage of respondents who are unfamiliar with the specific project or are uninterested in providing feedback on project planning and decision processes.

Benefits and Burdens

Once the existence of low-income and minority communities in a project area has been established, it is critical to accurately assess the known and potential impacts (both beneficial and adverse) as early in the process as possible. Findings from this study also indicate that there may be a need to provide more scientific and other information to communities in order to make accurate determinations of project impact. In the Devil's Lake case, such information would include data on water quality and quantity (particularly with regard to the Sheyenne and Red Rivers), engineering design and evaluation of the outlet's expected effectiveness, logistical and financial management of the proposed outlet structures, compensation and easement rights that would affect private property and tribal lands, and the impact of upper basin drainage on flooding at Devils Lake.

Disproportionate Impacts

Once the range of potential benefits and burdens for a proposed project has been assessed, we can determine whether the distribution of these impacts is proportionate to all groups or is unevenly distributed. An environmental justice situation arises when a disproportionate share of adverse environmental, health, economic, cultural, or other impacts would affect low-income or minority communities. It is critical, therefore, that such determinations are made prior to permitting decisions or project construction.

Similarly, if the majority of benefits will go to middle-income, wealthy, and nonminority groups or individuals, there is an opportunity to more closely examine whose values and preferences are being promoted by the proposed project, and at whose expense. It is often difficult to raise and address such questions, and some would argue that projects should be evaluated on the basis of *total* benefits outweighing *total* impacts regardless of their distribution (see Gary Bryner's discussion of distributive justice in Chapter 2). However, if agencies can strive to be objective about the distribution of impacts, and are willing to use this information to avoid or mitigate adverse impacts to environmental justice communities, the intent of the executive order will have been served.

Findings from the case study indicate that specific adverse impacts to environmental justice communities may need to be viewed as disproportionate impacts to these communities. Such impacts should be carefully considered in the NEPA decision-making process. If the result of a proposed project is likely to have disproportionate impacts, then a number of options could be considered. Such considerations in this case could include monetary compensation for property damage or loss, investment in comprehensive water treatment facilities, development of viable alternatives to an outlet (which could include an in-depth assessment of the impacts of upper basin drainage into Devils Lake), or a no-build alternative that included permanent relocation of residents in flooded areas, as well as other mitigation measures or alternatives. As Helfand and Peyton argue, "If remedies do not address root causes, they may not achieve desired goals."[28]

Environmental justice assessments provide an opportunity to examine a wide variety of impacts of a proposed project on affected communities and regions. If such assessments are initiated early in the process, the views and concerns of community members can be integrated into the planning process and can even point to gaps in information that are important to the decision-making process.

Stakeholder Involvement

Author Lorna Salzman points out that "public participation in the environmental process has in fact had a profound democratizing effect on our society."[29] She notes that such inclusion of the public has provided a number of benefits, including information becoming more freely available; increased media attention; the integration of broad social concerns into the regulatory and enforcement process; an enhancement of public oversight of administrative and enforcement agencies; and an activation of citizens. In general, such inclusion has taken environmental awareness and concern far beyond the classroom, hearing room, or courtroom. The inclusion and involvement of all stakeholders at all phases of the planning and decision-making processes is the final component in the four-point framework and plays a critical role in effective environmental justice assessments.

Although the Devils Lake assessment was effective even though it was conducted *after* the initial scoping process occurred, such assessments initiated earlier in the process would provide an opportunity to shape the nature of the scoping process itself, guiding the direction of preliminary project meetings and planning sessions. Additional issues are likely to arise, however, as project planning and implementation proceeds. For this reason, effective environmental justice assessments should continue throughout the life of the project, addressing new issues as they arise.

Several recommendations for better stakeholder involvement processes can be gleaned from the Devils Lake study. Initially, the format and range of scoping meetings should be broad enough to consider the needs and perspectives of diverse communities, so that all participants are given the opportunity to have their views included as part of the initial decision-making processes. A project may require more focused outreach, considering different types of involvement for different populations. In addition, local knowledge of the environment that is embedded within rural or tribal cultures can play an important part in formulating more effective strategies for natural resources management. Only by creating an inclusive process for stakeholder involvement can community knowledge and expertise in these areas be fully utilized in the decision-making process.

In addition to environmental and physical impacts, early scoping efforts should include a sensitivity to cultural differences and the unique character of individual communities. Before scoping meetings are held, focused outreach efforts of the lead agency should include assessing the cultural values, character, and needs of each community involved. Meetings and presentations should be specifically geared to address the concerns of diverse communities, collecting valuable input from residents and members, and providing information specific to their respective needs. CEQ guidelines for NEPA direct agencies to "acknowledge and seek to overcome linguistic, cultural, institutional, geographic, and other barriers to meaningful participation, and should incorporate active outreach to affected groups."[30] In some cases, it may be beneficial to have nontechnical persons make presentations—individuals who have familiarity with a specific community (such as a tribal community or other cultural or ethnic group) and who understand the traditions and values of those communities. Cultural sensitivity and inclusiveness should be an integral component of the information-sharing process.

Specific recommendations for effectively involving tribal communities include an acknowledgment that cultural views, traditions, and values are likely to be distinct from those of nontribal communities. Similarly, consideration of, and sensitivity to, land uses and spiritual practices are important in accurately assessing whether the impacts of a proposed project are disproportionate and would result in an unequal share of benefits. Values and perspectives are likely to be unique among each tribal group. For this reason, lead agencies and regulatory agencies should not assume that tribal ways of thinking about the land and about natural resources are identical to their own, or to those of the larger culture. In addition, although a lead agency's government-to-government relationship is primarily with the tribal government, it is important that the perspectives and concerns of the larger tribal community are also considered.

Finally, effective public participation in the NEPA process requires that detailed information on potential effects and mitigation measures be provided to and developed in consultation with the affected communities. The concerns mentioned by community members can easily be integrated into initial scoping processes if lead agencies make an effort to recognize the importance of in-depth community feedback at a project's inception.

Conclusion

Regulatory and land management agencies have an important role to play in environmental justice assessments involving natural resources management and other land use issues. These agencies are generally responsible for permitting decisions at the local, state, or federal level, and they often have regulatory authority for oversight of construction and operation of facilities or land use projects. Since it is critical that considerations of environmental justice be examined well before permitting or siting decisions are made or construction begins, it is the agencies' responsibility to ensure that potential impacts to minority communities and low-income communities are carefully assessed.

The four-point framework presented in this chapter provides a tool for conducting such assessments and can be applied to proposed projects involving natural resources management as well as other projects where environmental, health, or cultural impacts may potentially impact low-income or minority communities. Ideally, this framework is most effective if applied at the beginning of a project, to help direct the scoping process and subsequent analysis. However, as illustrated by this case study, the framework can also be applied after the fact by EPA and other regulatory agencies to analyze how well the lead agency has performed the NEPA analysis and met the objectives of the executive order.

Some federal agencies have developed agency-specific guidance on incorporating environmental justice considerations into the day-to-day work of their agencies. In addition, a number of states have developed (or are in the process of developing) their own statutes on environmental justice. If regulatory agencies are sensitive to the needs of traditionally disadvantaged populations, historical patterns of land use and natural resources decisions resulting in discrimination and disproportionate impacts to environmental justice communities can be reversed, and more equitable decision making can become an established practice.

Regulatory agencies are charged with serving all citizens. It is critically important, therefore, that environmental justice considerations be taken seriously by federal, state, and local governments to ensure that the interests and well-being of those citizens who have traditionally been underrepresented are recognized and represented in all phases of project design and implementation. Their voices should be heard early in the process, and their views integrated as fully as possible into the decision-making process. No civilization that discounts the quality of life and health of its most vulnerable populations can evolve in a sustainable manner. Actively engaging in considering the environmental justice impacts of land use and natural resources decisions will help agencies to better represent the people they are directed to serve, and to better fulfill the larger missions of assuring a high-quality environment for all communities. This framework for environmental justice assessment can contribute to this goal.

Acknowledgments

I am grateful to the Environmental Justice Program, U.S. Environmental Protection Agency, Region 8, for sponsoring this research. Particular recognition is due to Deldi Reyes, Elisabeth Evans, and Nancy Reish of Region 8 for their expertise and guidance on research design, editing, and mapping, to Manitoba Conservation for use of the map in Figure 1, and to Dave Dettloff of the University of Colorado–Boulder Department of Geography, Cartographic Lab for preparation of the final figures. Thanks is also due to Dr. Gene Reetz with the Ecosystems Protection and Remediation Program in Region 8 for his assistance with background and history of the Devils Lake outlet project. Additional recognition is owed to Kathryn Mutz of the Natural Resources Law Center, who provided insightful editing and thoughtful, constructive feedback on ways to best present the research for this volume.

Notes

Note: At the time this case study was completed, Jan Buhrmann was working as a social scientist and postdoctoral researcher for the Environmental Justice Program, U.S. Environmental Protection Agency, Region 8. The views expressed in this article are the author's own and do not necessarily represent the views or policies of the Environmental Protection Agency.

1. Executive Order No. 12898, 59 *Federal Register* 7629 (1994), 3 C.F.R., sec. 859, reprinted in 42 U.S.C., sec. 4321. Available at www.epa.gov/docs/oejpubs/.
2. See Barry Hill and Nicholas Targ's introduction to federal agency responsibilities in Chapter 12.
3. Ray Clark and Larry Canter, eds., *Environmental Policy and NEPA: Past, Present, and Future,* (Boca Raton, Fl.: St. Lucie Press, 1997), 22.
4. U.S. Environmental Protection Agency, Office of Federal Activities (July 1999), 2, 5.
5. As of the time of publication, the emergency outlet at Devils Lake is still

in the planning stages, with the NEPA review process not yet completed. Although draft and final scoping documents have been issued by the Corps, a draft environmental impact statement has yet to be developed. Details of the proposed project can be found in the *Draft Scoping Document*, Devils Lake Emergency Outlet Environmental Impact Statement, U.S. Army Corps of Engineers, St. Paul, Minn., District (June 1998).

6. Executive Order No. 12898, sec. 1-101: "Each Federal agency shall make achieving environmental justice part of its mission by identifying and addressing, as appropriate, disproportionately high and adverse human health or environmental effects of its programs, policies, and activities on minority populations and low-income populations."

7. In cases in which the household median income is significantly below the state average, it may be used as an additional criterion to determine low-income communities within a region.

8. Native Americans, or American Indians, are among those individuals recognized as minorities by the U.S. Census. For purposes of this study, federally recognized tribes are referred to as "minority communities."

9. The term *stakeholder* is used here (in place of the term *communities*) since benefits or burdens may accrue to industries, interest groups, or individuals, in addition to communities.

10. Adapted from *Guidelines and Principles for Social Impact Assessment*, Interorganizational Committee on Guidelines and Principles for Social Impact Assessment (December 14, 1993).

11. Adapted from Council on Environmental Quality, *Environmental Justice: Guidance under the National Environmental Policy Act*, app. A (December 10, 1997).

12. Gloria Helfand and L. James Peyton, "A Conceptual Model of Environmental Justice," *Social Science Quarterly* 80 (March 1999): 68–83.

13. Devils Lake Online, North Dakota State Water Commission, available at www.swc.state.nd.us/projects/devilslake.html.

14. The State of North Dakota has proposed an additional channel from Devils Lake to Stump Lake as a temporary measure to relieve flooding in Devils Lake. Although respondents in this study expressed their views of and preferences for the Stump Lake channel in comparison to other outlet options, the focus of the present study is the proposed west-end outlet.

15. Council on Environmental Quality, *Environmental Justice: Guidance under NEPA*, sec. 1508.14 (December 10, 1997).

16. Clark and Canter, eds., *Environmental Policy and NEPA*, 238.

17. A purposive sample is one in which participants are selected based on specific experience or characteristics, in order to obtain specific kinds of data, and is not considered a random or probability sample.

18. U.S. Army Corps of Engineers, St. Paul, Minn., District (June 1998).

19. If this study had been conducted prior to initial scoping efforts, a similar sampling technique could have been used, developing an initial group of

respondents by contacting community groups, examining local newspapers for articles on local citizens active in the proposed projects, and working with program staff in public agencies who are involved with the affected communities.

20. Snowball sampling involves obtaining additional respondents for a study based on the recommendations or referral of other study participants. This is done to include a larger number of respondents who have similar experience or characteristics in the sample.

21. The executive order directs agencies to focus attention on potential impacts or burdens to low-income and minority *populations*. The selection of the unit of analysis should, therefore, reflect the potential impacts to environmental justice communities as a whole. For this reason, assessments should be based on community, municipal, or regional levels of data. In this study, location of the proposed outlet routes, as well as downstream impacts to the Sheyenne River, could potentially impact such communities. Therefore, it is more effective to assess impacts to various *communities* in the Devils Lake Region, by using the *collectivity of responses* from individuals in those communities, rather than by focusing on specific impacts to individual respondents.

22. Adapted from U.S. Environmental Protection Agency, Office of Federal Activities, *EPA Guidance for Consideration of Environmental Justice in Clean Air Act Section 309 Reviews* (July 1999), 5.

23. The percent minority for the state of North Dakota, as a whole, is 5.9 percent. 1990 U.S. Census Bureau, Census Tract Group Level.

24. U.S. Fish and Wildlife Service, North Dakota Field Office, "Devils Lake Feasibility Study: Lake Stabilization, Devils Lake, North Dakota," Planning Aid Letter and Substantiating Report, Bismarck, N.D. (October 3, 1997).

25. A number of respondents from various communities felt strongly that much of the acreage in the upper basin was not being drained legally, and that construction of the outlet would encourage illegal practices to continue.

26. The State of Minnesota and the Canadian Government have expressed similar concerns regarding water quality and potential biota transfers (potentially affecting fisheries).

27. A separate project has been proposed that would channel water from Devils Lake into Stump Lake. If that project is approved, this community could be significantly affected by flooding and other structural and economic impacts. A separate environmental justice analysis for the Stump Lake project was provided to the Corps Office in Bismarck, North Dakota, in October 1999. See U.S. Environmental Protection Agency, Region 8, Environmental Justice Program, *Summary of Devils Lake Flooding Issues Affecting the Stump Lake Area* (October 25, 1999).

28. Helfand and Peyton, "A Conceptual Model of Environmental Justice," 68–83.

29. Lorna Salzman, "Ecology and Social Change," *New Politics* (summer 1997): 35.
30. Council on Environmental Quality, *Environmental Justice: Guidance under NEPA*, 9.

Chapter 12

PROTECTING NATURAL RESOURCES AND THE ISSUE OF ENVIRONMENTAL JUSTICE

Barry E. Hill and Nicholas Targ

There is an axiom that goes as follows: protect the natural resources—the air, the land, and the water—upon which all life depends, and you will have protected the health of the public and the various species that inhabit the earth. A clean environment and an intact ecology are indicators of a healthy population. The converse is also true: unhealthy natural resources will have a negative impact on the health of the public and the species, which can cause either or both to become endangered. This recognition of the relationship between natural resources and man and animals is not new. Marcus Vitruvius Pollio, a Roman architect and engineer, recognized this relationship as far back as the first century B.C. With respect to the selection of springs as sources of water, Vitruvius realized that natural resources need to be protected in order for humans and animals to survive and prosper. Vitruvius wrote:

> Springs should be tested and proved in advance in the following ways. If they run free and open, inspect and observe the physique of the people who dwell in the vicinity before beginning to conduct the water, and if their frames are strong, their complexion fresh, legs sound, and eyes clear, the spring deserves complete approval. . . .
>   And if green vegetables cook quickly when put into a vessel of such water and set over a fire, it will be proof that the water is good and wholesome. Likewise if the water in the spring is itself limpid and clear . . . and if its bed is not polluted by filth of any sort but has a clean

285

appearance, these signs indicate that the water is light
and wholesome in the highest degree.[1]

This is the link between man and nature.

Unfortunately, natural resources have not been adequately protected over the centuries, and consequently, certain species and
humankind, in some respects, have become endangered. Through
enactment of a panoply of modern environmental laws, government
(federal, state, and tribal) has sought to protect not only the natural
resources and the environment but also the health of humankind,
imperiled species, and their habitat.

Endangered species, species listed under the Endangered Species
Act (ESA),[2] have been likened to the proverbial "canary in the coal
mine." The ESA informs us not only as to the state of listed species'
condition but also that there is something seriously wrong with its
habitat.[3] The ESA requires people within the listed species' habitat to
modify their behavior, to the extent that it creates injury, and requires
the government to consider how actions can make the species' habitat
more "wholesome," to use Vitruvius's words.[4] To respond and aid in
the species' recovery, the ESA requires humans to look at the environment not only from our own perspective but from that of the threatened or endangered species itself, and, consequently, to modify our
behavior for its benefit and the benefit of its habitat.

Environmental justice, as a public policy issue, shares common-
alities with the ESA at levels metaphoric and physical. First, environmental justice is attentive to all communities—defined as "fair
treatment and meaningful involvement of all people regardless of
race, color, national origin, or income with respect to the development, implementation, and enforcement of environmental laws, regulations, and policies."[5] Environmental justice also shares the ESA's
special concern over environmentally burdened populations. The
Office of Environmental Justice defines the term *environmental justice*
as follows:

> Environmental Justice is the fair treatment and meaning-
> ful involvement of all people regardless of race, color,
> national origin, culture, education, or income with
> respect to the development, implementation, and
> enforcement of environmental laws, regulations, and
> policies. *Fair treatment* means that no group of people,
> including racial, ethnic, or socioeconomic groups,
> should bear a disproportionate share of negative envi-

ronmental consequences resulting from industrial, municipal, and commercial operations or the execution of Federal, state, local, and tribal programs and policies. *Meaningful involvement* means that: (1) potentially affected community residents have an appropriate opportunity to participate in decisions about a proposed activity that will affect their environment and/or health; (2) the public's contribution can influence the regulatory agency's decisions; (3) the concerns of all participants involved will be considered in the decision-making process; and (4) the decisionmakers seek out and facilitate the involvement of those potentially affected.[6]

Because of the continuing effects of historical overt discrimination, as well as passive, race-neutral permitting and other regulatory actions, these populations tend to be minority or low-income populations. (See David Getches and David Pellow's review of the history and literature of the environmental justice movement in Chapter 1.)

This chapter first outlines how authority under existing environmental law can be used by federal regulators to address a broad spectrum of environmental justice concerns. By taking action under the broad regulatory standards established by the major environmental statutes, the needs, experiences, values, and circumstances of residents of various communities can be addressed, and disproportionate impacts can be avoided. The following section explores in some greater detail three examples in which the federal government is using existing laws to begin to address environmental justice concerns and, by so doing, is buttressing the natural resources and ecological systems upon which the residents of the various communities depend. The examples draw from three different statutes or statutory provisions: Clean Water Act (CWA) provisions on water quality standards;[7] the National Environmental Policy Act (NEPA),[8] which requires analysis of impacts in the decision-making process; and Section 404 of the CWA,[9] which requires analysis of the public interest in permitting the use of specific resources.

The case studies are organized so as to build on one another. The first demonstrates how a race-neutral standard can nonetheless have disproportionate impacts on different communities. It also shows how natural resources are better protected by taking into consideration differences among communities. The second example explores how the requirements of NEPA can expose disproportionate impacts. Finally, the third case study illustrates how an analysis conducted under NEPA for a permit to dredge and fill under the CWA can produce environmentally just and ecologically wise natural resources choices. The chapter concludes with the observation that when the experiences, needs, and values of all communities are addressed in environmental and natural resources decisions, healthier, more robust communities and ecologies are the consequence.

Statutory and Regulatory Authority

Although environmental justice requires justice for all, special attention to minority and low-income communities is necessary because actions that adequately protect the general population may not always protect discrete segments of the population.[10] A host of race-neutral factors and, in some cases, the legacy of historical discrimination can lead to disproportionate impacts on minority and low-income communities. These factors include the following:

• Cumulative risks due to exposure to the aggregation of risks from multiple sources of pollution in addition to a new source
• Unique exposure pathways and scenarios
• Vulnerability of populations because of the lack of investment in infrastructures
• Lack of meaningful participation in decision-making processes.

Thus, the agencies' use of large-scale population averages and mainstream cultural values and experiences in making decisions may create risk gradients and other disproportionate environmental burdens across variously situated populations and communities.

Many of the statutes that the U.S. Environmental Protection Agency (EPA) implements provide the EPA with the authority to consider and address environmental justice concerns and support the integrity of the environment and natural resources upon which communities depend.[11] These laws encompass the breadth of the EPA's activities, including setting standards,[12] permitting facilities,[13] awarding grants,[14] and reviewing actions taken by other federal agencies, states, and tribal authorities.[15] These laws require the EPA to consider a variety of factors, which generally include one or more of the following: public health, cumulative impacts, social costs, and general welfare. Other statutes direct the EPA and other executive branch departments and agencies to consider special risks posed to vulnerable populations in setting standards, which may include people of color or low-income communities.[16] In all cases, how the EPA chooses to implement and enforce its authority (whether on a case-by-case basis or through more general policy) can have substantial effects on the natural and environmental resources and the health of all communities.

The Environmental Justice Executive Order and its accompanying presidential memorandum also recognize that existing environmental and civil rights statutes provide many opportunities to address environmental hazards in minority communities and low-income communities.[17] Implicit in the executive order is the message that the environmental and natural resources upon which each community depends need protection. Recently, the Environmental Appeals Board (EAB) has begun to review EPA actions to determine whether the EPA has indeed taken environmental justice concerns into consideration when they arise. This review has included examination of such issues as the adequacy of public participation and the disproportionality of impacts on minority or low-income communities.[18] The EAB's review, one permit at a time, is checking and determining on a case-by-case basis what the executive order indeed requires: environmental resources that are protective of every community.

The EAB review of a Resource Conservation and Recovery Act permit issued by Region 5 in *In re: Chemical Waste Management of Indiana* is typical of the EAB's consideration of environmental justice concerns.[19] That case emphasizes the important point that environmental justice concerns relate, at least in the first instance, not to a community's demographic characteristics (for example, racial composition or income status), but rather to attributes frequently associated with low-income or minority communities that may place such a community at special risk—what the community needs from its resources of air, water, and land to thrive. Because environmental risk factors in minority or low-income communities may differ from the general population, the EAB noted that an assessment of effects that looks only at "a broad analysis might mask the effects of the facility on a disparately affected minority or low-income segment of the community."[20]

The EAB ruled that the EPA should "as a matter of policy" exercise its discretion to ensure early and ongoing opportunities for public involvement in the permitting process. Further, the EAB ruled that where there is at least a superficially plausible claim that a facility will have a disproportionate impact on a minority or low-income segment of the affected community, the EPA should also, as a matter of policy, exercise its discretion to focus its impact analysis on the minority or low-income community whose health or environment is alleged to be threatened by the facility.

These policies can, and have been, incorporated by both the EPA and other agencies. The following case studies illustrate the use of existing law—both substantive statutes such as the CWA and the procedural requirements of NEPA—to help protect communities and the resources upon which they depend.

Fish Consumption under the Clean Water Act

Humans reside at the top of the food chain. Thus, when we protect the natural resources that sustain our health, we take a step toward maintaining a healthy environment. By contrast, if we degrade the resources upon which we rely, we expose ourselves through the food chain to the accumulated contamination of each link that ultimately finds its origin in that natural resource. Starting from the most basic natural resource, water, this connection to natural resources is Vitruvius's message.

This message is quite clear with respect to our exposure to pollution through fish consumption. Contaminated rivers and streams create unhealthy fish and, ultimately, unhealthy fish consumers. Human tolerance for contaminated fish and, thus, rivers and streams is subject to multiple factors, including, most importantly, the amount of fish consumed and the parts of fish consumed. Environmental justice advocates frequently criticize the EPA's evaluation of consumption of fish in the establishment of national ambient water quality criteria (AWQC)—criteria upon which permitting authorities may establish water quality standards.[21] Assumptions used to establish the criteria do not take into account the amount of fish or portions of fish certain populations typically eat. Critics argue that the problems associated with using low or inaccurate consumption values is amplified because, historically, the methodology has not accounted for the bioaccumulation of contaminants in fish resulting from the fish's consumption of contaminated food. Thus, environmental justice advocates argue that by not taking into account how both fish and certain communities interact with their environments, those populations are less well protected than the general public.

The EPA publishes AWQC that can be, and often are, used as default criteria by permitting authorities. The regulatory authority uses the criteria to establish acceptable ambient levels of pollution based on the water body's designated use. The regulatory authority must next identify waters that are so polluted that the technology-based federal discharge controls will be insufficient to bring the water into compliance with the water quality standards. For these water bodies, the regulatory authority (the EPA or the appropriate state or tribe) sets the total maximum daily load (TMDL) for each pollutant. The TMDL is then divided among point sources, and each source's limit is incorporated in its National Pollutant Discharge Elimination System (NPDES) permit(s).[22]

The establishment of national AWQC requires the EPA to make decisions at the cutting edge of science. However, large data gaps exist around the variability of consumption habits of different populations. Thus, definitively assessing the effect of the release of any one particular chemical into a water body is not possible given current knowledge and information.

Another difficulty, and the point frequently seized upon by environmental justice advocates whose communities depend on fish as a major source of protein, is that the establishment of the AWQC is inherently "political," involving issues of risk distribution. While the CWA requires the EPA to establish recommended national AWQC that, when implemented, will produce standards protective of public health, the meaning of the phrase *protective of public health* is not self-defining. The CWA does not define what levels of risk are protective in an absolute sense, much less identify which communities should represent the public. Therefore, if some level of pollution is to be tolerated, the risk to communities will differ depending on their sensitivities and vulnerabilities as well as on the relationship between the community and its river or estuary resources.[23]

In reviewing these difficult policy and scientific decisions, courts have given the EPA wide discretion, acknowledging the EPA's technical expertise. Moreover, the courts have also sanctioned risk gradients across differently situated populations so long as the standards are "protective" of all communities. In *Dioxin/Organochlorine Center v Clarke*,[24] environmental and industry plaintiffs challenged the EPA's establishment of TMDLs for discharges of dioxin into the Columbia River. The environmental groups—Dioxin/Organochlorine Center and Columbia River United (hereafter, "DOC")—claimed that the TMDLs established by the EPA would fail to conform to the state's water quality standards, which permit no more than a one-in-a-million risk of cancer in the general population. DOC argued that because the EPA based its TMDLs on the average American fish consumption rate of 6.5 grams of fish per day,[25] the Native American populations, who consume more than this amount, would not receive adequate protection.

In response, the EPA made two different arguments. First, the EPA argued that the extremely conservative "potency estimates" (the amount of contamination per fish) would adequately protect the

Native Americans. Second, the EPA asserted that it was unlikely that each fish eaten would be fully contaminated. Thus, based on these uncertainties, the EPA argued that there is no reason to believe that the Native Americans would have a higher risk of cancer than the general population. Second, even assuming that the Native Americans consumed 150 grams of fish per day, as asserted by DOC, and that the fish were fully contaminated, the EPA argued that the risk level would be twenty-three in a million for the Native American population, which is protective of health. While this risk is higher than the one-in-a-million level set for the general population, the EPA posited that the "risk level mandated by the state water quality standards for the general population does not necessarily reflect state legislative intent to provide the highest level of protection for all subpopulations but could reasonably be construed to allow for lower yet adequate protection of specific subpopulations."[26]

The Ninth Circuit upheld the EPA's position, finding that the "ambient dioxin concentrations cannot be considered arbitrary and capricious with regard to the effect of dioxin on human sub-populations, nor was the decision based on an unreasonable interpretation of state water standards."[27] Thus, the court both deferred to the EPA's expertise and adopted the "lower yet adequate" protection standard for the fish-consuming Native American populations.[28]

Despite judicial deference to its standards, the EPA has recognized that there are significant equity issues associated with fish consumption based on variation among different populations.[29] The EPA has also improved its understanding of the way water pollution enters the food stream.[30] Based on this information and a recent fish consumption study, the EPA has proposed revising the default fish consumption rate used for establishing AWQCs by almost threefold, to 17.80 grams per day.[31] This value represents the 90th percentile for consumption of freshwater and estuarine fish by the general population. At the same time, recognizing variations among populations, the EPA has also proposed a new default fish consumption rate of 86.30 grams per day for "subsistence fishers/minority anglers." This value represents the 99th percentile for consumption of freshwater and estuarine fish by the general population.

In order to ensure increased protection of the entire population, the EPA has also proposed a preference for state and tribal water quality criteria determinations to be based on local data and offers their default values as a last resort, ensuring that the fish intake level chosen be protective of highly exposed individuals in the population.[32] To this end, the EPA suggests the following four-tier hierarchy of preferences: (1) use of local data, (2) use of data reflecting similar geo-graphic-population groups, (3) use of data from national surveys, and (4) use of proposed default intake rates. By looking to circumstances within specific communities and urging that standards be based on the actual relationship between the use of the natural resources and the community, all communities can receive equal protection based on protection according to their needs.

While the EPA has not deviated from the "lower but adequate" position adopted in *Dioxin/Organochlorine Center v Clarke,* the EPA's proposed recommendations recognize the problems with using broad averages and present a framework for addressing differences between populations. Combined with the recently affirmed right of designated tribes to set water quality standards on tribal lands (see the discussion of "TAS" by Sarah Krakoff in Chapter 7), the proposed AQWC point the way for improved health in subsistence and other communities based on improved quality of the resources on which they depend.

National Environmental Policy Act—Evaluation of Impacts

Federal agencies are increasingly attentive to the differences among experiences, cultural values, and vulnerabilities of communities when the agencies conduct reviews under NEPA. The result of the government's attention to these differences, as specifically required under NEPA and as emphasized in the president's memorandum accompanying the executive order, is that residents of low-income or minority communities and their environments are being better protected. (See the discussions of the problems and potential for use of NEPA in Indian country by Dean Suagee in Chapter 10 and in the mining context by Kathryn Mutz in Chapter 13. See also the discussion of an EPA framework for incorporating an environmental justice analysis into NEPA documents by Jan Buhrmann in Chapter 11.)

NEPA mandates that for every proposed major federal action, government decision makers must consider the "environmental impact . . . , any adverse environmental effects which cannot be avoided . . . , alternatives, and any irreversible and irretrievable commitments of resources which would be involved in the proposed action should it be implemented."[33] These requirements accommodate easily the consideration of vulnerabilities and differences among communities (and the natural resources upon which they depend), which, in part, define how environmental burdens will be distributed. If these differences are considered, NEPA analysis can identify the effects that government action will have on a vulnerable community's environment. Moreover, by looking directly at the distribution of adverse impacts, additional environmental and natural resources burdens on minority or low-income communities can be identified and avoided. Without considering the social, economic, and environmental impacts on minority or low-income communities, decision makers cannot accurately conduct the balancing of costs and benefits that NEPA requires nor protect the community or resources upon which it depends.

Observers have long commented on the breadth of NEPA's scope and upon the opportunities it provides to consider and address adverse impacts on affected communities. However, many people— including some environmental justice advocates—have criticized the federal government's record of considering socioeconomic effects that may not be felt equally among communities and populations.[34] The president's memorandum accompanying the executive order addresses directly the environmental justice community's criticism of NEPA's implementation. The president's memorandum directs federal agencies to undertake three specific actions:

1. Analyze environmental effects, including human health, economic, and social effects, of federal actions, including effects on minority communities and low-income communities, when such analysis is required by NEPA
2. Develop mitigation measures outlined or analyzed in environmental assessments (EA), environmental impact statements, or records of decisions, whenever feasible, which address significant and adverse environmental effects of proposed federal actions on minority communities and low-income communities
3. Provide opportunities for community input in the NEPA process, including identifying potential effects and mitigation measures in consultation with affected communities and improving accessibility of public meetings, official documents, and notices to affected communities.[35]

The president further directed the EPA to ensure, under its authority pursuant to Section 309 of the Clean Air Act, that involved agencies have fully analyzed environmental effects on minority communities and low-income communities.

Implementing the executive order, the president's Council on Environmental Quality (CEQ) issued guidance. While the guidance, by its own terms, is not intended to be used as a formula, its principles respond to the criticisms of environmental justice advocates. The guidance provides that federal agencies should, in their NEPA analysis:

- Determine whether there are vulnerable populations present in the affected area and, if so, whether there may be disproportionately high and adverse effects on those populations
- Determine whether there is the potential for multiple or cumulative exposure to human health or environmental hazards
- Determine whether there are interrelated cultural, social, occupational, historical, or economic factors that may amplify the physical environmental effects of the proposed action
- Assure meaningful community representation in the process and develop effective public participation strategies.[36]

These principles direct federal agencies to take into consideration the context, values, experience, practices, and vulnerabilities of the subject populations and their relationships with the environment. From the perspective of the community, federal agencies can then take actions that maintain the natural and environmental resources upon which communities depend.

The executive order explicitly does not "create a right of judicial review against the United States."[37] Therefore, no federal court has remanded a federal action based upon an agency's failure to consider disproportionate impacts in the NEPA process.[38] However, at least two administrative tribunals have held that agency actions must adequately consider environmental justice issues, pursuant to the executive order, as part of the agency's NEPA analysis.[39] In these cases, the agency tribunals have expressed a willingness to review agency NEPA analyses for disproportionate impacts caused by agency actions to the environment and natural resources. Like the EAB, however, the agency tribunals look only to the nexus between the community and the environment and the way in which the government action affects that relationship. They will not examine allegations of outright discrimination on the part of the state or local regulatory agency responsible for approving a facility's siting.

A proposal for development of a visitor center in the canyon country of southern Utah provides one example of how NEPA can be used to protect communities and their environments. In *Southern Utah Wilderness Alliance, et al.*,[40] the Department of the Interior Board of Land Appeals (IBLA) reviewed and remanded a Bureau of Land Management (BLM) decision to construct a visitor station at Kane Gulch on the Grand Gulch Plateau, Utah. In so doing, the IBLA helped ensure that BLM would evaluate the proposed project's impacts on ecological integrity, cultural values, and traditional uses of the lands.

In that case, environmental organizations and the Navajo Nation, among others, objected to BLM's decision to construct a visitor center in Utah's canyon country because of possible harm to cultural and natural resources. Specifically, the appellants objected to BLM's failure to consider, in an EA prepared for the facility, the potential harm to natural and cultural resources from a potential increase of visitors to the area. Increased use has caused substantial degradation to significant portions of the Utah canyon lands. The loss of desert habitat is of special concern to local tribes who "gather pinyon nuts from the canyons for food and collect herbs indigenous only to [Cedar Mesa] for traditional medicines and blessing rituals."[41]

Preparing the NEPA analysis for the visitor center, BLM identified potential impacts to resources as a concern and entered into a dialogue with local tribes. However, BLM expressly decided not to address the possibility that new facilities would increase visitor use, because the agency assumed that visitor use would increase regardless of facility construction.[42] Consequently, BLM did not consider the facility's impact on cultural values caused by increased use and damage to natural resources. Consistent with this position, BLM also declined to address environmental justice concerns, stating that a "new visitor contact station would have no adverse impacts to minority or low income populations."[43] Further, rather than completing consultation with the tribes, BLM decided to respond to issues on a continuing basis, because it concluded that the facility would not injure any natural or cultural resources.

Noting that BLM had described the proposed visitor center as an "effective portal to the world-class resources of the Cedar Mesa outdoor museum," and planned to provide potable water in the high desert canyon land,[44] IBLA found that the EA should have determined whether the facility would, in fact, attract more visitors. Perhaps presupposing an answer, IBLA expressed concern that the EA did not consider the direct effect or indirect effects on cultural resources of the increased number of visitors. Moreover, IBLA was "troubled by BLM's treatment of Native concerns, since it expressly declined to address these issues and effectively acknowledged that, as of the issuance of the decision to go ahead, it had not fully resolved those concerns, but that it would do so in the future."[45] Remanding the decision to BLM, IBLA ordered BLM to complete the dialogue entered into with the tribes, to consider the effect of increased visitors to the area, and to identify vulnerable cultural resources likely to be impacted by increased use of the area. Thus, if BLM constructs the visitor center, the impacts to the land will be understood and addressed from the protective point of view of the local community.

Resource-Specific Analysis

Regulation of specific natural or environmental resources can protect ecosystems and people whose lives are intertwined with them.[46] Such regulation typically limits resource use to those actions that are found to be in the public interest.[47] Based upon common cultural understandings and executive branch policy, as stated in the executive order, government actions that disproportionately impact minority or low-income communities may be viewed as counter to the public interest. Thus, the public interest determination requirement, imbedded in most place- or resource-based acts, can give substance to NEPA's procedural requirements. An example of this is provided in a dispute over the issuance of a controversial CWA Section 404 permit to dredge and fill wetlands in Virginia.

Planning for expected regional growth, a group of municipalities and counties in Virginia's lower peninsula formed a consortium to develop a municipal water source that would satisfy estimated water demand through the year 2040. Projecting a water supply deficit of 39.8 million gallons per day, the consortium proposed a 1,526-acre water impoundment on Cohoke Creek—the King William Reservoir. The site was selected, in part, because of the unusual, deeply incised valley between the Mattaponi and Pamunkey Rivers. The suitability of the river valley for impoundment purposes and the availability of supplemental raw water from nearby Mattaponi River made the location desirable from an engineering perspective. The consortium concluded that without the reservoir the region would experience a severe water shortage.

According to an Army Corps of Engineer's (hereafter, "Corps") analysis, the King William Reservoir would have a substantial effect on regional ecological resources. The impoundment would create a 1,526-acre lake and result in a loss of a total of 437 acres of "highly diverse wetlands and uplands." The proposal, in fact, would rank as the "largest single destruction of wetlands and their associated habitat ever evaluated in the Norfolk District."[48] Animal and plant species would be significantly impacted by the project as well. The Fish and Wildlife Service found that two threatened plant species and a nest of bald eagles were located near the proposed dam and impoundment sites. Further, the project raised concern over the potential effect to the local shad population both from direct effects and, potentially more seriously, from the indirect effects of changes to instream salinity.

Two Native American tribes recognized by the State of Virginia,[49] the Mattaponi and the Pamunkey, would also be impacted.[50] The members of the Mattaponi have subsisted on a 150-acre reservation on the banks of the Mattaponi River since entering into a treaty with the then-colony of Virginia in 1677.[51] The river for which the Mattaponi Tribe is named and the surrounding land have special meaning to the Tribe, at cultural, spiritual, and physical levels. The area that would be impacted contains archaeological sites potentially eligible for inclusion in the National Register of Historic Places.[52] Among other spiritual and cultural resources, the Tribe revealed that the potentially impacted area includes a sacred site, which the Corps found to "have extreme importance to the sciences of archaeology and anthropology."[53]

From a physical needs standpoint, the potential diversion of water from the Mattaponi River and the impoundment and inundation of the Cohoke Creek and the surrounding river valley were perceived by the Tribe as having a catastrophic effect on the Tribe's way of life. The Corps characterized the Tribe's view of the impacts as follows:

> The reservoir would destroy their way of life through the loss of hunting, gathering and fishing habitat, by changing the rural setting from increased residential growth around their reservations, and by severing ties to their ancestors. . . . Also, the Mattaponi people believe that their subsistence shad fishery and hatchery operation will be lost or irreparably harmed by changes in salinity and impacts to shad eggs and fry associated with the raw water intake on the Mattaponi River.[54]

Because the Mattaponi are profoundly connected to the ecological resources surrounding them, it follows that affecting the natural resources would also have an adverse impact on the Tribe.

The Corps' final environmental impact statement, on January 24, 1997, recommended a preferred alternative that would have permitted the construction of the reservoir. In July of that year, the Corps accepted comments submitted by, among others, the Mattaponi Tribe, a number of environmental and natural resources organizations, the Georgetown Law Center (an environmental law clinic), and the EPA Region 3, which filed comments pursuant to Section 309 of the Clean Air Act. The environmental and natural resources organizations submitted studies that called into question the assumptions that the project proponents used in deriving the anticipated future demand for water. In addition, the groups raised a host of concerns relating to the proposed project's impacts to the ecology of the watershed and the indirect effects on the Mattaponi Tribe.[55]

Deferring to the Corps' analysis for water supply issues, EPA Region 3 focused its analysis on the project's direct and indirect effects on cultural, water quality, hydrology, fisheries, and wetland resources. Further, in its comments, the EPA addressed extensively, under the rubric of environmental justice, the intricate relationship between the local ecology and the Mattaponi. On this issue, the EPA found that the executive order, and the accompanying memorandum, "sets up a clear mandate for the Army Corps of Engineers to look seriously at this issue within the context of the . . . NEPA document."[56] While finding that the proponents had made a good faith effort to achieve some of the stated principles, the EPA found that "key components of *identifying* and *addressing concerns, in consultation with the affected communities* have yet to be completed."[57]

Significantly, the EPA found that the Corps should prepare a supplement to the environmental impact statement to address unresolved questions related to the impact on the affected Native American communities caused by the ecological modifications. In anticipation of this additional analysis, the EPA urged the Corps "to work directly with the affected [environmental justice] communities as well as seek professional assistance in this matter as they would any other environmental issue."[58] In particular, the EPA recommended examination of the following:

- Impacts or possible violation of a community's customs or religious practices
- Impacts to cultural and/or historic properties and areas and the degree to which the effects of the actions can be absorbed by the affected population without harm to its cohesiveness
- Impacts to fish and wildlife on which a minority population or low-income population depends, cultural differences in environmental expectations (endangered species vs traditional hunting or ceremonial use)
- Impacts on the health and sustainability of ecosystem or watershed within which a population is located (e.g. religious use of natural resources)
- degradation of aesthetic values.[59]

In response to comments received, the Corps prepared supplemental studies and conducted additional public outreach. In addition, the deciding official of the Corps met with the Mattaponi and Pamunkey Tribes directly, heard their concerns firsthand, and visited the cultural sites identified by the impacted communities.

The Corps also sought the services of its research arm, the Institute for Water Resources, to evaluate the need for, and alternatives to, the proposed reservoir. The institute concluded that the consortium "significantly overestimated future demand and that the stated need is not supported by their data."[60] Rather than the deficit of 39.8 million gallons per day predicted by the consortium, the institute estimated that a deficit of only 17 million gallons per day would exist in 2040. Using this lower measure, the deficit roughly corresponded to the amount of water the consortium estimated that it could obtain through conservation measures (7 to 11.1 million gallons per day) and the amount that could be developed from fresh and brackish groundwater supplies (10.1 million gallons per day).

On June 4, 1999, the Corps issued a letter stating its position to deny the consortium's request for permits to construct the proposed reservoir. The Corps issued the position to deny based on regulations governing wetlands and the information compiled as part of the NEPA review.[61] For such projects, two broad findings must be met before the Corps will issue a federal permit to dredge and fill a wetland. The regulations implementing Section 404 of the CWA provide that the Corps must determine (1) whether a practicable alternative exists that would have less adverse impact on the environment, and (2) that the project is not contrary to the public interest.[62]

Grounding its position to deny the permit in the supplemented environmental impact statement and the institute's analysis of water demand, the Corps found that the consortium had overstated the projected need by more than a factor of two, and that conservation and "non-reservoir [sources] would meet the 2040 deficit."[63] Thus, the Corps found that there did not appear to be a supportable, demonstrated need for the destruction of the wetland. The Corps also found that the reservoir would not be in the public interest. The position to deny first enumerated the ecological and cultural impacts of the proposed reservoir project, then looked at these resources from the Tribes' perspective. The Corps found the following:

> The project has the potential to impact a sacred site, traditional hunting, gathering and religious practice, subsistence fisheries, and the way of the Mattaponi. . . . Because the proposed reservoir is located between Virginia's only two American Indian Reservations, and the proposed intake is located upstream of the Mattaponi Reservation, the project has the potential to result in disproportionately high and adverse environmental effects

to this minority population as described in Executive Order 12898.[64]

The legal weight given to the executive order by the Corps can be debated. For example, it is not entirely clear whether the Corps interpreted the executive order as creating a policy finding that disproportionate impacts are necessarily or presumptively against public interest. However, among other bases for the position to deny, the Corps' decision was solidly based on the principle that actions which disproportionately impact low-income or minority communities are against the public interest. In the case of the Mattaponi, the Corps clearly found that environmental justice concerns have great bearing on the public interest determination under Section 404 of the CWA.

Conclusion

These examples do not define the universe of environmental statutes that have environmental justice implications for natural resources. To the contrary, the point is that all environmental laws have environmental justice implications embedded within them. The only question is, how will we use them? If statutes are applied using broad, generic averages, minority and low-income communities may be disproportionately impacted, and environmental injustices may result. However, if regulators view the communities' environmental resources from the communities' point of view, both the residents' health and that of the resources upon which they depend will be maintained.

Notes

Note: The views expressed in this article are solely those of the authors. No official support or endorsement by the U.S. Environmental Protection Agency or any other agency of the Federal government is intended or should be inferred.

1. Vitruvius, *The Ten Books on Architecture,* trans. Morris Hicky Morgan (New York: Dover, 1960), 241–42.
2. Endangered Species Act of 1973, 16 U.S.C., sec. 1521 et seq.
3. Zygmundt J. B. Plater, "The Embattled Social Utilities of the Endangered Species Act: A Noah Presumption and a Caution against Putting Gas Masks on Canaries in the Coal Mine," *Environmental Law* 27 (spring 1997): 845.
4. See Endangered Species Act, sec. 1538(a)(1)(B), making it illegal to "harass, harm . . . , or to attempt to engage in any such conduct."

5. U.S. Environmental Protection Agency, Office of Environmental Justice, *Final Guidance for Incorporating Environmental Justice Concerns in EPA's NEPA Compliance Analyses* (April 1998) (emphasis added).

6. U.S. Environmental Protection Agency, *Final Guidance for NEPA Compliance Analyses*.

7. Clean Water Act, 33 U.S.C., sec. 1251 et seq.

8. National Environmental Policy Act, 42 U.S.C., sec. 4321 et seq.

9. Clean Water Act, 33 U.S.C., sec. 1344 (permits for dredge or fill material).

10. See generally Samara F. Swanston, "Race, Gender, Age, and Disproportion Impact: What We Do about the Failure to Protect the Most Vulnerable," *Fordham Urban Law Journal* 21 (spring 1994): 577.

11. Memorandum to Bob Berman, Barbara Burr, Kirsten Levingston, Department of Justice, from Paul Tao, Department of Justice (July 25, 1994), concluding that the federal government can play an active role in eliminating a broad array of environmental justice problems. See also Richard Lazarus and Stephanie Tai, "Integrating Environmental Justice into EPA Permitting Authority," *Ecology Law Quarterly* 26 (winter 1999): 67, reviewing EPA authority to consider environmental justice concerns.

12. See, e.g., Clean Water Act, sec. 304(a)(1), 33 U.S.C., sec. 1314(a)(1).

13. See, e.g., Resource Conservation and Recovery Act, RCRA, sec. 3005(c)(3).

14. See, e.g., Comprehensive Environmental Response, Compensation, and Liability Act, sec. 117(e). This provision authorizes the EPA to make technical assistance grants of up to fifty thousand dollars to groups of citizens affected by Superfund sites.

15. See, e.g., Clean Air Act, sec. 309, directing the EPA to review and comment on the environmental impacts of actions of other federal agencies, including proposals for legislation, proposed regulations, and projects subject to Section 102(2)(C) of NEPA.

16. See, e.g., Federal Food, Drug, and Cosmetic Act, 21 U.S.C., sec. 346a; see also Safe Drinking Water Act, 42 U.S.C, sec. 300(g)-1.

17. Executive Order No. 12898, "Federal Actions to Address Environmental Justice in Minority Populations and Low-Income Populations," 59 *Federal Register* 7629 (1994), 3 C.F.R., sec. 859, reprinted in 42 U.S.C., sec. 4321. Presidential Memorandum Accompanying Executive Order 12898, Weekly Comp. Pres. Doc. 30 (February 11, 1994): 279, 280.

18. This review has been conducted pursuant to EPA policy and the executive order, rather than as a requirement of statutory law. See, e.g., *Sur Contra La Contaminacion v Environmental Protection Agency*, 202 F.3d 443, 2000 WL 132655 (1st Cir. 2000). Because the executive order explicitly does not create any substantive or procedural rights or a right of judicial review against the United States, no federal court has overturned a federal action based solely upon an underlying defect in an environmental justice analysis conducted pursuant to the executive order; see also *Morongo Band of Mission Indians v FAA*, 161 F.3d 569, 575 (9th Cir. 1998); *Air Trans. Ass'n of Am. v FAA*, 169 F.3d 1, 8–9 (D.C. Cir. 1999). Courts do, of course, review allegations relating to environmental justice concerns pursuant to

underlying environmental laws, other state and federal statutes, and common law causes of action, just as they would any other issue in dispute. The *Sur Contra La Comtamincacion* court, for example, reviewed many of the issues raised by the petitioning community group under Section 165(a)(2) of the Clean Air Act.

19. *In re: Chemical Waste Management of Indiana, Inc.*, RCRA Appeal Nos. 95-2 and 95-3 6 E.A.D. 66 (June 29, 1995).

20. *In re: Chemical Waste Management*, *5-6.

21. See, e.g., Catherine A. O'Neill, "Variable Justice: Environmental Standards, Contaminated Fish, and 'Acceptable' Risk to Native Peoples," *Stanford Environmental Law Journal* 19 (January 2000): 3, 55–57; see also Brian D. Israel, "An Environmental Justice Critique of Risk Assessment," *New York University Environmental Law Journal* 3 (1995): 469, 501.

22. See 33 U.S.C., sec. 1314 (publication of AWQCs); 33 U.S.C., sec. 1313(c)(2) (water body's designated use); 33 U.S.C., sec. 1313(d) (TMDLs); and 33 U.S.C., sec. 1314, and 40 C.F.R., sec. 123.45 (incorporation of TMDLs into NPDES permits).

23. O'Neill, "Variable Justice," 28–33. In addition to consideration of variability, Professor O'Neill suggests (see "Variable Justice," 25) that risk to high-fish-consuming communities may be compounded based on data gap uncertainties. She suggests that where professional judgment is exercised in the absence of knowledge, the values, experience, and biases of the expert decision makers will tend not to reflect those of high-fish-consuming communities.

24. 57 F.3d 1517, 1524 (9th Cir. 1995).

25. The EPA's current AWQC are based on the assumptions that a person consumes 6.5 grams of a fish fillet per day, and that this person weighs 70 kilograms (about 154 pounds). The fish consumption number of 6.5 grams represents the national average fish consumption calculated from data collected in a national U.S. Department of Agriculture (USDA) 1977–1978 survey. USDA National Purchase Diary Survey, cited in U.S. Environmental Protection Agency, "Environmental Equity: Reducing Risks for All Communities" (June 1992)(EPA-230-R-92-008), 13.

26. U.S. Environmental Protection Agency, "Environmental Equity," in which the EPA asserted that the potency factors used by other agencies or foreign governments would have resulted in a numerical between 5 and 1,600 hundred times less stringent.

27. *DOC v Clarke*.

28. O'Neill, "Variable Justice," 55–57. See also *Natural Resources Defense Council v EPA*, 16 F.3d 1395 (4th Cir. 1993), stating that subsistence fishing communities would not be injured because of low fish consumption values underlying the AWQCs.

29. U.S. Environmental Protection Agency, "Environmental Equity," 12–13.

30. The EPA is considering changing its methodology for calculating pollution levels in fish, focusing primarily on bioaccumulation for "certain chemicals where uptake from exposure to multiple media is important."

U.S. Environmental Protection Agency, Draft Water Quality Criteria Methodology, Human Health: Federal Register Notice, EPA 822-Z-98-001 (August 14, 1998), 214.

31. Notice, Draft Water Criteria Methodology Revisions, 63 *Federal Register* 43756, 43762 (August 14, 1998). This value is derived from a diet recall study conducted by the U.S. Department of Agriculture, "The Continuing Survey of Food Intake by Individuals for the Years 1989, 1990, and 1991."

32. Notice, Draft Water Criteria Methodology Revisions, 43892.

33. 42 U.S.C., sec. 4332(C).

34. Robert D. Bullard, "Building Just, Safe, and Healthy Communities," *Tulane Environmental Law Journal* 12 (spring 1999): 373, 374–78, criticizing the EPA and arguing that the "EPA was never given the mission of addressing environmental policies and practices that result in unfair, unjust, and inequitable outcomes," and pointing to the executive order's focusing "the spotlight back on [NEPA]" as a hopeful sign that the identification and prevention of disproportionate impacts may increase.

35. Presidential Memorandum Accompanying Executive Order 12898.

36. Council on Environmental Quality, *Environmental Justice: Guidance under the National Environmental Policy Act*, 8–10, 13. The CEQ Guidance states that "these factors should include the physical sensitivity of the community or population to particular impacts; the effect of any disruption on the community structure associated with the proposed action; and the nature and degree of impact on the physical and social structure of the community." With respect to public participation, the CEQ Guidance notes that "barriers may range from agency failure to provide translation of documents to the scheduling of meetings at times and in places that are not convenient to working families."

37. Executive Order No. 12898, sec. 6-609.

38. See, e.g., *Morongo Band of Mission Indians v FAA*, 161 F.3d 569, 575 (9th Cir. 1998); see also *Air Trans. Association of Am. v FAA*, 169 F.3d 1, 8–9 (D.C. Cir. 1999).

39. See, e.g., *San Carlos Apache Tribe et al.*, 149 IBLA 29 (May 21, 1999); *In Re: Louisiana Energy Services (Claiborne Enrichment Center)*, Docket No. 70-3070-ML (May 3, 1998); and *Antonio J. Baca*, 144 IBLA 35 (April 30, 1998). By contrast, another agency, the Federal Energy Regulatory Commission, has found that the "order does not apply to independent agencies, such as the Commission, and the President's memorandum that accompanies it states that it is intended to improve the internal management of the Executive Branch, and does not create any legally enforceable rights. Therefore, [an] EIS is not deficient for failing to include a specific discussion of this issue." City of Tacoma, Washington, Project Nos. 460-011 and -014, 86 FERC P 61,311 (March 31, 1999).

40. 150 IBLA 158 (August 29, 1999).

41. Christopher Smith, "Folks Flock to Site the Anasazi Once Fled in S. Utah," *Salt Lake Tribune*, January 20, 1997, D1.

42. *Southern Utah Wilderness Alliance*, 150, 167–68. BLM also neglected to con-

sider the management of visitors coming to the area, relying instead on an overall plan.

43. *Southern Utah Wilderness Alliance,* 161, n. 9 (internal punctuation omitted).

44. *Southern Utah Wilderness Alliance,* 162.

45. *Southern Utah Wilderness Alliance,* 168–69.

46. Resource protection would include the protection of specific types of natural or environmental resources based on an ecological or place-specific basis. This type of regulation includes, for example, management of public land under the Federal Land Policy and Management Act, 43 U.S.C., sec. 1701 et seq.; Wild and Scenic Rivers Act, 16 U.S.C., sec. 1271 et seq.; and Section 404 of the Clean Water Act, 33 U.S.C., sec. 1344, pertaining to permits for dredge or fill material.

47. See, e.g., Federal Land Policy and Management Act, 43 U.S.C., sec. 1712.

48. U.S. Army Corps of Engineers, "Briefing Paper Prepared by the Norfolk District Army Corps of Engineers for Assistant Secretary of Army for Civil Works" (May 28, 1999).

49. See Frank S. Ferguson, deputy attorney general, letter to John Dosset, Esq., June 3, 1997, acknowledging that the Mattaponi and other Indian tribes in the Commonwealth of Virginia stand in a position somewhat different for other citizens; citing 1917-1018 Op. Va. Att'y Gen 161, 1919 Op. Va. Att'y Gen. 179, and 1976-1977 Op. Att'y Gen. 107.

50. John R. Pomponio for Stanley Laskowsi, U.S. Environmental Protection Agency, Region 3, letter to Col. Robert H. Reardon Jr., district engineer, Norfolk District, Corps of Engineers, commenting on the final environmental impact statement for the King William Reservoir Water Supply Project. While both the Mattaponi and the Pamunkey would be substantially impacted, the analysis herein is limited to the Mattaponi, which have been the more active of the two tribes in opposing the reservoir.

51. Treaty of 1677, between the Mattaponi Indian Tribe and the Pamunkey Tribe, known as the "Treaty at Middle Plantation." The Commonwealth stands as the successor to the Crown. See 1976-1977 Op. Va. Atty. Gen. 107, 108–109, see also *Barker v Harvey,* 1881 U.S. 481 (1901).

52. Corps, "Briefing Paper"; see also Pomponio letter, commenting on final environmental impact statement for the King William Reservoir Water Supply Project. Artifacts found to be "Traditional Cultural Properties" are eligible for inclusion in the National Register because of "their association with cultural practices or beliefs of a living community that (a) are rooted in that community's history, and (b) are important in maintaining the continuing cultural identity of the community." U.S. Department of the Interior, National Park Service, "Guidelines for Evaluating and Documenting Traditional Cultural Properties," National Register Bulletin Number 38.

53. Corps, "Briefing Paper." The Briefing Paper also notes that the "Tribe only revealed the presence of this site when they felt they had no choice if the site was to remain undisturbed," and on the condition of confidentiality.

54. Corps, "Briefing Paper."
55. Pomponio letter, commenting on the final environmental impact statement for the King William Reservoir Water Supply Project.
56. Pomponio letter, 9.
57. Pomponio letter, 10 (emphasis in original).
58. Pomponio letter, 10. The EPA noted that the methods used to engage the affected populations may need to be tailored to the communities' culture and experiences. Because the tribes engaged in traditional and cultural practices not well understood by the government, direct communication with the Tribe was viewed by the EPA as essential to determine the effects of the proposed project. See Chapter 11 for Jan Buhrmann's recommendations for developing an adequate NEPA analysis involving potential environmental justice communities.
59. Pomponio letter, 11.
60. Institute for Water Resources, U.S. Army Crops of Engineers, "Evaluation of Conflicting View on Future Water Use in Newport News, VA" (May 1999). The use of the Corps' Institute for Water Resources appears to be directly responsive to the water demands critiques submitted by commentors on the environmental impact statement. See Corps, "Briefing Paper," 3–4.
61. Col. Allan B. Carroll, district engineer, U.S. Army, letter to R. W. Hildbrant, assistant city manager, City of Newport News (June 4, 1999).
62. 33 C.F.R., sec. 320.4 (j); 40 C.F.R., sec. 230.10(a); 33 C.F.R., sec. 320.4(a)(1).
63. Carroll, U.S. Army letter, 2.
64. Carroll, U.S. Army letter, 3.

Chapter 13

MINERAL DEVELOPMENT

Protecting the Land and Communities

Kathryn M. Mutz

A miner trudges slowly beside his mule up the narrow, rocky trail to his claim high in the Rocky Mountains. With a pick axe, explosives, and enough grub for a week, he is ready to make his fortune. Hoping to strike it rich, he lowers himself into the small shaft to pick, blast, and shovel out the mother lode. He is the quintessential miner—a symbol of the American West. Congress passed the 1872 General Mining Law to facilitate mining for his benefit and for the benefit of a nation in need of minerals and anxious to settle the West.

Today, this miner is only a romantic image and, arguably, environmental protection and restoration are as important as mineral development. Promoting settlement of the West has certainly not been a priority for decades. But the law conceived to protect and encourage the miner's entrepreneurship has remained relatively unchanged. The old prospector has been replaced by multinational corporations. Modern mining techniques range from sophisticated underground extraction with high-tech milling to huge open pit excavations that move more tons of rock per ounce of minerals than the nineteenth-century miner could have imagined.

Like other industries, the modern mineral industry can operate in either a destructive or an environmentally responsible manner. And like other industries, its environmental record has improved over the years. This transformation can be attributed in large part to the passage of environmental statutes applicable to mining, beginning with the National Environmental Policy Act of 1969 (NEPA), which established a broad environmental policy for the federal government and created requirements for analysis of federal actions "significantly affecting the quality of the human environment." The 1970s through 1990s followed with many environmental statutes that regulate mining impacts to air, land, and water.[1]

Despite the environmental protections that followed passage of these statutes of general application, there came a realization, as explained by David Getches and David Pellow in Chapter 1, that all communities were not benefiting equally from the nation's environmental progress. Consequently, in 1994 President Clinton issued the Environmental Justice Executive Order, *Federal Actions to Address Environmental Justice in Minority Populations and Low-Income Populations*,[2] and regulatory agencies slowly began to consider how their programs, policies, and activities might be disproportionately impacting—or unequally protecting—communities.

This chapter begins with examples of environmental problems and claims of environmental injustice at existing mine sites located in the vicinity of low-income and minority populations—those populations designated by the executive order as requiring special attention to avoid being disproportionately burdened. By confining the discussion of environmental justice to these populations, my discussion fits within Getches and Pellow's definition of environmental justice in terms of the communities served. I address these populations in settings more rural than the toxic waste siting cases of the traditional environmental justice context, but most of the environmental impacts of mining—for example, degradation of water and air quality and exposure to hazardous substances (such as cyanide), lack of enforcement of environmental statutes, lack of adequate information to inform decisions, and failure to address the unique impacts of development on specific populations—are all recognizable as traditional environmental justice concerns. Following these examples—which are intended to raise potential issues of environmental injustice rather than necessarily to characterize the mineral development industry—the remainder of the chapter focuses on the laws and regulations that allow federal land managers to control environmental degradation related to hardrock mining on federal lands.[3] The chapter concludes by considering how agencies might use their authority and discretion to ensure that minority and low-income populations are not disproportionately impacted by mining.

Environmental and Social Justice Issues

If we look at some of the failures of environmental protection in mining, environmental justice issues seem evident. While mining has provided jobs and economic development in many communities in the West, it has also left behind economically and environmentally battered communities. Many of these communities are rural and poor, and they often have a significant minority population. Yet mines cannot generally be "sited" in the same manner as are hazardous waste facilities, chemical processing plants, petroleum refineries, or even highways. Because mines must be located at the source of the mineral resource, mining companies cannot simply choose to locate a mine in a politically weak, low-income or minority community in order to minimize scrutiny or compliance with environmental regulations. Consequently, intentional targeting of vulnerable populations for the siting of facilities is likely to be a relatively minor concern for mineral development. Nonetheless, there may be issues of environmental justice once a mineral is located and mine permitting, construction, and operation begin.

The following case studies describe the claims of environmental injustice leveled by communities at three mine sites. These sites were chosen because they involve explicit claims of environmental injustice or racism and because they illustrate a range of environmental issues evident at mines. I do not attempt to evaluate the validity of these claims or the extent to which they characterize the mining industry. Rather, I use them to suggest the types of impacts and decision processes that raise environmental justice concerns and that might be addressed through statute and regulation.

Zortman-Landusky Mine, Montana

The most specific charges of environmental injustice in the hardrock mining industry have been made by the Assiniboine and Gros Ventre Tribes of the Fort Belknap Indian Reservation in Montana (hereafter, "the Tribes"), neighbors to the now-abandoned Zortman-Landusky (Z-L) gold mine. Pegasus Gold established the open pit, heap leach gold mines on a mixture of private and public lands in the Little Rocky Mountains of north-central Montana in 1979. With development of the mines, Spirit Mountain, previously a peak with spiritual and cultural importance to the Gros Ventre and Assiniboine, has disappeared and been replaced by a huge open pit. Since the mine opened, the Tribes have endured numerous environmental problems, including cyanide spills and water pollution from acid rock drainage. Despite multiple problems, the Z-L Mine was issued only one fine, for fifteen thousand dollars between 1979 and 1995, and in 1992, Pegasus submitted a proposal for significant expansion of its mine and waste rock facilities.[4]

After more than a decade of relative inaction on water pollution complaints, government agencies finally responded. In 1993, the U.S. Environmental Protection Agency (EPA), the Montana Department of Environmental Quality (Montana DEQ), and the Bureau of Land Management (BLM) all cited the Z-L Mine for water quality violations. That same year, BLM and the Montana DEQ required Pegasus to modify its existing operating and reclamation plans to address water quality impacts of acid mine drainage. In 1994, BLM prepared an environmental impact statement (EIS) that combined analysis of Pegasus's new reclamation plan with consideration of its proposal for mine expansion. In 1995, both the State of Montana and the EPA sued Pegasus for water quality violations. But while the case was still pending and many unresolved issues remained around the mine's responsibility to address water pollution in the Fort Belknap area, BLM finalized the EIS, approving Pegasus's plan to triple the size of its operation.[5]

The Tribes appealed BLM's approval of the Z-L expansion permit to the Interior Board of Land Appeals (IBLA), the Department of the Interior's administrative review board. The Tribes alleged that the NEPA review failed to sufficiently recognize and evaluate the impacts of the proposed mining, including impairment of water rights, groundwater quality degradation, destruction of cultural and religious sites, and interference with the Tribes' cultural practices.[6] The Tribes demanded that BLM reconsider the decision after preparing a more adequate supplemental EIS. Before any decision was reached, the threat of mine expansion ended in January 1998, when Pegasus Gold declared bankruptcy and closed the mine, leaving the state with millions of dollars in reclamation and cleanup costs not covered by the company's inadequate reclamation bond.[7]

In citing the many specific inadequacies of the EIS, the Tribes charged that BLM failed both to uphold its trust responsibilities and to fulfill its duties under the executive order. Specifically, they charged that BLM's "rush to approve the mine expansion in the face of missing information reflects the same lack of concern for the health of Tribal members and the quality of their physical environment" that was revealed in pollution studies that prompted the president to issue the executive order. The Tribes argued that approving expansion of the mines in the face of ongoing violations of environmental laws "continues this nation's history of inadequate enforcement of environmental laws in areas affecting minorities." Further, they asserted that BLM was required under the executive order to disclose in the EIS whether the mine expansion would disproportionately impact minority communities and to discuss how approval of any expansion could comply with the executive order in light of ongoing Clean Water Act violations.[8]

BLM responded to these allegations by claiming both process and substantive compliance with the requirements of the executive order. BLM argued that the EIS analyzed potential negative and positive impacts to the Tribes. They concluded that both the majority of economic benefits and the environmental risks were directed to the non-Indian community. The exception to this balance was that Native Americans would be more susceptible than others to impacts of mine development on traditional cultural practices and heritage values. BLM recognized that these impacts could not be mitigated if the mine were to be expanded yet chose to approve the expansion in spite of them.[9]

The IBLA eventually agreed with many of the Tribes' arguments and criticized BLM for dealing with the environmental justice issues only in a response to a public comment rather than in the analytical section of the EIS. But the IBLA declined to address the substance of the environmental justice claims in light of Pegasus's decision to cancel the mine expansion plans.[10] In April 2000, the Tribes sued the federal government for past and continuing environmental damages at the site, demanding full reclamation of the area. The Tribes argued that BLM failed to protect tribal health from mining impacts and to prevent degradation of public lands. They said cleanup is owed to them because the federal government failed to ensure protection of reservation water quality and quantity and of spiritual and religious interests in and around the mine area.[11]

In May 2001, the BLM issued a draft supplemental EIS for reclamation of the mine, examining five cleanup alternatives. The preferred alternative called for covering up most of the vertical pit highwalls, which can contribute to acid mine drainage, and revegetating most disturbed areas. This would cost about $22 million more than the state has available in the reclamation bond, but far less than the complete reclamation favored by the Tribes.[12]

Midnite Mine, Washington

The Dawn Mining Company (DMC), a subsidiary of the Denver-based Newmont Mining Company, mined uranium at the Midnite Mine on the Spokane Indian Reservation for twenty-six years. It also processed the uranium on the reservation at its mill near Ford, which lies along State Route 231 in Stevens County, Washington.[13] In 1982, demand for uranium dropped, and DMC assumed care and mainte-

nance status at the mine. Subsequently, DMC resumed minimal operation in order to reclaim uranium from water that continually seeped
from the mine. Groundwater at the mill site was contaminated as
well, and DMC initiated a groundwater remediation program in February 1992. Since then, it has pumped over 30 million gallons of water
out of the underlying Walker's Prairie Aquifer in an attempt to capture the polluted plume and remove radionuclides and sulfates. The
water is evaporated in plastic-lined pools covering over one hundred
acres. DMC has estimated that 92 million gallons of contaminated
water will have to be removed over about a twenty-year period.

Water pollution at both the mill site and the mine requires remediation, but the $1 million reclamation bond for the mill site is inade-
quate for reclamation, which is estimated at $20 million for the mill
site and from $100 to $200 million at the mine. The EPA proposed listing the Midnite Mine as a Superfund site in February 1999.[14]

Environmental justice claims surround the remediation planning.
Starting in 1986, DMC approached the Washington State Department
of Health (DOH) with a series of proposals to partially reclaim the site
by converting the mill site into a repository for various types of low-
level radioactive waste. DMC argued that filling a twenty-eight-acre
below-ground tailings impoundment with radioactive waste transported to the area from throughout the country would remediate the
most expensive single element of the mine-mill development. Proceeds from the commercial disposal site would also provide funds for
cleanup of the mill and perhaps even part of the mine.

The DOH evaluated the waste disposal proposal through a State
Environmental Impact Statement process, but in 1991, DOH
announced its preferred alternative that, instead, clean fill dirt should
be used to fill the abandoned tailing impoundment. Clean fill could
be transported to the site with less impact to the area's road system
and with less potential for accidents with expensive price tags for
their own cleanup. But rather than developing a closure plan using
clean fill, as recommended, DMC submitted a revised radioactive
waste disposal proposal for imported waste materials. A new state
administration approved this proposal despite Washington's policy to
limit the amount of radioactive waste flowing into the state.

One of the main community concerns for the waste dump project
was related to the transportation of radioactive wastes to the DMC
site, including damage to State Route 231, a two-lane rural collector
route that connects the area's small communities to one another, to
major highways, and to Spokane. The community was primarily con-

cerned with the "danger, stigma and inconvenience" of having the radioactive materials from across the country transported to Ford.[15] Plans and funds to offset impacts to infrastructure and to ensure safety had not been finalized, and the community feared that they would be ignored in the rush to close the facility. The community was also concerned with the precedent that would be set by allowing DMC to use government disposal contracts, supported by federal tax dollars, to pay for the reclamation of the mine site.

A member of the Spokane Tribe of Indians and Dawn Watch accused the company of "environmental racism" for refusing to clean up the messes left on the reservation by its uranium mine and mill.[16] The Tribe argued that use of the mine site for disposal of waste material would have a disproportionate impact on the Native Americans of the Spokane Reservation.[17] The Tribe also asserted that public participation in the decision-making process was deficient due to inadequate public notice, and that traffic safety questions were not addressed early in the process despite the fact that they were raised during the EIS process. While this claim was made specifically for the Tribe at public meetings, the Tribe has noted that the claim might also be made for residents of Stevens County, Washington, one of the poorest counties in the state.

Many of the Tribe's concerns were ultimately addressed in a final reclamation plan released in July 2000. After DMC was unsuccessful in bidding on the radioactive materials to be used in its disposal plan, the company agreed to fill the pit with "clean fill" plus demolished buildings and equipment from the mill site and unprocessed radioactive sludges from the mine's water treatment plant. This newest plan will reduce the radioactivity at the site, because no additional mill tailings will be buried there, and will allow for earlier closure of the mill site.[18]

Molycorp Mine, New Mexico

In the town of Questa in northern New Mexico, the environmental issues—primarily water pollution—are similar to those at the Z-L Mine site, yet the social justice issues differ. First, the mine is much older and, while the mine originated on former Spanish land grant lands, the site is now private property, patented in the 1920s under the 1872 Mining Law, within the Carson National Forest.[19] In 1964, Molycorp significantly expanded its existing facilities when it converted from an underground mine to an open pit operation. The conversion greatly increased the amount of tailings waste produced, and Molycorp responded by constructing and enlarging their tailings facilities to handle massive amounts of contaminated slurry. The existing tailings facility holds over 85 million tons of waste. In the late 1980s and 1990s, Molycorp sought permits to store 250 million more tons of waste but abandoned these efforts in the face of stiff community opposition.[20]

The predominately Hispanic town of Questa is surrounded by the mine-mill complex—located between the mine pit to the east and the tailings facility to the west—with slurry pipelines running along the Red River and across irrigation ditches to move the contaminated waste from the mine and mill to the tailings facilities. The Red River and its groundwater are the only water sources for the town, which has historically relied on them for agricultural, domestic, and cultural uses. For three decades, the town and its people have suffered from over one hundred documented slurry spills into the Red River, clouds of lead-contaminated tailings dust blowing through the town, acid mine drainage, and heavy metal contamination, which have left the town with at least eight miles of biologically dead river. The severity of the pollution near the town is apparent in recent efforts to have the mine listed as a Superfund site.

As described by some of the people of Questa and by environmental advocates at Amigos Bravos, the environmental justice issues at the Molycorp Mine amount to three decades of pollution of the Red River, a failure of the EPA and the State of New Mexico to vigorously enforce the Clean Water Act, and the inability, for economic reasons, of the poor, minority community to force regulatory action. Central to this problem has been the community's, as well as the state's and the EPA's, dependence on technical studies by the mine operator to determine the causes of water pollution. The community lacks both the expertise and the funds to independently evaluate the water quality problems. While it is clear to the residents that the river is dead, they have been unable to prove the cause of the pollution.[21] Molycorp has continually argued that their waste rock dump is not the main source of the river pollution. Only recently, in 1998, EPA completed a study of the hydrological connections associated with the mine development, and the New Mexico Environment Department (NMED) charged Molycorp with violation of New Mexico's Water Quality Act for illegally discharging pollutants from the waste rock piles into the groundwater.[22] After nearly two more years of wrangling, Molycorp, NMED, and Amigos Bravos agreed to a settlement to be monitored by the NMED. Molycorp agreed to upgrade water collection and treatment for the waste rock discharge and to pay for additional investigation into the extent of pollution attributable to the mine. Molycorp also put up over $150 million in bonds to cover cleanup of its tailings ponds and reclamation of the site after mine closure.[23]

Regardless of the availability or certainty of data on the cause of pollution, response to a polluted river is not a straightforward issue for a community like Questa. Relying on the mining industry for jobs and tax revenue, the community is divided on actions that would avoid risk to health and the environment at a cost to the industry. Before the Molycorp Mine transformed Questa into a mining-dependent town, the community was rural and agricultural. Fishing, irrigation, and domestic uses were the community's central needs, and the Red River met them. With expansion of the mine, Questa has become dependent on Molycorp and its "boom and bust" economy, with many Molycorp Mine workers feeling that they are "at the mercy of the mine."[24] This relationship between the mine and the community forces many Questa residents to choose between putting food on the table and speaking out against pollution of the river. Others are pragmatic and resigned to accepting both the benefits and the burdens that the mine development provides. As one Questa resident stated: "The mine or an oil well or I don't care what kind of industry you bring into a town, a community, a city, you're going to have the pollution. . . . If you want the jobs, [you're] going to have to deal with it, and pray to God nothing happens to you."[25]

Lessons from the Mine Sites

These case studies illustrate some of the basic issues of environmental justice that can arise in the mineral development context. While mine developments may not be intentionally sited in low-income or minority neighborhoods, there may still be environmental injustice in the mining context. Specifically, as illustrated in the Z-L Mine case, severe and disproportionate impacts to the community may result because the mine site location has a special value to the community—in this case, religious or cultural value. Once the mine development is located, inadequate enforcement of environmental laws can lead to inadequate protection of the environment and the health of the community—the principal issue at the Molycorp site. And finally, as suggested by the Midnite Mine example, reclamation of a mine at closure can be unjust if the reclamation plans do not meet the standards that might be applied in a more affluent or Anglo-American community.

Controlling Mining Impacts under Current Laws and Regulations

Given this country's array of environmental laws and the Environmental Justice Executive Order, no residents should have to "pray to God" that they and their communities are protected from environmental degradation and related health effects of mining. But how well do our current laws and regulations protect land and communities? The principal laws for regulating hardrock mining on federal lands are the General Mining Law of 1872, the Federal Land Policy and Management Act (FLPMA), the U.S. Forest Service's 1897 Organic Administration Act, NEPA, and individual environmental laws like the Clean Water Act.[26] This section describes the authority that these statutes and their regulations give to land managers to regulate the impacts of mining and to assure adequate reclamation after mine closure. With a basic understanding of how mining can be regulated, we can then determine how our most vulnerable populations—minority and low-income communities—can be protected from bearing an unfair burden of mineral development.

Land and Resource Management Laws and Regulations

The General Mining Law authorizes the development of hardrock minerals on federal lands. This law gives miners exclusive rights to mine on federal lands after establishing a valid mining claim. Lands are removed from this rule of "free access" only through a formal withdrawal under FLPMA.[27]

In order to develop and operate a modern, commercial hardrock mine on federal lands under the free access rule, companies must establish a valid claim through discovery of a valuable mineral deposit and prepare a mine plan (plan of operations) in compliance with the statutes and regulations of the appropriate land management agency.[28] The agency or its contractor then prepares an environmental assessment (EA) or EIS under NEPA, analyzing the potential impacts of the mine and developing appropriate mitigation measures.

The threshold condition that a mineral deposit be "valuable" before it is accessible under the free access rule allows some control over initiation of mineral development. Whether a mineral deposit is valuable is evaluated on the basis of a "marketability test," which requires the claimant to show that the mineral can be developed at a profit. In evaluating profitability, BLM considers the costs of mining, transport, and compliance with environmental regulations.[29] Consequently, a proposed mine must be able to comply with all environmental statutes if it is to take advantage of the free access rule. The panoply of general environmental statutes, including the Clean Water Act, Clean Air Act, Endangered Species Act, and Resource Conservation and Recovery Act, are all applicable to mining operations except when they specifically exclude mining operations from their purview or provide for specific exemptions. While the marketability test is likely to deter only marginal operations or operations in the most sensitive, relatively expensive to mine locations, it can give communities some degree of control over siting of mines.

The General Mining Law, relatively unchanged after more than a century, contains no explicit environmental protection language, but it does provide that mineral deposits are to be accessed "under regulations prescribed by law."[30] Consequently, the Forest Service has authority to manage mining on the national forests under the 1897 Organic Act, which authorizes the secretary of agriculture to promulgate rules to regulate "occupancy and use and to preserve the forests thereon from destruction."[31] FLPMA provides the Secretary of the Interior with organic authority to manage the public lands (federal lands under BLM jurisdiction), requiring that BLM "take any action necessary to prevent unnecessary or undue degradation of the lands."[32] Further, FLPMA directs the Secretary of the Interior to promulgate rules and regulations to carry out the purposes of FLPMA and other laws, like the General Mining Law, applicable to the public lands.

Pursuant to these statutes, BLM and the Forest Service have developed separate regulations for controlling mining operations on the lands they manage. BLM's FLPMA mandate to prevent "unnecessary or undue degradation" appears to give the agency wider latitude than the Forest Service to protect its lands. The requirement makes protective action mandatory rather than discretionary; it authorizes action by a variety of means; and it uses the conjunctive "or" to indicate that degradation should be prohibited regardless of whether such environmental degradation is necessary to extract minerals. But despite this broad statutory language, BLM's regulatory interpretation of the "unnecessary or undue degradation" provision has, since the regulations were promulgated in 1981, severely limited the agency's ability to deny or condition plans of operation. The 1981 Section 3809 regulations, under which all existing mines on BLM lands have been permitted, gave BLM some opportunity to deny or condition a permit on environmental grounds, but the regulatory definition of "unnecessary or undue" created a "prudent operator" standard.[33] Under this standard, BLM evaluated the potential environmental degradation from a proposed mine as compared to what might be perpetrated by a "prudent operator" at a similar mine, rather than by any absolute standard. Even when enforced, this standard prevents only the most egregious environmental degradation, that is, degradation beyond what is acceptable by industry standards. But short of this, BLM cannot under the 1981 standard evaluate the potential impacts of a mine and disapprove or condition the plan of operation based on the value of the resources affected or the specific community impacted.

After a long, contentious rule-making process, BLM finalized new, more stringent regulations in the final days of the Clinton administration (the 2001 regulations). These regulations were, however, immediately contested by the mining industry, and Secretary of the Interior Gale Norton began a process to reevaluate and revise them.[34] The regulations are likely to be in contention for years, but the following discussion compares the implications of the 1981 regulations and the 2001 regulatory changes for resource protection and environmental justice.

Perhaps the most controversial change was in the definition of "unnecessary or undue degradation." The 2001 regulations would allow BLM both to deny a permit outright and to require compliance with a variety of environmental standards. Under these regulations, BLM must prevent mining that would cause "substantial irreparable harm to significant scientific, cultural, or environmental resource values of the public lands that cannot be effectively mitigated."[35] Such harm might include obliteration of a Native American sacred site by open pit mining, such as occurred at Spirit Mountain at the Z-L Mine. Beyond this ability to deny a permit outright, the new definition would require that any mine must also meet an array of outcome-based performance standards related to mining technology and practices, sequencing of operations to avoid unnecessary impacts, compliance with land use plans, mitigation measures specified by the BLM to protect public lands, concurrent reclamation, and a wide range of environmental parameters.

Both the 1981 and the 2001 regulations contain two additional means for controlling mining impacts. First, both require mine operators to comply with federal and state environmental statutes. Where specific environmental statutes apply, the agency responsible for implementing them—either the EPA or a state or tribe with delegated authority—issues permits and develops appropriate permit conditions for the mine development. Second, both versions recognize that specific statutes may contain language more protective of certain locations than FLPMA's unnecessary and undue degradation mandate is for BLM lands in general.

Such a more stringent standard was applied, before the BLM regulations were changed, in denying a permit to develop the Glamis Gold Mine in the California Desert Conservation Area (CDCA). Upon the recommendation of the solicitor of the Department of the Interior, BLM determined that the mine would cause "undue impairment" (the standard specified in the CDCA's enabling legislation), based on the nature of the particular resources at stake, and consequently denied approval of the plan of operation. While such specific statutory authority is uncommon, it does, where applicable, provide an opportunity for addressing environmental justice issues. In the case of the Glamis Gold Mine, it prevented serious and irreparable impacts to the religion, culture, and historical resources of the Quechan Tribe.[36]

The Forest Service's mining regulations and their standards for compliance are less stringent than both the original and the new BLM regulations. Operations must only "minimize adverse environmental impacts on National Forest surface resources" "where feasible." The Forest Service standard does, however, specifically require compliance with applicable state and federal environmental statutes. Additional specific requirements are couched in vague terms, such as "where practicable."[37]

Once a plan of operations is approved and a mine is operating, both agencies have authority to monitor and inspect the operations periodically and to force compliance with performance standards. The Forest Service can issue a notice of noncompliance with the plan of operations, however, only if the operator's actions are "unnecessarily or unreasonably causing injury, loss or damage to surface resources." The 2001 regulations provide for on-site inspections that may be accompanied by members of the public, as well as issuance of noncompliance orders, suspension orders for significant violations, or immediate temporary suspensions if necessary to protect health, safety, or the environment from imminent danger or harm. Under the 2001 regulations, BLM could also revoke a plan of operations or nullify a notice based on failure to correct a violation or based on a pattern of violations after providing an opportunity for an informal hearing before the BLM state director. If an operator fails to comply with an enforcement order, BLM could pursue a civil action in U.S. district court for an injunction or order to enforce its order, prevent the operator from conducting operations on the public lands, and collect damages resulting from unlawful acts. These inspection and enforcement provisions are an improvement over the original regulations, which required BLM to go to court in order to enforce its noncompliance orders.

Adequate financial guarantees (bonding) for mine developments can also help protect communities. The Forest Service requires a financial guarantee for all mines regulated under a plan of operations. BLM's 2001 regulations require bonding for all but the smallest "casual use" operations. Under these regulations, the bond must cover 100 percent of the estimated cost for the agency to perform reclamation according to the plan of operations if the operator fails to perform. These stricter safeguards could help prevent abandonment of mine sites without sufficient bonds to conduct adequate reclamation—a problem at both the Z-L Mine and the Midnight Mine, which were developed under the original regulations. Under the 2001 bonding regulations, a mine would have to increase its financial guarantee if it modified its plan of operations and the estimated reclamation cost increased or if financial market fluctuations eroded the security by more than 10 percent of its value.

NEPA Evaluation

The National Environmental Policy Act, described in more detail by Dean Suagee in Chapter 10 and Jan Buhrmann in Chapter 11, provides the principal mechanism for evaluating the impacts of a proposed mining operation on public lands and, ideally, directing an agency decision on whether or not to approve a specific plan of operations or how to condition it. Public involvement in the process can help identify alternatives to a specific mineral development proposal and its potential impacts. NEPA applies to mineral development, since approval of a plan of operations is considered a "major federal action." Unfortunately, application of NEPA is as limited in the mining context as it is for other development scenarios.

First, NEPA does not require an EIS for agency actions unless those actions will have significant impacts. These actions, as Dean Suagee explains, can be evaluated through an EA, which does not require public participation or comments, rather than an EIS. Furthermore, NEPA is primarily a procedural statute and little, beyond process, is required. If the proper process is followed, the decisions of an agency will be given deference. Even when the public or other agencies participate in the process and object to a proposed plan and its NEPA document, the agency need not agree with the commenters.

Failure to agree does not establish that the agency did not adequately consider the comments, and the agency's decision will be upheld.[38]

In a NEPA analysis, the agency has the responsibility to "study, develop, and describe appropriate alternatives." An affected community may object to the agency's selection of alternatives analyzed or to its preferred alternative, and, if the public does not have notice and ability to participate in the process from the beginning, a review court may remand it back to the agency for further analysis.[39] But, as mentioned, if the agency follows proper procedures, review courts will defer to the agency's decision. At a minimum, to mount a successful challenge to the range of alternatives considered in an EIS, it may be necessary for the community to offer a specific, detailed counterproposal that has a chance of success. The agency also has considerable discretion in identifying and evaluating impacts of the project and in determining the detail with which potential impacts are analyzed. For example, while compliance with state and federal environmental statutes is a prerequisite to demonstrating that a mine will not cause unnecessary or undue degradation, BLM need not independently evaluate potential compliance with the statutes. The agency can simply assume that the EPA or designated state agency or tribe will properly administer and enforce regulatory and permitting requirements under their jurisdiction.[40]

Obviously, protection of a community is only as good as the enforcement of its laws, as illustrated by the Molycorp Mine and Z-L Mine examples and by Suagee's discussion of NEPA in Chapter 10. While BLM's ability to control mining may have improved with the new regulations, most of the laws and regulations that permit the agencies to control mining were in effect when the problems described earlier in this chapter occurred. In reality then, these laws and regulations can only be considered as providing "potential" for the protection of lands and communities. Actual protection requires vigorous, and perhaps creative, use of available authority.

The Executive Order and Discretionary Action under Law and Regulation

The previous section described the overall potential for environmental protection in the context of mineral development—the requirements of law and regulations that apply regardless of the populations impacted. Taken as a whole, the General Mining Law, as amended by FLPMA and interpreted under the Forest Service Organic Act, provides BLM and the Forest Service with the statutory authority to protect the environment and all communities from some, but not all, of the impacts of mining. Neither agency has complete discretion to prohibit mining altogether in order to protect other resources. The agencies can, however, protect other resources and may deny permits to mine under four specific circumstances: (1) if the land has been withdrawn from mineral entry; (2) if the mine cannot comply with environmental laws or the proponent cannot establish a valid mining claim because he/she cannot produce minerals at a profit after accounting for the costs of compliance; (3) if other specific statutory authority, like the CDCA, requires attaining standards of protection that cannot be achieved during mining; and (4) if the mine cannot meet the agency's own regulatory standard for mine operation. The Forest Service's weak standard and BLM's 1981 standard are not likely to preclude mining. But if something comparable to the BLM's 2001 standard is eventually implemented, the agency might preclude—through either permit denial or permit conditions—mining that would result in substantial irreparable harm to significant resources if that harm cannot be effectively mitigated.

With this background, I turn now to the requirements for environmental justice. What additional consideration is required of—or what discretion is available to—land management agencies to avoid unduly burdening low-income and minority communities with the impacts of mining?

Mandate and Limits of the Executive Order

The Environmental Justice Executive Order is a mandate that commands federal agencies:

> To the greatest extent practicable and permitted by law [to] make achieving environmental justice part of its mission by identifying and addressing, as appropriate, disproportionately high and adverse human health or environmental effects of its programs, policies, and activities on minority populations and low-income populations.[41]

Both the Department of the Interior and the Department of Agriculture, host departments for BLM and the Forest Service, are specifically named in the executive order and charged with developing a strategy for implementing the order, including "(1) promot[ing] enforcement of all health and environmental statutes in areas with minority populations and low-income populations; [and] (2) ensur[ing] greater public participation."[42]

The EPA and the Council on Environmental Quality (CEQ) have developed guidance documents to aid agencies in incorporating environmental justice principles into their missions. These are considered important internal policy documents, given "great deference" as the interpretation of the officers or agency charged with administration.[43] While the mandate of the executive order is clear, the ultimate implementation of the order is at the discretion of the agency, the departments, and the president. The executive order, Section 6-609, is explicit that it does not create any right to judicial review for compliance or noncompliance with the order. Similarly, EPA and CEQ guidance documents include explicit disclaimer language designed to keep compliance issues out of the courts.[44] The Department of the Interior was less tentative, at least initially, than the EPA and the CEQ in its own guidance, emphasizing, without disclaimer language, the need to ensure that decisions "consider the impacts of our actions and inactions on minority and low-income populations and communities, as well as the equity of the distribution of benefits and risks of those decisions."[45]

When asked to review agency decisions on the basis of environmental justice claims, the courts have cited the executive order disclaimer language and declined to address the merits of these claims.[46] In contrast, administrative appeals boards of the Department of the Interior and the EPA, unaffected by the disclaimer of *judicial* review, have been willing to address the merits of environmental justice claims.[47]

While the executive order and guidance documents create a mandate for federal agencies, the documents' escape clauses suggest that social justice advocates should work directly with the agencies to address environmental justice issues. Administrative appeals boards may support advocates' positions, as eventually occurred in the Z-L Mine case, but there is little recourse in the courts for a claim that is specifically couched in environmental justice terms.

Current Mining Law and Regulation

Assuming there will continue to be departmental and executive branch support for implementation of the executive order, what specifically is, in the words of the executive order, "practicable and permitted by law" to ensure environmental justice in the development of minerals on federal lands? "Permitted" as opposed to "required" is the operative language addressed here.

First, there is potential for promoting environmental justice within the current legal framework through the application of general environmental statutes. As discussed above, ability to comply with these statutes is a prerequisite to authorization to mine because the validity of mining claims—which form the basis for the mine development—are evaluated based on the marketability test. Environmental justice considerations can also be interjected through the environmental permitting process in conjunction with the development of the mine plan of operations and mine reclamation plan. Compliance with environmental statutes is an explicit component or minimum condition of both the Forest Service and the BLM standards. State mining regulatory law also typically requires compliance with state and federal environmental statutes.[48]

Ensuring that enforcement of environmental statutes is as vigorous in minority and low-income communities as it is in more affluent and Anglo-American communities is the first step in protecting all communities. Enforcement of the Clean Water Act is, for example, central to the claims of environmental justice at the Molycorp Mine. Once equal enforcement is attained, however, the EPA and the states can use these statutes to give special consideration to environmental justice issues. In an analysis of several statutes, including the Clean Water Act, to determine whether the EPA has authority to condition or deny permits on environmental justice grounds, Richard Lazarus concludes that the EPA has authority to address environmental justice issues in their permitting decisions.[49] Lazarus does, however, note that the agency's discretion is much broader than its statutory mandate. Consequently, as with the implementation of the executive order discussed above, progress on environmental justice will require voluntary agency action because agencies will not be coerced by the courts to exercise their discretion.

Apart from compliance with environmental statutes, the Section 3809 regulations also require an operator to implement mitigation measures specified by BLM to protect public lands. BLM must determine, on a case-by-case basis, the mitigation required to minimize the impacts and environmental losses from operations. These measures can be developed through the NEPA process, and mitigation may include avoiding the impact altogether; minimizing impacts by limiting a proposed action and its implementation; rectifying the impact by repairing, rehabilitating, or restoring the affected environment; reducing or eliminating the impact over time by preservation and maintenance operations during the life of the action; and compensating for the impact by replacing, or providing substitute, resources or environments. Mitigation measures are not explicitly limited in the regulations to those that would be required to meet the agency's development standard. Consequently, as with implementation of environmental statutes, agencies appear to have some discretion to tailor mitigation to the needs of the community at risk.

The BLM's 1981 prudent operator standard for evaluating "unnecessary or undue degradation" created a major impediment to addressing environmental justice issues. With this standard, BLM evaluated mine plans and their implementation based more on whether they followed industry standards than on the severity of impacts to communities or the value of the resources affected by mining. Consequently, the agency has been limited in its ability to advance environmental justice in the mineral development context except where specific legislation provided a standard more stringent than FLPMA's resource protection standards.

If implemented, the 2001 Section 3809 regulations would have allowed BLM to consider whether a new mine development or an expansion of an existing development might result in substantial, irreparable harm to significant resource values. Were such an impact likely, either that impact would have to be mitigated or the BLM would have to deny mine approval. Should this fundamental regulatory change eventually be implemented, BLM will have the clear authority to base mineral development decisions, at least in part, on an evaluation of the area's nonmineral resources.

In light of the mandate of the executive order, the agency could , under these regulations, evaluate the harm to resource values, not only from the perspective and values of the nation's majority population but also from the particular perspective of any community that may be affected by the development. In this type of analysis, the clearest case might be one similar to that of the Quechan Indians of the CDCA or the Assiniboine and Gros Ventre Tribes near the Z-L Mine in Montana. As in these cases, it may be relatively clear that obliteration of a sacred landscape with a mine pit would cause "substantial irreparable harm" to a cultural resource. The more difficult case might be in assessing the degree of harm that a combination of environmental impacts, including clouds of blowing mine tailings and a dead river, has on a poor farming community such as Questa New Mexico. If it were determined to be "substantial and irreparable," at the very least the agency, subject to the 2001 regulations, would have to determine whether the harm could be mitigated.

In the spirit of the executive order and to ensure that all communities are equally protected, application of the 2001 unnecessary or undue degradation standard should take into account the community as well as the physical resource. The CEQ notes that it is important to recognize that "the impacts within minority populations, low-income populations, or Indian tribes may be different from impacts to the general population due to a community's distinct cultural practices."[50] What is "undue degradation" should, therefore, be defined in terms of the quality of the resources being impacted, the value of those resources to the community, and the relative distribution of burdens and benefits that would result from degradation of those resources to facilitate mineral development.

Creative Use of NEPA

Both the potential and the limitations of using NEPA for controlling impacts of mineral developments have been described above. While the executive order does not correct these limitations, or change the statutory interpretations or any legal thresholds under NEPA, nevertheless it provides the mandate to incorporate environmental justice considerations into the NEPA analysis where practicable. Guidance provided by the CEQ and BLM can help managers incorporate these concerns into analysis documents.[51] The EPA's four-point framework for environmental justice analysis, described by Buhrmann in Chapter 11, provides more specific guidance for conducting such analysis.

Specifically the agencies, through the departments, have a mandate from the executive order to "ensure greater public participation," and the CEQ provides specific recommendations for providing creative, meaningful public participation and representation for low-income and minority populations.[52] The statute itself provides agencies with discretion to use whatever "procedures as may be necessary to provide public comment in a particular instance."[53] The CEQ cautions that "community participation must occur as early as possible if it is to be meaningful" and recommends that, where there is potential for disproportionate burdens, "agencies should augment their procedures" to ensure that the process adequately addresses environmental justice concerns."[54]

The process of participation in decision making surrounding mineral development can itself be a benefit to the communities because it assures that they have a voice in their own future—a voice that can weigh the benefits and burdens of the mine development. Identification of special circumstance of minority and low-income populations would be essential to recognize those situations in which mining activities would result in "substantial irreparable harm . . . that cannot be mitigated" such that the mining operation would not be allowed on public lands. Short of permit denial, however, community involvement in the process can be useful in prompting specific impact analysis and formulating permit conditions that will keep impacts to an acceptable level.[55] Identification of pertinent environmental data and data gaps, analysis of impacts specific to the minority or low-income populations, and identification of disproportionate risks and benefits of a mining development can also lead to development of either mandatory or voluntary special permit conditions that can promote equity.

Whether or not an agency will recognize disproportionate impacts and design effective mitigation plans depends, in part, on what issues are analyzed and how impacts are evaluated. NEPA documents must analyze both direct or indirect impacts of the proposed project, but agencies have, nonetheless, been able to exclude seemingly relevant impacts from consideration under this requirement. For example, the IBLA has approved BLM's exclusion of impacts of mining from analysis of a land exchange proposal where the lands exchanged would be used to expand an existing copper mine.[56] On the other hand, the agency has discretion to include analysis of impacts regardless of whether the impacts are within the control of the agency proposing the action.[57] If a community wants to force an agency to use a particular type of analysis to do an environmental justice evaluation, the community must demonstrate why or how the desired analysis is likely to demonstrate the potential for disparate impact.[58]

A thorough cumulative impact analysis under NEPA may also be valuable for addressing environmental justice concerns because the community may have had to endure similar burdens of development in the past. It is not, however, sufficient for communities to complain of many similar projects in their area. To force a cumulative impact analysis, there must be the likelihood of an interaction between other projects and the proposed project that may result in an "enhanced or modified impact" that the agency is required to consider.[59]

While NEPA analysis can be creatively used to further the goals of environmental justice, its effectiveness depends both on the ability of traditionally disenfranchised communities to participate in the process and on the willingness of the agencies to use their discretion to ensure that community concerns are addressed. The problems inherent in public participation and the historical problems with agency commitment are discussed by Sheila Foster in Chapter 6 and by Dean Suagee in Chapter 10.

Summary

Communities that have felt the negative impact of mineral development have criticized mining companies and federal and state agencies for slow, inappropriate, or inadequate response to environmental degradation. When those affected are low-income or minority communities, the complaint may include a claim of environmental injustice. When the complaints involve hardrock mines on federal lands, BLM and the Forest Service can use the General Mining Law, FLPMA, NEPA (to a lesser extent), the Forest Service Organic Act, and an array of general environmental laws to help prevent negative impacts of mining.

The General Mining Law, as amended by FLPMA, is firm in its protection of mining interests and cryptic but receptive to environmental protection. Within the framework of these statutes and with the mandate of the executive order, specific environmental statutes can be applied to recognize and alleviate unique or disproportionately negative mining impacts. In addition, NEPA requires a process to evaluate impacts and provides agencies with flexibility to consider environmental justice issues. Agencies can provide for meaningful participation of communities, develop a wide range of alternatives for consideration, identify impacts that are specific or unique to those communities, and develop mitigation measures that will address many of their concerns. In addition, BLM will, if the spirit of the 2001 regulations survives, have the obligation to evaluate mine developments based upon their impact on significant scientific, cultural, and environmental resource values.

But much of what is "permitted by law" is truly only "possible." While regulatory changes may give BLM new flexibility, most of the laws and regulations governing mining have been in effect for decades. The executive order has merely charged the agencies with a new awareness and challenged them to review their mission and programs through an environmental justice lens. It is up to affected communities to continue to make their voices heard, and up to the agencies to use the law, the regulations, and their discretion to ensure that all peoples are treated fairly—that none suffer unduly from mineral development on federal lands.

Acknowledgments

I thank Gary Bryner and Todd Baldwin (of Island Press) for their helpful comments on drafts, Mary Elizabeth Murphy and Sarah Stahelin for their research assistance, and Chet Pauls for his gentle patience and support. I am also grateful to the Ford Foundation and the William and Flora Hewlett Foundation for their support of the Natural Resources Law Center's justice and natural resources project, including the opportunity their support gave me to prepare this chapter.

Notes

1. NEPA is codified in the U.S. Code (U.S.C.) at 42 U.S.C., secs. 4321–4347 (1988), available at www.law.cornell.edu/uscode/. See particularly 42 U.S.C., sec. 4332(2)(C); see also Clyde Martz, ed., *Environmental Regulation of the Mining Industry: From Second Edition of the American Law of Mining* (New York: Bender, 1996), for environmental statutes applicable to mineral development.

2. Executive Order No. 12898, 59 *Federal Register* 7629 (1994), 3 C.F.R., sec. 859, reprinted in 42 U.S.C., sec. 4321, available at www.epa.gov/docs/oejpubs/.

3. Hardrock minerals are minerals that are "locatable," that is, able to be acquired under the General Mining Law of 1872. They are neither leaseable (for example, oil, gas, or coal) nor saleable mineral materials (such as common sand and gravel) but include such minerals as copper, lead, zinc, magnesium, gold, silver, and uranium. Federal lands discussed here include both public lands administered by the Bureau of Land Management and National Forest System lands.

4. Mineral Policy Center, "Six Mines, Six Mishaps," *Regulatory Reform Report No. 1*, (1999), 6–8, available at www.mineralpolicy.org/publications/.

5. *Island Mountain Protectors*, 144 IBLA 168 (1998); Island Mountain Protectors Statement of Reasons: 1 (on file with the author).

6. *Island Mountain Protectors*, 176. BLM's selected alternative in the mine's expansion EIS plainly stated that the cumulative impact of mining operations will be "100 plus years of significant disruption to the Native American cultural practices." Parties to the appeal included Island Mountain Protectors, National Wildlife Federation, the Assiniboine and Gros Ventre Tribes, and the Fort Belknap Community Council.

7. Erin P. Billings, "Mining Reclamation Laws Need Changes," *Billings Gazette*, March 8, 2000; Mineral Policy Center, "Six Mines, Six Mishaps," 5.

8. Island Mountain Protectors Statement of Reasons, 12–14.

9. Bureau of Land Management, "Final Environmental Impact Statement on the Zortman and Landusky Mines Reclamation Plan Modification and Mine Life Expansion, Responses to Public and Agency Comments," 6–194, comment 26.

10. *Island Mountain Protectors*, 203.

11. Erin P. Billings, "Tribes Sue U.S. over Damage at Gold Mines," *Billings Gazette*, April 13, 2000; Bob Anez, "Fort Belknap Tribes Sue over Pollution from Mines," *Associated Press Newswires*, April 13, 2000.

12. "Preferred Alternative Will Cost $22 Million More Than State Has, Study Shows," *Associated Press Newswires*, May 4, 2001.

13. Information for this case study is drawn primarily from the Dawn Watch web site, available at www.dawnwatch.org. See e.g., "Responsibility for Transportation Impacts" and "The Dawn Story."

14. "Six Mines, Six Mishaps," 25, citing EPA News Release, "EPA Proposes Midnite Mine (Stevens County) for Inclusion on National Priorities List" (February 16, 1999).

15. "The Dawn Story," available at www.dawnwatch.org, the Dawn Watch web site.

16. John K. Wiley, "Mining Firm's Pond-Filling Plan Draws Fire," *Morning News Tribune*, December 9, 1999.

17. Testimony by Shannon Work, attorney for the Spokane Tribe of Indians, Wellpinit Public Meeting, Spokane Indian Reservation, DMC/DOT Transportation Public Meeting #3 of 4 (August 25, 1997), Wellpinit School, Wellpinit, Washington.

18. John K. Wiley, "State Recommends Approval of Modified Uranium Mill Closure Plan," *Associated Press Newswires*, June 13, 2000.

19. Because it has been patented (is now private land), the 1872 General Mining Law, Forest Service regulations, and NEPA no longer apply to the mine development.

20. Information for this case study was drawn from several sources, including Amigos Bravos' web site, available at www.amigosbravos.org, including *The Workbook*, vol. 15, no. 2, and the organization's Oral History Project. Amigos Bravos is a nonprofit river advocacy group dedicated to preserving both the ecological and the cultural richness of the Rio Grande watershed.

21. Amigos Bravos Oral History Project, at www.amigosbravos.org/Projects/oralhistory.html.

22. "Six Mines, Six Mishaps," 20–21; "Molycorp in Violation," *Bulletin* (winter 1998–1999), available at www.amigosbravos.org/Bulletin/bulletinarchives.html; U.S. Environmental Protection Agency, "Report on Hydrological Connection Associated with Molycorp Mining Activity, Questa, New Mexico," EPA Report (February 13, 1998).

23. "Mining Company, Environment Department Reach Agreement," *Associated Press Newswires*, November 15, 2000; "Mining Company Posts Bond to Cover Tailings," *Associated Press Newswires*, October 14, 2000.

24. Brian Shields, executive director, Amigos Bravos, telephone interview with Sarah Stahelin (February 9, 2000); Oral History Project, Roberto Vigil, July 22, 1998.

25. Oral History Project, Anonymous, "The Molybdenum Corporation of America Has Not Been a Good Neighbor"; John and Mary Valdez (pseudonyms) ("People are afraid to speak out against the mine for fear of making trouble for friends or relatives that work at the mine"); see also interviews with Moises Rael and Berlinda Trujillo.

26. Codification of these laws can be found in the U.S.C. at FLPMA: 43 U.S.C., sec. 1701 et seq.; General Mining Law of 1872: 30 U.S.C., secs. 21–42; 1897 Organic Administration Act: Act of June 4, 1897, ch. 2, 30 Stat. 34–36 (codified as amended at 16 U.S.C., secs. 473–481, 551; and NEPA: 42 U.S.C., sec. 4321 et seq. The U.S.C. is available at www.law.cornell.edu/uscode. See also National Research Council, *Hardrock Mining on Federal Lands* (Washington, D.C.: National Academy Press, 1999), for a summary of statutes applicable to hardrock mining.

27. See John D. Leshy, *The Mining Law: A Study in Perpetual Motion* (Wash-

ington, D.C.: Resources for the Future, 1987); and Michael Graf, "Application of Takings Law to the Regulation of Unpatented Mining Claims," *Ecology Law Quarterly* 24 (1994): 57.

28. For purposes of regulation, both BLM and the Forest Service differentiate between the size and the type of operations. Only the larger mines, which require a plan of operations, are discussed in this chapter. "Casual uses" (very low disturbance activities, such as rock sampling with hand tools) and "notice" operations (specifically small-scale exploration on BLM land or mines of less than five acres on national forest lands) are minimally regulated and do not require an approved plan of operations. Hardrock mines can be developed on federal lands even if a valuable mineral deposit cannot be established for the specific acres to be disturbed. This is an important issue for the huge, modern gold mines, for which large areas of nonmineral land are required for cyanide heap leach piles and wasterock piles. What standards should be applied to these areas is currently being litigated in regard to the new BLM Section 3809 regulations discussed later in this chapter. See *National Mining Association v Bruce Babbitt*, filed in the U.S. district court for the District of Columbia as Case Number 1:00CV02998, December 15, 2000.

29. *U.S. v Coleman*, 390 U.S. 599 (1968); *Clouser v Espy*, 42 F.3d 1522, 1530 (9th Cir. 1994) (increased operation costs due to environmental regulation compliance may affect claim validity); *Great Basin Mine Watch et al.*, 146 IBLA 248, 256 (1998) ("Under no circumstances can compliance be waived merely because failing to do so would make mining of the claim unprofitable"). A more flexible "comparative value" test for claim validity has been proposed, but whether it will be accepted by the courts is unclear. See *United States v United Mining Corp.*, 142 IBLA 339 (1998).

30. 30 U.S.C., sec. 22.

31. 16 U.S.C., sec. 551.

32. 43 U.S.C., sec. 1732.

33. The original Section 3809 regulations were codified in the Code of Federal Regulations (C.F.R.) at 43 C.F.R., sec. 3809 et seq., 45 *Federal Register* 78902–78915 (November 26, 1980). The regulations defined "unnecessary or undue degradation" as

> surface disturbance *greater than what would normally result when an activity is being accomplished by a prudent operator* in usual, customary, and proficient operations of similar character and taking into consideration the effects of operations on other resources and land uses, including those resources and uses outside the area of operations. Failure to initiate and complete reasonable mitigation measures, including reclamation of disturbed areas or creation of a nuisance may constitute unnecessary or undue degradation. Failure to comply with applicable environmental protection statutes and regulations thereunder will constitute unnecessary or undue degradation. Where specific

statutory authority requires the attainment of a stated
level of protection or reclamation, . . . that level of protection shall be met. 43 C.F.R., sec. 3809.0-5 (emphasis added).

34. *National Mining Association v Bruce Babbitt;* Scott Sonner, "Nevada Mining
Industry Cheers BLM Decision to Suspend Regulations," *Associated Press
Newswires,* March 20, 2001. For a brief history of the regulatory revision
process, see the "background" sections of the proposed rule, 64 *Federal
Register* 6423–6425 (February 9, 1999), and the final rule, 65 *Federal Register* 69998-01 (2000), 2000 WL 1723734, available at www.access.gpo.gov/
su_docs/aces/aces140.html. See also *Public Land News* 26 (July 20, 2001):
1.

35. 43 C.F.R., sec. 3809.5. The 2001 regulations were to be numbered as follows at 43 C.F.R., sec. 3809 et seq.; definitions at sec. 3809.5; performance
standards starting at sec. 3809.400; inspection and compliance starting at
sec. 3809.600; and bonding starting at sec. 3809.550.

36. Regulation of Hardrock Mining, memorandum from Interior Solicitor
Leshy to the acting director of the BLM (December 27, 1999).

37. Forest Service mining regulations are found at 36 C.F.R., sec. 228 et seq.,
available at http://www.access.gpo.gov/nara/cfr/cfr-table-search.html.

38. See, e.g., *Vermont Yankee Nuclear Power Corp. v Natural Resources Defense
Council,* 435 U.S. 519, 555 (1978) (deference) and *Okanogan Highlands
Alliance et al., v Robert Williams, et al.* 1999 WL 1029106 (D. Or.)(agency
comments).

39. *Island Mountain Protectors* (agency's analysis was insufficient to choose
among alternatives); *National Parks and Conservation Association, et al. v
Federal Aviation Administration,* 998 F.2d 1523, 1531–33 (10th Cir. 1993)
(notice must be provided to the minority population but need not be
comparable to that provided to the white populations).

40. *Okanogan Highlands v Robert Williams* (government agencies are presumed
to act lawfully within their regulatory and statutory mandates) (citing *In
re Hergenroeder,* 555 F.2d 686 (9th Cir. 1977)).

41. Executive Order No. 12898, sec. 1-101.

42. Executive Order No. 12898, sec. 1-102.

43. *Udall v Tallman,* 380 U.S. 1, 16 (1965).

44. See, e.g., U.S. Environmental Protection Agency, *Final Guidance for Incor-
porating Environmental Justice Concerns in EPA's NEPA Compliance Analyses*
(April 1998): 1, available at http://es.epa.gov/oeca/ofa; Council on
Environmental Quality, *Environmental Justice Guidance under the National
Environmental Policy Act* (December 10, 1997).

45. Memorandum from Secretary of the Interior Bruce Babbitt to Solicitor, All
Assistant Secretaries, Inspector General and Heads of All Bureaus and
Offices, Environmental Justice Policy, August 17, 1994; in addition, the
director of BLM has stated that "consideration [of environmental justice
impacts] should be specifically included in National Environmental Policy Act (NEPA) documentation on our decision-making." Instruction

Memorandum No. 93- (expired 9/30/94) from BLM Director to ADs, SDs and SCD, "Policy of Promoting Environmental Justice in Public Lands Decisions."

46. *Citizens Concerned About Jet Noise v Dalton,* 48 F. Supp. 2d 582 (E.D. Va. 1999); *Sur Contra La Contaminacion v Environmental Protection Agency,* 2000 WL 132655 (1st Cir. 2000); *Morongo Band of Mission Indians v Federal Aviation Administration,* 161 F.3d 569, 575 (9th Cir. 1998).

47. Some administrative judges have recognized existence of the disclaimer and have proceeded to evaluate the claims. See *Antonio J. Baca* 144 IBLA 35 (1998): 39. Others have simply ignored the disclaimer language and have either chastised the agency for their inadequate implementation of the executive order or otherwise addressed the substantive claims. See *Island Mountain Protectors,* 203 n. 8; *In Re: Ash Grove Cement Company,* 7 E.A.D. 387, 1997 WL 732000 (E.A.P), 18.

48. See Martz, ed., *Environmental Regulation of the Mining Industry,* chap. 173 (examples of Colorado and Nevada).

49. See Richard J. Lazarus and Stephanie Tai, "Integrating Environmental Justice into EPA Permitting Authority," *Ecology Law Quarterly* 26 (1999): 617–78. The authors address the Clean Air Act, Clean Water Act, Resource Conservation and Recovery Act, Safe Drinking Water Act, and Toxic Substance Control Act, as well as other statutes not applicable to mining. See also EPA Office of General Counsel Memorandum, EPA Statutory and Regulatory Authorities under Which Environmental Justice Issues May Be Addressed in Permitting (December 1, 2000).

50. Council on Environmental Quality, *Guidance under NEPA,* 14.

51. Council on Environmental Quality, *Guidance under NEPA,* 10; Bureau of Land Management, *Incorporating Environmental Justice into the NEPA Process,* Training Manual.

52. Council on Environmental Quality, *Guidance under NEPA;* see also U.S. Environmental Protection Agency, *Final Guidance for NEPA Compliance Analyses.*

53. 43 U.S.C., sec. 1702(d).

54. Council on Environmental Quality, *Guidance under NEPA,* 9–17. While this recommendation refers to situations in which no EIS or EA is needed, it may be considered applicable when only an EA is required but does not seem adequate to address community concerns.

55. *Sur Contra La Contaminacion v Environmental Protection Agency,* 2000 WL 132655 (1st Cir.), 5 (permit that is issued may be "particularly stringent due in large part to the participation of the area residents"); see also U.S. Environmental Protection Agency, *Final Guidance for NEPA Compliance Analyses* ("presence of disproportionately high and adverse effects may or may not necessarily change the final decision, but will change the focus of the analysis and may result in additional mitigation measures").

56. *San Carlos Apache Tribe et al.,* 149 IBLA 29, 30 (1999).

57. Council on Environmental Quality, *Guidance under NEPA,* 9.

58. *In Re: Ash Grove Cement Company*, 7 E.A.D. 387, 1997 WL 732000 (E.P.A.), 18.

59. *Wyoming Outdoor Council et al.*, 147 IBLA 105, 109 (1998). See *Kleppe v Sierra Club*, 427 U.S. 390, 409–14 (1976).

CONCLUSION

Chapter 14

HOPING AGAINST HISTORY

Environmental Justice in the Twenty-first Century

Patricia Nelson Limerick

Discussions of environmental justice never drift far from questions of history. History records the injuries—whether disproportionate impact of environmental hazard or restricted access to resources—which environmental justice sets out to rectify. History defines and designates the groups that have been underprivileged, and who are therefore eligible for inclusion in the provisions of the movement. History sorts through the very difficult questions of identifying intent, since proving intent to injure can be a key component of some environmental justice claims. In the largest sense, history helps us to reconstruct the routes of change that delivered us to our present circumstances. And, while history, on one side, sobers us up with the record of the determination with which those with power and privilege hold on to their advantages, history, on the other side, reacquaints us with the fact that courageous opposition has slowed, and sometimes even reversed, longrunning patterns of injustice.

Most of the essays in this collection are powered by hope, hope that refuses to defer to the burdens of history. These writers offer stark assessments of historical and contemporary injustices, but most of them move away from that disheartening territory and steer toward a positive and hope-filled conclusion. The hope has several dimensions: that historical injuries can be addressed and repaired; that social justice and environmental well-being will prove to be compatible goals; that existing environmental and civil rights laws and regulations can serve as tools to advance this merged cause; and that democratic participation in decision-making, especially of the people who have been historically excluded and disenfranchised, will act as a corrective for the problems of the past and a preventative for problems in the future. If you have ever wondered what became of the visions and hopes that characterized a number of social movements thirty years ago, reading this book gives you one answer to your question: many of the dreams of the 1960s and 1970s seem to have migrated to and found a home in the movement known as environmental justice.

Why would hope be so prominent in this volume? As a "relatively new movement," environmental justice has the advantages of fresh energy.[1] Recent change has created a new and novel channel for activism on behalf of the oppressed. The movement has rapidly rallied many to its cause, and solidly challenged oppressive practices that were once entirely taken for granted. Thus, it sets a spirit-raising example, offering exhilarating evidence that human beings do not have to suppress their protests and submit to conditions of injustice. No wonder scholars who study or practice in the field of environmental justice are susceptible to repeated episodes of cheer and hope! The stories of communities refusing to be overpowered and, instead, actively seeking remedy or compensation for unfairly imposed burdens surely raises the spirits of those who write about this field. Considered in a longer framework of time, the rise of the environmental justice movement has indeed been a remarkable development, offering its own heartening proof that historical change does not follow a predictable, fatalistic path of development.

And yet, not surprisingly, the two articles most oriented toward history offer the strongest challenge to optimism. Sketching the origins of the conservation movement, Jeff Romm notes that it arose in a time of white supremacy, when an elite of well-placed white men made the consequential choices that created the practices we now know as nature preservation. Segregation—whether of whites from minorities, or of natural environments from "improper" users—was an operating strategy running through American society. The hardening of restraints on people of color and the growth of conservation were, Romm declares, "synchronous formations of racial and resource policies."[2] In this context, the idea that social justice and environmentalism could ever come anywhere near each other is its own measure of miracle.

Drawing similar lessons from an international framework, Tseming Yang puts the spotlight on colonialism, a process in which the paternalism and coercive power of resource-extractors from Europe and the United States found their successor and match in the paternalism and coercive power of postcolonial conservationists and environmentalists imposing a First World agenda on the Third World. The international situations that Yang describes bear a close resemblance to the reservation situations described by Sarah Krakoff and Dean Suagee; Indian people, after all, underwent a process of conquest and colonialism with striking similarities to the exercises of European power over Africans, Asians, and Australian aborigines.[3]

In the starkness of their portraits of the origins of today's environmentalism in historical circumstances of white privilege, both Romm and Yang raise a forceful challenge to the hope that the environmental justice movement can provide a remedy or corrective—domestically or internationally—for these deep, systemic inequalities of power. Nonetheless, in the spirit of this book, both Romm and Yang conclude their articles with their own expressions of hope. Romm imagines a "just forest," in which all forest-affected constituencies would receive "respectful, full, and fair control of the basic terms, rules, standards, and processes of governance."[4] Meanwhile, Yang offers a vision of a transnational world in which we would take "more, and even full, responsibility for the consequences of and impacts on others of our own actions. . . ."[5]

The history of conservation is thoroughly connected to a hierarchy of racial inequity, though the connection is sometimes well-obscured from public recognition, even though, as Romm observes, "America's racial inequality and its 'environment'" may be "kept separate because they are so tightly bound together."[6] At the turn of the last century, the beginnings of federal conservation—the creation of the Forest Reserves, the presidency of Theodore Roosevelt, the passage of the National Antiquities Act—coincided with the founding of the National Association for the Advancement of Colored People and the influential early writings of advocates like W. E. B. DuBois. Simultaneous or not, concern about a "timber famine," fueled by alarm over the devastation of forests in the upper Midwest, seemed to exist in an entirely different sphere of life from concern about race terrorism, fueled by alarm over a siege of lynchings of African Americans in the South. Of course, in the mind of an individual like Theodore Roosevelt the issues of race and conservation did "cohabit": to Roosevelt, the status and security of native-born white Americans were jeopardized by the reproductive power of Blacks and immigrants. Along with exhortations to white women and men to have larger families, the conservation of natural resources and the maintaining of opportunities for outdoors experience found their places in the larger project of protecting the position of white Americans in a rapidly changing world.

To take another telling example, in the early history of most national parks, a major project was the removal of Indian people so that those areas could be properly free of human habitation and thereby qualified as intact nature. Recent books by Robert Keller and Michael Turek, Mark Spence, Theodore Catton, and Philip Burnham have told the story of the removal of Indian people from the locales that would become parks.[7] Before white nature-lovers could begin to imagine the national parks as places of pristine nature with no significant human impact, they had to drive out the human beings whose presence compromised that pristineness. In books with a similar moral to the story, Louis Warren and Karl Jacoby have written about the tie between the protection of fish and wildlife populations and the "criminalization" of hunting and fishing practices that had been normal parts of subsistence for a variety of local peoples—Indian, Mexican American, immigrant, and native-born whites.[8] With these studies in mind, it is hard to remember how we were ever led to separate studies of human relations with nature from studies of relationships between and among people.

A number of writers in this volume note what Getches and Pellow call "the exclusion of people of color and low-income communities from the dominant environmental movement."[9] In our times, an awareness of both the early twentieth century racial attitudes of early conservationists and the racial exclusivity of the current mainstream environmental movement is fairly widely distributed. But comparatively few scholars have commented on the active indifference to issues of race that appears in the writing of influential environmental thinkers of the mid-twentieth century. Recognizing this pattern is an important way of helping mainstream environmentalists reach a recognition that the low numbers of people of color in conventional environmental groups is not a historical accident. On the contrary, a habit of taking white privilege for granted runs deeply in the currents of their movement.

Consider, for instance, what a reader with a strong interest in the history of American slavery and segregation might make of the influential Aldo Leopold essay, "The Land Ethic." People, Leopold argued, should extend to the natural world the ethics that call for good behavior between and among human beings. For many environmentalists, Leopold's call for a recognition of natural entities as members of a community, a community in which humans would be only one group of citizens, has been a very high-powered inspiration.

Read in terms of U.S. race relations, the passage has some odd features, especially its famous opening passage. Rather than begin with an invocation of wildlife or landscape, Leopold began with a discussion of slavery, noting that ethics had evolved to the point where the idea of holding humans as property was understood to be wrong. He then called for an extension of that ethic "to land and to the animals and plants which grow upon it."[10] Strikingly, Leopold confined his references to the practice of slavery to the ancient Greeks: "When God-like Odysseus returned from the wars in Troy," Leopold declared in his powerful opening sentence, "he hanged all on one rope a dozen slave-girls whom he suspected of misbehavior during his absence."[11] Not a word in the essay offers any recognition that slavery was a practice, not just of ancient Greece, but of the United States, too, a practice ended less than a century before Leopold wrote his essay. Even more strikingly, not a word in the essay suggested that the end of slavery left any unfinished business in the United States. Leopold's presumption seemed to be that the ethical obligations of one person to another had been addressed and resolved with emancipation. The subordination of the slave girls to Odysseus could thus serve Leopold's rhetorical purposes as a reminder of a very different, and very distant, stage in the evolution of human society.

In 1949, the year of publication of "The Land Ethic," segregation was still established national practice, de jure in the South and de facto in the North and West, and African Americans who defied that arrangement put themselves at risk of physical violence. At the time that Leopold spoke warmly of a land ethic that would "enlarge the boundaries of the community to include soils, waters, plants, and animals," most American communities kept African Americans (and often Mexican Americans, Asian Americans, and Indian people) in a separate and subordinate place within those boundaries.[12] As an inspirational model for the relationship between humans and nature, with its hierarchical assumptions of superiority and inferiority, segregation was not a great improvement over slavery. Nonetheless, Leopold evidently felt that history had given him a simple point to make: human societies had reached the recognition that people should not be treated as property, without rights or self-determination, and it was time to apply the same understanding to plants, animals, and land.

In launching his argument for a land ethic with a reference to the Greek practice of slavery, Aldo Leopold seemed either indifferent or oblivious to the legacy of slavery in his own nation. The striking fact is not that a man preoccupied with nature and wildlife could pay so little attention to the heritage of slavery, although it was indeed a heritage visible in many aspects of American daily life in Leopold's time.

The far more telling fact is that so many have found inspiration in Leopold's "land ethic" essay over the last half century, and so few have been troubled by the missing recognitions in his opening analogy between the ethics governing the holding of property in humans and the holding of property in plants, animals, and lands. Although I have read many references to Leopold's call for extending the ethic of emancipation from human beings to nature, I have never seen any discussion of Leopold's incomplete reckoning with the lasting legacy of American slavery.

A more direct example of active indifference to the dilemmas of African American people comes from the great naturalist and environmental writer Joseph Wood Krutch. Often cited and excerpted for his eloquent descriptions of the adaptation of plants and animals to desert conditions and of the need for humans to restrict their self-indulgence on behalf of natural preservation, Krutch was a leading voice for nature in the mid-twentieth century. In his autobiography, published in 1962, Krutch became one of the few twentieth century, white nature-writers to discuss his racial attitudes explicitly, writing warmly of his memories of his hometown, Knoxville, Tennessee. His birth certificate, he said, described him as "White, legitimate, born alive." In the 1890s in Knoxville, as Krutch wrote, "not to be white was frankly admitted to rightfully entail some pretty severe penalties." The belief in a fundamental difference between blacks and whites was, accordingly, "one of the very first of the things which I took for granted." While life could be "unadventurous" and dull in his hometown, Krutch found much to value in the ways things were: he could not help remembering, he said, "how relatively free [Knoxville] was from both the public and private pressures, tensions, and anxieties of today. . . . We are now accustomed to seeing our world as a concatenation of 'problems'; few living before World War I took any such view of it."[13]

Writing during the early years of the civil rights movement, Krutch declared that the pleasant, leisured life of the white middle class in his childhood was made possible by "the greatest labor-saving device of all, namely servants—almost invariably black." "Neither I nor anyone else," he went on, "ever thought of 'a Negro problem' or supposed that the *modus vivendi* which seemed accepted without reservation by both groups need ever be disturbed." Subordination, Krutch suggested, offered the benefits of stability and tranquility. "Whether or not the Negroes actually believed themselves to be natural inferiors, I do not know," he said, "but they accepted with apparent cheerfulness and often with humor the assumption that they were." With that acceptance shattered, "life has now become a series of problems," as African Americans "exchanged a possibly degrading acceptance of things as they are for anxiety, anger, and a corroding sense of wrong."[14]

Joseph Wood Krutch was an accomplished nature writer and environmental advocate. His example is also a powerful reminder of the obstacles that block the path to merging civil rights with environmentalism. Many of the heroes of environmentalism carry very thin credentials in the field of civil rights. In truth, Krutch's approval of the workings of nature and his nostalgia for segregation were well matched. Looking out at the flora and fauna of deserts, or looking back at the people in early twentieth century Knoxville, Krutch admired a stable system in which individuals kept to their proper places in a spirit of cheerful acceptance. He offers one focused example of the kind of white privilege that, as Jeff Romm tells us, is intrinsic to the founding principles and practices of mainstream environmentalism.

Leopold and Krutch, some readers will instantly respond, were "men of their times," and there is no particular benefit in drawing attention to the fact of their tone-deafness on the matter of racial justice. Of course, a recognition of the unfinished business of slavery was very much on the minds of people of those same times, people like A. Phillip Randolph, Thurgood Marshall, and Rosa Parks. More important, an interpretative stance that categorizes white indifference to racial injustice as simply "the way things were" offers its own grim danger of fatalism. Indeed, by challenging that fatalism, a door opens to a more positive, potentially more hope-sustaining way of configuring and structuring the history of conservation and social justice. The twentieth-century movements of conservation, preservationism, and environmentalism did indeed form in a partnership of racial exclusiveness, and they have had a heck of a time breaking free of that relationship. And for that very reason, a different way of structuring the history of conservation might offer more cheerful prospects for change.

In this reshaped history, Leopold's and Krutch's indifference to racial injustice would stand out as a *change*, perhaps even a decline, and not a longstanding tradition in the practice of environmental thought. Writing a century before Leopold and Krutch, and often cast in the role of environmentalism's founding thinker, Henry David Thoreau was a determined opponent of slavery. Nature-loving and slavery-hating were compatible and matched projects in Thoreau's mind; it was the peculiar achievement of twentieth-century environmentalism to subtract his opposition to slavery from Thoreau's remembered work, leaving the celebration of nature to stand as his primary, and even exclusive, legacy to the future. And yet, unlike Leopold, Thoreau recognized that slavery had not ended with the ancient Greeks, but continued to be practiced in his own nation, and much of his intellectual and personal energy went into opposing that practice. In that context, by their indifference to racial justice, thinkers like Leopold and Krutch altered and narrowed environmentalism's heritage. Located deeper in time than either of them, Thoreau's joining the commitment to human rights and the commitment to nature could be repossessed as a point of origin, when the environmental movement so chooses.[15]

If it is possible to reconnect social justice and nature-loving at a moment of origin for environmentalism, it is equally possible to reconnect them in more recent history. Attempts at remedy, too, fell into the odd pattern of disconnected simultaneity. In 1964, the United States Congress passed both the Civil Rights Act and the Wilderness Act. The connections between these two pathbreaking acts of legislation remain dramatically understudied. Did they share any of the same sponsors? Did the debates that preceded their passage feature any qualities or common issues? Was there some sort of "spirit of the times" that drove both sets of advocates and made possible their legislative success? Did advocacy of "states' rights" figure in the opposition to both bills? Did any member of Congress in 1964 declare that these two causes stood in some relationship to each other? Whatever answers to these questions scholars may uncover, the Civil Rights Act and the Wilderness Act *did* appear in the same year, passed by the same Congress.

Accent Thoreau at the start, and accent the simultaneity of important reform legislation in 1964, and it is possible to offer a reconfigured, and more promising, history of the relationship between environmentalism and social justice. Yes, the two movements have often been disconnected from each other, and they have sometimes even collided head-on. But they have also had their moments of intersection, and even of compatibility.

As a moment of intersection, and in some ways a recovery from the backward steps taken by thinkers like Leopold and Krutch, the issuing of Executive Order 12898 in 1994 would certainly register as a high point. President William Jefferson Clinton has had some trouble maintaining design control over his legacy. And yet, when it comes to getting the attention of historians and the gratitude of many of the voters who had supported him, Clinton scored big with Executive

Order 12898. Creating a federally backed mandate for environmental justice (or "EJ"), Clinton formally joined the two causes of environmentalism and social justice. The order directs each federal agency to "make achieving environmental justice part of its mission by identifying and addressing, as appropriate, disproportionately high and adverse human health or environmental effects of its programs, policies, and activities on minority populations and low-income populations."[16] Of course, as with any administrative or legislative action, this order has had to run the usual gauntlet of conflicting interpretations, uneven implementation, and outright opposition. Still, even if Clinton's Environmental Justice Executive Order may never equal Abraham Lincoln's Emancipation Proclamation in fame or impact, it is in itself firm proof of the fact that, citizen fatigue with the election process aside, presidential power still can add force and legitimacy to a deserving cause.

The environmental justice movement did not, of course, have to wait for presidential recognition to receive force and legitimacy. Many authors in this collection describe the process by which grassroots groups merged the cause of enhancing environmental health with the cause of increasing racial and class equity. Long before the existence of Executive Order 12898, community activists had recognized—and challenged—the arrangements of power that placed a disproportionate burden of environmental hazard on communities of limited political and social influence.

And yet the historical timing of this merged movement presents some distinctive challenges. By the late twentieth century, both civil rights and environmentalism faced strong backlashes. In the early twenty-first century, with a new Republican administration installed in Washington, D.C., neither civil rights nor environmentalism is riding high in the saddle. For environmental justice, this situation is a particularly precarious one, since Executive Order 12898 is, as Kathryn Mutz tells us, "explicit that it does not create any right to judicial review for compliance or noncompliance with the order"; that is, whatever actions are taken must be taken voluntarily at the agency level because "agencies will not be coerced by the courts to exercise their discretion."[17] But how likely is the continuance of voluntary action from the agencies? Will public opinion demand that the president and his Cabinet maintain a commitment to the executive order?

When it comes to these questions, David Getches and David Pellow convey considerable cheer in their assessment of contemporary political opinion. "Racial discrimination and environmental insult," they declare in the opening chapter, are "both eschewed in modern political rhetoric and public opinion."[18] Indeed, few public figures these days make open declarations of racial prejudice, and they usually land in the soup when they do. Similarly, few citizens will say directly that they would prefer to have their environmental burdens borne by less privileged people. Still, some observers may wonder if these modifications in rhetoric and opinion will lead those with greater wealth and power to put real substance behind their improved sentiments, especially if action required self-sacrifice. Even though the penalties now attached to outright expressions of racism have reduced public statements of prejudice considerably, unspoken racism continues to exercise an unfortunate power, sometimes made harder to challenge because of its concealment. Getches and Pellow seem willing to take declarations of good principle at their face value, and, in truth, this strategy of "taking people at their word" can sometimes dispose even the hypocritical to honor that word in action. "There has been a growing consensus," Getches and Pellow affirm, "that there is something wrong when communities of color and poor people are the involuntary hosts for the rest of the nation's garbage."[19] Will this consensus prove powerful enough to persuade well-off communities to be "hosts" to their own garbage, or even to reduce their production of garbage? Will sympathetic feeling produce consequential action, or only an oral performance of pleasantly phrased virtue?

If this movement has its origins in both civil rights and environmentalism, and both those undertakings now face backlashes, will environmental justice thereby face a doubled—or even squared—dose of opposition, making the historical timing of its emergence a matter of bad luck? Or is environmental justice sufficiently different from both of its "origin movements," so self-evidently its own entity, that it may be positioned to skirt the attacks now directed, for instance, at affirmative action and wilderness preservation? Since environmental justice is, in many ways, something new under the sun, might it be that effective strategies for opposing it will take some time to develop, giving the movement a valuable period of grace before it, too, encounters its own backlash? With years of struggle, both civil rights and mainstream environmental activists are at risk of fatigue from the sense of years and years invested in holding the line against further loss. Environmental justice has a quite different air of just having rolled up its sleeves and gotten started.

Strategy and a certain ideological agility might well permit environmental justice to sidestep some of the more forceful forms of opposition to environmentalism and civil rights. Consider the often-deployed critique of "mainstream" environmentalism: that it seeks to separate nature from humanity, as if humanity were an alien parasite sent to infect and drain the planet's rich ecosystems. This critique misses its target entirely if it is directed against environmental justice. With this movement, after all, the point is to increase or restore the quality of human life in its material setting, not to minimize or eliminate human presence. Whatever its opponents may argue, no one can say that environmental justice is misanthropic, a charge that is all too easy to bring against environmentalist writers like Edward Abbey, or against the rhetoric of wilderness, with its drive to make humanity, at best, a peripheral and fleeting presence.

Participants in the environmental justice movement can present themselves in ways that might well neutralize a number of the more time-tested attacks on the environmental movement, perhaps especially the declaration that environmentalism is an elitist operation, giving primacy to the desires and whims of an already overindulged segment of society. Like many of the industrial and commercial critics of conventional environmentalism, environmental justice advocates themselves have been spirited critics of the unfairness of making recreation and aesthetic pleasure into primary values, giving leisured visitors to the outdoors a place of privilege far above local people trying to pursue their livelihoods. Similarly, environmental justice's focus on local interests and particular communities works well to counter the negative image of environmentalism as a mandate imposed by a set of distant and ill-informed federal policymakers.

In a similar way, environmental justice may be able to neutralize a number of the standard objections to and criticisms of civil rights measures, especially the charges brought against affirmative action. For cases where people of color have been denied access to natural resources or forced to live with a disproportionate burden of pollution, the injury requiring compensation or remediation is immediate and unmistakable. For Americans who cannot make their peace with the idea of making up for longer-term injuries left over from slavery or conquest, the immediacy and material reality of environmental justice cases may prove compelling and persuasive.

Perhaps most persuasive of all, in terms of moving public opinion, environmental justice advocates seem to be among the most committed of believers in well-established American ideals of democracy. It is hard to think of where one might look to find more earnest expressions of faith in the promise of democracy as a political practice that delivers just and fair results. This, surely, is an advantage when it comes to making a case to garner public support. To take the example before us, the articles in this collection are full of discussions—sometimes, really, celebrations—of "community" and "participation," of the productive value of having a voice and being heard.

And yet, among the writers here, two present themselves with some detachment from this value system. Tellingly, it is one of those—Sheila Foster—who, in her critique of devolved community decision-making, explicitly and coolly describes this faith in democracy. She notes that "the 'democratic wish'—the imagining of a single, united people bound together by consensus over the public good which is discerned through direct citizen participation in community settings—has a long tradition in America." But as Foster remarks, "Disparities in representation and influence among interests in collaborative processes are inextricably linked to the same set of social relations that make pluralistic decision-making processes problematic."[20] In other words, even in democratic participation, wealth carries an advantage, and poverty carries a disadvantage.

Tseming Yang, in his clearheaded appraisal of the limits of postcolonial governance, offers comparably cautious appraisals of the outcomes of what seem to be democratic processes. Self-government, in the form of national sovereignty, "can give developing countries significant leverage to achieve equity while also protecting differing cultural values. . . ."[21] And yet sovereignty "can also serve as a means of escaping accountability when, at their best, internal disagreement or, at their worst, corruption and exploitation by elites lead to decisions that are patently short-sighted and exploitative of the environment and local or indigenous communities." Still, "as a theoretical matter, when such decisions are controlled by democratic political processes, they have a legitimacy that is otherwise lacking."[22]

While it is still a very appealing idea for winning the good opinion of voters and officeholders, the ideal of democracy has, by this very power, a capacity to elicit uncritical support from its advocates. Letting the "community" participate in the making of environmental decisions that will affect community members' lives seems a self-evidently virtuous approach. Most environmental justice activists believe very strongly in the necessity of involving people of color and the poor in democratic decision-making. The reminder, offered effectively here in Krakoff's and Suagee's articles, to recognize tribal sovereignty in environmental issues involving Indian country, presents a heightened example of this desire to let the local community play the key role in deciding how resources will be used, or risks mitigated. The hope of environmental justice advocates to replace the pattern of decisions imposed from outside with local, democratic deliberation is in many ways admirable.

And yet democratic self-government, small-scale or large-scale, has proven to be quite a can of worms. Local communities can be, and often are, factionalized and divided, and enhanced powers for decision-making can widen and deepen the existing divisions. While the arbitrary exercise of overly centralized authority is a lamentable practice, it has inspired a reaction which romanticizes and exaggerates the fairness and effectiveness of community-based politics. Democratic decision-making is perfectly capable of producing, or furthering, environmental messes. A democratic community can choose short-term extraction of resources, status as a host for waste disposal, or postponement of costly cleanups and remediations. As Sarah Krakoff, Dean Suagee, and Tseming Yang point out in different ways, recognizing the sovereign and self-defining powers of communities, tribes, or nations can also require accepting an outcome of environmental degradation. Twentieth-century history, after all, is rich in episodes in which idealistic believers in self-government found themselves deeply disappointed in the decisions reached by democratic procedures.

The commitment of the writers in this volume to the democratic inclusion of community groups carries another paradox, noticeable in matters of terminology. In these essays, words come freighted with special and particular meanings, meanings which a generalist dictionary will not always disclose: impact, intent, mitigation, remedy, compensation, equity, equality, externalizing, disproportionate, distributive. Acronyms—NEPA, ESA, EIS, EA, FONSI, TAS, FLPMA, and, for that matter, EJ—draw a sharp line between insiders and outsiders. In a field of inquiry and advocacy so preoccupied with increasing participation and inclusion, one unexpected and paradoxical development has been the rapid creation of a new subdialect, familiar to some and unfamiliar to many. This language draws a line that runs through all the usual divisions of humanity—of ethnicity, race, nationality, gender, class, and generation, making it possible for humanity now to arrange itself into two categories: the acronymically adept and the acronymically befuddled.

And yet becoming a skilled and fluent user of the terms and acronyms of "EJ" is, potentially, an empowering and consequential talent, and it is the admirable intention of these authors to make the powers packed into those words and abbreviations available to the people who need them. When made available to people who have not been given many such occasions of access, those terms could serve as the keys to assertion and self-protection. It would be worth the while of environmental justice scholars to put a little more time and effort into "watching their language," making sure that it does not have the inadvertent effect of discouraging the democratic participation they so much want to support.

Whatever the locale and scale of the decision-making body, how subject to democratic reform are matters like the distribution of wealth and the habits of overconsumption? Describing the philosophy of sustainability, Gary Bryner states that "one of [its] fundamental tasks . . . is to decrease poverty and increase consumption or access to goods and services, while at the same time decreasing the level of pollution produced and nonrenewable resources used."[23] Of course, he is right in recognizing that social equity has no real meaning unless greater opportunities for wealth and consumption become available to people who have been denied those opportunities.

This goes right to the heart of the troubled turf where environmental conservation intersects with issues of social justice, domestically and internationally. Can people who have "made it"—prosperous white Americans living in material comfort—credibly ask other people (either underprivileged Americans or citizens of underdeveloped nations) who have not yet reached a state of prosperity to restrict their material desires on behalf of the planet's well-being? Or is it actually possible for material consumption to expand dramatically, letting the poor match the wealthy in material comfort, without eroding environmental quality or depleting natural resources? If this is a viable direction for human economic activity, it will require an enormous shift from the customs of production and consumption that have come to seem so "normal" in the two centuries since the Industrial Revolution. In the meantime, until the privileged themselves undertake this shift, references to the admirable alternative values we can learn from "traditional societies" can sound like a way of suggesting to the poor that they have reason to prefer and treasure the humility, modesty, and simplicity of their material conditions, leaving the lion's share of the planet's resources to those who are already using them.

The question here could not be more fundamental: what can the environmental justice movement do to address a situation in which a small percentage of the world's population lives in great material comfort, and a huge percentage very understandably aspires to have access to many of those amenities and indulgences? Social justice has to mean increasing material well-being for the disadvantaged, and yet the idea that giving the poor better opportunities for consumption will be compatible with the goals of reduced pollution and sustainable resource use is a difficult one to swallow.

Questions about the distribution of wealth inevitably direct us to the topic of social class. Repeatedly in these articles, the writers raise the familiar question of whether environmental injustices afflict people because of race or class. As Bryner poses the question, "Should environmental justice focus only on people of color, or should impacts on low-income people also be addressed?"[24] In their article on water, James Wescoat and his co-authors shift outside this framework by writing directly about poverty, and mentioning race only in asides. When they declare that the homeless have no water rights, to use one example, it seems entirely unnecessary to inquire as to whether the white homeless are also to be included in this statement. Frequently combining the phrases, "people of color and the poor," many of the authors seem at peace with accepting a paired set of meanings for what Getches and Pellow refer to as "traditional characteristics of disadvantage—where high poverty levels and/or people of color populations are concentrated."[25]

Indeed, there are good reasons to anticipate a future when references to race may become more and more problematic, and the ability to discuss social class may be at a premium. It is, after all, a striking twist of historical timing: at the very same time that a social movement joining the topics of race and nature rose to visibility, those two words—*race* and *nature*—had become two of the world's most unsettled and destablilized terms. Race, most scholars recognize, is a biologically irrelevant quality; to people studying human genetics, racial differences are simply insignificant. Racial differences could play such a powerful role in human affairs only because human beings went to a lot of trouble to give meaning to skin color, and to arrange the distribution of power and wealth in response to that meaning. Race, in other words, is a very minor biological characteristic that human beings have made into a matter of enormous social, economic, political, and cultural importance. This mental and cultural behavior has had very serious, and very material, results in day-to-day life. Thus, it would be pointless to say that race was not a "real" thing and that we should be able, by an act of will, to choose to live in a "color-blind" society. Nonetheless, race is no longer a term to use with any complacency or with any sense of security in knowing its meaning; as a way to divide human beings into categories of membership and identity, race has become a questionable device.

Given the shifting status and meaning of the idea of "race," it seems particularly important to address and resolve the persistent question of the relationship of environmental justice to social class. In light of the need to bring every workable strategy to bear on the project of enhancing environmental justice's prospects in a not particularly favorable political climate, it seems the path of wisdom to recognize that, while race and poverty often intersect (and thereby can produce burdens of doubled impact), some poor white Americans have still landed in the category of people who are unfairly burdened by environmental hazard.

Rather than waste any energy in a battle over the primacy of race versus class as a category of disadvantage, it seems more productive to focus our attention on Bryner's description of an important aspect of U.S. jurisprudence:

> Race is well established in constitutional law as a suspect classification, requiring heightened or strict scrutiny by courts and a showing of compelling government interest when it serves as the basis for policy making. In contrast, federal courts do not recognize class as a suspect classification or any kind of a problematic distinction at all. Poor people simply have fewer options than wealthy ones. They also bear more risks because they have less money to protect themselves against some risks. Neither constitutional nor statutory provisions provide any basis for claims that class or income status constitutes an actionable claim.[26]

Here is a matter asking for our close and creative attention. Given the importance of poverty as a factor making communities vulnerable to both higher risks of pollution and lower opportunities of access to natural resources, if class cannot now be invoked as a basis for a claim of injury and vulnerability to injustice, then it has to be a high priority for environmental justice theorists to launch long-range efforts to figure out a way around this obstacle. The project will be as difficult as it is important. Race may be a subject of some discomfort in public discourse, but searching and productive discussions of class division are, for Americans, even more difficult to come by.

At the same time that the meaning of *race* has been contested and questioned, the word *nature* has been getting a workout of its own. Environmental historians have vigorously challenged the idea that "nature" was a world "out there," existing in separation from human beings.[27] Rather than a pristine wilderness delivered straight from the hand of the Creator to the arriving colonists from Europe, North America was clearly a place very much shaped by human activities like the Indian use of fire to create ecosystems more productive of game. What preservationists had wanted to see as nature untouched by human ambition or manipulation is now recognized as a material world very shaped by human action.

While no historian has gone all the way to the full relativism of making the operations of material reality purely a matter of "cultural construction," many recognize that what people have called "nature" or "the environment" varies enormously according to culture, historical experience, and ambition. A number of authors in this collection make this point. As Henry Carey puts it, "A challenge underlying any discussion of environmental justice is that the concept of environmental quality varies from culture to culture."[28]

In a number of ways, the contested status of the word *nature* could work to the advantage of environmental justice advocates. With "nature" no longer a hard and fast category separating humanity from a set-apart network of flora, fauna, soil, air, and water, the door stands open to exactly the kind of understanding environmental justice supporters ask for: a recognition of the ways in which human well-being is entirely woven into concerns and matters that we once relegated to the category "natural."

In his study of the ways that early efforts to protect nature served to confirm patterns of ethnic and social injustice in rural America, the historian Karl Jacoby writes these concluding lines, summing up the challenges to hope contained in the historical record:

> As conservation's hidden history reveals, Americans have often pursued environmental quality at the expense of social justice. One would like to imagine that the two goals are complementary and that the only way to achieve a healthy environment is through a truly democratic society. But for now these two objectives remain separate guiding stars in a dark night sky, and we can only wonder if they will lead us to the same hoped-for destination.[29]

In a number of passages in this collection of essays, these twin stars combine in the cause of making the world a brighter place. In times when both social justice and environmental well-being face stiff challenges, let us hope that we can keep both of them in our view.

Notes

1. David Getches and David Pellow, 5.
2. Jeff Romm, 119–20.
3. For an overview of worldwide similarities in the history of conquest, see

Patricia Nelson Limerick, "Going West and Ending Up Global," *Western Historical Quarterly*, Spring 2001.

4. Jeff Romm, 127, 131.
5. Tseming Yang, 106.
6. Jeff Romm, 124.
7. Robert H. Keller and Michael F. Turek, *American Indians and National Parks* (Tucson: University of Arizona Press, 1998); Mark Spence, *Dispossessing the Wilderness: Indian Removal and the Making of the National Parks* (New York: Oxford University Press, 1999); Theodore Catton, *Inhabited Wilderness: Indians, Eskimos, and National Parks in Alaska* (Albuquerque: University of New Mexico Press, 1997); and Philip Burnham, *Indian Country, God's Country: Native Americans and the National Parks* (Washington, D.C.: Island Press, 2000).
8. Louis Warren, *The Hunter's Game: Poachers and Conservationists in Twentieth-Century America* (New Haven: Yale University Press, 1997); and Karl Jacoby, *Crimes against Nature: Squatters, Poachers, Thieves, and the Hidden History of American Conservation* (Berkeley: University of California Press, 2001).
9. David Getches and David Pellow, 19.
10. Aldo Leopold, *A Sand County Almanac, with Essays on Conservation from Round River* (1949; reprint, San Francisco: Sierra Club, 1970), 238.
11. Leopold, *Sand County Almanac*, 237.
12. Leopold, *Sand County Almanac*, 239.
13. Joseph Wood Krutch, *More Lives than One* (New York: William Sloane Associates, 1962), 23.
14. Krutch, *More Lives than One*, 24, 26.
15. Peter Coates, "From Discord to Concord: The Reunification of Henry David Thoreau," in *The Nature of Justice: Racial Equity and Environmental Well-Being*, ed. Patricia Nelson Limerick (in preparation).
16. Executive Order No. 12898, 59 *Federal Register* 7629 (1994), 3 C.F.R., sec. 859, reprinted in 42 U.S.C., sec. 4321, available at www.epa.gov/docs/oejpubs/.
17. Kathryn Mutz, 323–24.
18. David Getches and David Pellow, 4.
19. David Getches and David Pellow, 10, 12.
20. Sheila Foster, 155.
21. Tseming Yang, 99.
22. Tseming Yang, 99.
23. Gary Bryner, 52–53.
24. Gary Bryner, 38.
25. David Getches and David Pellow, 5.
26. Gary Bryner, 38.
27. See, especially, William Cronon, ed., *Uncommon Ground: Toward Reinventing Nature* (New York: W. W. Norton, 1995).
28. Henry Carey, 219.
29. Jacoby, *Crimes against Nature*, 198.

About the Authors

Gary C. Bryner is a research associate at the Natural Resources Law Center at the University of Colorado School of Law. He has bachelor's and master's degrees in Economics from the University of Utah, a Ph.D. from Cornell University in Government, and a J.D. from Brigham Young University. Gary has been a guest fellow at the Brookings Institution, the National Academy of Public Administration, and the Natural Resources Law Center. Before coming to the Center as director in 1991, he directed the Public Policy program at Brigham Young University. His research interests include international environmental law and policy, air pollution law, and public lands and wilderness policy and law.

Jan Buhrmann is an environmental sociologist specializing in qualitative research on natural resources and other environmental issues. Her background includes policy analysis, research design, and a focus on the human dimensions of environmental issues. Jan worked as a post-doctoral researcher with the Environmental Justice Program at the U.S. Environmental Protection Agency in Denver and the National Renewable Energy Laboratory in Golden, Colorado. She received her doctorate in Sociology from the University of Colorado at Boulder, as well as graduate certification in Environmental Policy. She currently works for Conocer, a public-spirited research and consulting organization in Louisville, Colorado, emphasizing qualitative research on environmental, public policy, health care, and other issues. Her work with Conocer includes providing strategic thinking support to help public sector organizations fulfill their leadership potential.

Henry H. Carey is founder and executive director of the Forest Trust, founded in 1984. Henry directs its programs in community forestry and forest protection, a land stewardship division, and a land trust. In the early years of his career, he worked in the farming and ranching trades in rural New Mexico. Since then, he has managed numerous conservation properties in New Mexico, Colorado, and Hawaii. As a forest scientist with the John Muir Institute, he conducted research on timber harvest scheduling and on the relationship between national forest resources and community stability and welfare in rural areas. Subsequently, he spent two years as a forest planner with the U.S. Forest Service. Henry also sits on the boards of the Land Trust Alliance, the Sapelo Foundation, and the Forest Stewards Guild. He is a graduate of St. John's College and has master's degrees in Arts from Goddard College and in Forestry from Colorado State University.

Luke W. Cole is director of the California Rural Legal Assistance Foundation's Center on Race, Poverty and the Environment in San Francisco. He represents low-income communities throughout California who are fighting environmental hazards, stressing the need for community-based, community-led organizing and litigation. Through the Center, he also provides legal and technical assistance to attorneys and community groups involved in environmental justice struggles nationwide. Luke served for four years on the U.S. Environmental Protection Agency's (EPA's) National Environmental Justice Advisory Council, chairing its Enforcement Subcommittee. He also served on the EPA's National Advisory Council for Environmental Policy and Technology's Title VI Implementation Committee. Luke is the cofounder, editor, and publisher of the journal *Race, Poverty and the Environment* and has taught seminars on environmental justice at Stanford Law School, University of California–Berkeley, Boalt Hall School of Law, and University of California, Hastings School of Law. He graduated cum laude from Harvard Law School and with honors from Stanford University.

Sheila Foster is a professor of Law at Rutgers University in Camden, New Jersey. She received her B.A. in English, with honors, from the University of Michigan–Ann Arbor and her J.D. from the Boalt Hall School of Law at the University of California–Berkeley. Sheila is the author of numerous publications on environmental justice, including the recently released book *From the Ground Up: Environmental Racism and the Rise of the Environmental Justice Movement* (New York University Press, 2001) (with Luke Cole of the Center for Race, Poverty and the Environment).

David H. Getches is the Raphael J. Moses Professor of Natural Resources Law at the University of Colorado School of Law. He was the founding executive director of the Native American Rights Fund and formerly served as executive director of the Colorado Department of Natural Resources. David teaches and writes in the fields of Indian law, water law, public lands, and environmental law. He has consulted and lectured throughout the United States and in several Latin American, Asian, and European countries. David is a graduate of Occidental College and the University of Southern California Law School.

Sarah Halvorson is an assistant professor of Geography at the University of Montana. She took her Ph.D. at the University of Colorado at Boulder in 2000 with a dissertation on "Geographies of Children's Vulnerability: Households and Water-Related Disease Hazard in the Karakorum Mountains, Northern Pakistan." She has written articles on teaching water resources courses and the development of the Indus basin in Pakistan. Sarah teaches courses on water resources, mountain geography, and gender and development.

Lisa Headington is a doctoral candidate in Geography at the University of Colorado at Boulder. She is conducting dissertation research on the effects of urban river restoration and improvement on homeless and low-income social groups, with an emphasis on the South Platte River parks in Denver, Colorado. She is asking whether the social effects of urban riverfront redevelopment constitute the "other tragedy of the commons." Lisa has a master's of Urban and Regional Planning from the University of Colorado at Denver and has worked as a land use planner in metropolitan Denver.

Barry E. Hill is the director of the Office of Environmental Justice of the U.S. Environmental Protection Agency. He has also served as the acting associate solicitor, Division of Conservation and Wildlife; as director of the Office of Hearings and Appeals of the Department of the Interior; and as the department's representative on the Enforcement and Compliance Interagency Task Force created as a result of President Clinton's February 11, 1994, Environmental Justice Executive Order. Barry has taught both law and political science courses at various institutions, including the Antioch Law School, Vermont Law School, and the American University Washington College of Law, and served as counsel to the international law firm of Dickstein, Shapiro and Morin, where he practiced in the area of environmental law and energy law. He has written several articles on environmental law and policy and environmental justice in scholarly and professional journals and is currently writing a textbook for law students in the area of environmental justice. He earned a B.A. in Political Science from

Brooklyn College, an M.A. in Political Science from Howard University, and a J.D. from the Cornell Law School.

Douglas S. Kenney has been a member of the University of Colorado School of Law's Natural Resources Law Center's research faculty since 1996. He has a broad interdisciplinary background in natural resources policy and administration, with degrees from the University of Colorado, the University of Michigan, and the University of Arizona. His research is generally confined to water and public lands issues in the western United States and emphasizes the evaluation of institutional arrangements for decision making and governance.

Sarah Krakoff is an associate professor of Law at the University of Colorado School of Law, where she teaches and writes in the areas of Indian law and natural resources. Sarah clerked on the Ninth Circuit Court of Appeals, worked for three years on the Navajo Nation for DNA–Peoples Legal Services as director of their Youth Law Project, then served as director of the Indian Law Clinic at the University of Colorado, representing Indian tribes and individuals in a range of Indian law and environmental matters. She continues to represent Navajo schoolchildren pro bono in ongoing civil rights litigation. Sarah received her bachelor's degree from Yale and her J.D. from University of California–Berkeley, Boalt Hall School of Law. She currently lives in Boulder, Colorado, with her husband and daughter.

Patricia Nelson Limerick is a western American historian with particular interests in ethnic history and environmental history. From 1980 to 1984, she taught at Harvard University as an assistant professor before joining the faculty at the University of Colorado at Boulder, where she teaches a variety of courses on the American West. Patricia is the chair of the board and cofounder of the Center of the American West, an interdisciplinary regional studies center. She received her B.A. in American Studies from the University of California–Santa Cruz, and her Ph.D. in American Studies from Yale University. In 1995, she was named a MacArthur Fellow.

Kathryn M. Mutz joined the research staff of the Natural Resources Law Center at the University of Colorado School of Law in September 1996 with a background in both law and natural resources management. She holds a bachelor's in Geography from the University of Chicago, an M.S. in Biology/Ecology from Utah State University, and a J.D. from the University of Colorado, concentrating in natural resources and environmental law. As a biologist, Kathryn worked throughout the West for state and federal government and private industry on scientific and public policy issues related to natural resources development, specializing in wetlands, endangered species, and reclamation of disturbed lands. At the Center, her research focuses on forestry, minerals, and environmental justice issues.

David N. Pellow is an assistant professor of Ethnic Studies and Sociology at the University of Colorado at Boulder. David currently serves on the boards of directors of several community-based organizations that are dedicated to improving the living and working environments for people of color and low-income groups and has recently worked with the National Environmental Justice Advisory Council's Subcommittee on Waste Facility Siting on urban revitalization and brownfield redevelopment and with the President's Council on Sustainable Development. David writes and publishes on environmental justice issues, including garbage, recycling and Silicon Valley electronics/computer industries, in communities of color and in the workplace. He received his B.A. from the University of Tennessee, Knoxville, and his M.A. and Ph.D. in Sociology from Northwestern University.

Jill Replogle earned her B.A. in Geography at the University of Colorado at Boulder in 1999 with a summa cum laude honors thesis, "The Geographic and Social Dimensions of Acute Water Problems in Southern Costilla County, Colorado." She has since lived in Mexico and published articles on the Zapatista movement in Chiapas, including, "Caravan of Hope: Marching for Indigenous Dignity, the Zapatistas Open a New Era," in *Toward Freedom*. Jill currently teaches English and works with Project Mosaic Guatemala, which places volunteers in humanitarian, environmental, and human rights projects.

Jeff Romm is a professor of Resource and Environmental Policy at the University of California–Berkeley. He has served there as the director of the Center for South and Southeast Asia Studies, the chair of the Energy and Resources Group, and the chair of the Division of Resource Institutions, Policy and Management. Prior to joining the Berkeley faculty in 1980, he served in the Ford Foundation in South and Southeast Asia for a decade, developing programs in water, land, and forest management, and in the Nepal Forest Department for several years before that. He holds his undergraduate degree in forestry from Berkeley and graduate degrees in resource economics from Cornell.

Dean B. Suagee, a member of the Cherokee Nation, is a professor of Law at Vermont Law School, where he is director of the First Nations Environmental Law Program and the Indian Country Environmental Justice Clinic. He writes on environmental and cultural resources law in Indian country. He has a J.D. from the University of North Carolina and an LL.M. in international legal studies from American University. Previously he was an associate with Hobbs, Straus, Dean & Walker, a Washington, D.C., firm that specializes in acting as legal counsel to tribal governments and organizations. He has also held positions with the National Congress of American Indians and the Bureau of Indian Affairs. As a member of the American Bar Association, he serves as a vice chair on both the Committee on Native American Resources and the Diversity Task Force. He is also on the Indigenous Peoples Sub-committee of the National Environmental Justice Advisory Council, an advisory committee to the Environmental Protection Agency.

Nicholas Targ is counsel to the Office of Environmental Justice, U.S. Environmental Protection Agency. He is the principal legal/policy adviser to the Office, addressing a wide variety of environmental, civil rights, permitting, and regulatory issues. He previously practiced law as an attorney adviser in the Office of the Solicitor, U.S. Department of the Interior, where he worked extensively with the Bureau of Reclamation and Bureau of Land Management on matters involving the public lands, water resources, privatization, regulatory takings, and hazardous substances. Nicholas earned his J.D. from Boston College Law School. He also attended the Massachusetts Institute of Technology, Department of Urban Studies and Planning, and received his B.A. from the University of California–Santa Cruz, in Politics/Legal Studies and Economics.

Gerald Torres is the H.O. Head Centennial Professor of Real Property Law at the University of Texas Law School. He has been vice provost at the University of Texas as well as a professor and associate dean at the University of Minnesota Law School and a visiting professor at Stanford and Harvard Law Schools. He has written and lectured extensively on the intersection of issues of race and politics, being among the first scholars to address the disparate impact of environmental regulation on different racial, ethnic and socioeconomic groups. He has also been directly involved in the debate over the management and legal protection of Native American land and religion. Before moving to Texas he served in the Department of Justice, first as deputy assistant attorney general for environment and natural resources and then as counsel to Attorney General Janet Reno. In these positions, he was charged with developing what became Executive Order 12898 on environmental justice and with establishing the Office of Tribal Justice to coordinate Indian legal issues at the department. He received his B.A. in Political Science from Stanford University, his J.D. from Yale Law School, and his LL.M. from the University of Michigan.

James L. Wescoat Jr. is professor of Geography at the University of Colorado at Boulder and a faculty associate in the College of Architecture and Planning, the Peace and Conflict Studies program, and the Institute of Behavioral Sciences. He teaches courses on urban water resources, western water, world water, comparative environmental studies, and the history and theory of geography. Jim has written about spatial aspects of western water law and policy conflicts and about long-term interactions among U.S., South Asian, and Islamic water systems. His research in South Asia has received support from the Smithsonian Institution and the U.S. Environmental Protection Agency. His research in this book is part of a three-year study, "Water, Poverty and Sustainable Livelihoods in Colorado," funded by the National Science Foundation.

Tseming Yang is associate professor of Law at Vermont Law School. His areas of legal scholarship center on civil rights, environmental law, and international law. He teaches courses in torts, environmental justice, international environmental law, and race and the law. Before he joined the Vermont Law School faculty in 1998, he served as an attorney in the Policy, Legislation and Special Litigation Section of the U.S. Department of Justice's Environment and Natural Resources Division, where he worked on domestic and international environmental issues. He graduated with a B.A. in Biochemistry from Harvard University and received his J.D. from the University of California–Berkeley, Boalt Hall School of Law, where he was an articles editor for the *California Law Review* and a member of the *Ecology Law Quarterly*. Tseming is currently a member of the Environmental Protection Agency's National Environmental Justice Advisory Committee and serves as a vice chair of the International Subcommittee.

Index